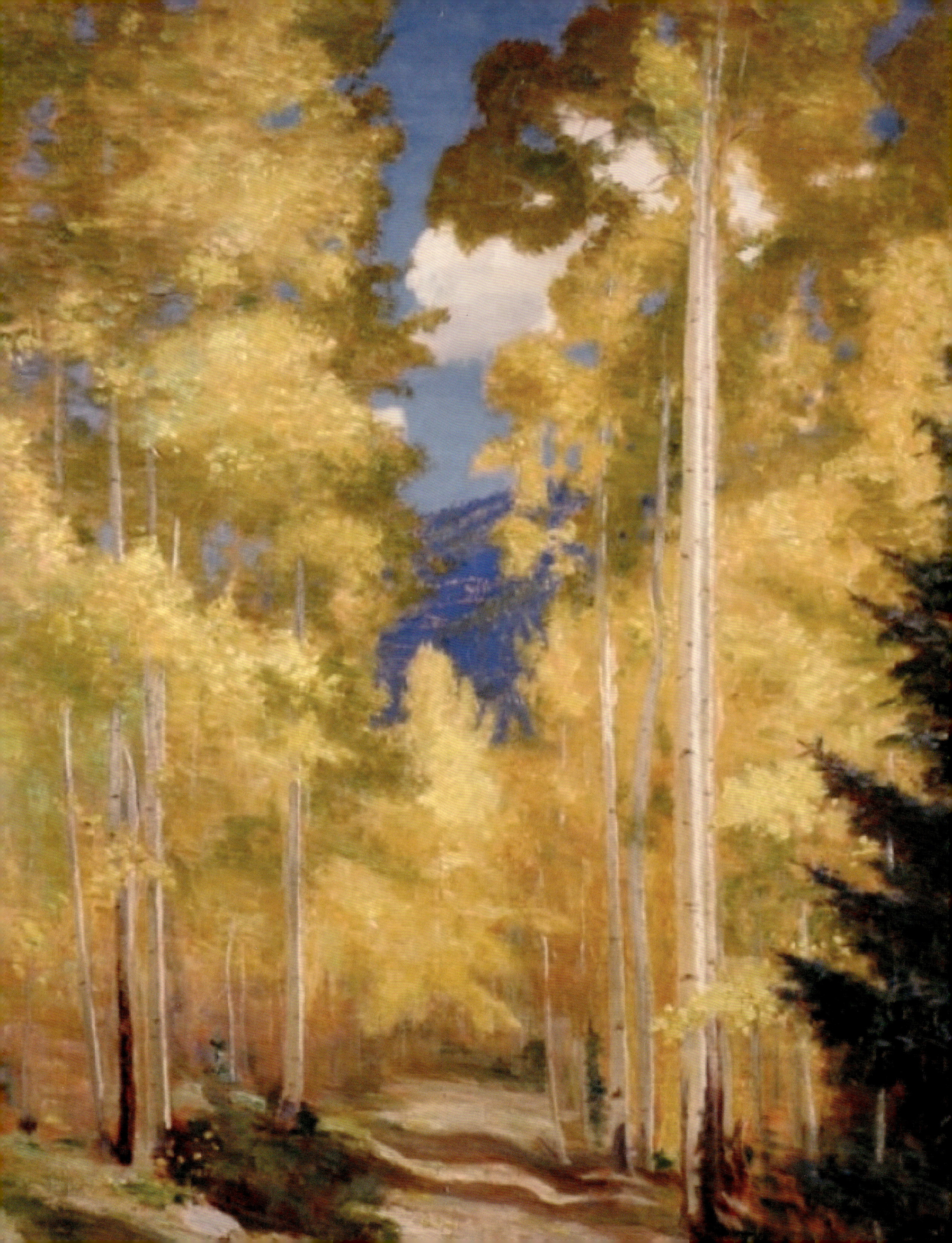

THE KLAUER FAMILY OF DUBUQUE, IOWA
A Story of Patronage

Dean A. Porter, Ph.D.

With contributions by the Klauer family

and Friends

Project Director Christine Fowler Shearer, Ph.D.

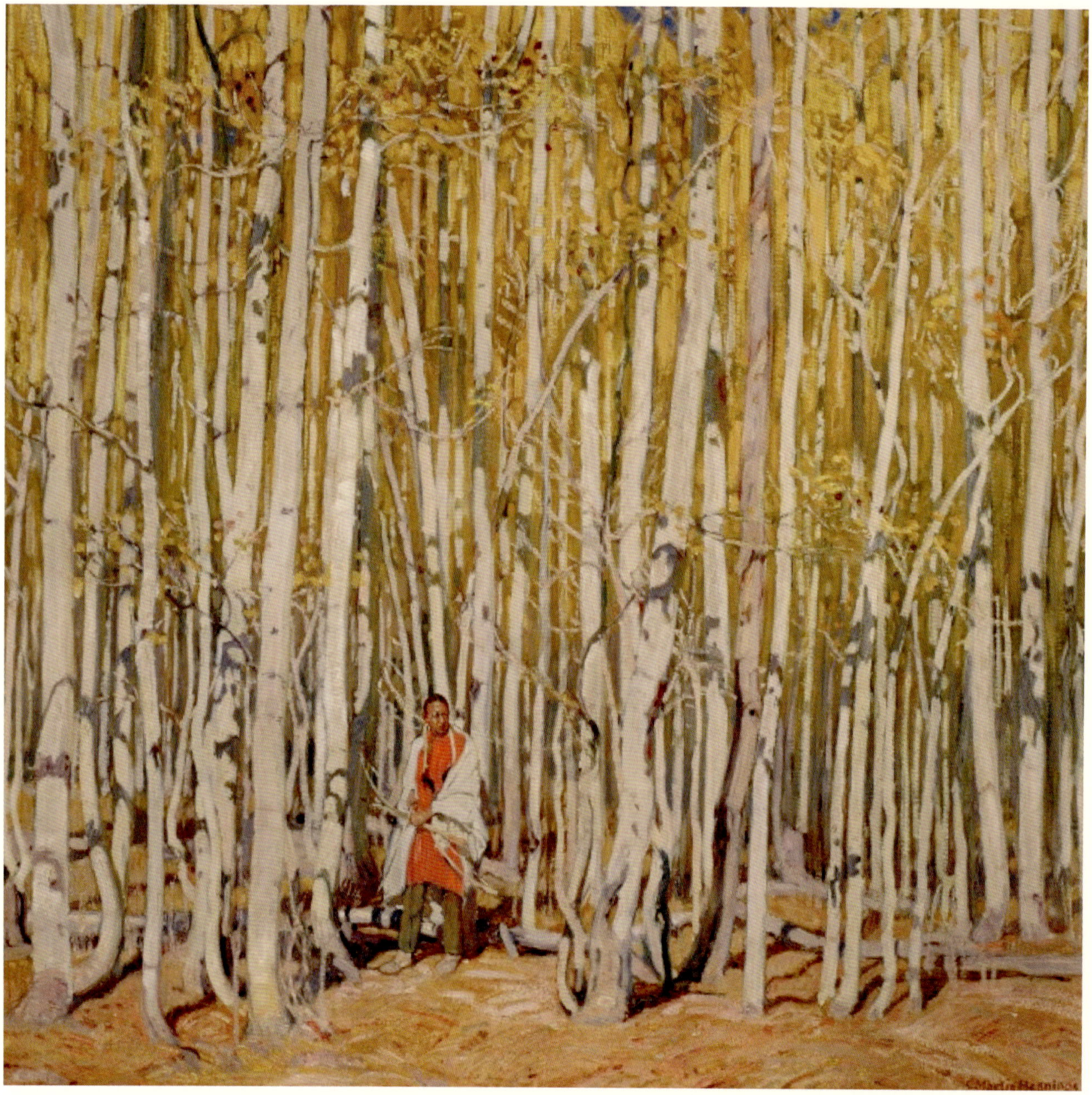

Figure 1. E. Martin Hennings. *Silver and Gold*, before 1926. Oil on canvas, 29.5 x 29.5 inches. Collection Klauer Manufacturing Company.

Jacket Front: Walter Ufer. *My Studio Entrance*, 1927. Oil on canvas, 50 x 40 inches. Collection Klauer Manufacturing Company.

Facing title page: Bert Phillips. *Trail Through the Aspens*, c. 1920s. Oil on canvas, 39 x 29 inches. Collection Klauer Manufacturing Company.

ISBN 978-0-692-19706-6

THE KLAUER FAMILY OF DUBUQUE, IOWA: A STORY OF PATRONAGE

Project Director Christine Fowler Shearer, Ph.D.,
with editorial assistance from Carol A. Porter

Design by Christine Fowler Shearer, Ph.D.

Photography Credits: Stephen Moriarty, John Jay Anderson, Michael Wright

Includes bibliographical reference

Typefaces: Winchster New ITC, Frutiger LT Std

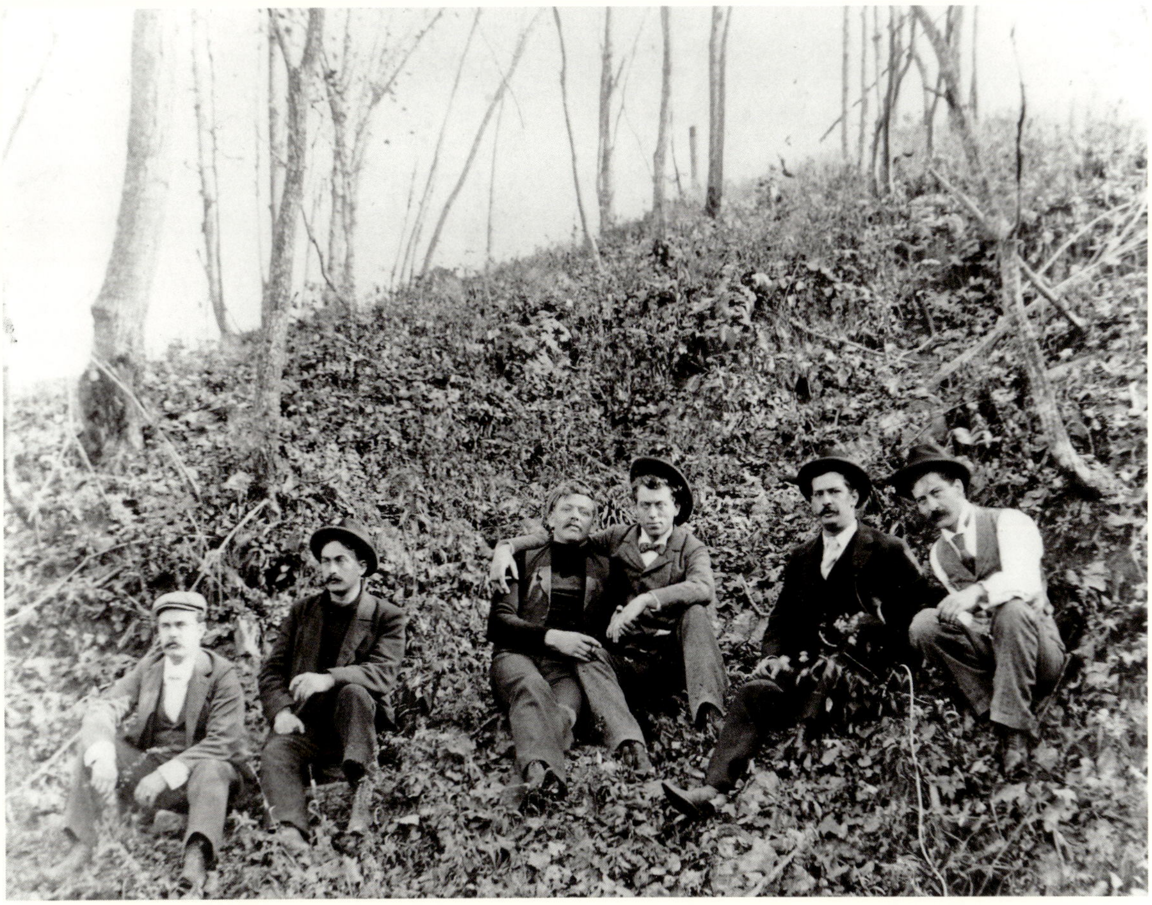

Figure 2. *William H. Klauer (second from left) and Friends*, c. 1890. Photo courtesy Klauer Family.

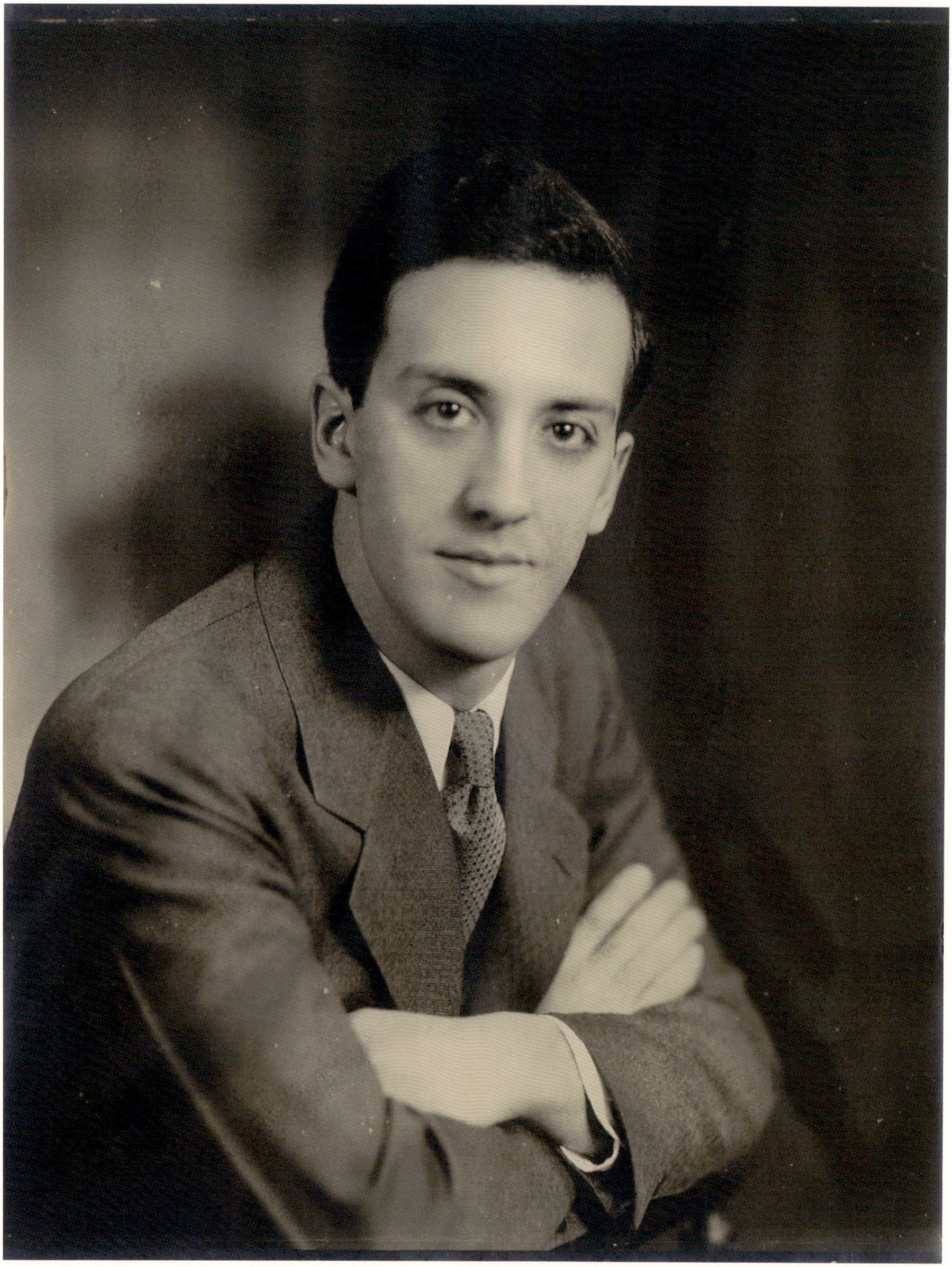

Dedicated to William J. Klauer

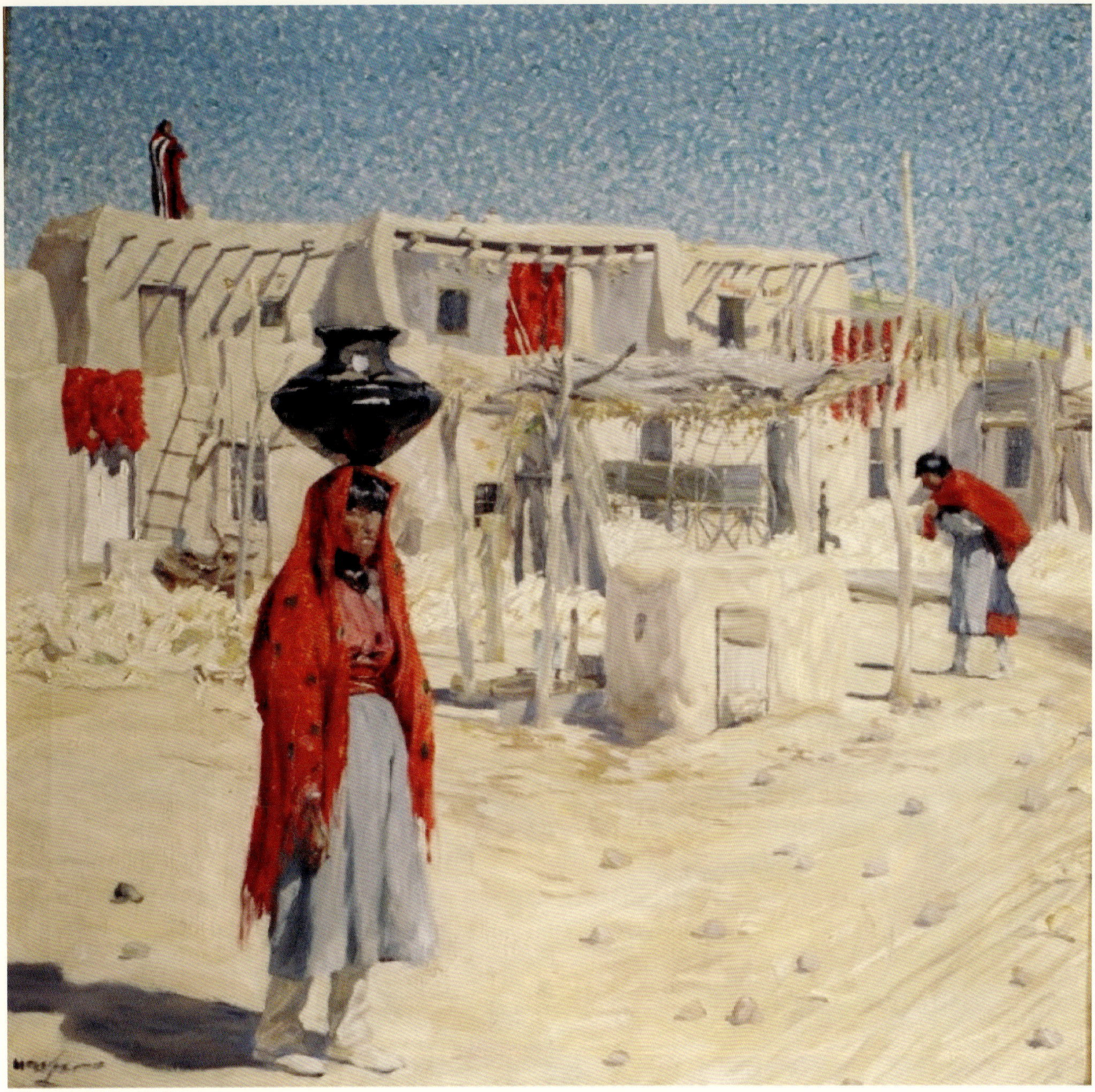

Figure 3. Walter Ufer. *Isleta Water Carriers*, 1915. Oil on canvas, 30 x 30 inches. Collection Klauer Manufacturing Company.

The Klauer Family of Dubuque, Iowa: A Story of Patronage

By Dean A. Porter, Ph.D.

Table of Contents

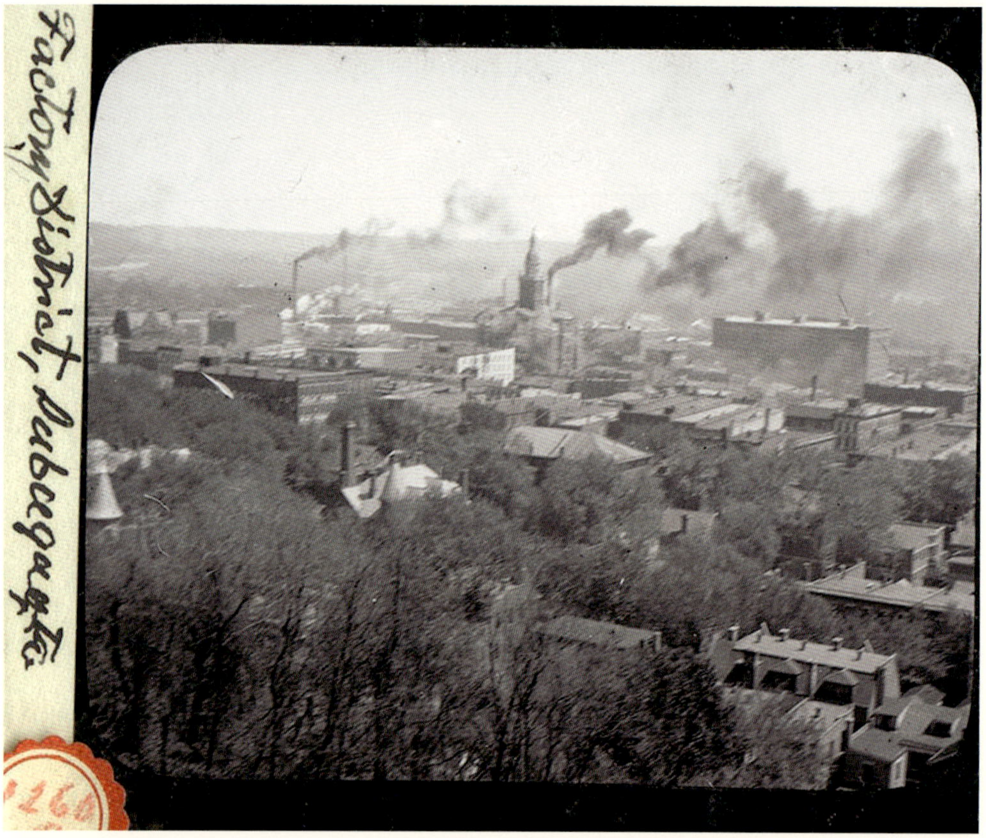

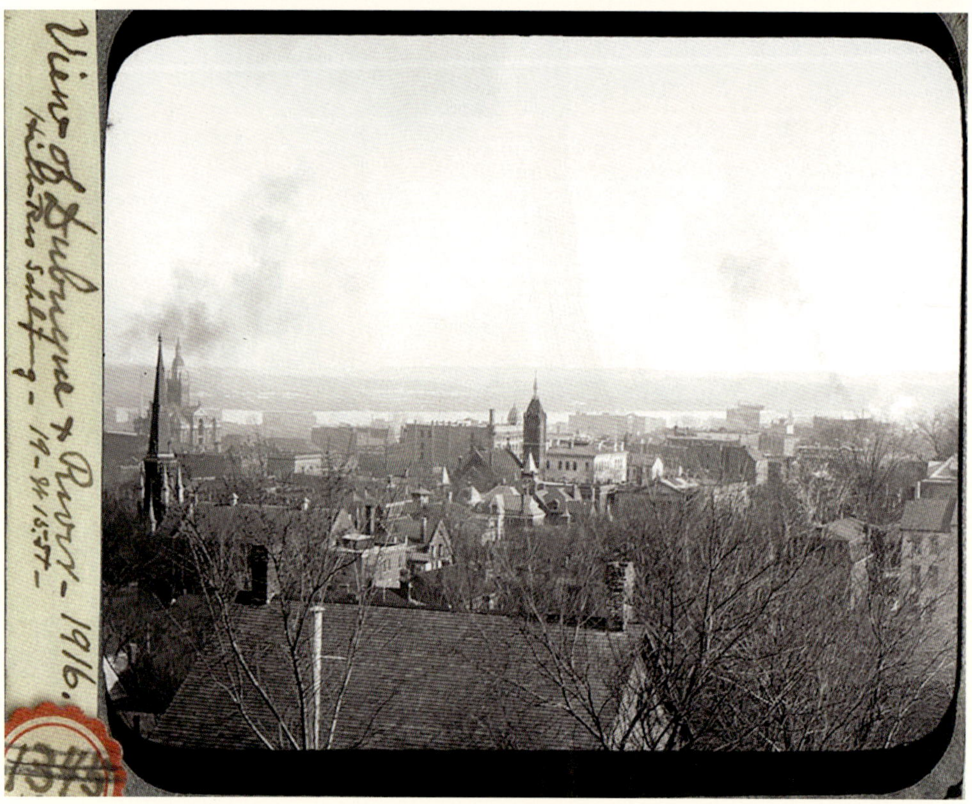

Figures 4 and 5. Reverend H. J. Loemker. *Factory District, Dubuque, Iowa*, 1916 (top) and *Downtown Dubuque, Looking East*, 1916 (bottom).
Rev. H.J. Loemker Collection, Loras College, Center for Dubuque History.

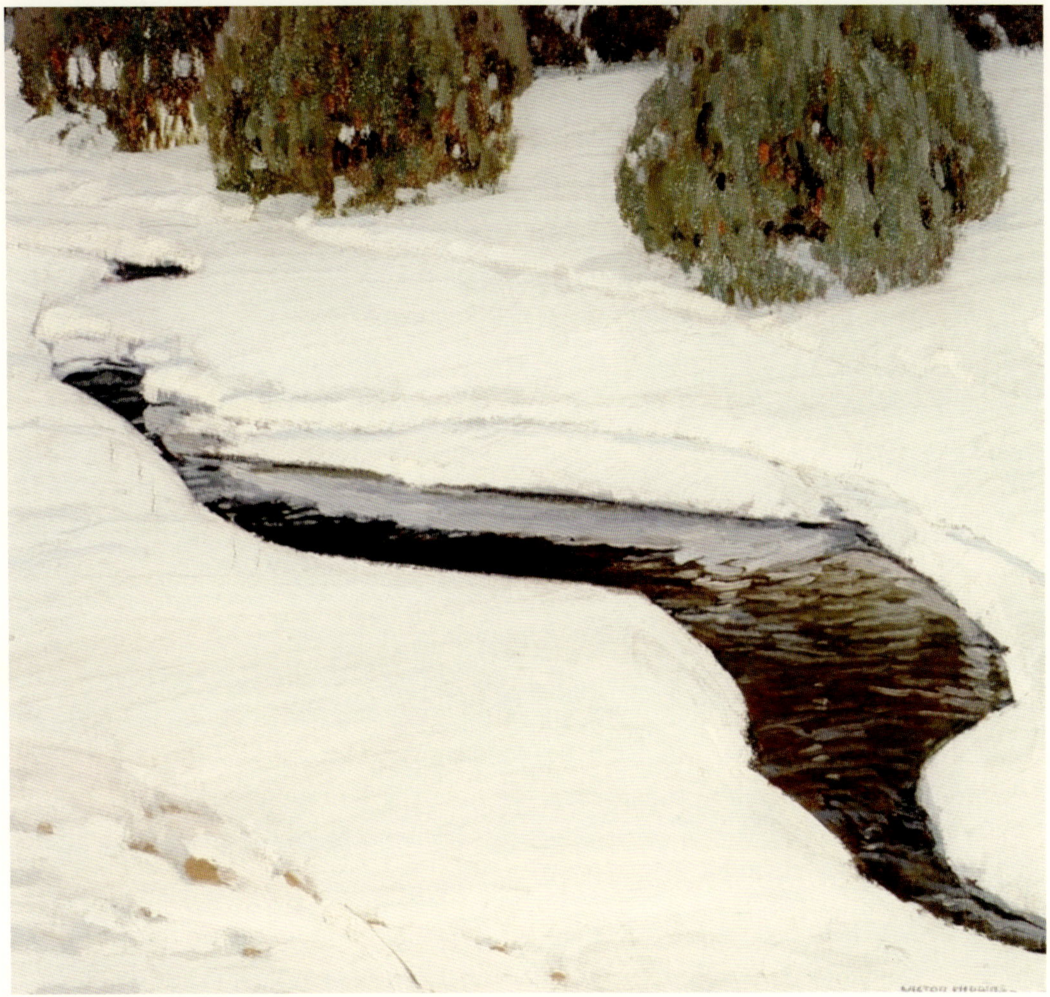

Figure 6. Victor Higgins. *Stream in Winter*, c. 1920. Oil on canvas, 18 x 18 inches. Collection Klauer Manufacturing Company.

FOREWORD

How often does the head of a corporation develop a close relationship with a group of relatively unknown artists, an association which would impact his and their lives for over two decades? William Henry Klauer and several members of the Taos Society of Artists developed a special kind of relationship, one that would advance their careers while also forming an important private collection for the industrialist. William Henry Klauer's name would be cited as provenance of nearly seven or eight-dozen paintings by Walter Ufer, Victor Higgins, E. Martin Hennings, and Bert Phillips.[1] In subsequent years, the collection was curated by William J. and Walter J. Klauer, and today, by the grandsons of William Henry Klauer—William, Robert and James Klauer. In fact, for a short time in my professional career (1966-1969), I curated nineteen paintings by Walter Ufer that bore the William Henry Klauer provenance. Ufer was a relatively unknown artist at that time, and his paintings were of little interest. Today, scholars consider *Going East*, *Indian Corn–Taos*, *Santuario de Chimayo*, *Their Audience–Laguna*, and *Where the Desert Meets the Mountains* to be among the most important works created in Taos, New Mexico. They are considered icons of American painting and were once owned by the Klauer family.

[1] "Provenance" denotes those objects once owned or in the care of William H. Klauer.

For the summer of 1967, the Notre Dame Art Gallery, needing a summer show, displayed all nineteen Ufers, identifying them with tombstone not didactic labels—the artist's name, title, media, and "Gift of William J. and Walter J. Klauer." Working on the blockbuster exhibition *The Age of Vasari*, I had little time to research the paintings. Consequently, the show was hung and dismantled with little fanfare. For years, I likened it to a party where invitations were sent and very few came. Little did I realize that I was curating the most important collections of Ufer's art ever assembled. While the exhibition turned out to be my Taos 'appetizer,' the main course wouldn't be served until 1974 when I made my first trip to Taos. I immediately became one of New Mexico's strongest advocates.

While few knew Walter Ufer's paintings, over the next forty years interest soared from relative obscurity to one of national importance. Key to this meteoric rise has been three generations of the Klauer family working in concert with scholars like Stephen L. Good, Teresa Hayes Ebie, Suzan Campbell, members of the Southwest Art History Council, a half a dozen graduate students from the University of Notre Dame, including Christine Fowler Shearer, and myself. Fortuitously, there are young scholars who are continuing our work. They are already serving as apostles of Walter Ufer and his Taos Society of Artists' peers.

The focus of this study is the Klauer family of Dubuque, Iowa, beginning with Peter and including three generations of sons who formed and cared for a remarkable collection of Southwestern art. Today, grandsons, William, Robert and James are curating over two dozen paintings by Ufer, Higgins and E. Martin Hennings collected by William Henry Klauer and belonging to Klauer Manufacturing Company. There is also a group of American paintings that Klauer, a founding member of Grand Central Art Galleries, acquired between 1924 and 1940.

Remarkable was the impact that the Klauer family has had on four communities: Dubuque, Iowa; Grand Island, Michigan; Taos, New Mexico; and the University of Notre Dame, Indiana. William H. Klauer formed an early partnership between Chicago and Dubuque with Taos, New Mexico. Important was the ease by which he formed friendships with the five-term mayor of Chicago, Carter H. Harrison IV, and a group of prominent Chicago businessmen. Apparent will be William Klauer's interaction with the artists Walter Ufer, Victor Higgins, and E. Martin Hennings; the role he played in the cultural life of Dubuque, Iowa; as well as his twenty-year membership in New York City's Grand Central Art Galleries and friendship with its manager Erwin S. Barrie. Significant was Klauer's interaction with individuals who joined him in his retreats to his cottages south of the Picuris Mountains in the Sangre de Cristo Mountain Range, a half dozen miles south of Taos, New Mexico, and to Grand Island, located on Lake Superior, a short boat ride from Munising, Michigan.

Fueling the reader through the riveting chapters on art in this book are the papers of Mary and Walter Ufer and William Henry Klauer and his family that are held by the University of Notre Dame Archives. Along with other collections—including interviews and printed materials—we are able to reconstruct the fascinating story about a family who made, and continues to make, a difference.

Chapter I
The Klauer Family, Dubuque

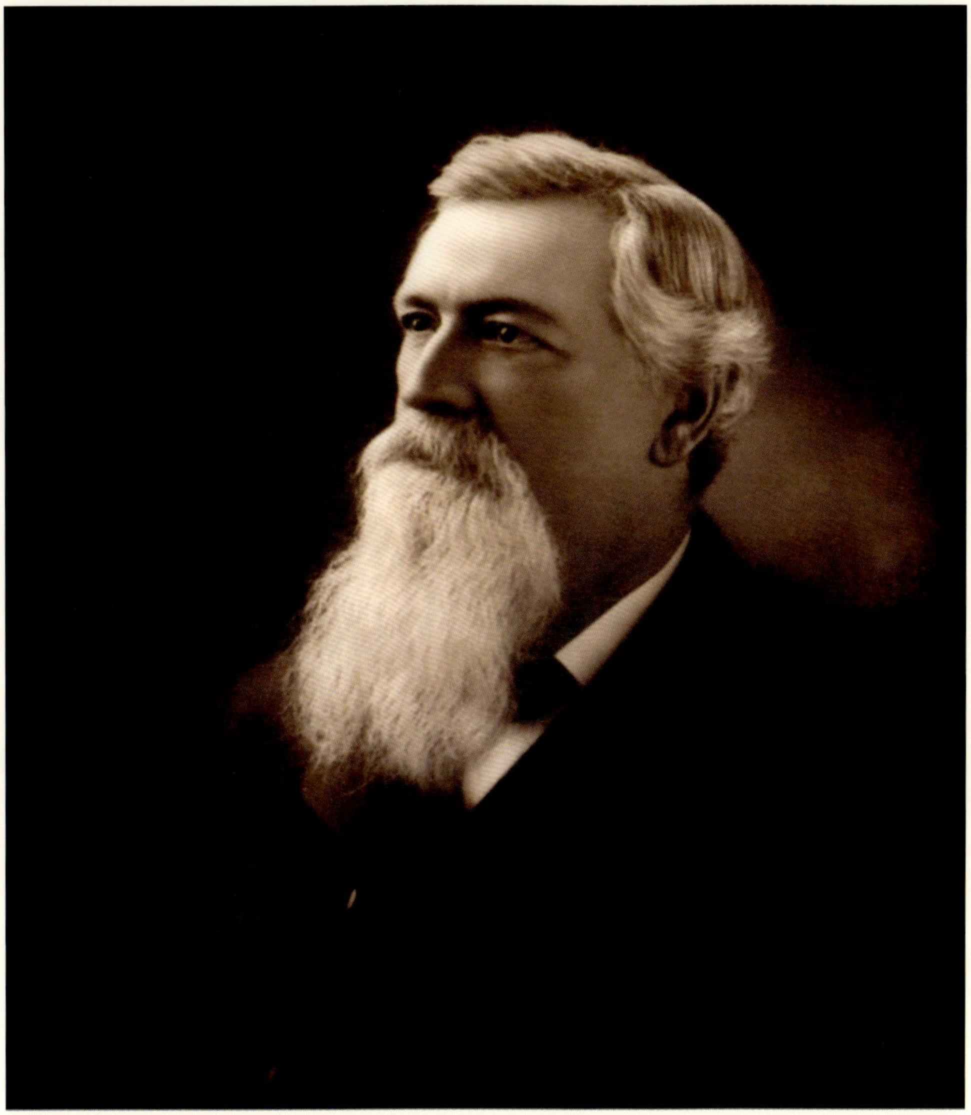

Figure 7. *Peter Klauer.* Photo courtesy Klauer Family.

PETER KLAUER, BEGINNINGS OF A DYNASTY

Peter Klauer (1842-1919) [fig. 7] was one of the thousands of Germans who immigrated to Dubuque, Iowa, during the nineteenth century. A population explosion caused by over-crowded conditions on the East Coast drove immigrants west to the industrial town called Dubuque, the first settlement in what would become the state of Iowa. Located along the Mississippi River, and at the junction of Iowa, Illinois, and Wisconsin, Dubuque was initially important for French-Indian fur trading, later becoming a major lead-producing center as well as a center of transportation.

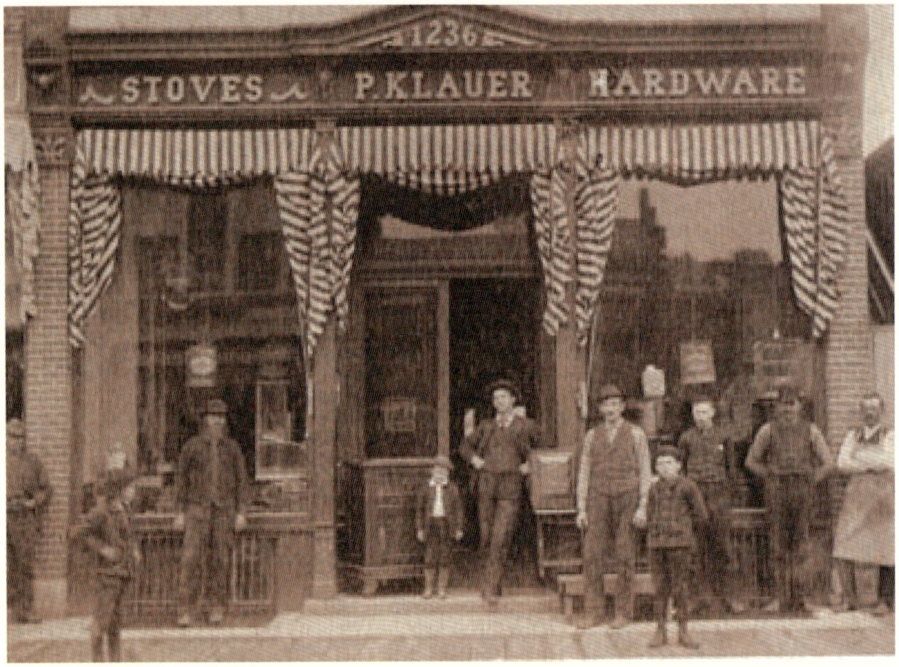

Figure 8. *Peter Klauer's Hardware Store*, c. 1870s.
Photo courtesy *Encyclopedia Dubuque*.

Peter Klauer was born in Coblenz, Germany, November 28, 1842, moving to Dubuque in 1855. His marriage to Ludmilla (Millie) eventually produced a son, William Henry Klauer (1870-1952). Soon after arriving in Dubuque and seeking a better life, Peter served an apprenticeship as a coppersmith with the firm of Dries and Hennock before taking a job as a tinsmith with Thomas Hennie. In 1870, not satisfied working for others, Klauer opened his own business, the P. Klauer Stove and Hardware [fig. 8]. His firm produced galvanized iron cornices, stoves, home furnishing goods, hot-air furnaces, and tin roofs..."[1]

Peter became active in Dubuque's political, social and cultural life. Besides his involvement with the Democratic party, in 1886 he became one of the founders of the German Trust and Savings Bank. Klauer, along with a group of businessmen, satisfied the need for a banking institution in the predominantly German section of north Dubuque. The bank opened "for business in the building known as the Bell Block" on January 20, 1887.[2] Peter and his fellow businessmen were commended for "starting at the bottom," and "through thrift and industry" had achieved success, while commanding the "confidence and respect of the community."[3] In January 1899, Peter was selected president of the bank and served in that position until his death in 1919.[4] During his lifetime, he was also involved with the St. Francis Orphans Home, a trustee of St. Mary's Parish, and vice president of the Iowa Coffin Company. When it came to building the Dubuque County Courthouse, Peter Klauer was on the board of supervisors and chairman of the committee directing its construction.

[1] "Peter Klauer," *Encyclopedia Dubuque*, accessed July 1, 2018, http://www.encyclopediadubuque.org/index.php?title=KLAUER,_Peter.

[2] "Thirty-eight Years of Progress," *Union Trust and Savings Bank, Dubuque, Iowa*, 20 January 1923, 3.

[3] Ibid.

[4] "In Memoriam," *Union Trust and Savings Bank*, 1923, 20.

An expert marksman and avid outdoors man, he organized the Dubuque Shooting Society. A shooting contest was held annually, and the winner of the 'King Shoot' was given the title 'King of the Gesellschalt,' holding it until the following year's competition. Peter's son, William Henry Klauer [fig. 16] was among the title-holders.[5]

Peter's influence on the community's educational and cultural life was even more important. He was one of the first directors and trustees of the Dubuque City Library, a role that successive members of the Klauer family, in particular his son, William, accepted. While the Klauer family, beginning with Peter, forged a long history of philanthropy and patronage in Dubuque, their preservation of a collection of glass photographic plates of historic Dubuque is particularly relevant to this story [figs. 10 through 15].

In the spring of 1912, two itinerant photographers arrived in Dubuque with a large format camera. For three weeks they took roughly 440 extraordinary photographs that documented the city at work. The photographers made prints from the glassplates with a plan to sell them to the people and businesses of the city.[6] The collection thoroughly documented life in Dubuque six years before America became involved in World War I. It captured images of professionals in their offices, holiday events, retail stores,

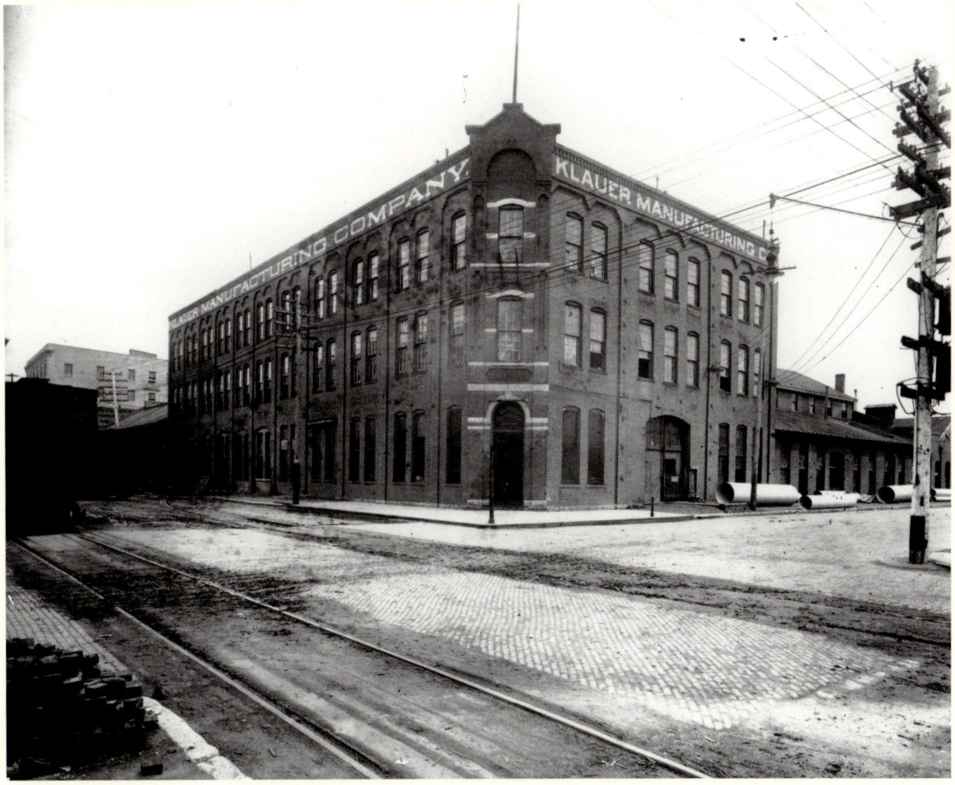

Figure 9. *Klauer Manufacturing Company*. c. 1915.
William J. Klauer Collection, Loras College, Center for Dubuque History.

[5] "Dubuque Shooting Society," *Encyclopedia Dubuque,* accessed July 1, 2018, http://www.encyclopediadubuque.org/index.php?title=DUBUQUE_SHOOTING_SOCIETY.html.

[6] Tim Olson, *A City at Work: 1912 and 2012* (Dubuque Museum of Art and Loras College Center for Dubuque History, 2012), 1.

churches, and factories. General views of the city illustrate a flourishing metropolis and a major industrial center. Among the images were early photographs of the Old Hotel Julien—its lobby, bar, and cigar stand—taken before the hotel was rescued from bankruptcy by the Klauers in 1930.

The collections included images of the Klauer Manufacturing Company employees at work. Peter Klauer acquired approximately fifteen of the prints, and Tim Olson suggests that Klauer "must have sensed the value of the entire set of images shot in Dubuque and so he bought the plates and stored them in a Klauer Manufacturing (Company) warehouse."[7] When he died in 1919, the plates remained in storage for the next sixty years—"occassionally thumbed through by the curious, but mostly forgotten..."[8] Finally, in the 1980s, Peter's grandson, William J. Klauer, had the plates "removed from storage and two sets of contact prints were made."[9] All of the prints were eventually donated to the Loras College Center for Dubuque History.

For historians of the city of Dubuque, it is fortunate that the Klauer family preserved the images created over a century ago. All too often, after the plates were used, they were scrapped and reused. The Klauer's early munificence offers a unique opportunity to view an earlier time in Dubuque.

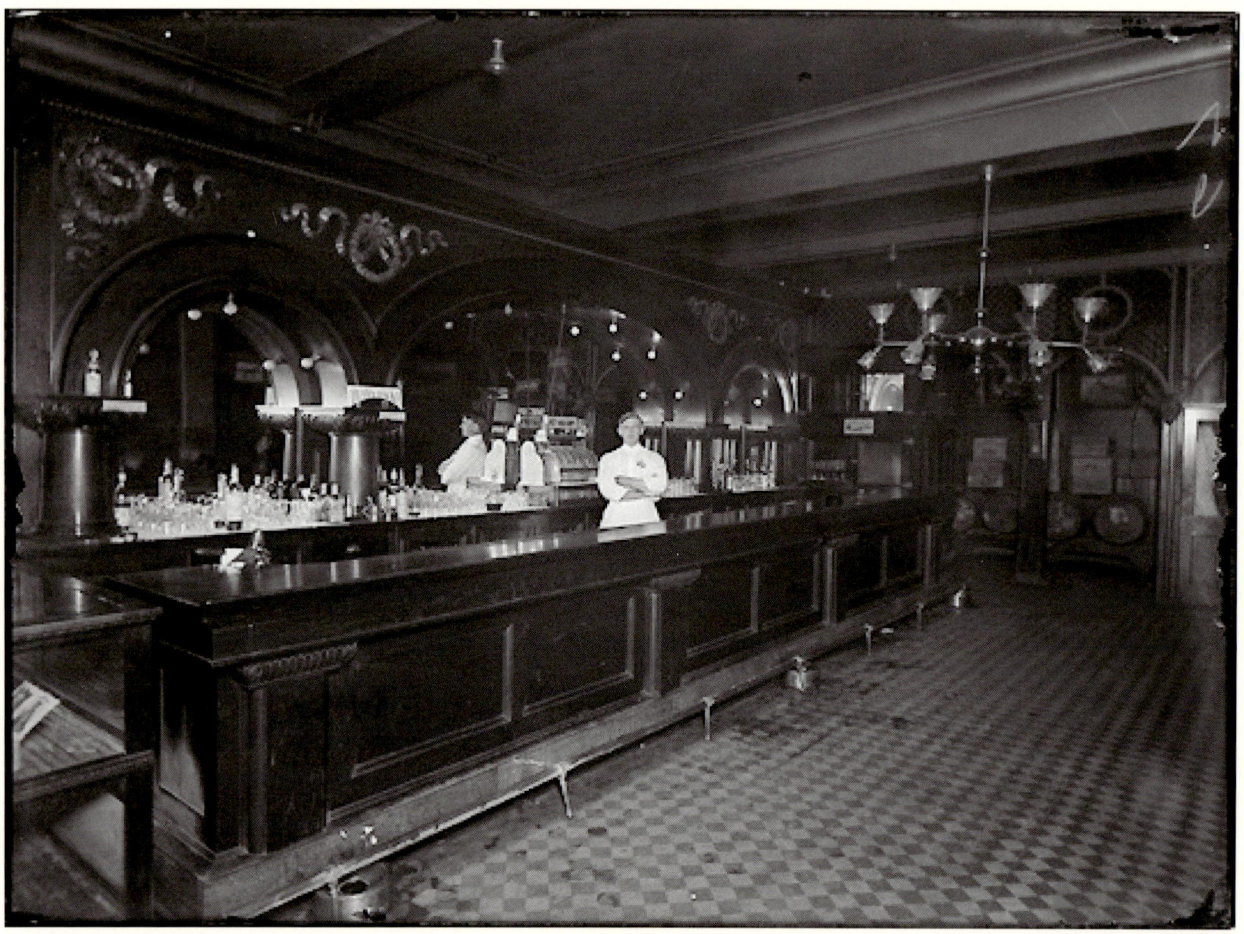

Figure 10. *Bar at the Old Julien Hotel.*
William J. Klauer Collection, Loras College, Center for Dubuque History.

[7] Ibid.
[8] Ibid.
[9] Ibid.

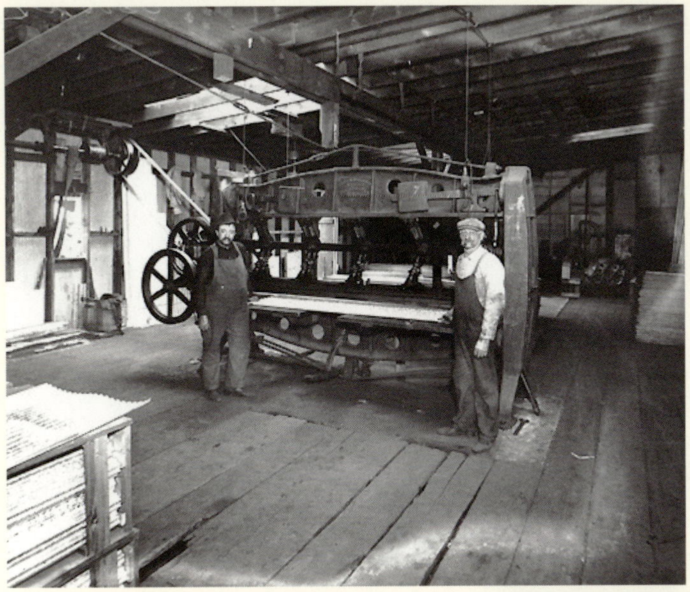

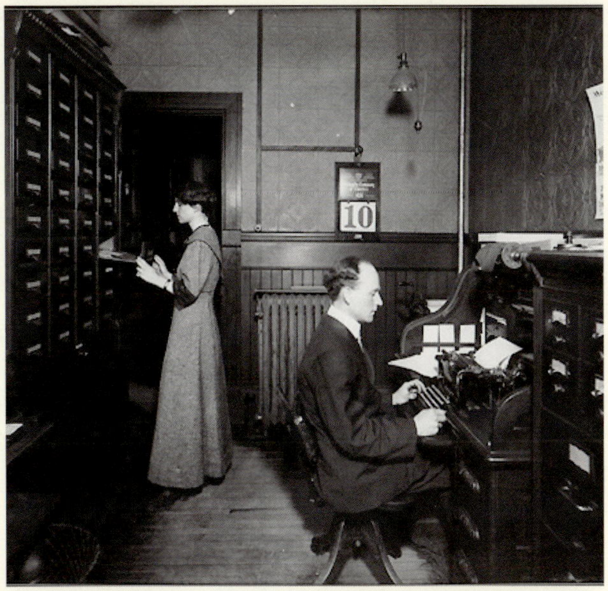

Figures 11 and 12. *Two Workers Klauer Manufacturing Company* (top left) and *Klauer Manufacturing Company Office* (top right), William J. Klauer Collection, Loras College, Center for Dubuque History.

Figure 13: *Whelan Brothers Grocery Store* (middle), William J. Klauer Collection, Loras College, Center for Dubuque History.

Figures 14 and 15: *Unidentified Barbershop* (bottom left) and *Two men filling kegs at Dubuque Brewing and Malting Company* (bottom right), William J. Klauer Collection, Loras College, Center for Dubuque History.

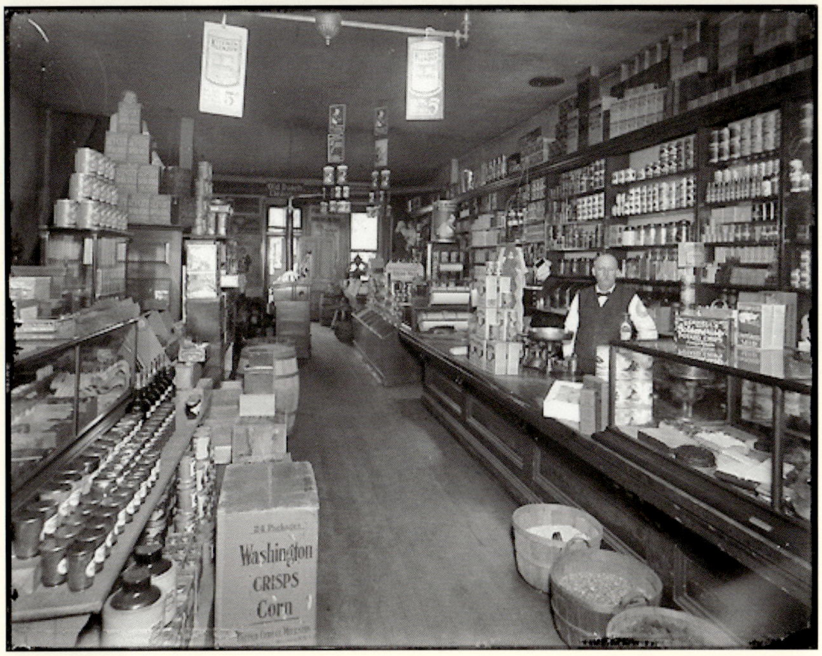

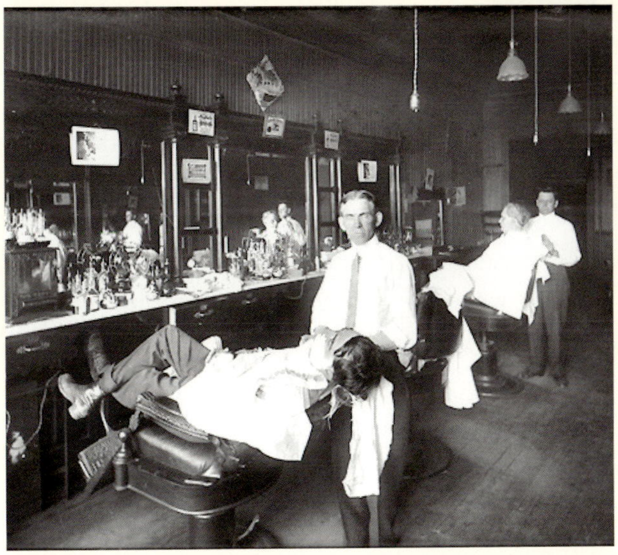

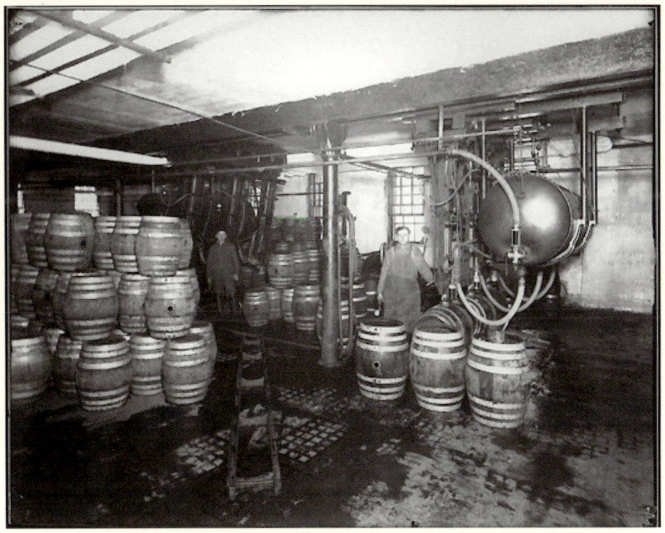

WILLIAM HENRY KLAUER: EARLY YEARS

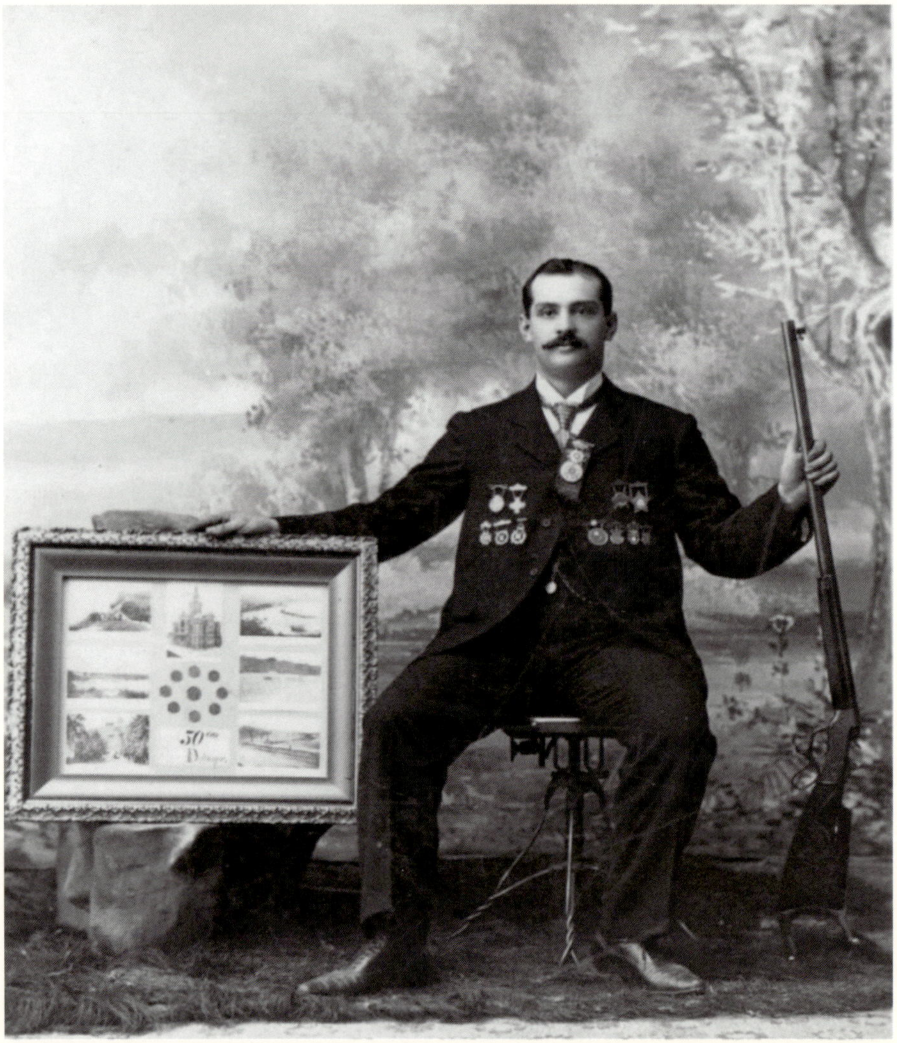

Figure 16. *William Henry Klauer as a Member of the Dubuque Shooting Society*, before 1900. Photo courtesy Klauer Family Papers, University of Notre Dame Archives.

Peter and Ludmilla gave birth to William Henry Klauer on the 18th of August in 1870. From his youth, William followed in his father's footsteps. Peter made his son a partner in the Klauer Manufacturing Company, beginning a tradition that continues today. William became a member of the Dubuque Shooting Society, and like his father, and the generations of Klauer men to follow, William worked and played hard. Klauer men have always brought balance to their lives. The Klauer Manufacturing Company prospered and became one of Dubuque's most successful enterprises, even during the most difficult of times, including two world wars framing the Great Depression. To Peter and his three generation of heirs, the family played an important role in the life of the Dubuque community. Members of the Klauer family have always enjoyed a strong, close relationship. They have partnered in Dubuque's social, political, religious and cultural affairs. With all their obligations, Klauer men found time for annual, sometimes semi-annual, hunting retreats. By 1914, William had built a cottage south of Taos, New Mexico, and in the late twenties purchased the Mather-Klauer Cottage on Grand Island, Michigan.

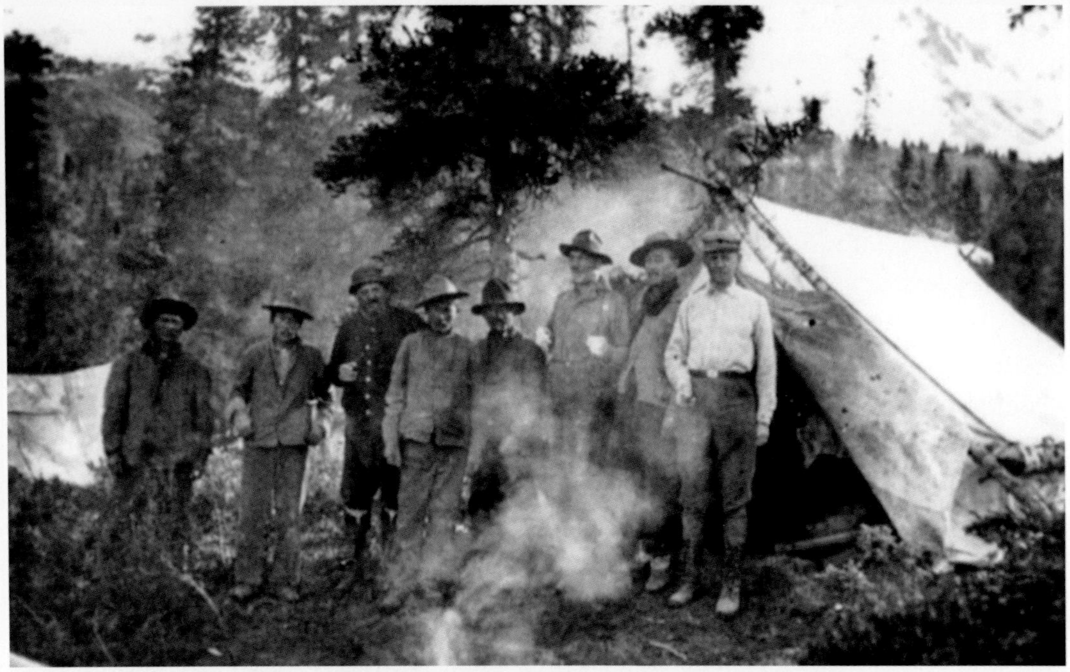

Figure 17. *William H. Klauer with Friends*. Klauer third from left smoking a pipe. Photo courtesy Klauer Family Papers, University of Notre Dame Archives.

By the time he died on December 2, 1952, Klauer had led a full life—one of success, prosperity and adventure. In business, he survived two world wars and twenty years working with a prominent but problematic, nearly impossible, artist. Operating the company in partnership with his father, he led the company through years of great expansion.[10] In 1885 the firm built a three-story structure onto the Klauers' factory shop at 1236 Iowa Street. With continual growth, the business moved to the corner of 18th and Washington Street. In 1896, the Klauer Company again moved, this time to 1353 Iowa Street. By 1911, already fabricating anything that moved water, the Klauers realized they needed more space and acquired additional property to manufacture culverts and irrigation flumes.

As the company's factory superintendent, William Henry Klauer travelled extensively to market product-flumes, plows, culverts, and other water related products. The company also produced stamped metal ceiling tiles.[11] In a 1995 interview with Klauer's oldest son, William, he described other types of equipment produced by Klauer Manufacturing Company. For example, the company developed a small heating burner that could be used on trains transporting wintertime fruit from California to points north. They sold for "six bucks a piece and we made a lot of money."[12]

RANCHOS ORCHARD AND LAND COMPANY PURCHASE

On December 1, 1914, Klauer Manufacturing Company entered into a contract "to buy all of the Ranchos Orchard and Land Company, lying above surveyed line of the irrigation ditch, 4,500 acres for $18,000."[13] It was the introduction and development of irrigation flumes to this property that brought

[10] "William H. Klauer," *Encyclopedia Dubuque*, accessed July 1, 2018, http://www.encyclopediadubuque.org/index.php?title=KLAUER,_William_H.

[11] Steve Fox. "Pesky Named for Arts Patron," April 15, 2009. Klauer Family Papers, University of Notre Dame (KFPUND)

[12] William J. Klauer interview with Dean A. Porter in Dubuque, December 1995.

[13] *Memorandum*, KFPUND.

William Klauer to Taos, New Mexico. The Company had developed a system of flumes and metal schutes with gravity that could move water from the mountains to the lowlands. Without water, the Ranchos Orchard's land would remain unusable desert. Located near Ranchos de Taos, irrigating the Ranchos Orchard property became one of the Company's most ambitious projects.

From 1915 to 1923, Klauer, with his friends and business associates, attempted to develop the land, making it commercially viable for growing apples and peaches. For Klauer, securing titles, meeting deadlines, paying taxes, developing funding sources, acquiring additional acres, and more, became a full-time job that often required trips to Taos. As his trips were both short and long-term, he decided to have a cottage constructed close to his property rather than finding housing in town. The construction of the cottage could satisfy two needs—business and recreation. He could adjourn to his cottage after a day of work to enjoy the fruits of the land, spectacular scenery, trout fishing in the streams flowing from the Picuris Mountains, and the camaraderie of his friends and business associates whom he invited to his cottage. By spending several weeks in his cottage, he could daily inspect the progress being made on the Ranchos Orchard property.

Klauer soon found that irrigating the 4500-acre upper tract was a major challenge and would take some time to complete. By 1921, Klauer Manufacturing would also own half of the lower tract. Eventually Klauer would own all 10,700 acres. From 1915 to 1921, Klauer focused on owning and irrigating all of the Ranchos Orchard and Land property. In order to own and irrigate the land, he formed partnerships—some successful, others not. Two of his close friends during this period of activity were Bert Barker from New York and John Hillman from Delta, Colorado. He also had extensive dealings with various Chicago businessmen.

By 1919, Klauer felt he had visual evidence to attract participation from a group of Chicago businessmen. He was able to send photographs to them "showing some of the flume work that has already been done on the Ranchos Orchard and Land Company property. They will probably be surprised to see what work has been done."[14] Unfortunately, the group was not interested. In September 1920, Hillman was contemplating buying the lower tract of Ranchos Orchard property and spent three days with an engineer inspecting "the ditches, flumes, etc., and found everything in better condition than expected..."[15] While Hillman was there he thought he could stay in Klauer's cottage, but "couldn't get inside. Everything looks to be in good shape. Some swell log cabin."[16] Klauer had campaigned repeatedly to form an organization to share the cost of installing an irrigation system that also included the construction of a dam. Despite heroic efforts, he failed to find a group that would join him in the project. By the following January 1921, Klauer with Hillman, owned all 10,700 acres of the Ranchos Orchard property. Klauer still owned his original purchase, the upper tract's 4500 acres. In January 1921, Hillman purchased the lower tract, 5500 acres, during the same month selling "one-half undivided interest" to Klauer.[17] In addition to funding the creation of an irrigation system, Klauer and Hillman also had to pay the annual taxes on the property.[18]

Klauer and Hillman continued their effort in irrigating the large tract of land, but eventually they realized that even with the expertise and work of Klauer Manufacturing Company, their efforts were futile.

---

[14] William Klauer to Fred J. Wegg, 8 July 1919, KFPUND.

[15] J. E. Hillman to William Klauer, 24 September 1920, KFPUND.

[16] J. E. Hillman to William Klauer, 28 September 1920, KFPUND.

[17] W. Barker to John Hillman, 6 January 1921, KFPUND.

[18] It took a major effort in establishing the annual tax fee per acre based on the quality of the land.

In an on-going issue involving taxes owned on the property as well as once again trying to get an extension on water rights, the future of the Ranchos Orchard property looked discouraging.

By June 1923, the prospect that Ranchos Orchard would ever produce fruit offered little hope. A letter from J. W. Booker to District Attorney Fred Stringfellow settled the issue of what the property's acres should be valued. Hillman and Klauer had been contesting the valuation of the property for tax purposes. Taxes for "uncultivated lands" were $2.25 an acre while "bad lands" were $1.00. Booker reported that the land was purchased with the intention "to irrigate it and plant an orchard but they did not succeed in getting any water for the land and probably never will and it is the poorest grade of grazing land as it now stands."[19] From that time on Klauer Manufacturing Company maintained the property as "bad lands." It wasn't until the 1990s that the property served a beneficial role for recreational and educational purposes—not commercial.

The inability to irrigate the Ranchos Orchard property did not deter Klauer from visiting Taos. He was also an avid outdoor's man, annually spending time hunting for big game... moose, deer, caribou, mountain sheep, elk, and in New Mexico, fishing for fresh water trout [fig. 18]. His extensive travels and intense passion for adventure led to exploration of much of America, including Alaska. His rotund shape suggests he had a voracious appetite for the spoils of the hunt. When he travelled to Taos, New Mexico, he found a country suited to his taste for the out-of-doors—wild and unspoiled.

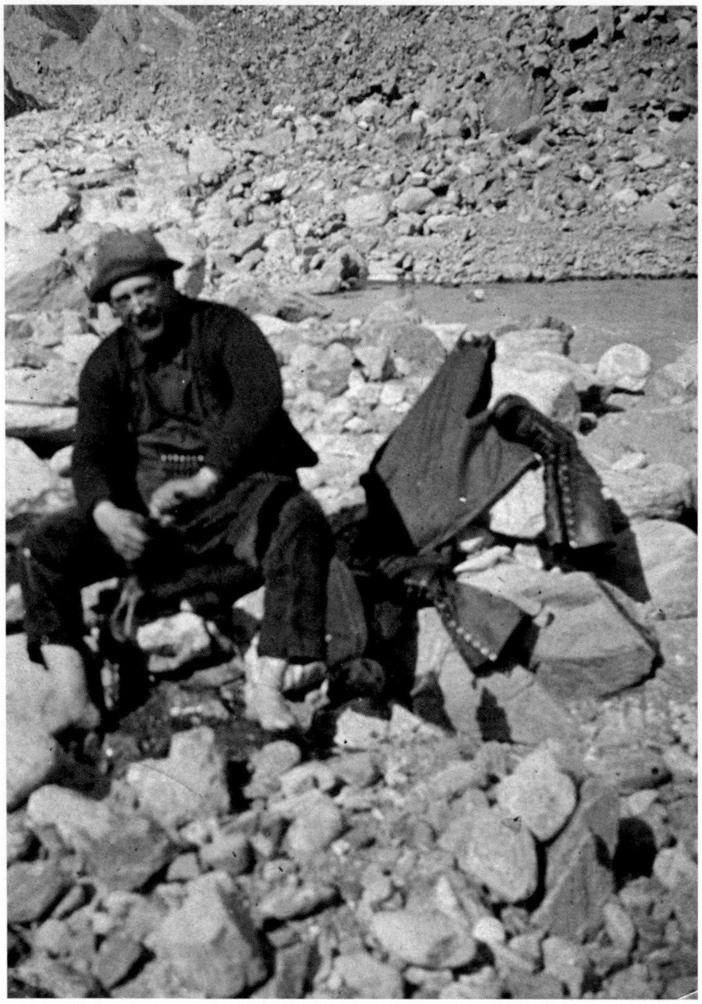

Figure 18.
William Henry Klauer in New Mexico, c. 1914.
Photo courtesy Klauer Family Papers,
University of Notre Dame Archives.

[19] J. W. Booker to Fred Stringfellow, 14 June 1923, KFPUND.

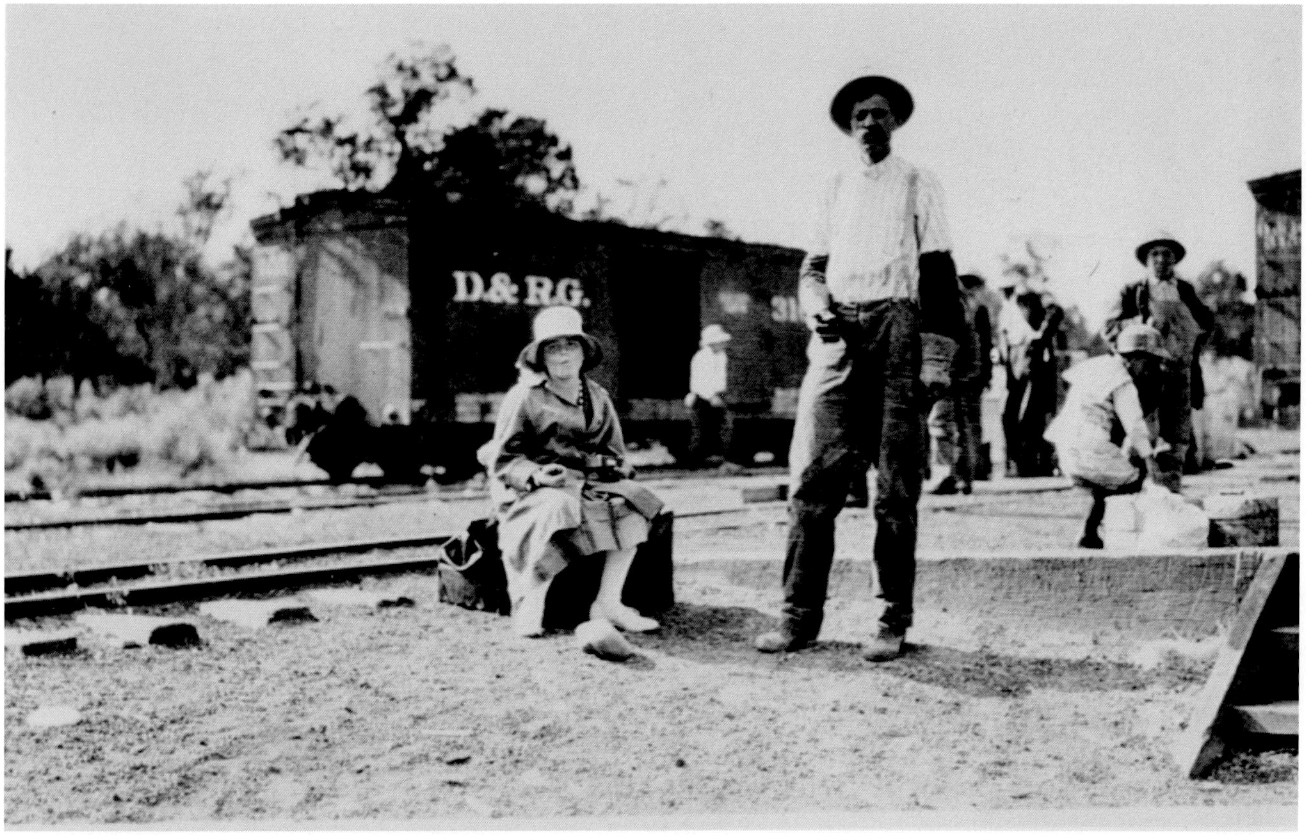

Figure 19. *Dorothy Berninghaus [Brandenberg] with Long John Dunn at Railroad Station at Servilleta.* Photo courtesy Mrs. John [Barbara] Brenner.

LONG JOHN DUNN OF TAOS: ENTREPRENEUR

Long John Dunn, one of New Mexico's most colorful entrepreneurs, greeted visitors coming to Taos at Taos Junction or Servilleta. After a 1200-mile train ride from Chicago, Klauer would also have experienced a trip with Dunn. Besides being a cattleman, escaped convict, and saloon-keeper, Dunn hauled passengers between the railroad line and Taos—in a stagecoach, buckboard or prehistoric Ford. John owned "the toll bridge (across the Rio Grande Gorge), several stages, and teams of horses. He built a hotel, or what he called a 'road-ranch,' at the mouth of Hondo Canyon…"[20] He also operated an infamous roulette wheel in the Columbian Hotel in Taos. Through his acquaintance with Dunn, it wouldn't be surprising if Klauer met Ufer in one of the entrepreneur's four saloons. The artist's reputation as a gambler and drinker was well-known.

In 1934, the *Taos Valley News* described Dunn as being "possessed of that keen, radical viewpoint known as common sense which he frequently supplemented with satirical wit…"[21] Virtually everyone, including Klauer, would have been transported "back and forth before we had our own cars, and never did he fail us."[22] John Dunn's riders would have been treated to a real taste of the Old West.

Dunn was given much credit to opening Taos to the rest of America. He "hauled" businessmen, entertainers, and, of course, artists and their families. Dunn would have shipped artist's supplies to Taos,

---

[20] Max Evans, *Long John Dunn of Taos: From Texas Outlaw to New Mexico Hero* (Santa Fe, NM: Clear Light Publishers, 1993), 113.

[21] "Kindly Karaicature: Long John Dunn," *The Taos Valley News*, 1934.

[22] Ibid.

and finished paintings from the "mud town" to points East. Dunn spoke of Walter Ufer during the artist's memorial service, describing their first trip together. Oscar Berninghaus and his daughter were passengers to Taos as can be seen by a photograph of the fifteen-year-old seated next to the standing Dunn [fig. 19].

During his first years traveling to New Mexico, Klauer stayed in the century old Columbian Hotel (now the LaFonda Hotel). According to Mabel Dodge Luhan the hotel was located on the east side of Don Fernando Plaza "where every other door is the entrance to a saloon," the long, low building featured shops with columned portals.[23] The hotel, was fronted with trees and hitching posts for saddle horses and wagons. Luhan reported that "...nobody ever comes here, except traveling men."[24] Artists met at the hotel for breakfast and to play cards and chess. Over the years, the environment didn't change. The aroma of hot stove-heat and burning lamp oil, mingled with cigarette and cigar smoke, contributed to an unpleasant environment. To the cigar-smoking Klauer, however, the environment likely posed little problem.

Klauer, who was in his mid-forties, had an eye-opening, challenging experience his first days in Taos. It was still an untamed, tri-culture community of Hispanics, Taos Indians, and a few Anglos. Max Evans described how the plaza was "lined with wagons, horses and buggies. The Spanish farmers and sheep men came to town to trade and gossip and the Indians did likewise. It was an oddity to see the three races, including Anglos, so peaceful after so much bloodshed in the past."[25]

Despite the picture Evans painted, at times it was dangerous to go to the post office, where everyone congregated. It remained an Old West town where it wasn't uncommon for Taosenos to carry six shooters. The town wouldn't have electricity, running water, and a modern sewage system until the late 1920s. For Klauer, Taos offered a dramatic contrast to Chicago, even Dubuque. Yet, it became his place to go to—his escape from an industrialized world. Taos's acceptance of Klauer was immediate and lasting.

We can't be sure when Klauer first met Walter Ufer or Victor Higgins. He could have met them in Chicago, perhaps introduced by Mayor Carter Harrison or meat baron Oscar Mayer. However, we can't discount Taos as a possible meeting place. Both artists were in Taos by 1914. Bert Phillips was an early friend of Klauer, and if stays by Ufer and Higgins overlapped with Klauer's visits to Taos, they would have met.[26]

THE KLAUER COTTAGE, TAOS, NEW MEXICO

By 1914, Klauer had solved his housing problem. He had built a cottage [fig. 20], that was too large to be called a cabin, south of Ranchos de Taos.[27] The cottage played a significant role in the lives of William Klauer as well as his family and friends. It enabled Klauer to conduct business or simply enjoy his friends with stimulating conversation, good food, hunting, fishing, games of chance, or the splendors of Mother Nature. He visited his cottage annually, often staying several weeks, and he invited many friends each year since he was happiest when people surrounded him. Everybody brought something special to his cottage, and he made certain that they enjoyed all of the comforts of "roughing it" away from Dubuque or Chicago.

---

[23] Mabel Dodge Luhan, *Edge of Taos Desert*, 3rd ed. (Albuquerque: University of New Mexico Press, 1991), 23.

[24] Ibid, 39.

[25] Evans, *Long John Dunn*, 107.

[26] Klauer usually visited Taos in November or December, while Ufer and Higgins left for Chicago before the snows fell in December.

[27] In the late 1920s he also rehabbed an existing structure, later named Mather/Klauer Lodge, on Grand Island, Michigan.

By the time William H. Klauer met Walter Ufer in 1914, he was an important business, cultural and political figure in Dubuque and well known on the Chicago scene. While Klauer's principle reason for being in Chicago was business, he also enjoyed socializing with a close coterie of friends. He always had a room reserved at the Bismarck Hotel [fig. 22] or the Chicago Club [fig. 21]. Klauer's son recalled, "When I came into the kitchen in the morning and dad's suitcase was not by the backdoor, I knew he had gone to Chicago."[28]

Emil Eitel was "a great friend of Klauers," as well as president of the Old Bismarck Hotel. "Everybody…the Germans would go to the Bismarck Hotel."[29] Because Klauer stayed at the Bismarck, Ufer also became a regular, staying weeks at a time. The Chicago Club, housed in a Burnham and Root building, was a private social club that catered to Chicago's most prominent businessmen, politicians and families. The members enjoyed meeting to play cards and drink.

As he was on the board of the Chicago and Great Western Railway, Klauer frequently had business in Chicago. As a board member, he was also provided transportation between Dubuque and Chicago.[30] On days when the board of the Railway met, a passenger car was sent to Dubuque to pick up Klauer, and the train would return Klauer after he had concluded his business.[31]

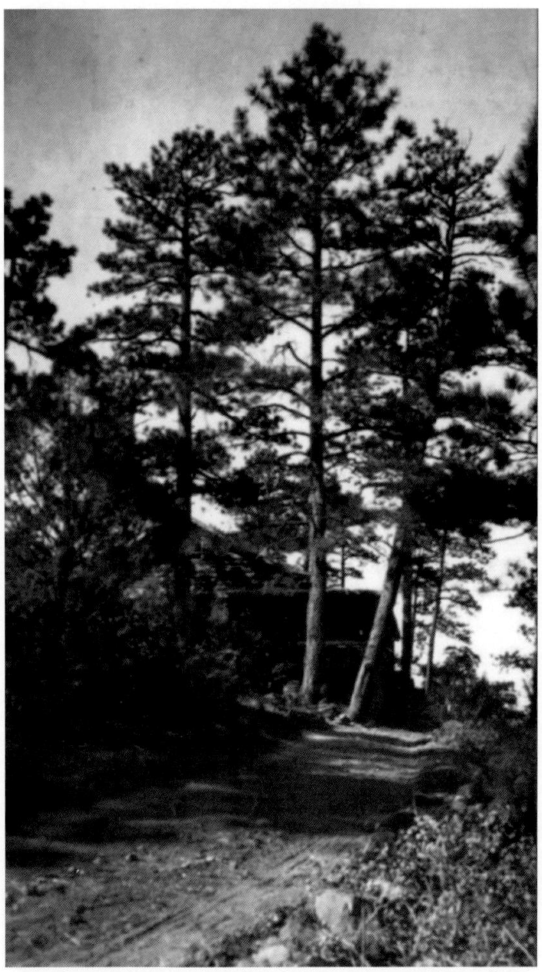

Figure 14. Carter H. Harrison.
Klauer Cottage, Taos, New Mexico, c. 1915.
Photo courtesy Klauer Family Collection, University of Notre Dame.

[28] William J. Klauer interview with Dean Porter in Dubuque, 1993.
[29] Ibid.
[30] Ibid.
[31] Ibid.

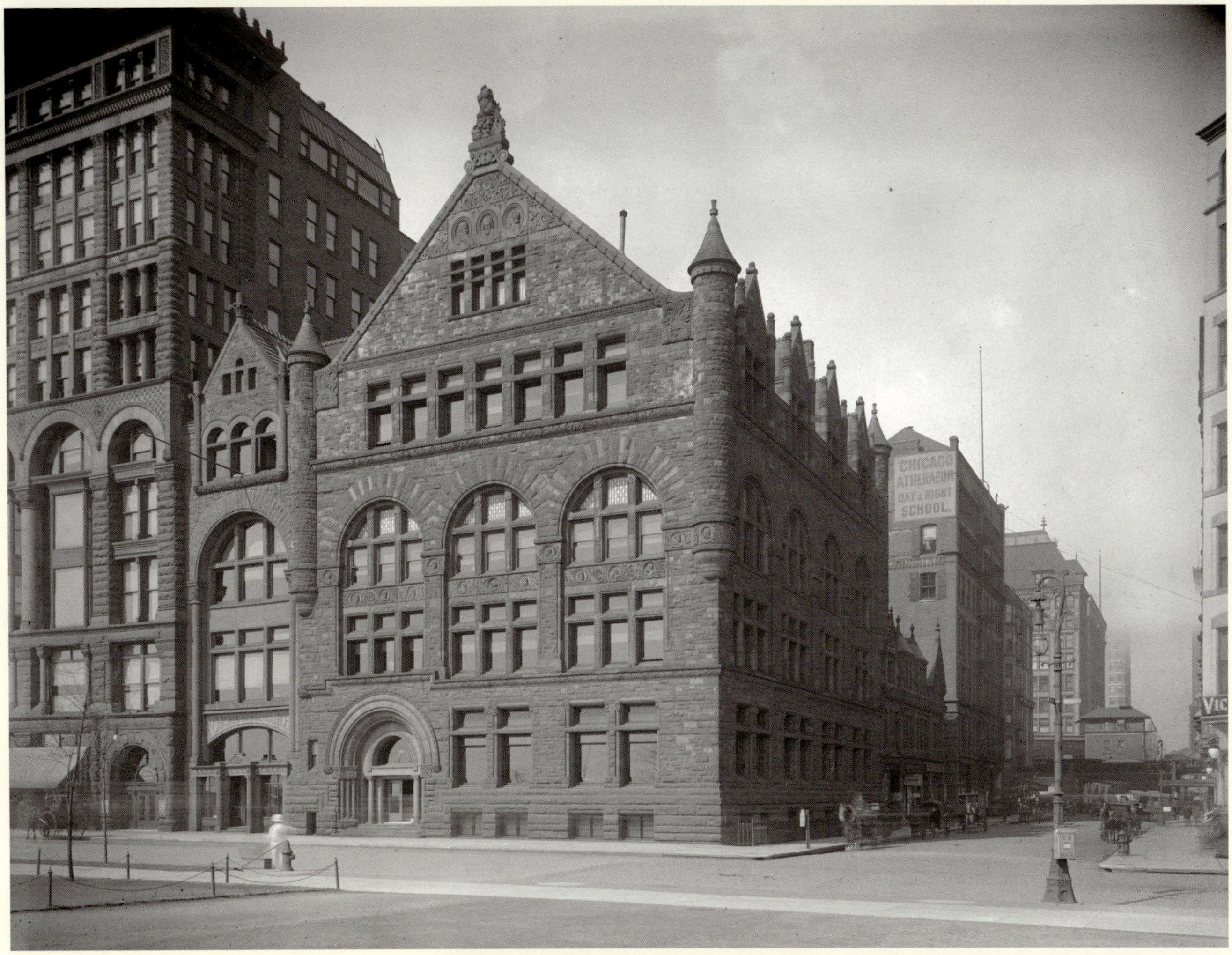

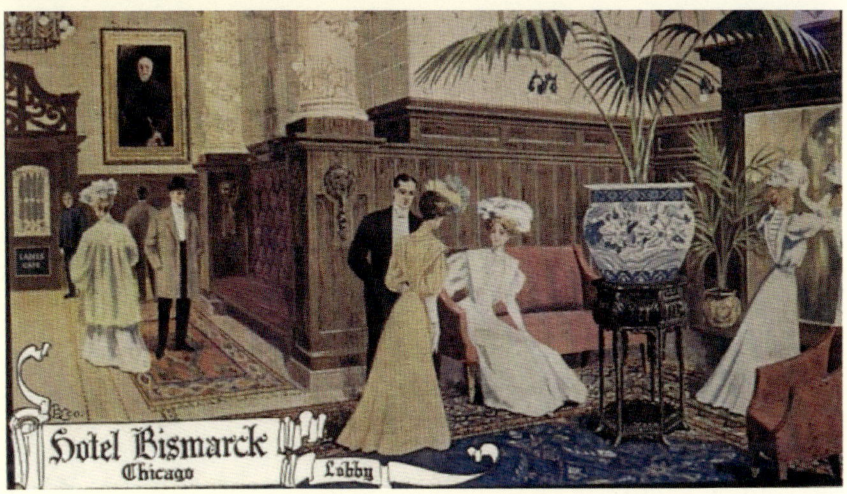

Figure 21.Detroit Publishing Co. *Chicago Club*, c. 1906. (top) Library of Congress, Prints and Photographs Division, [LC-D4-13261]. Gift of State Historical Society of Colorado.

Figure 22. *Hotel Bismarck Lobby, Chicago*. (bottom) Postcard courtesy the author.

Besides those serving on the board of the Chicago and Great Western Railway, Klauer had numerous friends—politicians, heads of major corporations, owners of hotels, and more. One of his friends was the five-term mayor of Chicago, Carter Henry Harrison, IV [fig. 23], who was to have a profound influence on Klauer's life as patron.

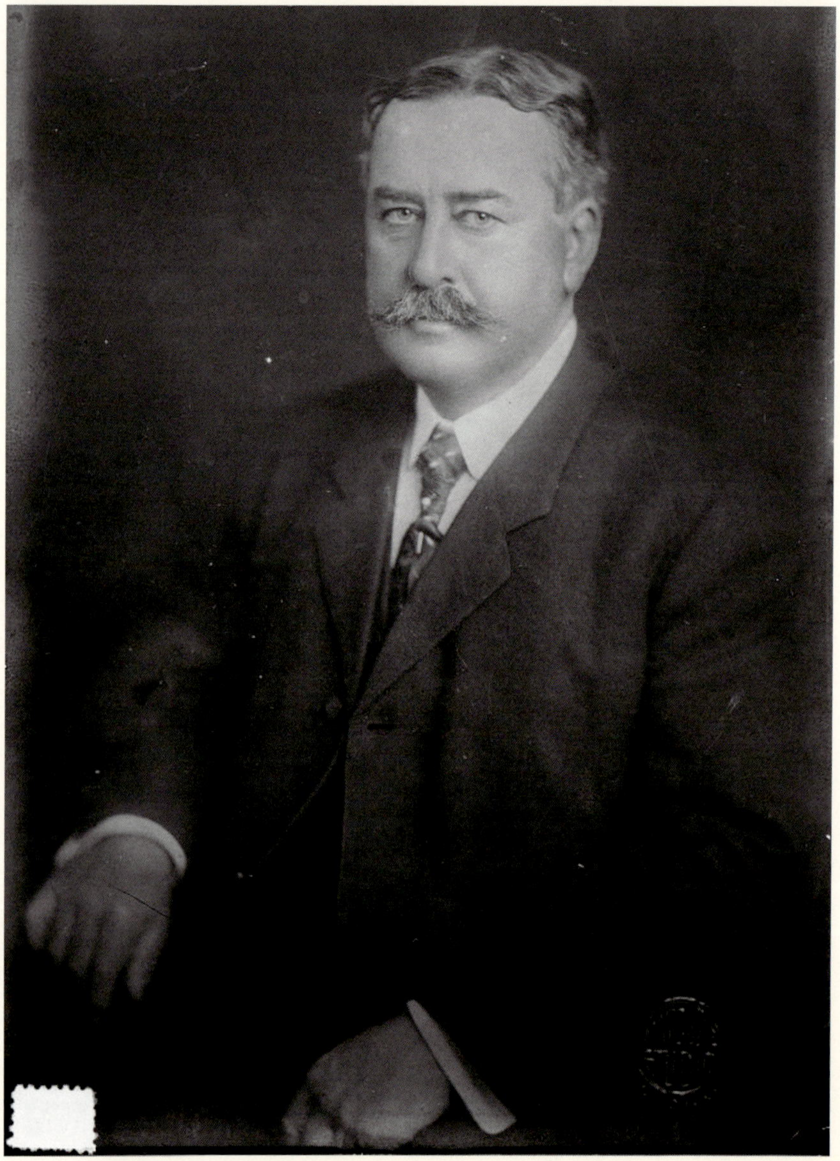

Figure 23.
Carter H. Harrison, IV in 1916.
Library of Congress, Prints & Photographs Division, [LC-B2-3764-6]

CARTER H. HARRISON, IV

Another key to Klauer's trips to New Mexico was his friendship with Chicago Mayor, Carter H. Harrison IV [fig. 23]. Long before Klauer made his first trip to Taos, the Harrison brothers had been frequent visitors to the area, and Klauer and Harrison shared their experiences in New Mexico. Like Klauer, Carter Harrison was an avid hunter and fisherman. He also was a fine photographer, documenting New Mexico's numerous pueblos and their inhabitants [fig. 24]. The mayor exhibited his large-scale, sepia tone photographs in solo exhibitions in Chicago. In fact, when Carter Harrison approached Walter Ufer about painting in New Mexico, he showed the artist several travel brochures of the Southwest, as well as his own photographs.[32] During Ufer's early years in New Mexico, Harrison counseled Ufer on what, how, and when to paint. His philosophy was reflected in his work with the camera.

[32] A large collection of Carter Harrison's photographs are now located in the Palace of the Governors in Santa Fe. The Klauer family also donated a selection of Carter Harrison's photographs to The Snite Museum of Art, University of Notre Dame.

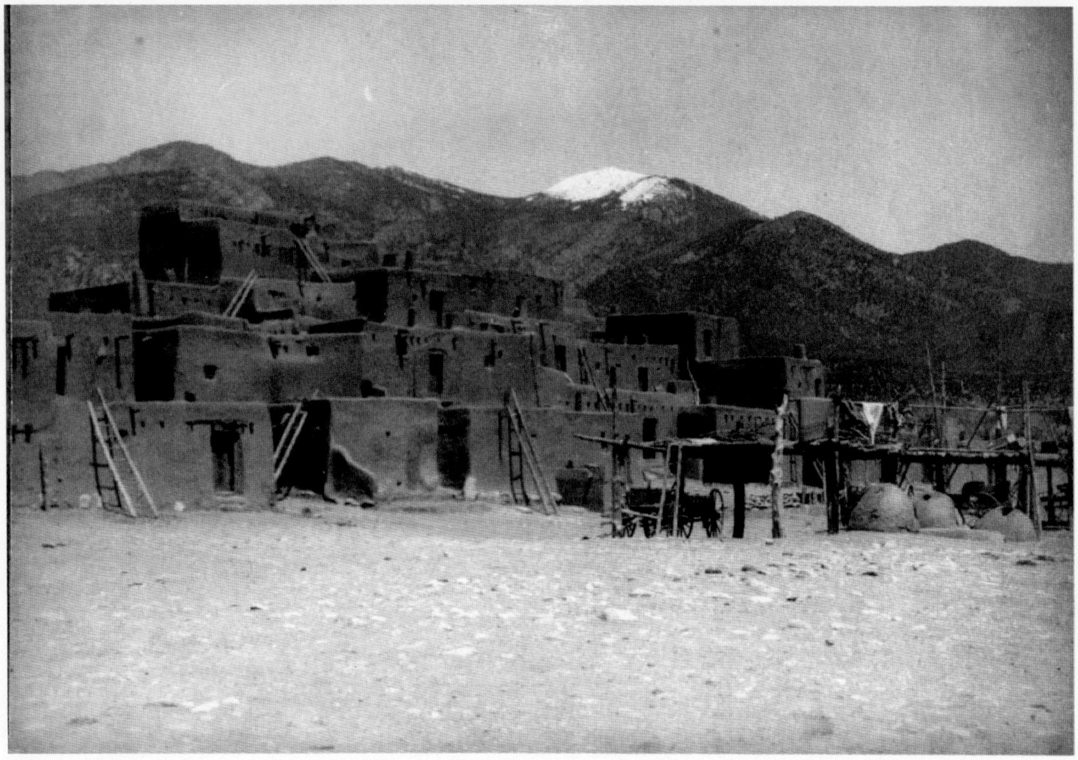

Figure 24. Carter H. Harrison, *Taos Pueblo,* c. 1906-1909. Photograph, 10.5 x 11.5 inches. Collection The Snite Museum of Art, University of Notre Dame. Gift of Klauer Family.

Harrison undoubtedly discussed his New Mexico experiences with Klauer. Knowing Harrison's attitude about his photographs, he certainly showed them to Klauer.[33] Harrison was too serious a photographer not to share his handsome, large-scale, sepia tone vignettes of pueblo life with Klauer and his friends. Klauer would have attended one of Harrison's solo exhibitions in Chicago. The former mayor invited his friends to exhibitions of personal photographs and portraits of himself created by Ufer, Hennings, and Louis Betts. Harrison had a track record of sharing exhibitions at The Art Institute with his friends. Surprisingly, even though Ufer was an accomplished portrait painter of Chicago notables, William Klauer never sat for the artist.

Until recently, the importance of Harrison's photographs to Ufer has been largely neglected. James C. Moore astutely observed that Harrison's photographs "...are not posed fictional stereotypes, however, but attempt to document everyday activities and contemporary circumstances."[34] Moore dates Harrison's photographs to the years of 1906 to 1909, a period when the mayor wasn't holding office and a time when Carter's wife Edith and their sickly son were forced to take up residence in Pasadena, California. During this period, Carter and his brother Preston visited Taos and the pueblos, which were seen as a primitive place, a holdover of the Wild West. It was a place where people could still see Indians in an "unspoiled condition."[35]

By 1914, Harrison was serving his fifth and final term as mayor and planning for his future, particularly in the arts. As Stephen Good states, "Harrison's passion for art, which had its inception at

---

[33] William Klauer eventually owned several of Harrison's photographs.

[34] James C. Moore, "That Man Out in the Mountains," in *A Place in the Sun: The Southwest Paintings of Walter Ufer and E. Martin Hennings* (Norman, Oklahoma: University of Oklahoma Press, 2016), 146.

[35] Ibid.

the Columbian Exposition in Chicago in 1893, blossomed into a distinguished career of collecting and patronage after his retirement from active political life."[36]

After experiencing the 1913 Armory Show at The Art Institute of Chicago, he became actively involved in the Chicago contemporary art scene. In November 1914, he fathered the Commission for Encouragement of Local Art, a program that budgeted city funds to acquire art to decorate public buildings in Chicago. Beneficiaries of this program were future Taos Society of Artists' painters Victor Higgins, Walter Ufer and E. Martin Hennings—all of who would eventually become friends with Klauer. Harrison appointed Higgins to represent the Palette and Chisel Club on the board of the Commission.[37] In fact, Harrison appears to have also played an influential role in the juried shows at The Art Institute. After Harrison and his syndicate sponsored Ufer and Higgins's trips to New Mexico, the two artists became frequent prizewinners at The Art Institute.

Outside of the political world, Carter Harrison helped his brother, William Preston Harrison, run the *Chicago Times*. They also enjoyed the friendship of a group of individuals, mostly of German descent, who they would involve in their scheme to support artists to paint the section of Southwest America that they loved. Included among their friends were Andreas Wackenreuter, Emil Eitel, Otto Demme, Charles Hermann, Oscar Mayer [fig. 25], and William Klauer. While Demme and Hermann purchased only one painting by Ufer, Wackenreuter acquired over two-dozen canvases, earning the reputation of being the artist's "angel." Several of his purchases were family portraits and pre-New Mexico canvases. The Harrison brothers acquired nearly thirty paintings, spending less than $1000. According to Ufer's sales cards, Mayer only purchased twelve paintings but spent more than $2000. Mayer was also Hennings's major patron and paid the artist top dollar. Even though he was the last member to join the syndicate, Klauer acquired an unbelieveable number of canvases. In 1919 and 1920 alone, he acquired sixteen paintings by Ufer at a cost of $4200. He also acquired five paintings by Higgins and at least six by Hennings between 1917 and 1930.

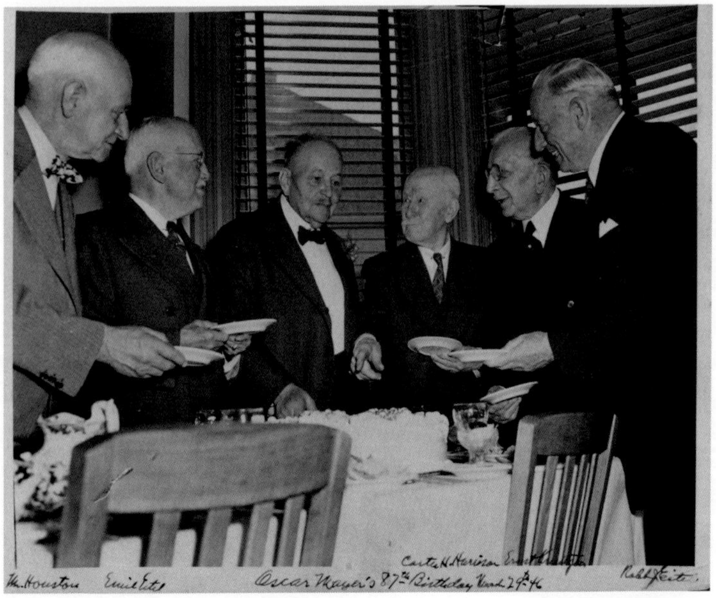

Figure 25.
Oscar Mayer Celebrating His 87th Birthday, 1946.
(Left to right: William Houston, Emil Eitel, Oscar Mayer, Carter Harrison, Ernst J. Kreutgen, and Robert Eitel).
Photo courtesy Klauer Family Papers, University of Notre Dame Archives.

[36] Stephen L. Good, "Walter Ufer: Munich to Taos, 1913-1918" in *Pioneer Artists of Taos*, revised and expanded edition (Denver: Old West Publishing Company, 1983, rev. 1985), 124.

[37] Carter H. Harrison in a letter to Victor Higgins. 19 November 1914, Joan Higgins Reed Estate, Museum of Fine Arts, Santa Fe.

Chapter II
Walter Ufer, Victor Higgins, and E. Martin Hennings: The Beginning

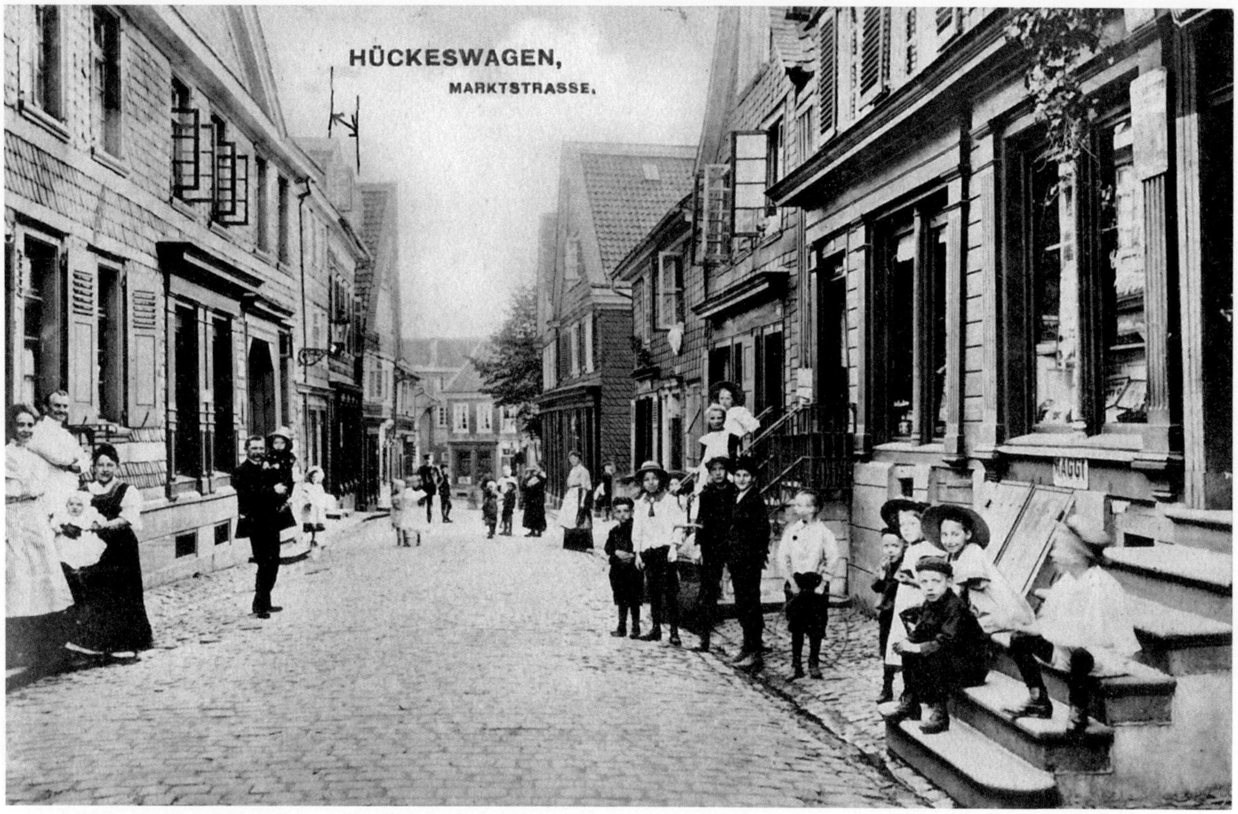

Figure 26. *Walter Ufer's Home, Hückeswagen, Germany*. Postcard courtesy Ufer Papers, University of Notre Dame Archives, gift of Stephen L. Good, Denver [Ufer identified his home with pencil on the upper left].

Three artists from Chicago, Walter Ufer, Victor Higgins, and E. Martin Hennings, followed a similar road in becoming beneficiaries of Klauer's patronage. Each began his professional life in Chicago and ended it in Taos, New Mexico. During their careers, William Henry Klauer played a critical role in their survival and success.

Walter Ufer was born in Hückeswagen, Germany in 1876, and his family moved to Louisville, Kentucky in 1880. He soon developed a strong passion for art. Ufer was one of three boys, and he was expected to work to help support an impoverished family since Ufer's father had been swindled of his money. At age seventeen, Ufer spent five years (1893-1898) as a journeyman apprentice and student in Germany. While he was in Dresden, Ufer painted *Portrait of an Old Man with Beard* [fig. 27]. The portrait hearkens back to the style of the Old Masters, painting alla prima, with oil applied in generous, thick, juicy strokes. It is reminiscent of one of America's great portrait painters and teachers, William Merritt Chase. After his five years in Germany, Ufer returned to America where he moved to Chicago to continue his career as an illustrator as well as his pursuit of being a fine arts painter.

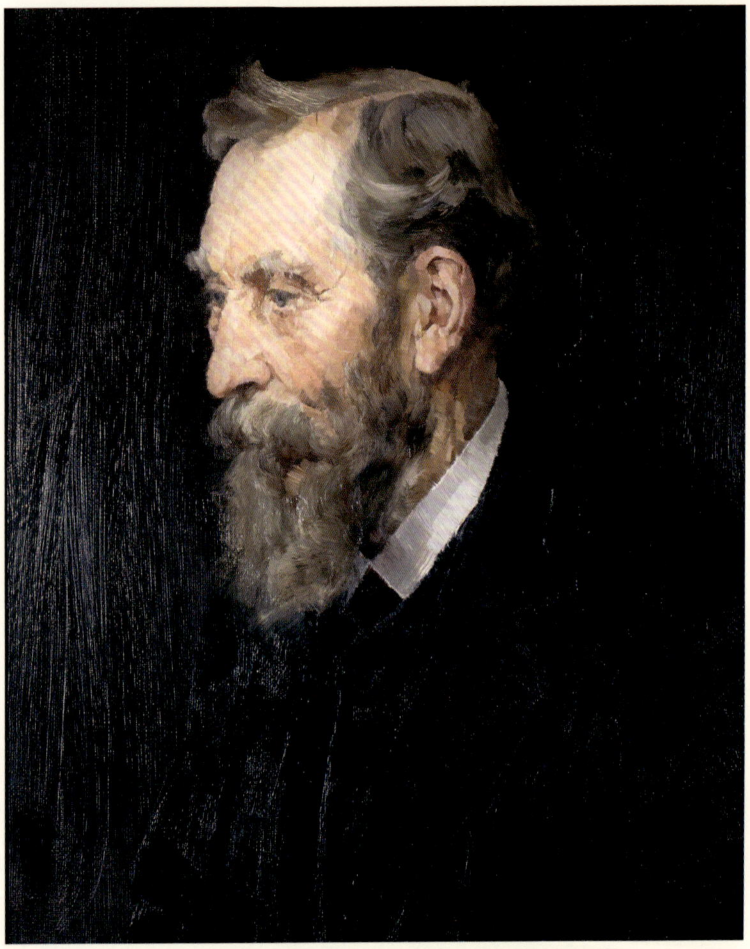

Figure 20. Walter Ufer.
Portrait of an Old Man with Beard, 1896.
Oil on panel, 22 x 18 inches.
Collection Klauer Manufacturing Company.

Victor Higgins was born in 1884 to an Irish-Catholic farming family in Shelbyville, Indiana. As a member of a family of eleven, he was expected to share in the chores. However, Victor was not happy unless he was painting. Any two-dimensional surface—the interior walls of the family barn, carriages, an old piece of fabric—were soon covered with images. His youngest brother John recalled seeing Victor scratch pictures on the frosted windows of their home. At fifteen, Higgins moved on to Chicago to work as an illustrator and begin his art education and career as an artist.

E. Martin Hennings was born in Penns Grove, New Jersey in 1886. His family came from Schleswig-Holstein, Germany. His father, a cement finisher, moved his family to Chicago in 1888. As a youth, Martin became a regular visitor to The Art Institute of Chicago, eventually enrolling in classes in 1890.

By the turn of the twentieth-century, Ufer, Higgins, and Hennings were living, studying and working at part and full-time jobs as illustrators in Chicago. While we can't be sure how well they knew each other at this early stage of their careers, they would eventually establish lasting relationships that grew stronger over time. All three travelled in the same circles, attended art shows and took courses at The Art Institute of Chicago.

Their ultimate goal was to become fine arts painters. Despite spending more than a decade in Chicago, their futures showed little promise. In fact, their careers as fine arts painters were at a standstill. They were surviving as commercial designers, studying and teaching part-time, and accepting any job that would earn them enough to survive on. Something had to change.

THE TRIO STUDIES IN EUROPE

Walter Ufer, Victor Higgins, and E. Martin Hennings travelled to Europe separately in 1911 to study in Munich. Each would remain there until 1913. While there is little evidence suggesting that they planned to meet, they were together in Munich in 1912 and 1913. Importantly, their trips would have an unmistakable influence on their careers and their goal to become fine arts painters.

Walter, with his wife Mary, first stayed with her family in Copenhagen. After a couple of weeks, they moved on to Munich to begin his studies. When they began to run out of money, Walter persuaded Mary to rejoin her parents in Copenhagen. In her absence, he strengthened his relationship with Hennings, Higgins, and other American artists studying in Munich.[1]

There were a number of teachers the American artists were attracted to while in Munich, many of whom were considered old school. Both Ufer and Hennings studied with Walter Thor (1870-1929) whose reputation for his portraits of Tyrolean peasants made him a master of the academic style of realism. Thor had a private school that both artists joined.[2] At the age of thirty-five, Ufer was too old to join the Academy, but managed to learn as much as he could from the opportunities available to him. Ufer enjoyed describing the duress he experienced while painting. He was thrilled to be in Thor's class. Working with the man he called a "great teacher," Ufer wrote about his painting *Woman of Dachau* [fig. 28]:

> *All of my fellow students liked it very much. Thor came in on Friday and immediately walked to my painting. He stood studying it. Asked me if I had a palette knife. I gave him one. One, two, three and he had scrapped it off. I was mad. He said that it was very good and this [was] to see if it was an accident. He said to the monitor 'This model poses another week and Ufer is to choose any position he wants.' I could hardly wait until Monday came. I chose my position and did it work! I'll say so. At the end of that week he came again complemented me, saying it was better than the first — 'Now I know you can paint Ufer.'*[3]

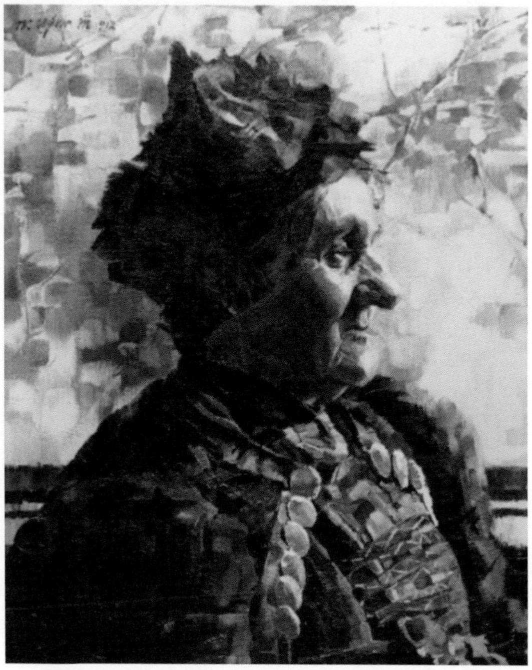

Figure 28. Walter Ufer. *Woman of Dachau*, 1912.
Oil on canvas, 22 x 18 inches.
Location unknown (former Klauer Family Collection).
Photo courtesy Ufer Papers, University of Notre Dame.

---

[1] E. Martin Hennings to Walter Ufer, 4 November 1913. Ufer Papers, University of Notre Dame, Gift of Stephen L. Good (hereafter UPUNDSG).

[2] The school also admitted women, and Mary Ufer studied there for a short time before returning to Denmark.

[3] Walter Ufer to Miss V. R. Purinton, 16 May 1935, 19, UPUNDSG.

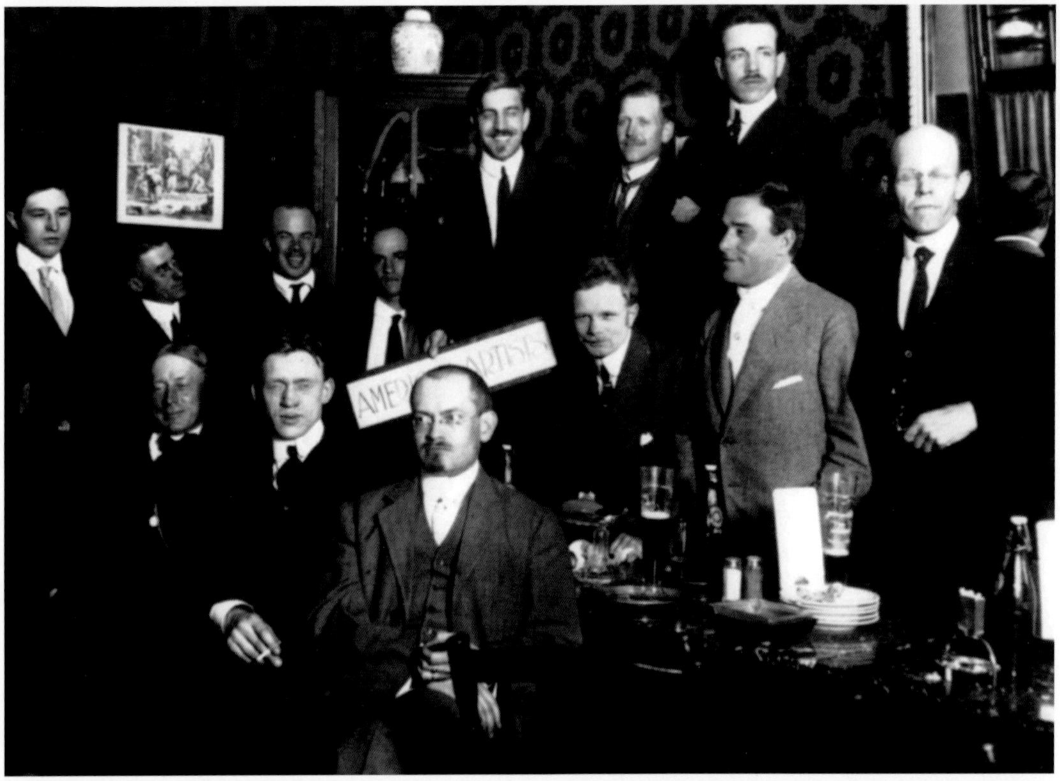

Figure 29. *American Artists Club, Munich (Walter Ufer, E. Martin Hennings and Others)*, 1912. Photo courtesy of Stephen L. Good, Denver.

A cabinet card made by Franz de Groote shows the three artists as members of the American Artists Club. They were photographed in the Kunstler Café Glasl in 1912 [fig. 29], a regular meeting place for the group. The card bears the inscription "Atelier Electra Kunst-u. Vergrosserungansstadt" and shows an unidentified artist holding the sign "American Artists." The main group from the club relocated to Chicago after America's involvement in the World War I became a reality.[4]

The purpose of the organization was "to assist American students of the fine arts in Munich."[5] The group met every Friday evening at the café, which was located at the corner of Theresien and Amalien Streets. The photograph suggests that the club was social in nature, but there was a report of an exhibition of the member's work in March 1914 at Brakl's Gallery.[6]

Another photograph [fig. 30] pictures Ufer and Hennings after they moved on to Paris. Based on letters between Walter and Mary, Ufer and Hennings enjoyed the bachelor's life. It even appears as though they enjoyed social life more than working at their easels. By November, Ufer and Higgins were in Chicago while Hennings was continuing his studies in Munich with Professor Jank and preparing for a Club exhibit.[7] Hennings returned to Chicago in 1915, their friendship remaining strong. By 1917, they were in Taos, New Mexico.

---

[4] The American Artists' Club in Munich was initially organized by William Merritt Chase in 1873-74 and included founding members Frank Duveneck and J. Frank Currier. By 1912 the club included Ufer, Higgins, and Hennings as well as other prominent figures such as Louis Grell.

[5] "Colleagues and Contemporaries," accessed July 15, 2018, http://www.louisgrell.com/artworks/colleagues-contemporaries/.

[6] Ibid.

[7] E. Martin Hennings to Walter Ufer, 4 November 1913, Klauer Family Papers, University of Notre Dame (Hereafter KFPUND).

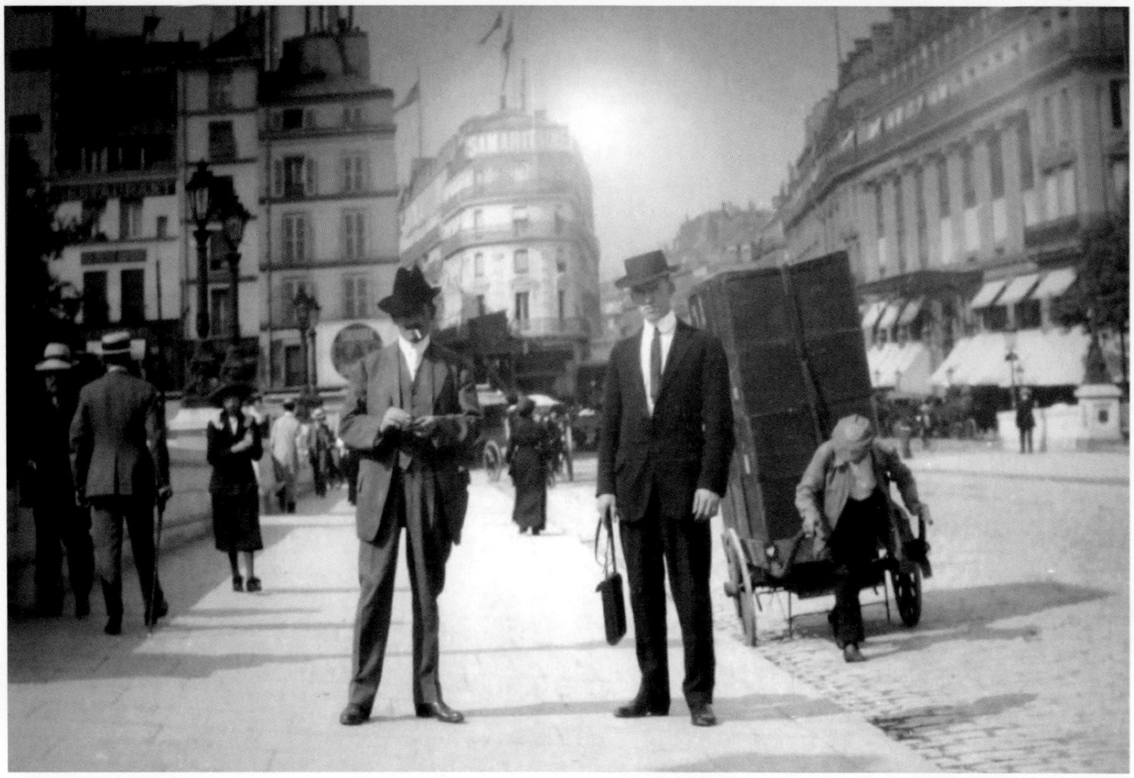

Figure 30. *Walter Ufer and E. Martin Hennings in Paris*, 1913.
Photo courtesy of Stephen L. Good, Denver.

They all returned from Europe with their trunks filled with paintings. Higgins was offered a one-man show at the Palette and Chisel Club soon after reaching Chicago. Initially denied a show, Ufer had to wait until March 1914 for his exhibit.[8] There is no record that Hennings ever had a solo show at the Palette and Chisel Club, even though he was a prominent member.

PALETTE AND CHISEL CLUB, CHICAGO

The Palette and Chisel Club provided welcomed exposure. The club was founded in 1895 and was the second oldest artists' organization in America. Its purpose was to provide a place for work and study as well as a venue for exhibitions. Among its membership were Charles Marion Russell and George Bellows, later joined by Higgins, Ufer and Hennings. All three held administrative posts in the organization, with Ufer serving as President in 1917.

The Palette and Chisel Club played a critical role in attracting key patrons to their paintings. During Ufer's March 1914 show, he sold paintings to the Harrison brothers, Andreas Wackenreuter and their friends. Even though several of the sales only netted between $20 and $50, Ufer had been discovered. His career as a fine arts painter, like that of Higgins, had been launched.

Ufer made a major commitment of time and energy to the club. He organized programs for the club, invited an impressive number of lecturers, and organized circuit exhibitions of the members' art. Despite his efforts, he found he had to resign his presidency. In his letter of resignation, he claimed he had been

[8] Higgins exhibited thirty-five paintings and was awarded the Club's Gold Medal in the first of two Palette and Chisel Club exhibits. He was awarded a gold medal in the Club's Gold Medal Show in 1913 followed by a Silver Medal the next year.

"grossly misjudged by his fellow members and finds this an insult to his good service as President."[9] Ufer's difficulties may have resulted from his dominating-style of leadership as well as his personality, which could be abrasive at times.

Ufer included *Woman of Dachau* in his exhibition in March 1914. However, it remained unsold until 1919 when Klauer added it to his collection. Ufer's sales card for *Woman of Dachau*, #6, reads: "This went in with a lot of pictures for which Klauer paid $1200."[10] In 1919, Klauer purchased "two lots" of paintings—each at $1200.

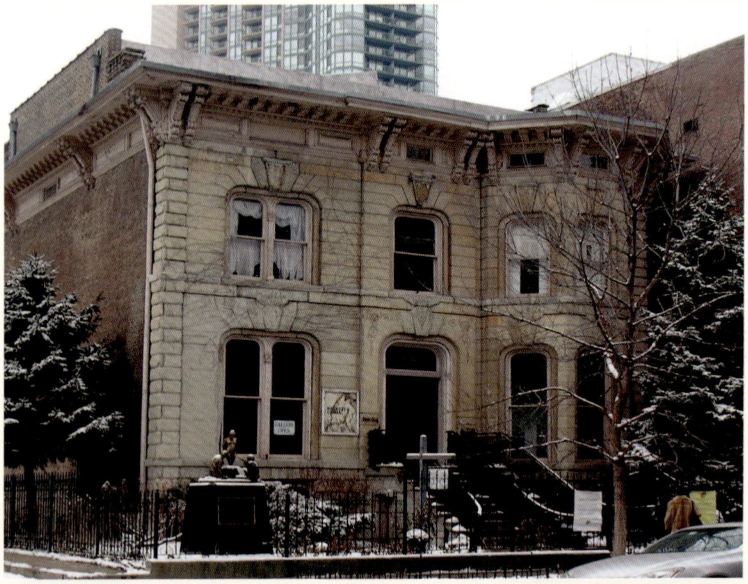

Figure 31.
Del Hall, *Palette and Chisel Club, Chicago*.
Photo courtesy of The Palette and Chisel Academy of Fine Arts.

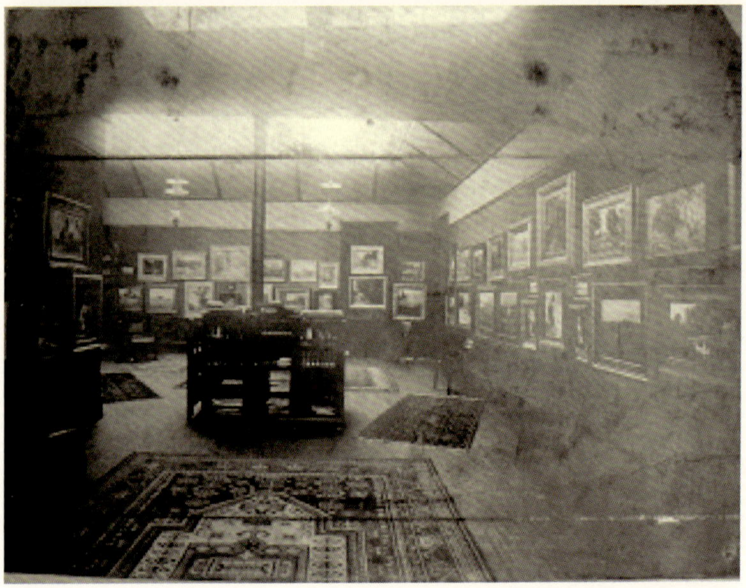

Figure 32.
Exhibition Room of the Palette and Chisel Club, Chicago.
Exhibition catalog of 1916 Annual Exhibition.
Photo courtesy Higgins Papers, University of Notre Dame Archives.

[9] Good, "Walter Ufer, Munich to Taos," 160.
[10] Ufer's Sales Card. UPUNDSG.

Chapter III
The Syndicate and William Henry Klauer

Interest in the Southwest was not a passing fancy for William Preston Harrison and Carter H. Harrison. Over the next three years, from 1914 to 1916, the Harrison brothers and their syndicate became important promoters of a newly "discovered" indigenous American art created in Taos.[1] How could syndicate members like Oscar Mayer, William Klauer, and others not respond favorably to the impassioned proposal of the Harrison brothers? Everybody, weary of a world war, were turning their backs on anything European and seeking art forms that were uniquely American.

Chicago's passion for the art of the American West was apparent to artists and their patrons. Ufer, Higgins and Hennings were exposed to art focusing on the Native American; Carter H. Harrison's photographs; the annual Santa Fe Railway calendars featuring kneeling Taos Indians by Eanger Irving Couse; Western art and artifacts in The Field Museum; Frederic Remington bronzes in the George F. Harding Castle; and public sculptures by Alexander Phimister Proctor, Cyrus Edwin Dallin, Lorado Taft, and John L. Boyle, among others. Chicago was an environment that favored images of the Native American, an exciting introduction for those travelling West.

When William Klauer became a syndicate member at the invitation of Carter Harrison in the fall of 1916 and purchased his first paintings by Ufer, he probably didn't consider himself a collector of fine art. In fact, other than the Harrison brothers, none of the syndicate members considered themselves art collectors. However, like so many other businessmen, Klauer was attracted to the images of a disappearing culture as well as the death of the Old West. With his experiences in New Mexico, Klauer needed little encouragement to purchase one, perhaps two paintings by Ufer. He could easily justify spending $75 for paintings to hang in his home, and at this price, Ufer's paintings were well within his budget.[2]

UFER AND HIGGINS IN TAOS, 1914-1916

Ufer's first visit to New Mexico was a combination painting and scouting trip. His itinerary included stopovers in Santa Fe, Chimayo, and the pueblos of San Juan, Isleta and Taos. Arriving in Santa Fe, Ufer was enthusiastically "met at the train by the Governor [William C. McDonald]..." It was "customary in those days—and that evening he played bridge in the executive mansion."[3]

Ufer rode with John Dunn to Taos where he was left with his trunks in front of Mrs. Barker's American House (now known as Governor Bent's Place). Before turning in, Ufer spent his first night in Taos wandering dark streets illuminated only by occasional flashlights and oil lamps. Unfortunately, Mrs. Barker had washed Ufer's bed linens and had failed to thoroughly dry them. Waking up the next

[1] The syndicate was a group of the Harrison brothers' friends who sponsored Walter Ufer (1914-1916) and Victor Higgins (1914). The members of the syndicate agreed to acquire a predetermined amount of 25-by-30-inch paintings at the price of $75 each.

[2] $75 in 1916 would be worth $1732 in 2019.

[3] "Taos Painter Entertained on 60th Birthday" in *Taos Valley News*, 23 July 1936.

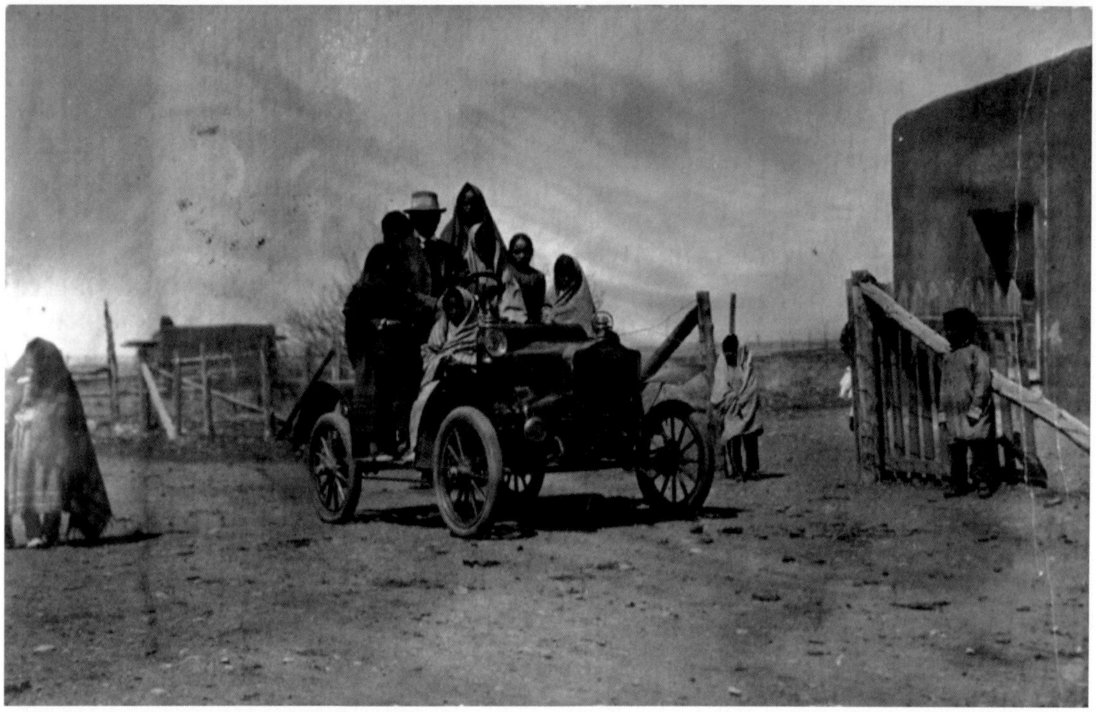

Figure 33. *"Doc" Martin in His Model T with Taos Indians*, c. 1920.
Photo courtesy of the author.

morning with a bad cough, Ufer made the acquaintance of the legendary Taos personality Doctor Thomas P. Martin [fig. 33]. After Ufer stayed in his doctor's home, they began a long friendship. Ufer returned, staying in "Doc" Martin's home until Mary travelled to Taos for the first time in 1916. From that time on, the Ufers were renters. Even though he had years where he enjoyed strong sales and a handsome income, the couple never owned a home in Taos.

Klauer had already been a frequent visitor to Taos and knew "Doc" Martin by the time Ufer met him. Both Ufer and Klauer welcomed the opportunity to share friendships. They enjoyed the man who was considered a "delightful character," and "Doc" Martin was one of the wittiest and most colorful physicians in the Southwest.[4] Everyone who came to Taos found "Doc" Martin to be "a great raconteur," and "his stories of the Wild West and the interesting characters would have filled many volumes."[5] Like Ufer and Klauer, Martin was a serious drinker and an "inveterate smoker," enjoying liquor—for social as well as medicinal purposes—and Havanas.[6]

Victor Higgins, by comparison, spent his first days in Santa Fe enjoying Thanksgiving dinner with Santa Fe painter Sheldon Parsons and his thirteen-year-old daughter Sara. The attractive Sara was a precocious artist who, at seventeen, exhibited her paintings along with Ufer, Higgins, Hennings, and her father in the November 24, 1917 grand opening of the Museum of New Mexico. During Higgins's visit with the Parsons, Sara prepared the meal while her father and Victor likely painted together. The thirty-year-old Higgins also found himself attracted to Sara, which led to their marriage in 1919. *New Mexico Dooryard* [fig. 41], the first painting Klauer purchased from Higgins, was created during one of the artist's early trips to Taos.

[4] Ibid.
[5] Ibid.
[6] Ibid.

E. Martin Hennings remained in Europe until 1915, when World War I drove him back to America. He wouldn't travel to Taos until 1917. After he returned to Chicago, Hennings taught for a year at the Academy of Fine Arts. He continued to paint and attracted the attention of Carter Harrison. As with Ufer, Harrison showed Hennings his photographs of Taos. Hennings also painted a portrait of Harrison during this time.

Harrison invited his friends, Oscar Mayer in particular, to support Hennings's first trip to Taos. Harrison gave Hennings a letter of introduction to Edgar L. Hewett (1865-1946), director of the Museum of New Mexico, and wrote to Ufer, explaining that he was sending Hennings to New Mexico with commissions for eight to ten paintings. By September 29, Hennings was painting in New Mexico. He managed to complete three canvases, which were seen in the inaugural exhibition of the Museum of New Mexico.[7]

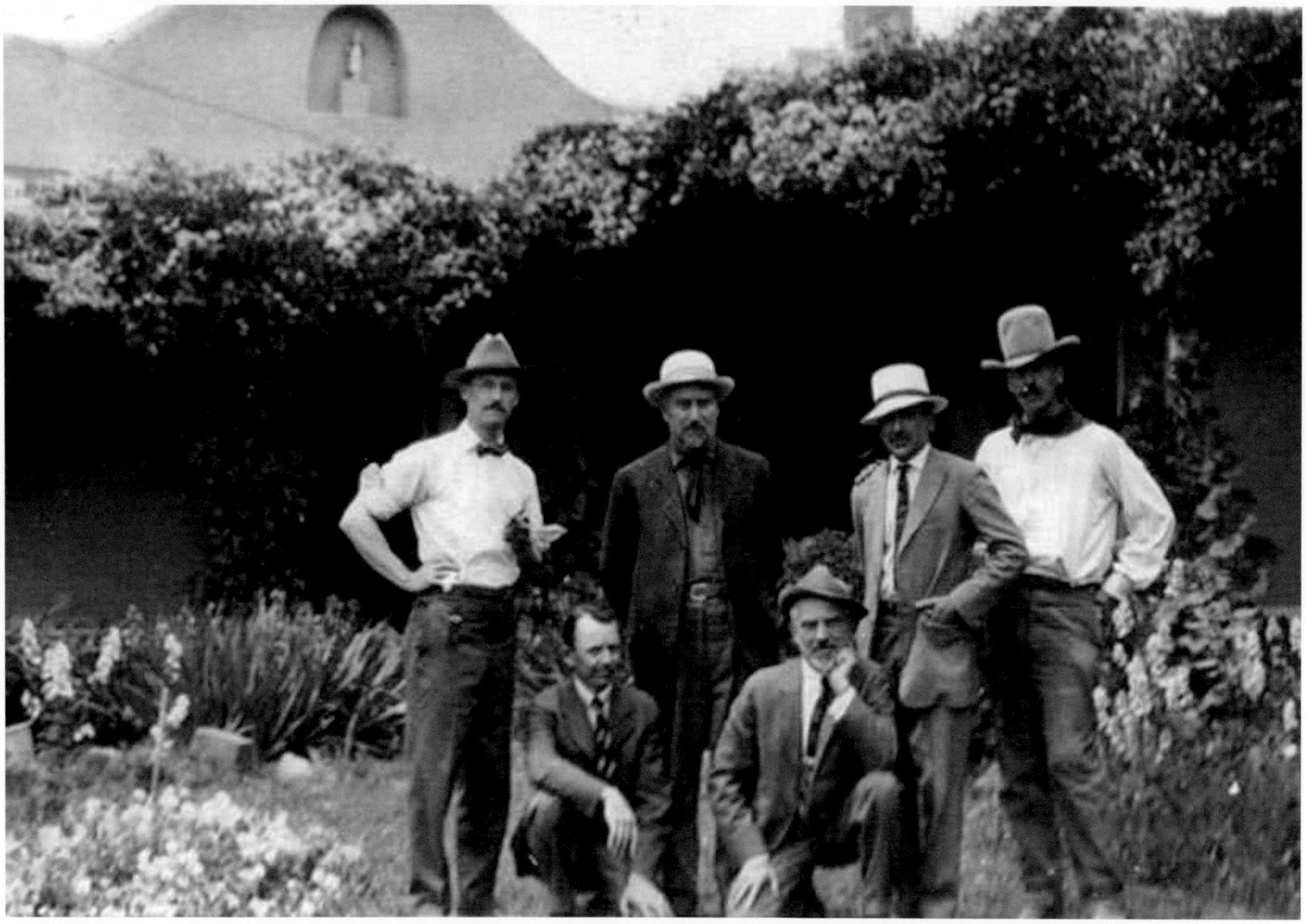

Figure 34. *The Six Founding Members of the Taos Society of Artists in Couse's Garden*, 1915. (Kneeling: Oscar Edmund Berninghaus and Joseph Henry Sharp. Standing Left to Right: Ernest Ludwig Blumenschein, Eanger Irving Couse, Bert Geer Phillips and William Herbert "Buck" Dunton.) Photo courtesy of The Couse Foundation.

7 Robert E. White, "E. Martin Hennings" in *Pioneer Artists of Taos* (Denver: Old West Publishing Company, 1983, rev. 1985), 197-198.

WILLIAM HENRY KLAUER AND WALTER UFER

Led by Bert Phillips, Irving Couse, Joseph Sharp, and other future members of the Taos Society of Artists [fig. 34], Ufer and Higgins were readily accepted by members of the Taos community. Phillips had arrived in Taos in 1898 and became the first artist to live there year-round, his studio on Pueblo Road becoming a beacon for others coming to Taos. He was a one-man reception committee, constantly recruiting other artists to join him. He felt there was enough work for twenty artists. For a decade and a half, he received newcomers, artists and patrons alike. Soon after William Klauer arrived in Taos, he developed a friendship with Phillips, a relationship that Carter Harrison wrote to Ufer about.[8]

Phillips's invitations to other artists to join him were answered. By the time Ufer and Higgins arrived in Taos in 1914, the six members who formed the Taos Society of Artists in 1915 were committed to Taos, some living year-round and some arriving in time for the painting season while wintering in New York, Chicago or other home cities.

As housing and studio space were difficult to find, artists had to locate homeowners willing to rent their spare rooms. Anglos were in the minority, complicating the artist's search for living space. As mentioned earlier, Klauer solved his housing problem by building a cottage shortly after making his first trip to Taos.

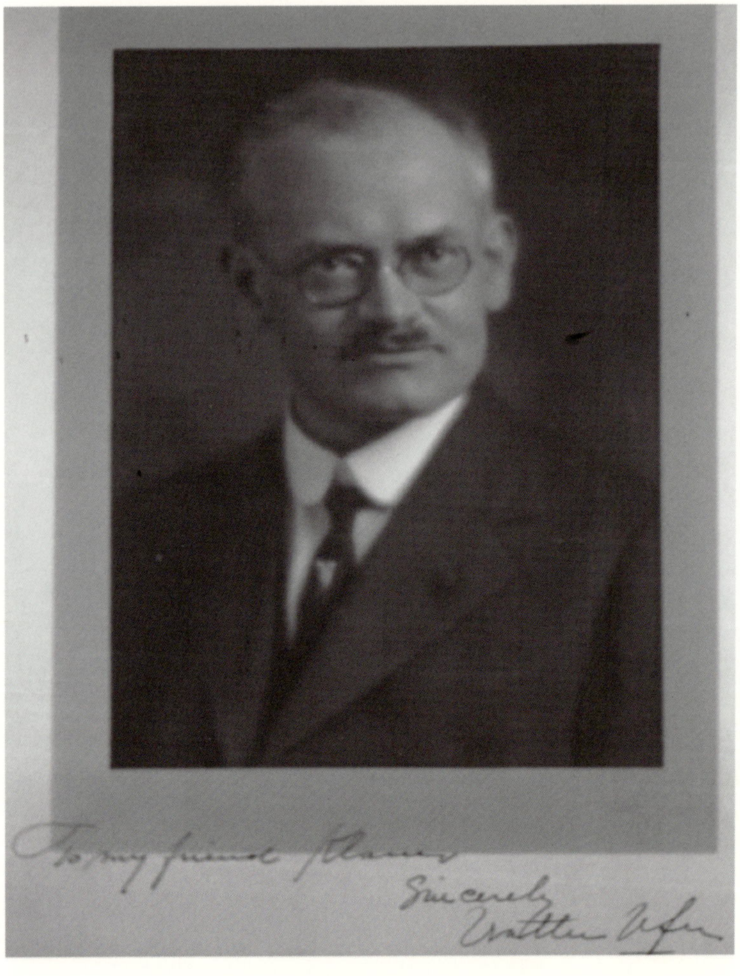

Figure 35.
Photographer Unknown. *Walter Ufer. "To My Friend Klauer/Sincerely/Walter Ufer."*
Photo Courtesy Klauer Family Papers, University of Notre Dame Archives.

[8] Carter Harrison to Walter Ufer, 2 November 1915, UPUNDSG.

While the exact date of Klauer's friendships with Ufer and Higgins is not known, they were certainly acquainted by the end of 1914. Klauer could have seen them painting in Taos or socializing in Chicago. By November 1915 they were doing business together. Documentation has Ufer as a guest in Klauer's cottage by 1917 and Higgins in December of 1918. The first of five paintings Klauer purchased by Higgins was painted in 1915, the same year Klauer began to assemble his large collection of Ufer paintings.

Wherever Ufer found himself—in Taos, Santa Fe, Laguna or Isleta—he was a tireless worker. Faced with orders from several members of the syndicate, he had to produce a substantial number of 25-x-30-inch paintings. He wrote to Harrison, "every spot and corner is a picture, and every figure, whether Indian or Mexican, is a study."[9] We can safely assign one painting [fig. 36] created in 1914 that was acquired by Klauer. Ufer maintained records of the paintings he created on 5-by-8-inch cards. He numbered the paintings as they were created, 1 through 264. Number 264 was the last painting he recorded in 1930.

In 1914 Ufer created *Kit Carson House* [fig. 36], one of the artist's earliest efforts in Taos to have his work enter the Klauer collection. The historic Kit Carson first appeared in Taos in 1826 and eventually settled there. The *Taos Valley News* called Carson "the greatest plainsman, mountain man, hunter,

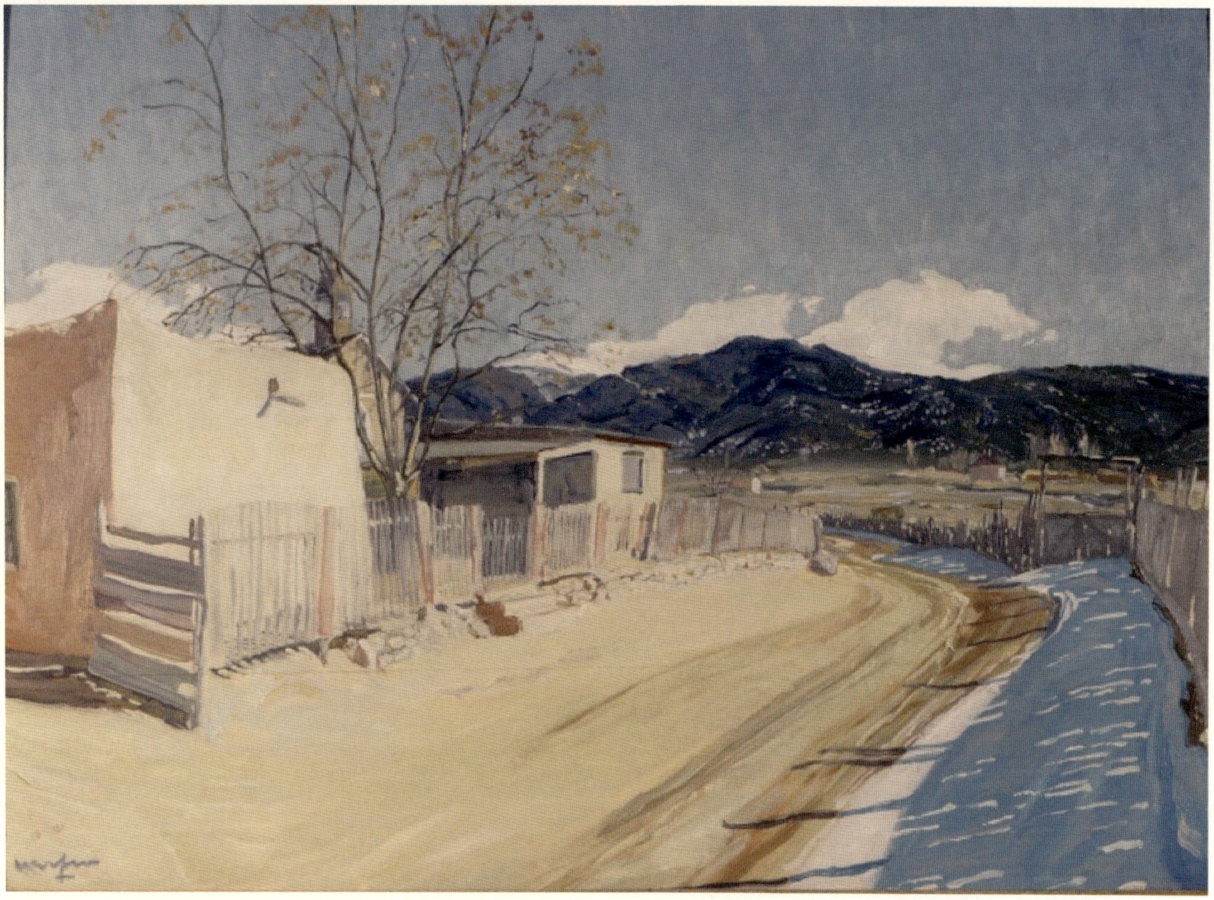

Figure 36. Walter Ufer. *Kit Carson House*, 1914. Oil on panel, 10.5 x 12.5 inches. Collection Klauer Manufacturing Company.

[9] Good, "Walter Ufer, Munich to Taos," 125.

trapper, and scout of the Southwest."[10] Ufer painted a relatively simple composition depicting the home that was built in 1844 for Carson's new bride Josefita. In a conversation with his grandfather, William J. Klauer reported, "When I mentioned the exploits of Kit Carson, Grandpa Klauer responded—that is a bunch of crap."[11]

Carson's home appears in more than one of Ufer's paintings in the Klauer collection [figs. 36 and 39]. It was a simple colonnaded adobe, not a grand palace. Despite its modesty, it became a tourist attraction in Taos. This was one of William Klauer's earliest acquisitions, an 18-by-18-inch painting he could easily transport back to Dubuque so that he could have a little of Taos and American history in his home.

UFER IN ISLETA AND TAOS, 1915

Ufer made trips to Isleta, New Mexico in 1914 and 1915. While his first trip was exploratory, he planned an ambitious itinerary in 1915. He spent two months in Isleta, followed by a trip to San Juan, Grand Canyon, Mojave Desert, and San Francisco where he was exhibiting three paintings in the Panama Pacific Exposition. Back in Taos, he concluded a summer trip that saw him create over sixty pictures. In 1916 he painted upwards of forty, and in 1917 about twenty. The dramatic decline in production was because Ufer began to paint larger canvases and fewer of the small paintings measuring 10.5 by 12.5 inches. By 1915, he had to focus more on 25-by-30-inch canvases or larger to satisfy his contracts with syndicate members as well as entries needed for competitive exhibitions.

Judging by the large number of canvases he painted in Isleta, including *Water Carriers—Isleta* [fig. 3; see frontispiece] in the Klauer Collection, Ufer was able to achieve a working relationship with his models, resolving a communication problem that he had experienced during his initial trip. Water carriers became a favored subject as it allowed him to paint the Isleta women in their environs. By 1915, Isleta Pueblo women were accustomed to photographers and artists encouraging them to change from ordinary daily wear to more colorful ceremonial costumes. Ufer's model stands balancing a black *olla* on her head. Even though he may have intended to suggest motion, she appears posed and almost stationary.

In *Water Carriers—Isleta*, Ufer was able to adapt to his new environment. Painted *en plein air*, the canvas is an early example of the artist's exploration of the principles of impressionism. Stephen Good suggested that Ufer's impressionist palette resulted from the "strong coloristic effects of the German Impressionists who started the Munich secession in 1892." He further stated, "the artists of Jugendstijl would have prepared Ufer for his eventual adaptation of a more stimulating approach to light and color."[12] *Water Carriers—Isleta* is characterized by lively brushwork as well as an emphasis on light and a color saturated palette. Using a pointillist technique, he created an impressionistic sky composed of dots of whites and pastel reds and blues.

Besides Ufer's Isleta painting, Klauer acquired Carter Harrison's photograph *Water Carriers* [fig. 37], which depicted two Taos pueblo women with *olla* pots on their heads. Both works, created at Isleta and Taos Pueblo respectively, represent a subject that fascinated Klauer. The photograph may have

[10] "Kit Carson, Greatest Frontiersman of Old West" in *Taos Valley News*, Ila McAfee Scrapbooks (3), Collection The Couse-Sharp Foundation Archives, Taos.

[11] William J. Klauer interview with Dean Porter, 2 April 2017.

[12] Good, "Walter Ufer, Munich to Taos," 128.

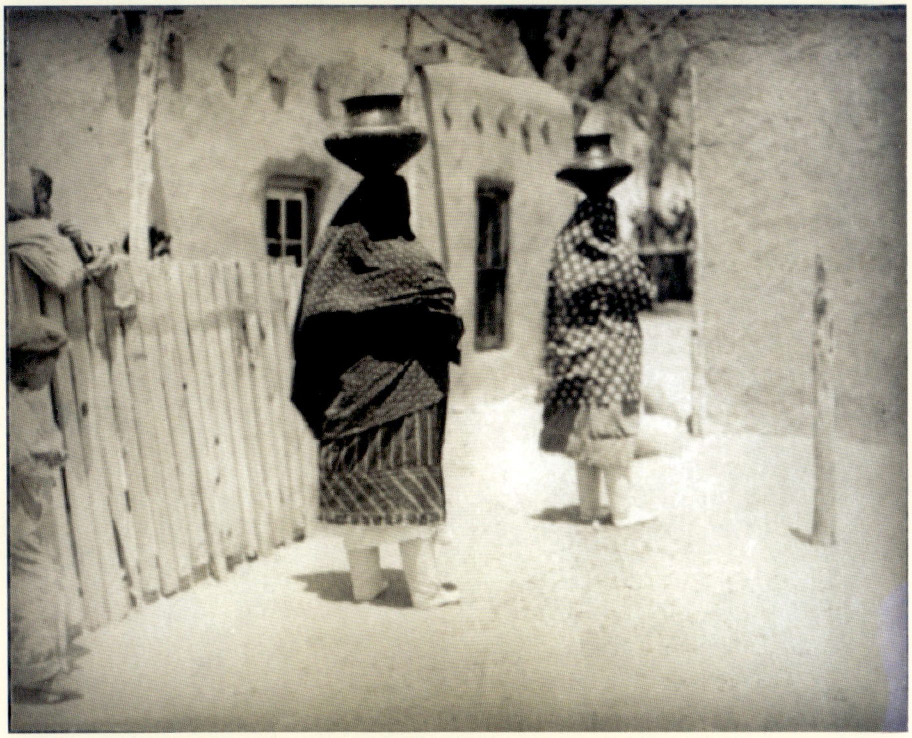

Figure 37.
Carter H. Harrison.
Water Carriers, c. 1906-09.
Sepia tone photograph,
10.5 x 12.5 inches.
Collection The Snite Museum of
Art. University of Notre Dame.
Gift of Klauer Family.

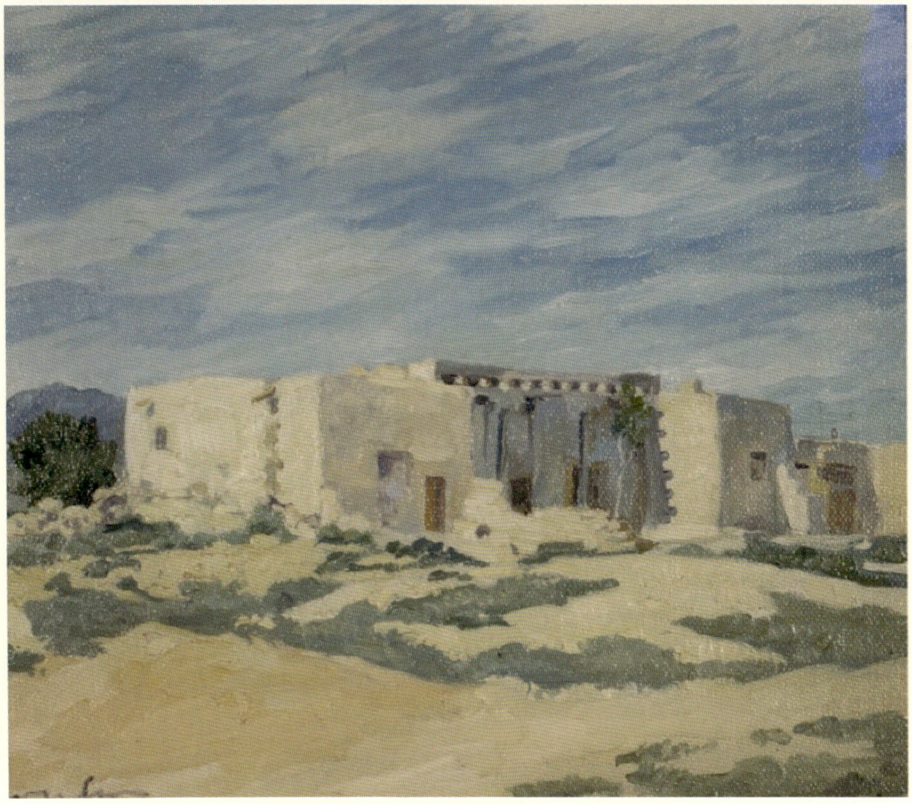

Figure 38.
Walter Ufer.
*Untitled [*maybe *An Old Adobe in Isleta],* 1915.
Oil on canvas,
10.5 x 12.5 inches.
Collection Klauer
Manufacturing Company.

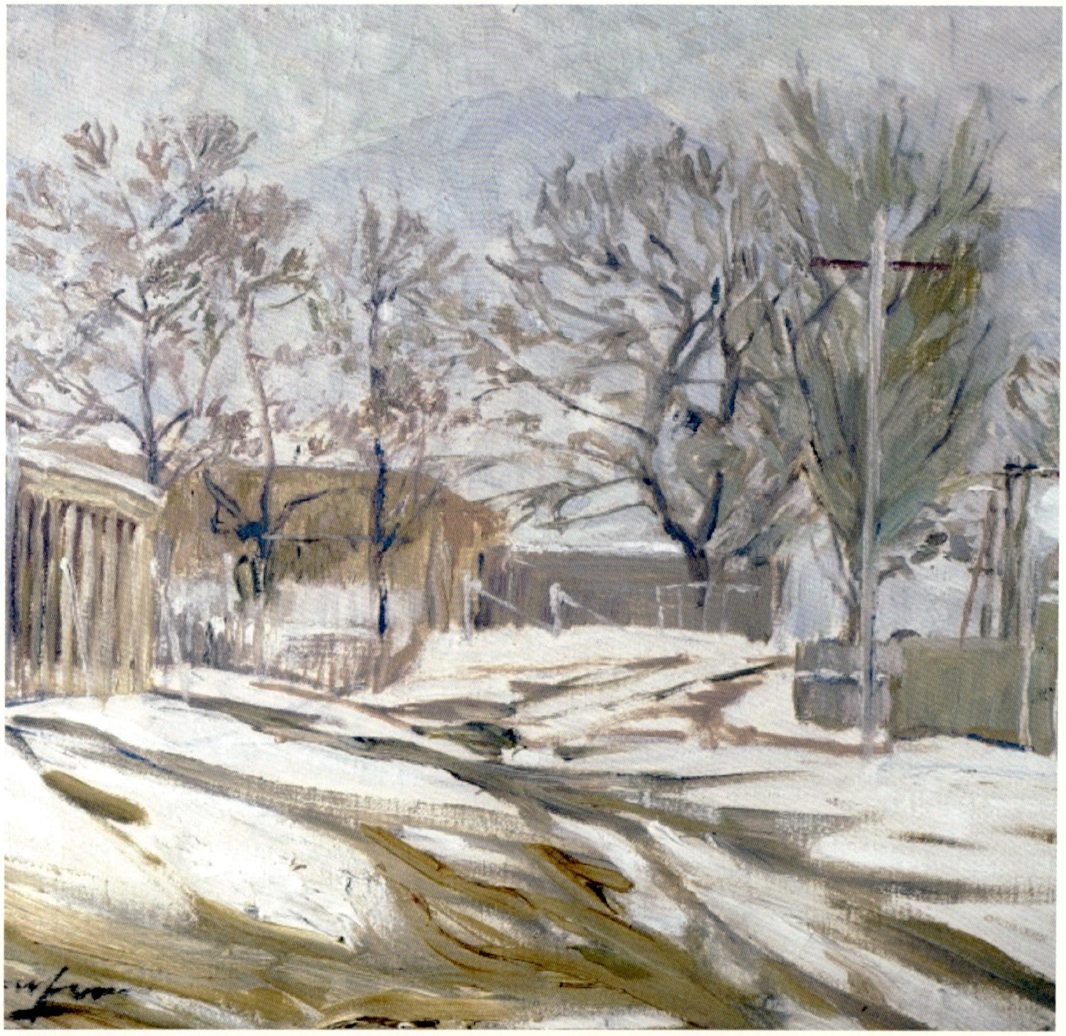

Figure 39. Walter Ufer. *Taos in Snow,* 1915. Oil on canvas, 18 x 18 inches.
Collection The Couse Foundation, Lunder Research Center for the Taos Society of Artists.
Gift of Klauer Manufacturing Company.

been a gift from the former mayor to Klauer; however, in Ufer's archives, there is a pencil list that includes the entry "Carter H. H. photos 6.00."[13]

Klauer acquired a second painting by Ufer of an old adobe building [fig. 38]. It is a typical structure that has been ravaged by sun, wind, rain and sand. Adobe homes in New Mexico were often built over years, with rooms added as needed. Painted in a bravura manner, Ufer adapted his palette to the creamy greys and tans of the textured adobe structure.

Following his trip to the West Coast in 1915, Ufer returned to Taos in time to paint *Taos in Snow* [fig. 39], a rare, early winter scene on Kit Carson Road. The painting represents why Taos earned the nickname "mud town." The only evidence of human activity is the calligraphic tracks created by wagons meandering through town on rutted streets once covered with freshly, fallen snow.

Ufer identified the scene on the painting's sales card as being "the Kit Carson house before it was spoiled by the masons." On the left of the composition, Ufer painted the colonnaded entry to the Carson

[13] Three-page list in pencil documenting Ufer's sales or pending sales with customers' names." UPUNDSG.

home. On November 27, 1924, he presented the painting to Klauer "in part payment of what I owe you."[14] This is but one of several examples of how Ufer satisfied his financial indebtedness to Klauer over the years.

As late as November 4, 1915, while Ufer was finishing his second season in New Mexico, Carter Harrison was still recruiting new syndicate members to cover the cost of Ufer's third trip to Taos. Again, Harrison had to secure subscriptions for a least eight Ufer paintings to make the arrangement viable. While the Harrison brothers, Andreas Wackenreuter, and Oscar Mayer had committed for multiple purchases, Carter Harrison was running into a predictable problem—how many Ufer paintings did a member need? Most collectors were satisfied with one or two paintings by an artist. When syndicate members had purchased what they considered to be their quota, Harrison had to identify new members and William Klauer became a prime candidate. Harrison wrote to Ufer,

> *W. H. Klauer, of Dubuque, Iowa, told me yesterday he would take one of your pictures. The reason why I did not include him in original list [syndicate members] was that he has a place near Taos, is a friend of Phillips & I was afraid might quote prices. He agrees if he gets a picture not to tell anyone what he paid for it. So far, I have not told him the price, but if he comes in it must be the same basis that others are included: $75.00. He does not care for the figures but likes the horseman. If you want to include him, paint him a picture on this order namely a horseman or some unobtrusive figures in foreground and a nice landscape or background.*[15]

Not surprisingly, it appears that Ufer listened to Harrison's advice. On more than one occasion Ufer created paintings that reflected the former mayor's recommendations; however, it wasn't until 1917 that the artist painted a "horseman," Jim Mirabal on horseback. In 1916, Mirabal, a handsome Indian from Taos Pueblo, began a twenty-year friendship with Ufer. In the 1920s, he painted several versions of Mirabal working as a freighter transporting goods—two paintings that would eventually bear the Klauer provenance [figs. 104 and 106].

Carter Harrison struggled to keep the syndicate a viable organization, one that would provide enough revenue to support the artist while satisfying the syndicate members' tastes. As early as September of 1915, distribution of paintings became a problem that would eventually lead to the dissolution of the syndicate. Would Harrison or Ufer make the decision over which painting each syndicate member would receive? Harrison, after a conversation with Mary, wrote to Walter, "I did not understand from her [Mary] whether you [Walter] had painted certain pictures for each of us or whether we were to make our own selection. From our talk in Albuquerque, I figured that you were painting certain pictures for my brother, a particular one for Mr. Wackenreuter, a particular one for Mr. Demme, and certain ones for me. Please let me know if this is the case."[16]

With virtually every syndicate member, Ufer would select the painting to hang in their home once he had the patrons' $75. Charles Herman, for example, wasn't interested in a painting of a water carrier, while the Harrison brothers and Oscar Mayer wanted a painting of a church. Preston Harrison, in a serious rife with Ufer, was forced to accept a desert scene while watching Mayer and Klauer enjoy paintings of the church at Chimayo. Klauer also repeatedly asked Ufer for a painting of his "cottage," which, judging by all standards, was a veritable castle in the pines. Eventually Klauer began to select the

---

[14] Walter Ufer to William Klauer, 27 November 1924, KFPUND.

[15] Carter H. Harrison to Walter Ufer, 2 November 1915, UPUNDSG.

[16] Carter H. Harrison to Walter Ufer, 28 September 1915, UPUNDSG.

paintings he wanted and not what someone else dictated. It is interesting to note, however, Ufer never painted the cottage, likely because it wasn't a subject that interested him.

According to Ufer's sales records, he created at least three paintings of Isleta water carriers. He sold the first two to Andreas Wackenreuter and Carter Harrison while the third went to William Klauer, all for the syndicate price of $75. While the sales record has not surfaced for Klauer's version, he probably acquired it in late 1915, shortly after becoming a syndicate member.

Essentially, the syndicate, as a formal organization, dissolved in 1916.[17] Its failure was primarily due to Ufer's falling out with William Preston Harrison over the "church picture" issue and continuing friction with other members. Prepaying Ufer for a painting they had not seen was certainly a reason for syndicate members to withdraw their support. Even though Ufer was creating impressive pictures, he soon found that he couldn't satisfy everyone.

Fortunately, after 1916, two syndicate members continued to purchase Ufer's paintings. Oscar Mayer remained a faithful client until 1920 while William Klauer never lost interest in the artist or his paintings. Mayer and Klauer were close friends, and they enjoyed mutual interests, in particular, the art created by members of the Taos Society of Artists. It brought excitement to their lives, whether it be in Chicago or Taos. Klauer and Mayer formed an incredible, unwavering friendship.

As early as November 1915, in a letter from Klauer to Ufer, it becomes obvious that the two were developing a special, lasting relationship. Klauer wrote, requesting a "painting before Christmas." He also invited Ufer to "visit him in his nice log cabin in Taos Mountains," hoping "to have the pleasure

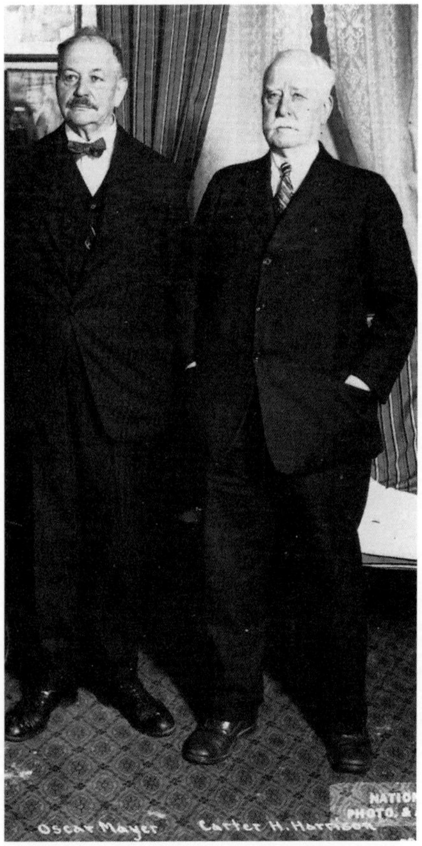

Figure 40.
Oscar Mayer and Carter Harrison, c. 1940s.
Photo courtesy Stephen L. Good, Denver.

17 The syndicate supported Ufer for three years and Higgins for one. In 1921, Carter Harrison wrote to Klauer about reviving the "skindicate" for E. Martin Hennings.

of entertaining you there the next time I am in the valley." He continued, "Geo.[rge] Neel, a member of Klauer Manufacturing Co., will be glad to have the opportunity of showing you the cottage and its surroundings at any time."[18] This would be the first of several invitations Klauer would extend to Ufer. For more than a dozen years, Klauer's cottage, surrounded by tall pines, became critical to their sustaining a close relationship. Whenever Klauer visited Taos, Ufer was not only a guest but also a facilitator in making the cottage ready for the Iowa owner's arrival.

KLAUER ACQUIRES HIGGINS'S TOWNSCAPE, 1915

Besides the several paintings Klauer had purchased from Ufer, the patron acquired *New Mexico Dooryard* [fig. 41] from Victor Higgins. Not long after Higgins visited Taos for the second and third times, he gravitated to the landscape and the flora that could be seen in the community's courtyards. Seemingly following the examples set by his future father-in-law, Sheldon Parsons, in *New Mexico Dooryard*, Higgins was attracted to the spectacular hollyhocks framing the entrance to an adobe home. It wasn't unusual for Higgins and Ufer to paint canvas after canvas of the streets they walked. While Klauer primarily collected Ufer's figurative paintings, he was attracted to Higgins's landscapes. In 1925, Klauer would add four more paintings by Higgins to his collection—all landscapes. *New Mexico Dooryard* remained Klauer's only townscape by Higgins.

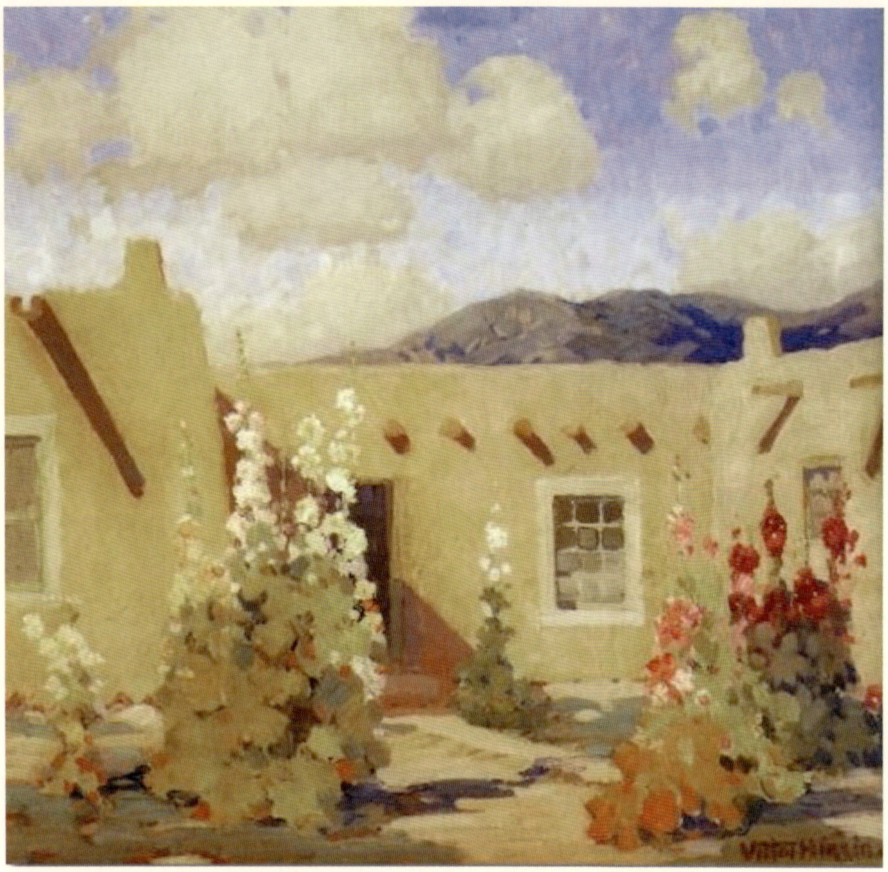

Figure 41. Victor Higgins. *New Mexico Dooryard*, c. 1915-1916.
Oil on canvas, 18.75 x 20.25 inches. Collection Klauer Manufacturing Company.

18 William Klauer to Walter Ufer, 30 November 1915, KFPUND.

Chapter IV
Klauer, Ufer and Chimayo, 1916

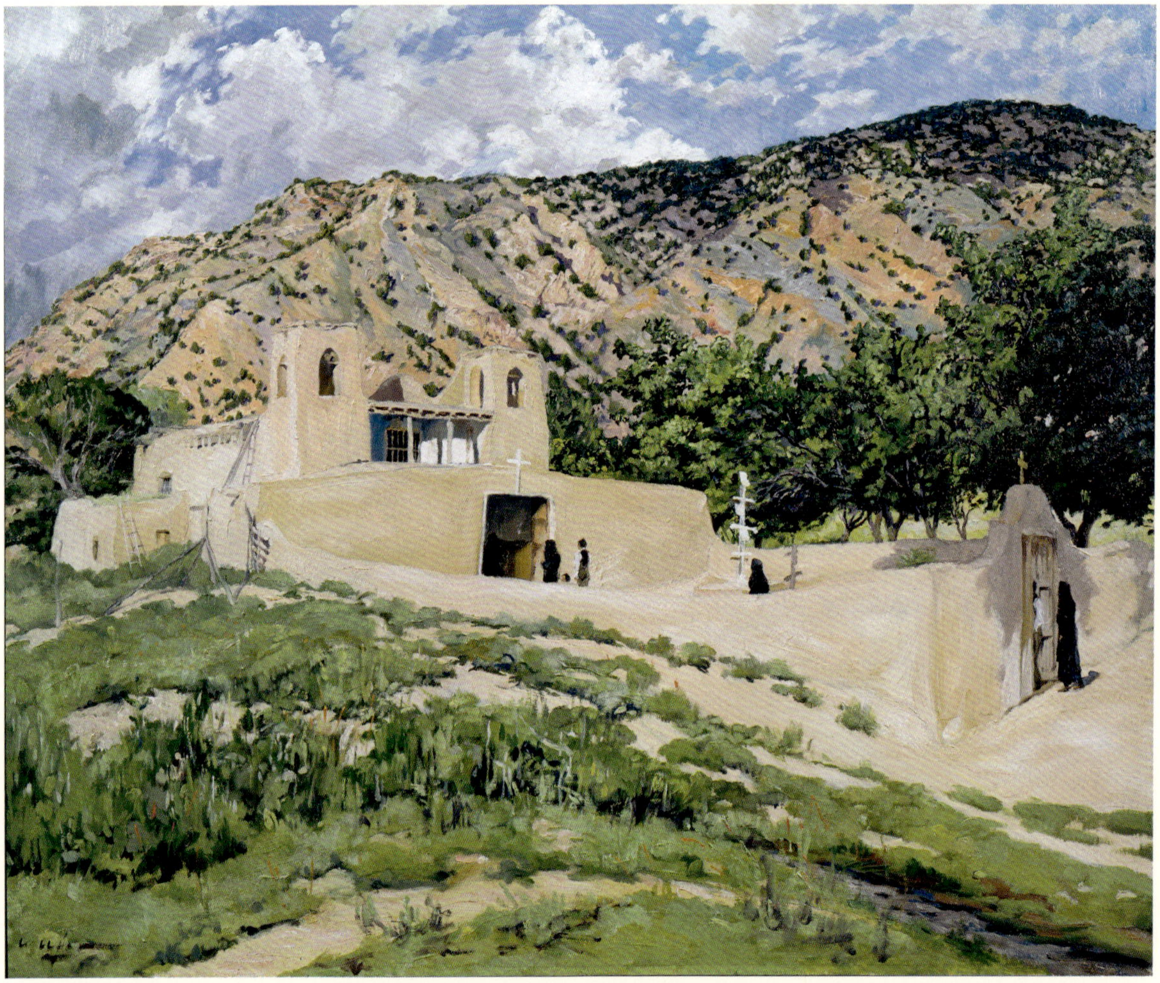

Figure 42. Walter Ufer. *Santuario de Chimayo* (also *Mission Church*), 1916. Oil on canvas, 25 x 30 inches. Collection Gilbert Waldman. (former Klauer Family Collection)

In January 1916, Ufer wrote Klauer regarding the possibility of having a solo exhibition in Dubuque.[1] Klauer responded, stating that he would refer Ufer's letter to his father Peter, chairman of the Dubuque Library's board. He "...will see that it is placed in the hands of the proper parties who will doubtless take up the matter with you."[2] In letters that followed, there is no further mention of a Dubuque exhibition until 1923, four years after Peter Klauer died.

Three weeks later, Ufer developed a problem with William Klauer. This wouldn't be the first, or the last, as Klauer had to contend with an artist who became increasingly self-centered. Ufer's unusual conduct, when it came to business matters, became a challenge for the patient Klauer. Ufer, even with

[1] Walter Ufer to William Klauer, January 1916, KFPUND.

[2] William Klauer to Walter Ufer, 3 February 1916, KFPUND.

matters of little consequence, like the sale of a one dollar photograph, had to make a point, particularly when he was dealing with a man (or woman) he considered stronger than himself.

Ufer considered Carter Harrison more than an amateur photographer. He acquired some of the photographs from the former mayor, and apparently some for resale. Harrison's photographs were attractive and suitable for anyone's home, particularly for those fascinated with the allure of the Southwest. Ufer, anxious to please Klauer, sold him a copy of a Harrison photo—its cost was one-dollar. On March 22, Klauer sent a check to Ufer for $2.87 covering the former mayor's invoice of $3.87, "as the picture of Mr. Harrison was to be $1.00."[3] Ufer had a copy of a Harrison photograph made to sell to Klauer. Two days later, Ufer upset Klauer by billing the industrialist again, for money not agreed on. "You [Ufer] told me, in the presence of Mr. Wackenreuter, that you would have one of the Harrison pictures reproduced for me for a dollar and that it would be the same as the original."[4] When Ufer sold Klauer the "copy," "no mention was made of any further charge." Yet, Ufer sent him a bill for $1.87 "for framing it."[5] Klauer maintained that he would have paid the bill had Ufer "informed me [Klauer] in the first place."[6] For Klauer it was simply not good business practice to make additional charges after a deal had been consummated. Somehow Ufer weathered this storm, the first of several that would follow.

UFER IN CHIMAYO, 1916

On July 25, 1916, with the Ufers ensconced in Chimayo, the *Taos Valley News* prophetically announced, there "is little doubt that Ufer will bring out of the Chimayo valley some paintings that will cause Chicago to trek to that out of the way charming Santa Fe county town, with its beautiful chapel and story of miracles."[7] Staying at a teacher's home, Walter did, in fact, create two handsome 25-by-30-inch paintings of the 100-year-old sanctuary—the first, *Oferta para San Esquipula* for Carter Harrison, and the second, *Santuario de Chimayo* [fig. 42] for Klauer. In both paintings Ufer painted families entering the walled sanctuary courtyard on their way to services.

The ancient structure is wonderfully organic in feeling, appearing as though it had sprung from the earth. In its uneven, textured surfaces, defined by gently curving, sinuous lines, Ufer captured the venerated, religious sanctuary, which was the destination point of thousands who travelled annually there in hope of salvation. In a small chapel, the pilgrims found the *tierra bendita* ("holy dirt"), believed to have healing powers.

As early as 1914, Preston Harrison had requested a church picture. In a letter to Ufer from that year, he wrote "I am anxious for a Pueblo picture—or an old church—with mountains in distance and Indians in foreground."[8] Even though Ufer undoubtedly remembered Preston's request, he created the painting for syndicate members who treated him well. Twice he disappointed Preston when he assigned the Chimayo church pictures to his brother and William Klauer. His relationship with Preston was always strained, something that Ufer unquestionably had in mind when assigning the Chimayo pictures to others.

---

[3] William Klauer to Walter Ufer, 22 March 1916, KFPUND.
[4] Ibid.
[5] Ibid.
[6] Ibid.
[7] *Taos Valley News,* 25 July 1916.
[8] William Preston Harrison to Walter Ufer, 31 August 1914, UPUNDSG.

In November, Ufer presented Carter Harrison with his church picture. Ufer was pleased with his Chimayo paintings. He wrote to Carter, "I believe that I got something new in your church picture and wish that [Robert] Henri or [George] Bellows could see it...I aimed for this peculiar Southwestern 'something' which is hard to describe but one sees it."[9] Even though he liked the picture, the former mayor could not be magnanimous. He wrote, "Pictures came—I like the church except I would have painted it according to prescription—no large figure but as a crowd galley hovered about the entrance."[10] He failed to follow Harrison's detailed description of what he expected because Ufer was uncomfortable painting crowds. Ufer's real strength was painting a figure or two. Whenever he attempted to paint multiple figures he had difficulty unifying them as a compositional whole. Eventually the painting intended for Carter Harrison entered the collection of Oscar Mayer. While it is not clear how Mayer received Harrison's "church picture," it appears as though Harrison's less then enthusiastic reaction drove Ufer to offer the painting to Mayer instead.[11]

When Ufer delivered *Santuario de Chimayo* [fig. 42] to William Klauer for a price of $200, he satisfied his contract with his patron. However, surviving Ufer literature doesn't explain why Ufer charged Klauer $125 more than the syndicate members' $75 price for a 25-by-30-inch painting.

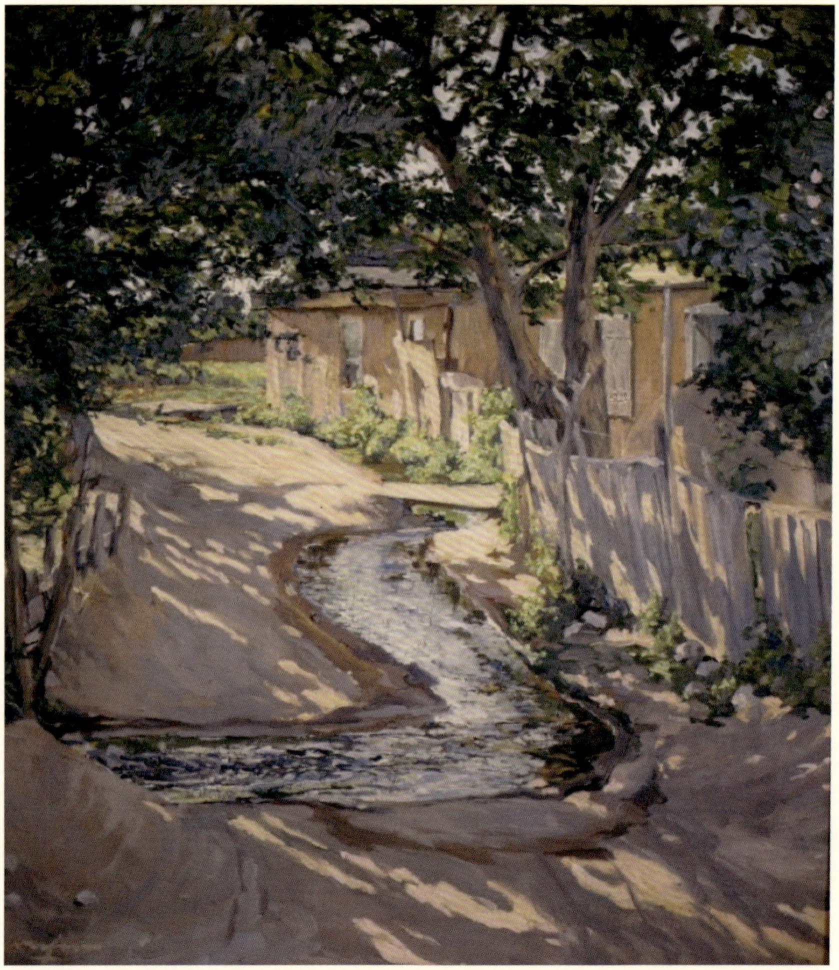

Figure 43.
Walter Ufer. *Acequia Madre*, 1916.
Oil on canvas, 30 x 25 inches.
Collection Klauer Manufacturing Company.

[9] Good, "Walter Ufer, Munich to Taos," 146. Good is quoting Ufer's letter to Carter H. Harrison, IV.

[10] Carter H. Harrison to Walter Ufer, 1 December 1916, UPUNDSG.

[11] According to Ufer's sales card, *Oferta para San Esquipula* was eventually sold to Oscar Mayer for reasons unknown.

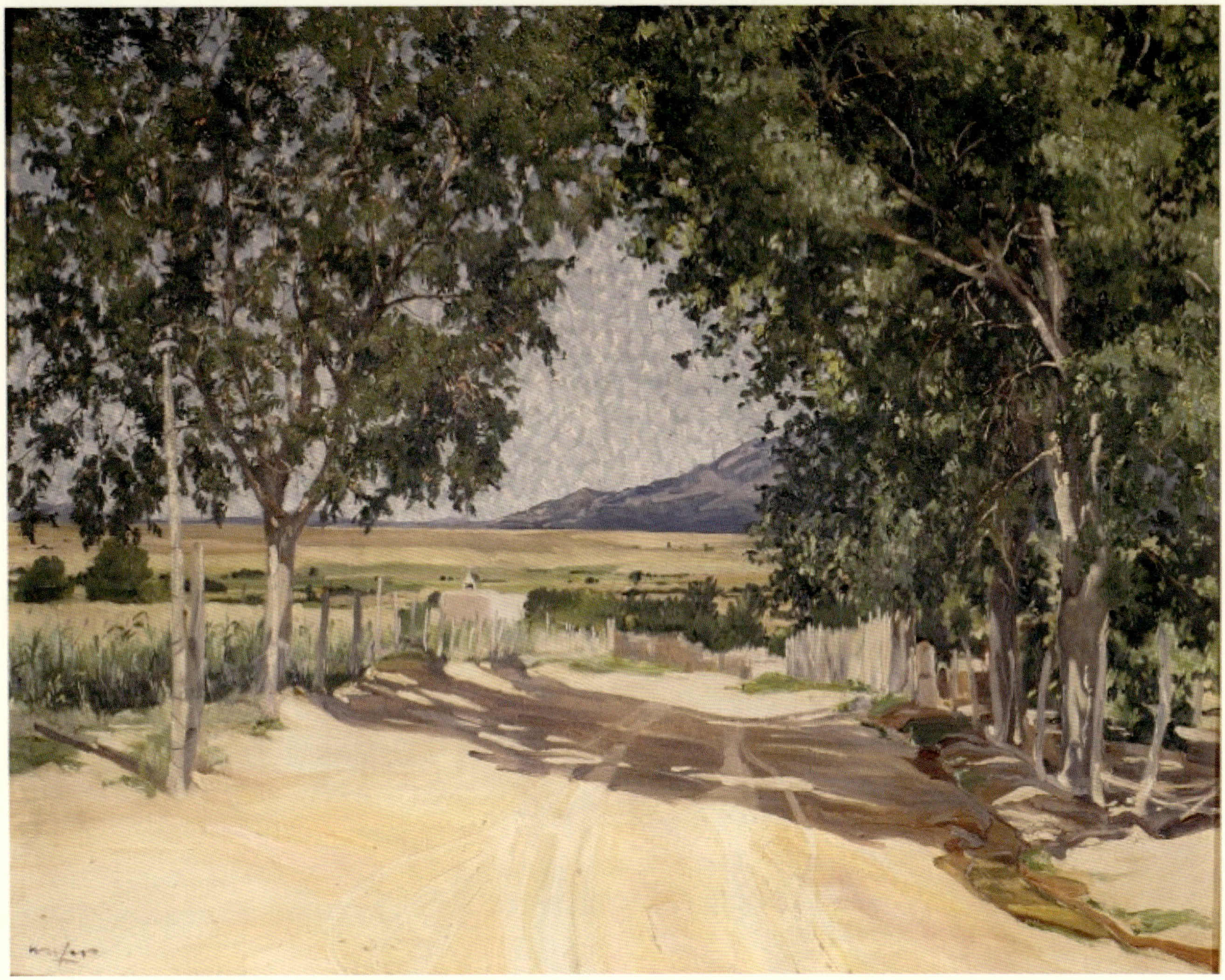

Figure 44. Walter Ufer. *September Morn*, 1916. Oil on canvas, 25 x 30 inches. Collection Klauer Manufacturing Company

UFER'S STREET SCENES: SANTA FE AND TAOS, 1916

During Ufer's third trip to New Mexico, he painted views of Hillside Avenue, "the Santa Fe that was, is but never again will be..." Three artists of the colony called them "the finest thing [sic] that has ever been done," and as "bully pictures which is about as high praise as one artist gives another."[12] Before leaving Santa Fe, Ufer enjoyed a solo show at the Old Palace.

By 1916, the press began giving Ufer and his paintings considerable ink. The *Taos Valley News* and *El Palacio* parroted articles from Chicago and New York newspapers, and Ufer provided enough press and photographs to promote his upward mobility in the art world. In August 1916, *El Palacio* published "The Santa Fe–Taos Art Colony–Walter Ufer." The author reviewed four exhibitions, each with paintings that would eventually bear Klauer's provenance. Three of note were *Woman from Dachau* [fig. 28], *Acequia Madre* [fig. 43] and *Taos in Snow* [fig. 39].

Acequia Madre, painted in Santa Fe, pictured "old fences, a lonely old adobe house sunning itself, tangled fruit trees through which the sunlight plays hide and seek, casting lovely shadows upon the

[12] *El Palacio*, 3 August 1916, 75-81.

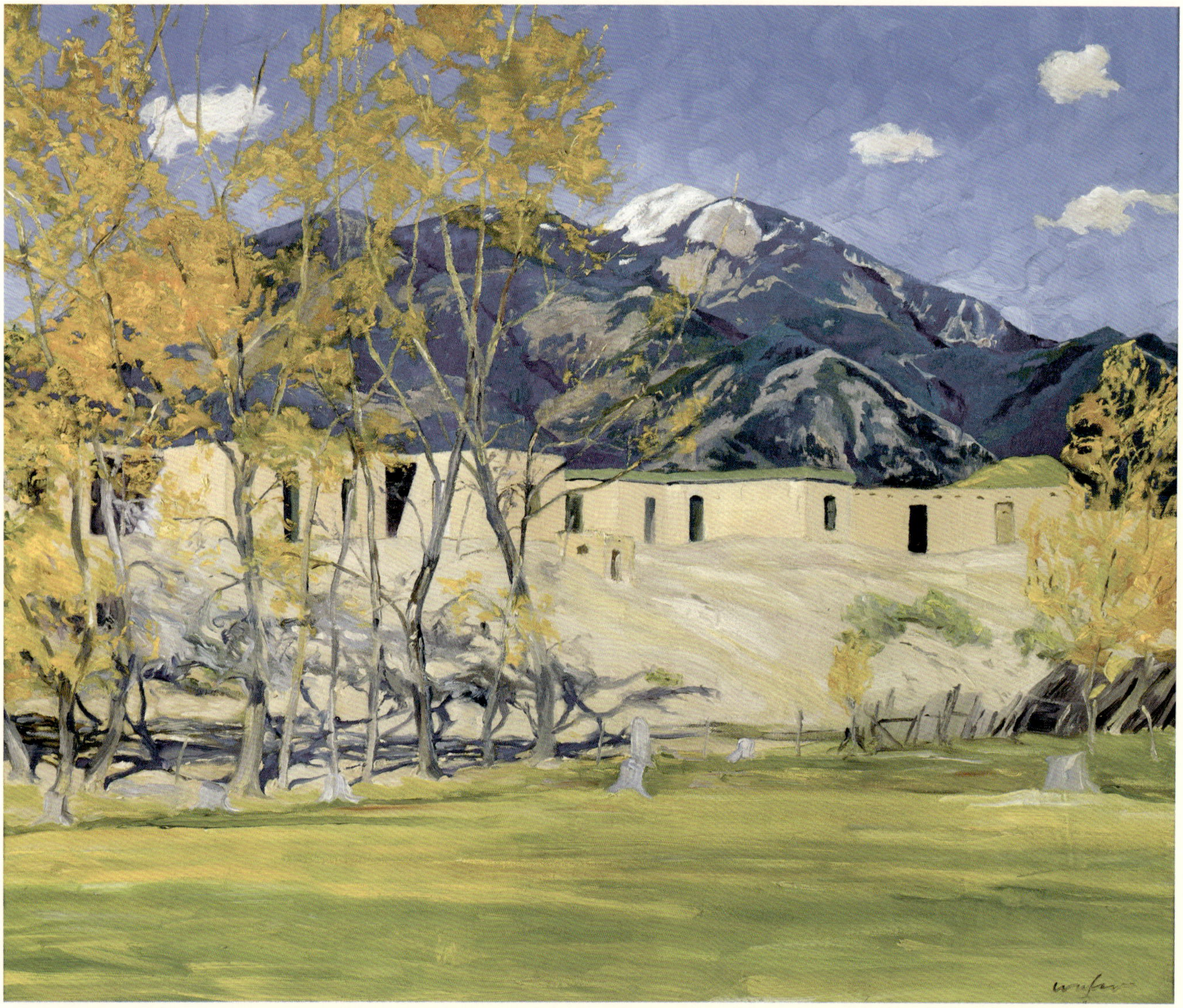

Figure 45. Walter Ufer. *Taos Loma*, 1916. Oil on canvas, 25 x 30 inches. Collection Matthew and Joyce Walsh. (former Klauer Family Collection)

narrow, yellow highway."[13] In another street scene titled *September Morn* [fig. 44], Ufer framed a fenced dirt street with towering trees while ushering the viewer's eye towards the morada, north of what would become the Mabel Dodge Luhan compound.

Taos Loma [fig. 45] is a fine example of Ufer painting a neighborhood that has settled into a New Mexico fall landscape under intense, bleaching light. Ufer no longer used the water rippling through an acequia or the wagon tracks on a rough dirt road to usher the viewer through his composition. He positioned the viewer on the outskirts of the village, allowing a panoramic view of the Sangre de Cristo Mountains as seen through a row of sparsely defoliated trees and over a street lined with adobes.

[13] Ibid.

Chapter V
Breaking Out, 1917

The year 1917 was Ufer's break out year. Without the support of the Harrison brothers and the syndicate, but with the patronage of the faithful Oscar Mayer and William Klauer, Ufer began to create some of his most important paintings in Laguna and Taos. His gross annual income was $6,900.[1] While he only finished sixteen canvases that year, they were larger and more important, and William Klauer would acquire a number of them.

LAGUNA PUEBLO, 1917

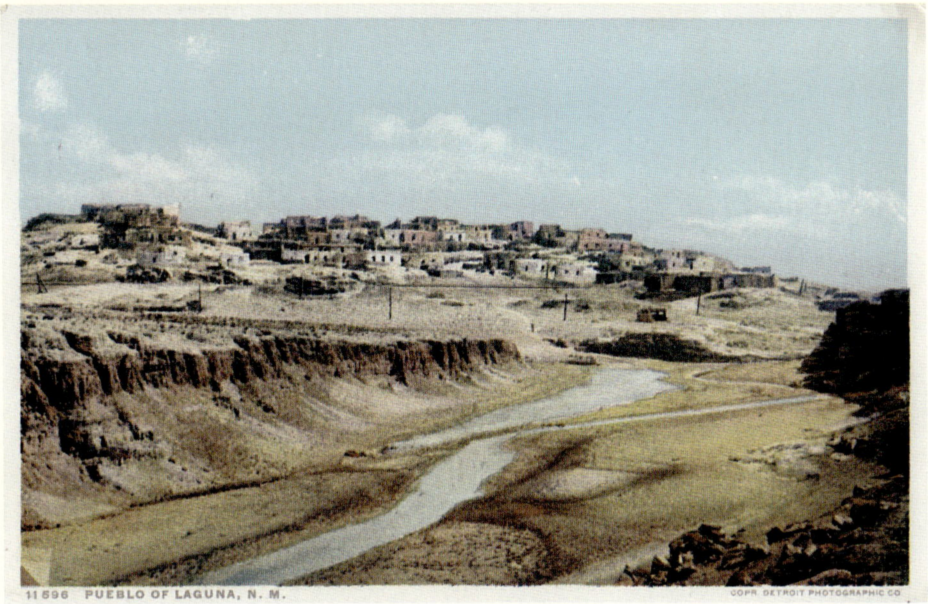

Figure 46. *Panoramic view of Laguna Pueblo*, 1902. Postcard courtesy of the author.

Noteworthy paintings that year were *The Bakers–Laguna* [fig. 48], *Indian Corn–Taos* [fig. 50], and *Going East* [fig. 52a], all of which would bear the Klauer provenance the following year. Until 1917, Ufer's largest painting had been 30 by 30 inches. Following Carter Harrison's advice, he started creating larger canvases, specifically to make a more powerful impact in juried shows. He painted *Mexican Well*, measuring 36 by 40 inches, followed by *Indian Corn–Taos* at 40 by 50 inches. Finally, *The Bakers–Laguna* and *Going East* became Ufer's largest canvases ever at 50 by 50 inches. All of Ufer's larger paintings were accepted into juried competitions. As happened repeatedly, Harrison's advice proved beneficial to Ufer's career. From 1917 through 1926, Ufer's large-scale paintings attracted seven awards in national juried exhibitions. Eventually, William Klauer acquired a significant percentage of his pre-1920 large canvases.

Ufer began the 1917 painting season at *Laguna Pueblo* [fig. 46], his second visit there. Historians often date the founding of Laguna Pueblo to 1688 or 1698 CE, a date that aligns with the founding of the

[1] $6900 in 1917 would equal $135,689 in 2019.

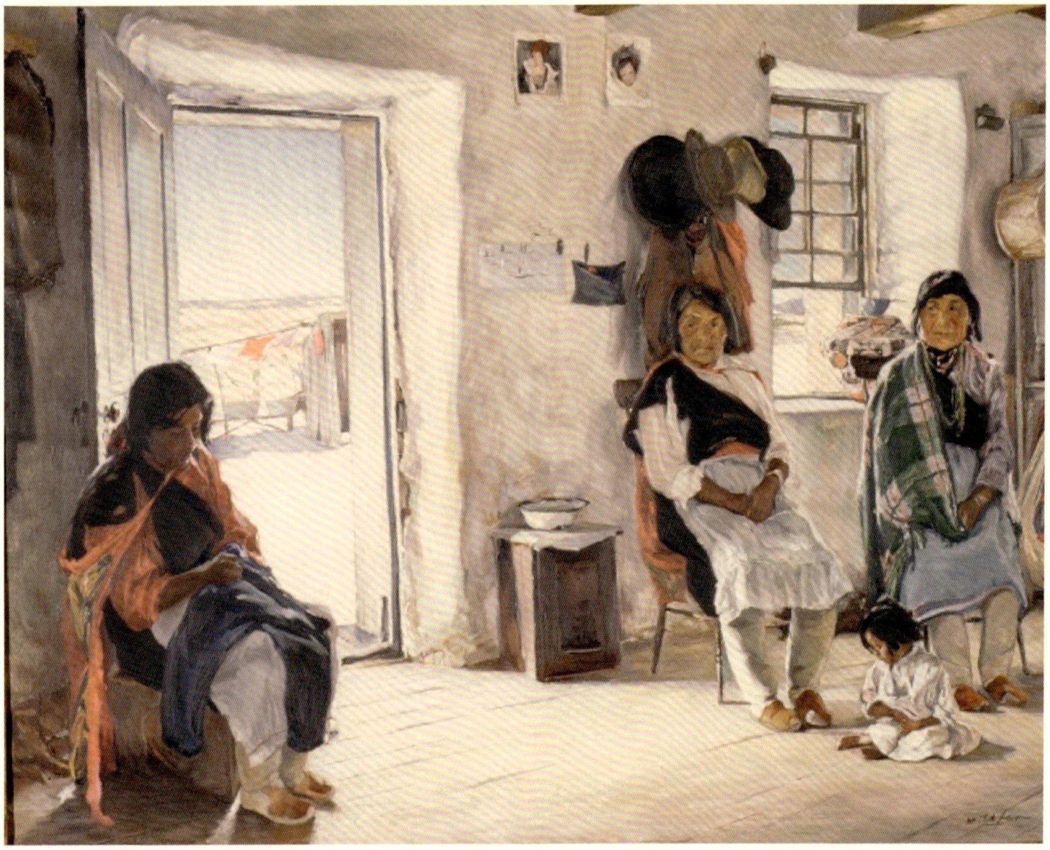

Figure 47. Walter Ufer. *Friends–Laguna Pueblo*, 1917. Oil on canvas, 40 x 50 inches. Collection Klauer Manufacturing Company.

Mission of San José de la Laguna by Father Miranda. However, the tribe was in its present location at least two centuries earlier "after migrating from the north because of a drought presumed to have been caused by lack of attention to religion."[2] The pueblo was built in a multi-storied apartment style with the ground floor usually reserved for storage. The lower level apartments, capped with ceilings made of poles, straw, and adobe served as the floor for the second level rooms. Entry to the original pueblo was through openings in the apartment's ceilings—each floor accessed by ladders. When there were threats, the ladders were pulled in and the ceiling openings sealed.

The natives welcomed Ufer at Laguna Pueblo and invited him into their home. By the time of Ufer's visit, entry to the pueblo was made through a conventional door rather than a ceiling opening. He was able to establish a special relationship as evidenced in *Friends–Laguna Pueblo* [fig. 47]. Fortunately, Ufer had befriended Mr. Robert Conroy, the Deputy Keeper of the Interior U.S. Indian Services, and his wife in 1915. The couple provided him with room and board and gave him a place to stay and paint while visiting and learning about the Laguna Pueblo culture.

While Ufer is usually celebrated for paintings he created in Taos, a significant number of his largest and most important works were created in Laguna. After his Laguna experience in 1915, he easily settled there and felt at home with the natives. In 1919, he again returned to Laguna, painting *Their Audience–Laguna* [fig. 59] which he also sold to Klauer for $465.

[2] Florence Hawley Ellis, "An Outline of Laguna Pueblo History and Social Organization," in *Southwestern Journal of Anthropology*, Vol. 15, No. 4 (Winter, 1959), 346.

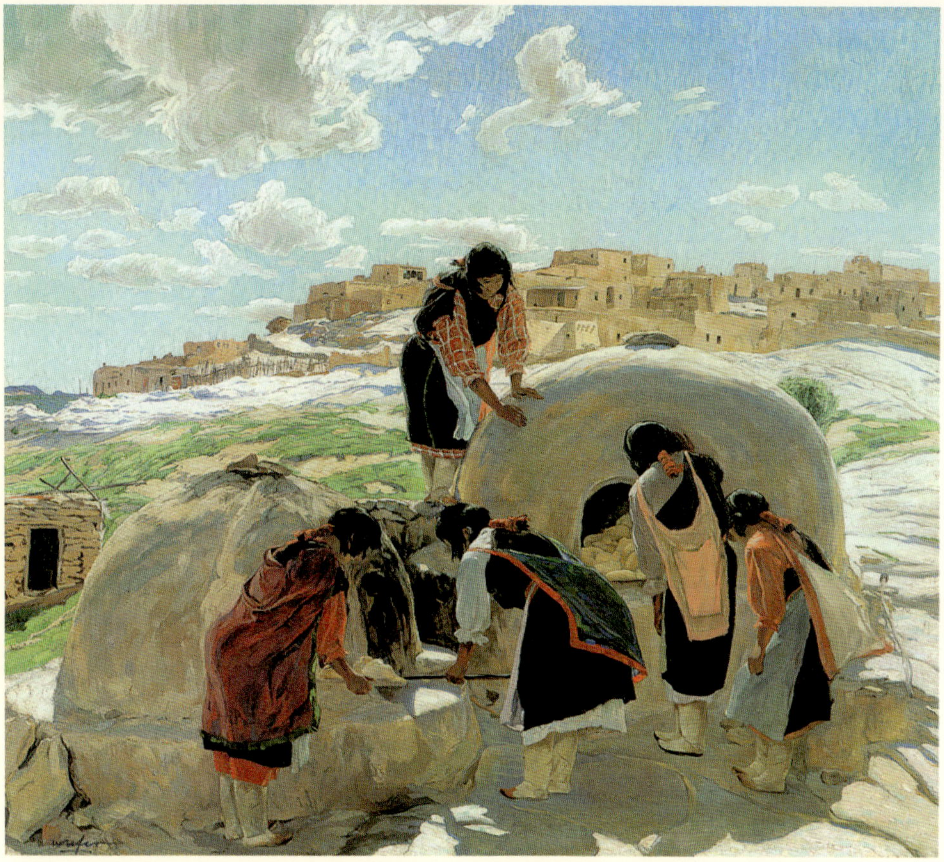

Figure 48. Walter Ufer. *The Bakers–Laguna*, 1917. Oil on canvas, 50.25 x 50.25 inches. Private Collection. (former Klauer Family Collection)

Friends–Laguna Pueblo reflects the simple lifestyle of its occupants, their home featuring only the barest of necessities. Brilliant sunshine flooding the interior through the open door highlights the family passing the time of day. Three women are seated in a world of their own, seemingly unaware of the man painting them. Their primary functions are sewing and babysitting for the youngster seated on the floor. Ufer treated them individually and made little or no attempt to create the feeling of interaction.

The Bakers–Laguna [fig. 48] is a classic Ufer painting. Creating a composition based on a triangle, five women are gathered around two *hornos* (ovens) and baking bread. They are positioned in shadows cast by clouds, silhouetting their forms against the sprawling, multi-story pueblo and brilliance of the sky. The strong light "seems to bless and clarify the simple domestic, communal activity below."[3] The result is a dramatic, eye-catching canvas that demonstrates his mastery at painting bluish-grey shadows. The length of the shadows suggests the painting was done in early morning, the time when baking was done to feed the pueblo and tourists.

For artist and photographer alike, Laguna Pueblo offered a myriad of pictorial possibilities. Even though Ufer demonstrated his mastery of atmospheric perspective, William Truettner claimed that Ufer's "vision did not, perhaps, penetrate far beneath dazzling surfaces..." However, "his ability to recreate the strong patterns and colors of southwestern light brought him considerable prominence during the 1920s."[4]

[3] William H. Truettner. "The Art of Public Life" in *Art in New Mexico, 1900-1945: Paths to Taos and Santa Fe* (New York: Abbeville Press), 85.

[4] Ibid, 84.

RETURN TO TAOS

After producing wonderful paintings of the church at Chimayo and being elected as a member of the Taos Society of Artists, Ufer was ready to create more prize-winning canvases. He now found critics, collectors, and jurors ready to accept his paintings. He no longer experienced the failure that had greeted him when he returned from Europe in 1913. Rather, by 1917, the same "critics" were awarding his paintings prizes—initially in The Art Institute of Chicago's regional shows, then nationally at the National Academy of Design in New York. His principal subjects in Europe and New Mexico were, more often than not, ordinary human beings living unpretentious lives. While Europe provided him with the technical ability to apply paint to a canvas, New Mexico inspired his use of exciting color applied in a pseudo-impressionistic style.

With *Down a Hill in Taos* [fig. 49], Ufer captured a Hispanic firewood vendor, a *leñador*, trailing three beasts of burden. The *leñador*, dressed in overalls, delivered packs of split cedar and *piñon* to vendors who would, in turn, sell them to housewives.[5] According to the *Taos Valley News*, "burro hauling was an ancient Spanish tradition."[6] As with other paintings in the Klauer Collection, notably *In Taos* [fig. 53], no event was unimportant to Ufer. Catherine Whitney saw Ufer's paintings of Hispanics and Taos Indians as "a revolt against refined and academic subjects in favor of humble subjects painted from life."[7]

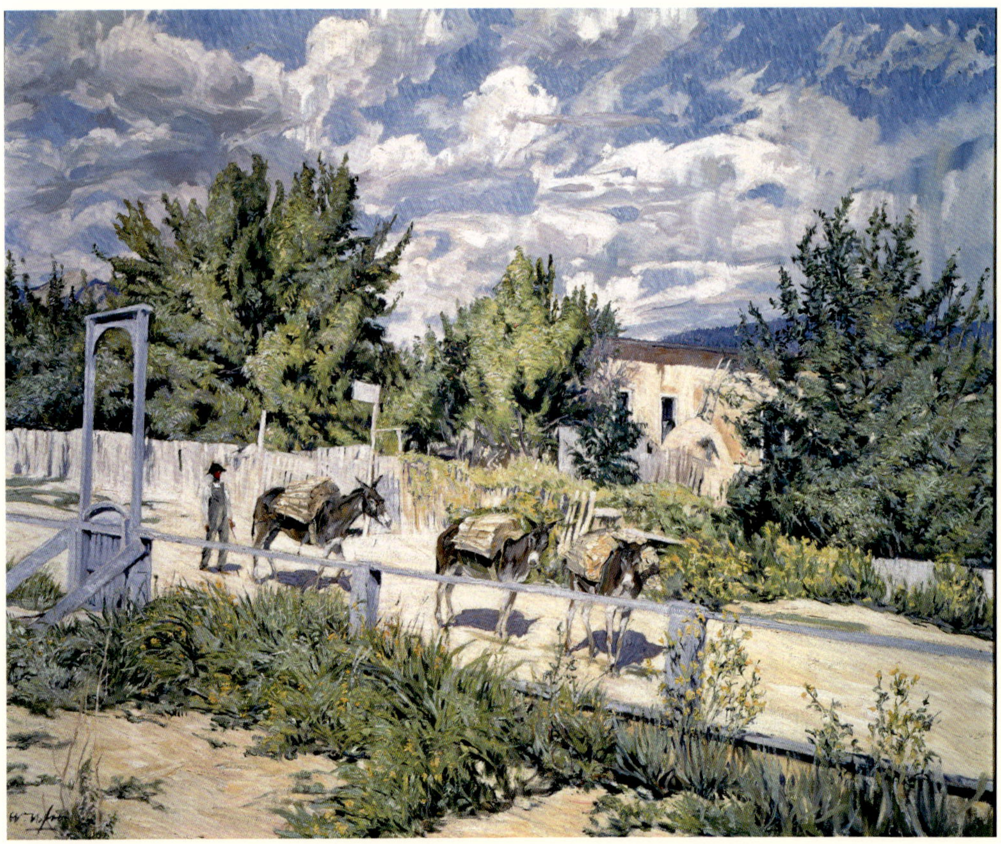

Figure 49. Walter Ufer. *Down a Hill in Taos*, 1917. Oil on canvas, 25 x 30 inches. Private collection. (former Klauer Family Collection)

[5] Arrell Morgan Gibson, *The Santa Fe and Taos Colonies: Age of the Museums* (Norman, OK: University of Oklahoma, 1983), 20.

[6] *Taos Valley News*. Ila McAfee Scrapbooks (3), Collection The Couse-Sharp Foundation Archives, Taos.

[7] Catherine Whitney, "Glimpsing Modernity" in *A Place in the Sun: The Southwest Paintings of Walter Ufer and E. Martin Hennings* (Denver, CO: Denver Art Museum, 2016), 137.

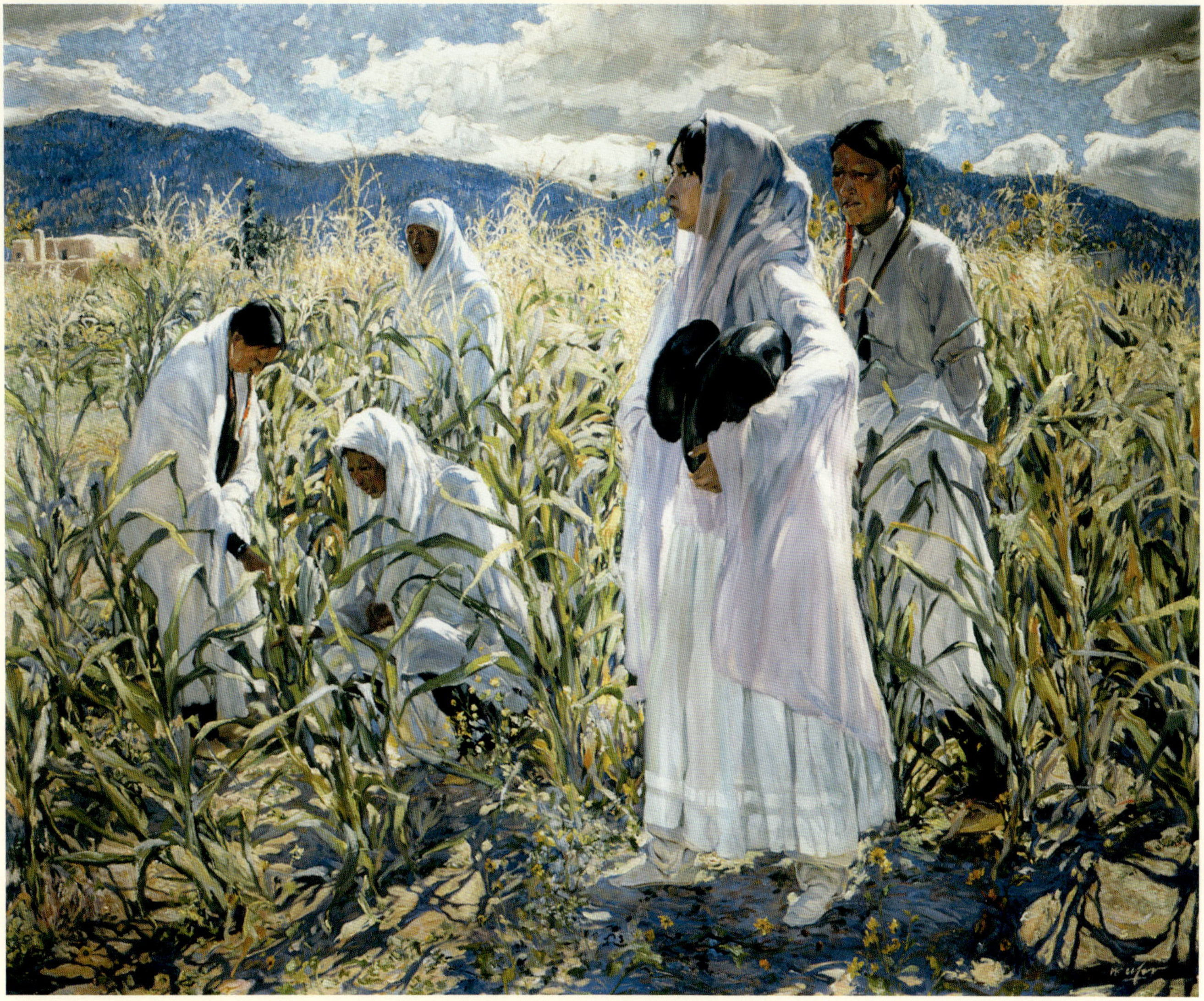

Figure 50. Walter Ufer. *Indian Corn-Taos,* 1917. Oil on canvas, 40 x 50 inches. Private collection. (former Klauer Family Collection)

Another subject enjoyed by Ufer was Taos Indians working in a cornfield. Growing corn was an important occupation of the Taos Indian. In fact, for the participants picking corn in *Indian Corn–Taos* [fig. 50], it was a solemn, sacred event. *Indian Corn–Taos* was the most ambitious of Ufer's cornfield pictures. In a rare composition showing multiple figures, Ufer pictured Jim Mirabel and his daughter in the foreground walking through a cornfield. As with compositions showing Jim by himself, Ufer relished the opportunity to paint the myriad shapes of lengthy leaves and the silk bursting forth from cornstalks. The cornfield became Ufer's playground where he could explore curvilinear shapes that controlled the flow of light and how it affected color.

Ufer achieved his full potential in 1917. Becoming the darling of the Chicago cultural scene, his paintings were praised by critics, museum professionals, and patrons alike. He won his first major prize at New York's National Academy of Design and, as mentioned earlier, was elected president of the Palette and Chisel Club [figs. 31 and 32]. Furthermore, after Ufer and Higgins participated with the Taos Society of Artists's (TSA) circuit exhibitions in 1915 and 1916, they became full members in 1917. In November

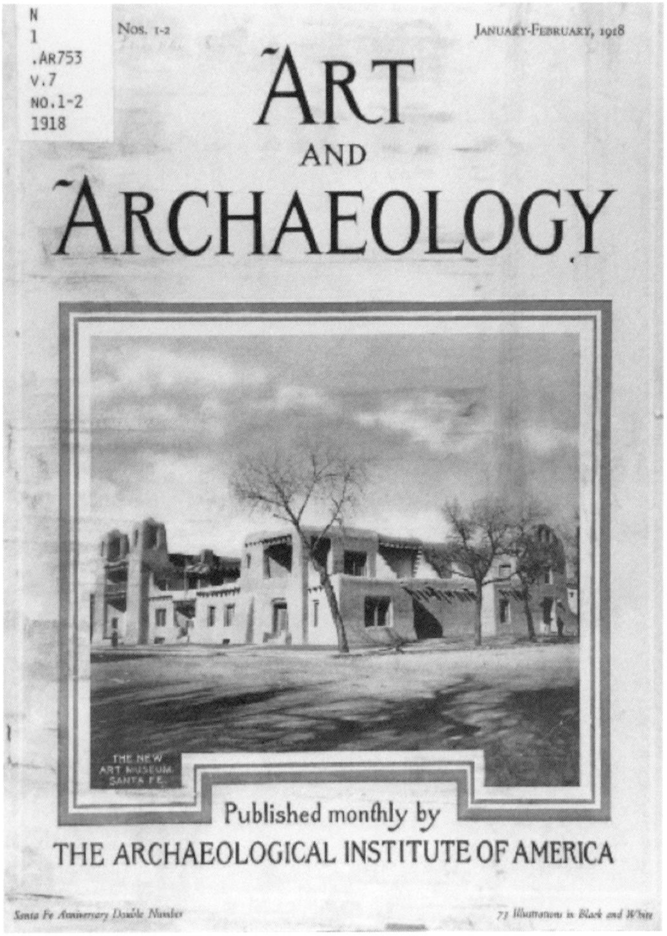

Figure 51.
"The New Art Museum, Santa Fe,"
Art and Archaeology (January-February, 1918).

they enjoyed seeing their paintings included in the inaugural, grand opening of the Museum of New Mexico in Santa Fe. As the seventh and eighth members, Ufer immediately became a major force in the TSA while Higgins, a "loner" and "sleepy-time joe," was a more laid-back member. When the positions of president and secretary were elected annually, Ufer served as both secretary and president, while Higgins always found excuses why he wasn't able to serve in the time-demanding posts. Essentially, the purpose of the TSA was to attract exposure for their paintings.[8]

This membership had a major impact on Ufer and Higgins's careers. They would find new success through their association with an art movement that achieved national recognition within a relatively short period of time. While they would continue to enjoy one-man shows and success in juried exhibitions, the circuit exhibitions of the TSA enabled their work to travel to major cities and be viewed by new audiences.

On Klauer's annual trips to Taos, artist and patron became better acquainted. Ufer saw his patron in Chicago socially, but at Klauer's Taos cottage, they spent several days together with their mutual friends. Besides providing an opportunity to hunt and fish, eat and drink, cottage life promoted the spirit of camaraderie. The cottage also provided Ufer with a stage to perform on. In Taos, he earned a reputation of telling, what he thought, were humorous stories. Unfortunately, his performances were often embarrassing, not only to himself, but also to the host. Still, Klauer invited Ufer to the cottage, year after year.

[8] The Society created annual circuit exhibitions that travelled to major cities like New York, Chicago, and St. Louis, among others.

GOING EAST, THE BIG PRIZE

While Victor Higgins and Ufer had been honored with earlier prizes in shows at The Art Institute of Chicago, from 1917 on they began to win the more important prizes in national competitions. Ufer entered *Going East* [fig. 52a and 52b] in the juried show at The Art Institute of Chicago, and it became a featured painting in competitive exhibitions at the National Academy of Design and The Pennsylvania Academy of the Fine Arts. When seeing *Going East* at the National Academy, colleague Ernest Blumenschein commented: "*Going East* is just a baby—and ought to attract a lot of attention and put you in the Academy as an associate member."[9] Blumenschein's prophesy came true when Ufer won the prestigious Thomas P. Clarke Prize in the Winter Show at the National Academy for the best figure painting in the exhibition.

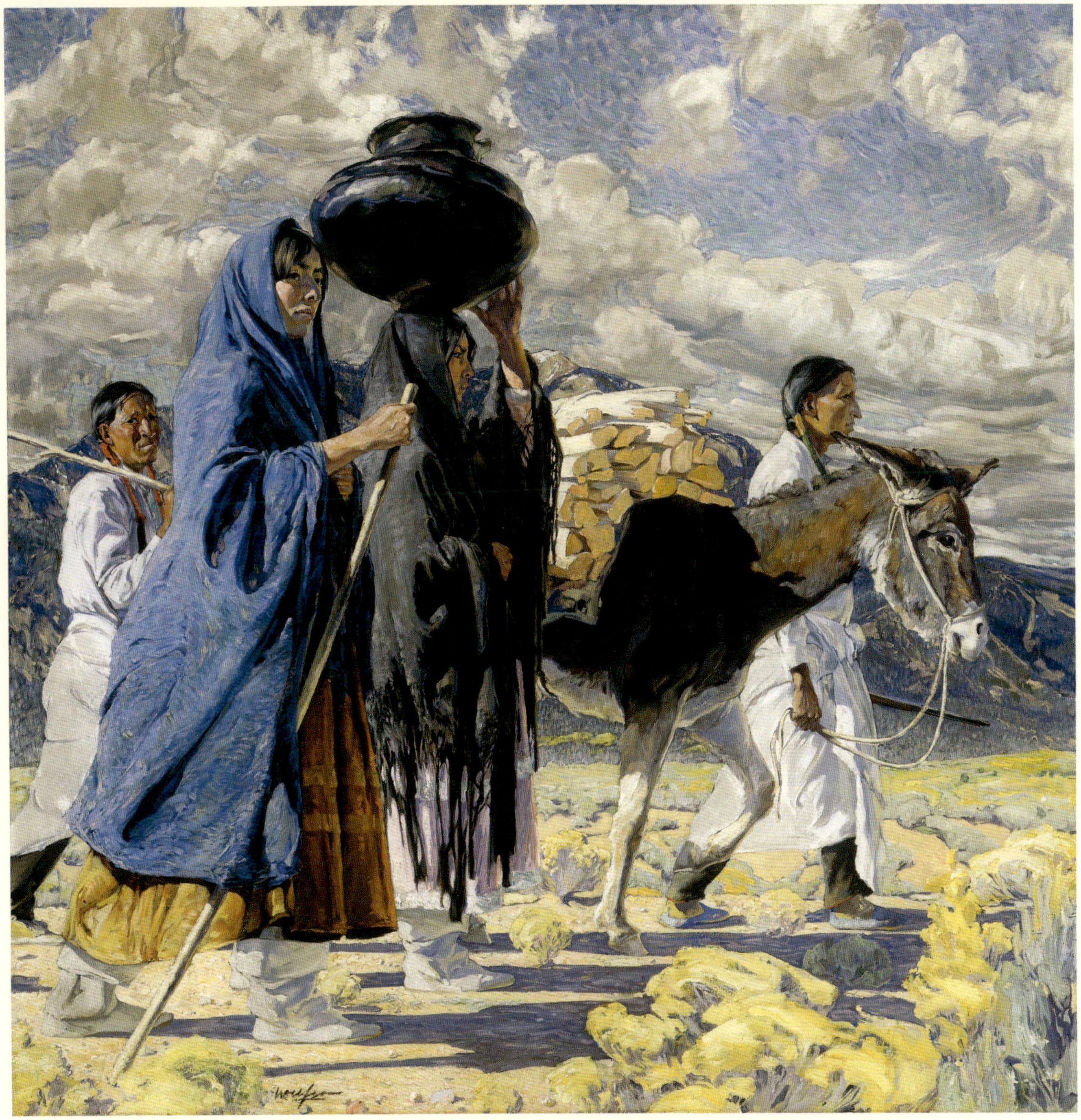

Figure 52a. Walter Ufer. *Going East*, 1917. Oil on canvas, 50 x 50 inches.
The Eugene B. Adkins Collection at the Fred Jones Jr. Museum of Art, the University of Oklahoma, Norman, Oklahoma and the Philbrook Museum of Art, Tulsa, Oklahoma.

[9] Ernest Blumenschein to Walter Ufer, 1927.

The painting thrust him into the limelight of American art. Finally, receiving the attention he felt he deserved, the *Chicago Examiner* rewarded him with the highest of praise, "Ufer is the first resident of Chicago to capture a national painting prize in the East. New York's cold attitude toward artistic effort emanating from west of Patterson, New Jersey, was broken down by Walter Ufer's brilliant composition *Going East* painted at Taos, N.M."[10]

Jim Mirabal and family are pictured traveling towards the Sacred Blue Lake in *Going East*. The group carries provisions for the twenty-mile trip. Ufer painted two young women, possibly Mirabal's wife and daughter, one supporting a walking stick, the second, balancing a large black *olla* for water on her head. According to Catherine Whitney, the burro carries split wood that will be used for fires to boil water for the ritual of body purification.[11]

The history of rituals and customs of the Taos Indian were not written, but rather communicated by mouth generation after generation. Taos Indians believe Sacred Blue Lake is the source "of all life." Quirino Romero, an official of the Taos community, wrote,

> *Blue Lake for our life is living. Blue Lake is where the spirit of the Indian God is living still today. We go over there to pray, and we go over there to worship. The stars, and the moon and the sun and the sky and the clouds and air and whatever nature has provided us, we do believe in this. To these people religion is central to their existence.*[12]

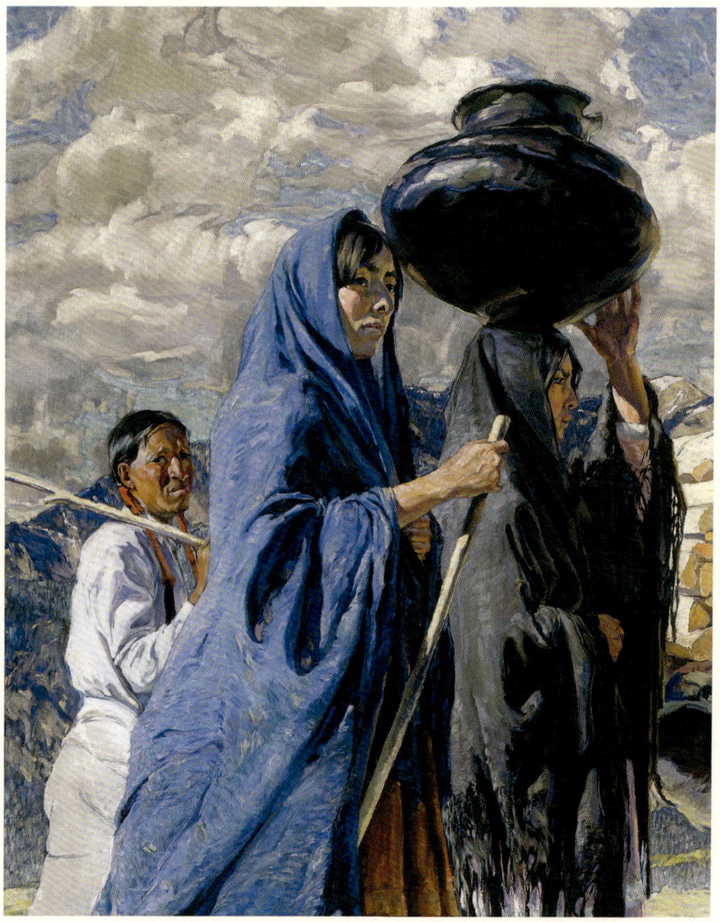

Figure 52b.
Walter Ufer. *Going East* (detail), 1917.
Oil on canvas, 50 x 50 inches.
The Eugene B. Adkins Collection at the Fred Jones Jr. Museum of Art, the University of Oklahoma, Norman, Oklahoma and the Philbrook Museum of Art, Tulsa, Oklahoma.

[10] *Chicago Examiner*. 16 March 1918. KFPUND.
[11] Whitney, "Glimpsing Modernity," 130.
[12] Marcia Keegan, *The Taos-People and Its Sacred Blue Lake* (Santa Fe, NM: Clear Lake Publishers, 1991), 14.

Chapter VI
The War Years

After experiencing relative prosperity, Ufer's market crashed. In the previous four years he watched his paintings sell for ten times the $75 the syndicate paid him for a 30-by-25-inch painting in 1914. World War I undermined his plans to continue selling at that increased rate. By 1918 Americans weren't in the mood to buy art—at any price. In fact, Americans, subscribing to "Hooverism," became ultra conservative, "eliminating inessentials and streamlining all activity toward the war effort..."[1] In 1918 the market crashed. Ufer exclaimed, "Art is dead...in Taos this year. Nobody doing much. War in the air. Yet I have finished about four fairly large paintings."[2]

In Dubuque, the Klauers were faced with operating Klauer Manufacturing Company during World War I and trying to determine how the company would aid in the war effort. The factory was equipped to fabricate virtually any type of metal-made object used to move water. While it was easy to claim that factories producing machinery used in the war effort made the company a profit, few companies had a reserve for retooling and producing equipment to be used by the military. Besides adaptation of equipment, the Klauers had to deal with a shortage of manpower. Finding men and women to operate machinery became a critical problem when America joined the Allies on July 28, 1918, and it was no different for the Klauer Manufacturing Company.[3]

As America became fully engaged in the European war, the nation spent monies on essentials only and certainly not on art created by artists with German surnames. The Ufers, living under a cloud of suspicion, found their mail opened and "edited" by censors which caused Walter to seek legal counsel. Despite this, Ufer demonstrated his patriotism by creating posters for the Fourth Liberty Loan Campaign and painting a World War I Range Finder. Ufer and several Taos artists also painted large-scale canvases of French landscapes, measuring 5-by-7-feet, designed to aid rifle shooters.

Besides the atrocities brought on by a world war, the devastating Spanish Influenza Epidemic was also killing people worldwide, and those living in Taos did not escape this disaster either. Mary and Walter Ufer became night nurses, assisting Dr. J. W. Bergman.[4] There are numerous horrific stories of graves being dug to accommodate the thousands who died. Even though Mary and Walter also became seriously ill, it was reported that "...they were washing babies and burying the dead in the same breath."[5]

---

[1] Good. "Walter Ufer," 158.

[2] Walter Ufer to Allan [?], 6 September 1918. UPUNDSG. Besides a couple of portraits and a sketch, Ufer was likely referring to: *In Taos* [30 x 25 inches]; *Jim* [36 x 40]; *Me and Him* or *Spring* [40 ¼ x 36 ¼]; and *His Song* [30 x 36]. A fifth canvas dated 1918, *The Gateway* [30 x 30], may have been painted between September 5 and Ufer's departure for New York in December.

[3] Records do not exist to confirm what changes were made in Klauer Manufacturing Company, Inc., and whether or not the company created a new line of products to aid in the war effort. In a telephone conversation on April 2, 2017, with Bill Klauer, he recalled that during World War II, the Federal Government had Klauer Manufacturing producing ventilators to be used in the hot Florida factories that were producing munitions. Klauer Manufacturing Company also fabricated sawed-off shotguns. According to Bill, the operation was highly secretive. He stated that no one at Klauer Manufacturing Company knew where the ventilators were going when they left Dubuque.

[4] 'Doc' Martin was serving the army troops in Austin, Texas, during the flu epidemic. The December 24, 1918 *Taos Valley News* thanked Mary and Walter "for excellent work they did during the flu epidemic." On December 3, the *Taos Valley News* mentioned Dr. J. W. Bergmans "who has been overworked in the recent flu epidemic."(My thanks to Robert Rankin White, Ph. D., for locating this material.)

[5] Good, "Walter Ufer," 165.

The *Taos Valley News* praised "the spontaneous and explosive Mr. Ufer and his gentile wife," promising that they "will be remembered in Taos for the excellent work they did during the flu epidemic."[6] William Klauer would have been aware of the Ufers' heroic activities because he was staying in his cottage in Taos at the height of the flu epidemic.[7]

IN TAOS, UFER'S REALISM

Even though Ufer faced unfavorable conditions during World War I, he managed to create a group of significant paintings before meeting at the cottage with Klauer in December of 1918. The first of these paintings was *In Taos* [fig. 53], and it was one of Ufer's earliest efforts depicting the plight of the Taos Indian.[8] It represented the kind of abject, brutal honesty normally associated with paintings created by Robert Henri and other members of the Ashcan School, who were appropriately nicknamed "apostles of ugliness." A writer for *El Palacio* described the Taos Indian in the painting as

> *standing against the closed door of an adobe barn while at his side, lounging against the adobe wall, sits a Hispanic, one foot shod, the other bare, in cheap overalls, and shirt and broad brimmed Stetson hat. Both men seem perfectly satisfied doing nothing. The scene is drenched in a sunshine that only Ufer knew how to bring to his canvases.*[9]

Jim Mirabal is the standing figure, but the seated Hispanic is unidentified. Able to identify Mirabal, Klauer was more interested in "the history of the Mexican." Ufer had told him that the Mexican "was some celebrated officer," and Klauer asked to "send me this description as soon as you can."[10] Unfortunately, if Ufer responded, it hasn't survived in Klauer's papers.

Ufer had painted the laborers whose job was posing for the artist, an occupation paying twenty-five cents an hour. It is not clear in this work if they are working as models or are taking a break. Either way, the writer's reference to "cheap overalls" is bothersome as it implies that the model should have dressed better for the occasion, completely missing Ufer's intentions. Their ruddy complexions are strong evidence that they spend every waking hour working in the searing desert heat. Jim wears the customary white sheet, gathered at the waist, draped over shirt and trousers. The seated Hispanic wears the usual blue overalls, bleached by wear and intense sunlight. His knees are covered with pads, covering holes or serving as cushions for a man who spent too much time kneeling. The Hispanic's shoeless foot reveals a painful corn looking like a volcano about to erupt.

Ufer's success was the result of painting the laborers, Indian or Hispanic, as he saw them. It is apparent that the ill-informed *El Palacio* critic had seen too many paintings of Taos Indians dressed in Plains Indian costume and looking like idealized, semi-clad, Greek gods. Even though Ufer should have rejoiced because of his success, his enthusiasm was dampened by the lack of sales. Totally frustrated, he needed to make a change. For several years, the Harrison brothers had recommended that he move to

---

[6] "Locals," *Taos Valley News*, 24 December 1918.

[7] The Bergmans were from Holland. He was the doctor for Taos Pueblo and in 1927, one of his patients, a young girl, was seriously ill. Bergman prescribed aspirin, advised the family to bath her repeatedly, and left for the night. She died of double pneumonia a few hours later. Mabel Dodge Luhan, an active spokesman for the Taos Indians, reported Bergman to his employer. His reputation destroyed, the Bergmans were forced to leave Taos, returning to their native Holland. The Bergman house, built in 1917, was sold to Nicolai Fechin.

[8] Ufer sold the canvas from his solo show for $500 to Klauer in 1922. Klauer eventually sold it to the Dubuque Art Association for $600. $500 in 1922 would equal $7491 in 2019.

[9] "The Taos Society of Artists Exhibit" in *El Palacio*, 30 September 1919, 135-136.

[10] William Klauer to Walter Ufer, 30 March 1923, UPUNDSG.

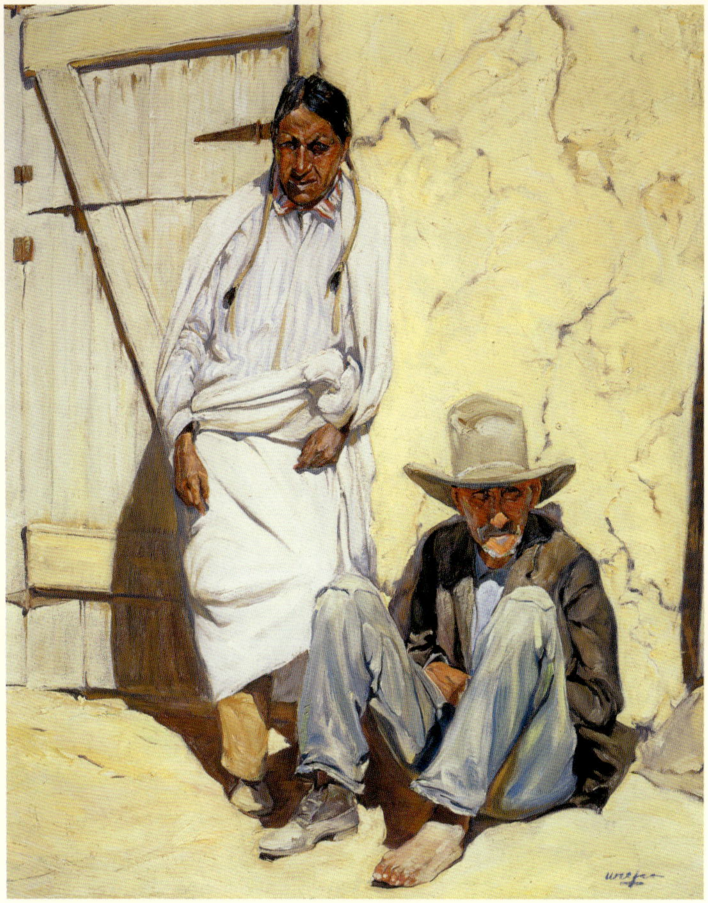

Figure 53.
Walter Ufer. *In Taos*, 1918.
Oil on canvas 30 x 25 inches.
Private Collection.
Photo courtesy Gerald Peters Gallery,
Santa Fe, New Mexico.
(former Klauer Family Collection
and Dubuque Art Association)

New York City and fresh subject matter, "where the ducats" were. However, it required funds to make the move to the most expensive city in America.[11]

In desperation, Ufer turned to the Peoria Art Association where he had previously exhibited paintings. In early September 1918, Charles A. Bennett approached Ufer about participating in a juried exhibition of Illinois painters.[12] Bennett was anxious to involve Ufer because he was an artist riding the crest of popularity. Bennett's goal was to attract artists from all over Illinois, bringing "to the surface some obscure and hidden talent as well as to bring to Peoria the work of our best artists."[13] Bennett sent letters "to five [artists] that have won the hearts of Peorians," and he felt that with contributions from three of these artists, "the success of the exhibition would be assured."[14] Ufer was the first of the five to agree and basically became the "bait" to attract other top artists.

On November 12, the jury accepted *Going East* and *Indian Corn–Taos*, and Bennett invited Ufer to "a very informal 'first view' of the exhibition…"[15] Five days later, on November 17, Ufer wrote a letter expressing his disappointment that neither painting was awarded a prize. He couldn't understand how the judges failed to award *Going East* a prize in an exhibition in Peoria. One of the jurors, Harold H. Brown, offered an explanation. Sarcastically, Ufer responded, "it [Brown's letter] should have been entitled 'You got it, but you didn't get it.' "[16] Bennett, attempting to placate Ufer, explained the jurors considered giving

[11] Carter H. Harrison to Walter Ufer, 31 October 1916, UPUNDSG.
[12] Charles A. Bennett to Walter Ufer, 6 September 1918, UPUNDSG.
[13] Ibid.
[14] Ibid.
[15] Charles A. Bennett to Walter Ufer, November 12, 1918, UPUNDSG
[16] Walter Ufer to Charles A. Bennett, 1 December 1918, UPUNDSG.

Going East a medal, expressing "the idea that they would be heaping a small medal on top of a big one if they gave the award to you or to one other [*Indian Corn—Taos*] in the exhibition."[17] Bennett further reasoned that Ufer would have thought less of them had they given him a medal. "You would have said either that it was throwing away good medals much needed by other artists or that the jury didn't know enough to have a mind of their own, and merely copied the jury in New York."[18]

Bennett continued by describing the hanging of *Indian Corn–Taos* which was "opposite the entrance to the room and was shown to excellent advantage. It had the best place in the exhibition."[19] At the same time, Bennett stated that *Going East*, despite being admired by "many of the leading people," was "out of our class for purchasing at present."[20] Bennett failed to realize how important it was for Ufer to make a sale in Peoria. He desperately needed funds for his December trip.[21]

THE COTTAGE, 1918

Ufer's only hope now was William Klauer. When Klauer announced he would be staying in his Taos cottage in November, Ufer took charge of planning for the visit. Ufer knew what he had to do when Klauer came to Taos. He would inform *Taos Valley News* of Klauer's pending visit, and he would also make arrangements to have Klauer's baggage picked up at Taos Junction or Servillita before organizing workers to ensure the residence was accessible. Mud slides, bringing rocks and other debris, kept the little travelled dirt road to the cottage impassable, and Ufer would contact Earl Brazelton to clear it. The cottage, of course, also had to be habitable. It had to be cleaned since it had been unoccupied for about a year. Besides cutting several cords of wood to burn in the fireplace and stove, the pantry and icebox had to be well stocked. Ice would have to be brought in to preserve meats, fish, and other foods. While much of the food and beverages would have been purchased in Taos, Klauer and his visitors also hunted and fished. Oscar Mayer also sent hams and other meats. Feasts in Klauer's cottage were legendary. Like so many sessions at the cottage, Klauer and his guests enjoyed a festive atmosphere. Ufer played a major role in choreographing activities that lasted as long as Klauer was in Taos. There is not even a suggestion that Ufer failed to live up to Klauer's high expectations.

The cottage was not modest by any standard. It was large and comfortable with a deck surrounding the main floor. Besides eating and drinking, the region offered Klauer and his friends excellent opportunities for hunting as well as fishing in fresh water streams. Klauer's lengthy stays always included guests—notably his close friend O. L. Barker, business associate Carter Harrison, and other friends from Chicago and Dubuque as well as the artists Ufer and Higgins. When Carter Harrison visited, he photographed the cottage and presented it to Klauer [fig. 54].

On December 3, *Taos Valley News* reported that Higgins and Ufer "spent Thanksgiving with William Klauer at his bungalow home in the mountains south of Taos."[22] One can only imagine what transpired during their gathering. Ufer's agenda during that visit was to request financial assistance

---

[17] Charles A. Bennett to Walter Ufer, 1 December 1918, UPUNDSG.

[18] Ibid.

[19] Ibid.

[20] Ibid.

[21] According to Ufer's records, the Peoria Artists Association never acquired a painting by Ufer and, three years later, still recalling his experience, terminated their relationship.

[22] "Locals," *Taos Valley News*, 3 December 1918.

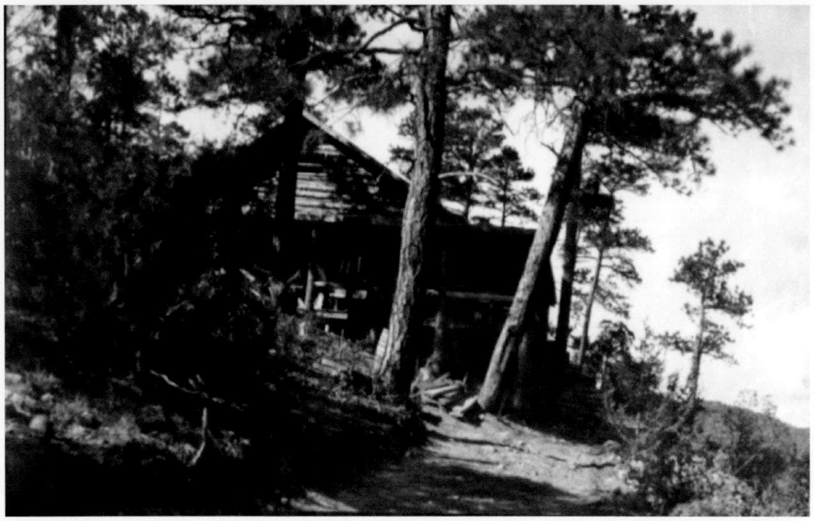

Figure 54.
Carter H. Harrison, IV.
William Klauer's Cottage, Taos, c. 1915.
Collection The Snite Museum of Art,
University of Notre Dame,
Gift of Klauer Family.

from Klauer. He needed to approach his patron for funds to cover expenses for an extended, perhaps permanent, stay in New York City. The only answer was to sell some of his most prized paintings.

Because Klauer undoubtedly knew of Ufer's situation before they began their visit, all that remained was finding a private moment when they could discuss specifics. Ufer knew that he would have to persuade Klauer to purchase a group of his paintings or cancel his New York trip. Because he had already attempted, unsuccessfully, to sell *Going East* for $2500, he probably realized that it would require more than one painting to consummate a favorable transaction.

Initially, the two focused on a purchase that included *Going East* along with *The Bakers–Laguna*, *The Mexican Well* and *Down a Hill in Taos*. A December 5 letter to Klauer recorded the values Walter placed on four paintings, "*Going East* 50 x 50 –2500; *The Bakers–Laguna* 50 x 50 –1800; *The Mexican Well* 36 x 40 –1000; *Down a Hill in Taos* 30x 36 –700."[23] Ufer offered four paintings originally priced at $6000 for $2500. Later, for reasons unknown, Ufer substituted *Indian Corn–Taos* for *The Mexican Well*.[24] There wasn't an immediate agreement on how much Klauer would pay for the four paintings. Ufer also made specific conditions for the sale, stating "I may have to ask you for them again when the Blumy, Higgins, Ufer, Proctor exhibition is on and will travel around the country under the auspices of the Museum Directors Association."[25]

Finally, on December 24, 1918 Klauer wrote from Dubuque; "For these four pictures I am willing to pay $1800 and permit you to exhibit them as you suggest. If this is not satisfactory to you just say 'no' and we will call the matter off."[26] Given little choice if he wanted to go to New York, Ufer still had a problem. He was concerned his colleagues would kid him when they learned the bargain price Klauer paid. Klauer assured Ufer, "under no circumstances is anyone going to know, for the present, that I have bought these pictures and it is mutually understood that no one will ever know what I paid for them."[27] In fact, Klauer suggested that Ufer tell his colleagues that he had "loaned these pictures to me, that they have

[23] Walter Ufer to William Klauer, 5 December 1918, UPUNDSG.

[24] Eventually Ufer was successful in selling *The Mexican Well* to Oscar Mayer, a painting that remained in the family until December 2, 2009, when it sold at a Christie's auction for $1,142,500.

[25] Walter Ufer to William Klauer, 5 December 1918, KFPUND.

[26] William Klauer to Walter Ufer, 24 December 1918, UPUNDSG.

[27] Ibid.

not been sold until such time you wish to make it known."[28] Little did Klauer realize that the paintings over the next fourteen years would spend more time travelling to exhibitions in America and Italy than in his home.

Klauer no sooner hung *The Bakers–Laguna* in his home than Ufer requested that it be lent to an exhibition. Ufer wanted *The Bakers–Laguna* and another [unidentified] painting sent to Newcomb Macklin, a shipping firm in Chicago. Klauer agreed to follow Ufer's instructions, reminding the artist that it was "going to be quite a lot of trouble to bring down and send it away. It is very unpleasant on account of having made a place for it."[29]

NEW YORK CITY: "WHERE THE DUCATS ARE"

With the $1800 from his sale and excited about the prospect of beginning a new chapter in his career, Ufer headed for New York City. He arrived in time to attend and enjoy the excitement of Varnishing Day at the National Academy. Unfortunately, Ufer's archives are relatively sparse when it comes to reconstructing his stay in New York. For the most part, what is to be learned comes from Mary's letters to Walter because his responses are missing. He made the trip with little preparation, leaving it to Mary to have his clothes cleaned, packed and sent. In early January she asked if he had received his clothes. She also reviewed his files, which were "bursting from fullness," sending them by Adams Express Money Department parcel. Remaining suspicious of the postal system, Mary wrote that they were "all sealed up and closed so no one can take a peek without your knowledge."[30]

An unidentified, undated newspaper clipping in Ufer's archives announced Ufer's intentions to remain in New York City permanently. The article, apparently written after Ufer had been there for several weeks, reported "with quarters at 96th Fifth Avenue, [Ufer] is finding Eastern subjects of decided interest to paint. He has been engaged with out-door subjects in the vicinity of N. Y. for several weeks and is getting some interesting results."[31] This is the only evidence that Ufer *may* have created more than one painting in what turned out to be a short, three-month stay in New York. If he created multiple paintings, only *Union Square: The Battery*, has survived [fig. 57].

In New York, Ufer became caught up in the wartime spirit. He was likely inspired by Childe Hassam who painted approximately thirty canvases of flags mounted on buildings along the streets of New York. During a series of fundraising campaigns, Fifth Avenue was decorated with hundreds of flags and known as 'Avenue of the Allies,' in sympathetic support of the war effort. Ufer couldn't avoid feeling the excitement generated by artists who had taken their brushes and paint to create images in their historic struggle against the Huns. Ufer approached the subject—a panorama overlooking an army recruiting station—with passion. He was determined to create a canvas of significance. While *Union Square: The Battery* has its political implications, it is not an image reflecting suffering brought on by a horrific war, but one of a peaceful world returning to some sense of normality. *Union Square: The Battery* was Ufer's final salvo in support of the war effort.[32]

---

[28] Ibid.

[29] William Klauer to Walter Ufer, 1 May 1919, KFPUND.

[30] Mary Ufer to Walter Ufer, undated early January letter, UFPUNDSG

[31] Newspaper clipping in Klauer Family Papers that is undated and unidentified, KFPUND.

[32] *Union Square: The Battery* is located on the southern shoreline of Manhattan. It was known as the Battery since it was part of the Dutch settlement of New Amsterdam.

In April, Klauer had grown suspicious that New York hadn't been all that the Harrison brothers promised Ufer it would be. Somehow Ufer managed to spend three months forgetting the work ethic that had served him so well. As a member of the Salmagundi Club [figs. 55 and 56], he spent time socializing instead of living up to the reporter's earlier claims of results. It remains a mystery how Ufer, with only a single painting on his easel, could give the impression that his trip was producing multiple paintings. He played cards and pool, attended exhibits, and hobnobbed with fellow artists. He also drank and took a few meals. As a bachelor, he could lose himself, doing anything but working at his easel. Ufer never had Mary join him while he was in New York. As he had in Munich and Paris, he was most comfortable when Mary was anywhere but with him because then he could enjoy the life of a bachelor.

For the most part, Ufer also kept Klauer in the dark concerning how little he was accomplishing in New York. After making a major investment sponsoring Ufer's trip, Klauer wrote, "Anxious to see your Union Square picture..." Accustomed to seeing Ufer finish a record number of canvases when the artist settled in a location for a few weeks, he questioned, "how many pictures you painted in the East and if you are satisfied with Eastern conditions. I heard you were not working as hard down East as you did in Taos. I rather take it that the New York trip is sort of a bumming trip for you."[33]

Union Square: The Battery was painted from an upper story apartment owned by Klauer's friend O. L. Barker.[34] The painting is a masterpiece of space and atmospheric perspective. It shows a panoramic, bird's-eye view of Lower Manhattan, a beehive of activity with crowds, horse-drawn wagons, trolleys, and

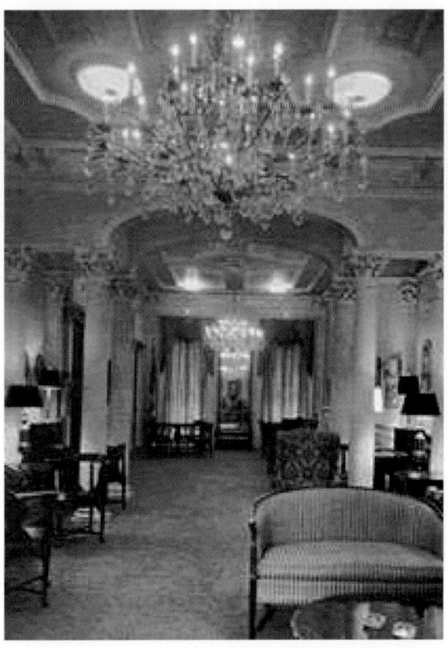

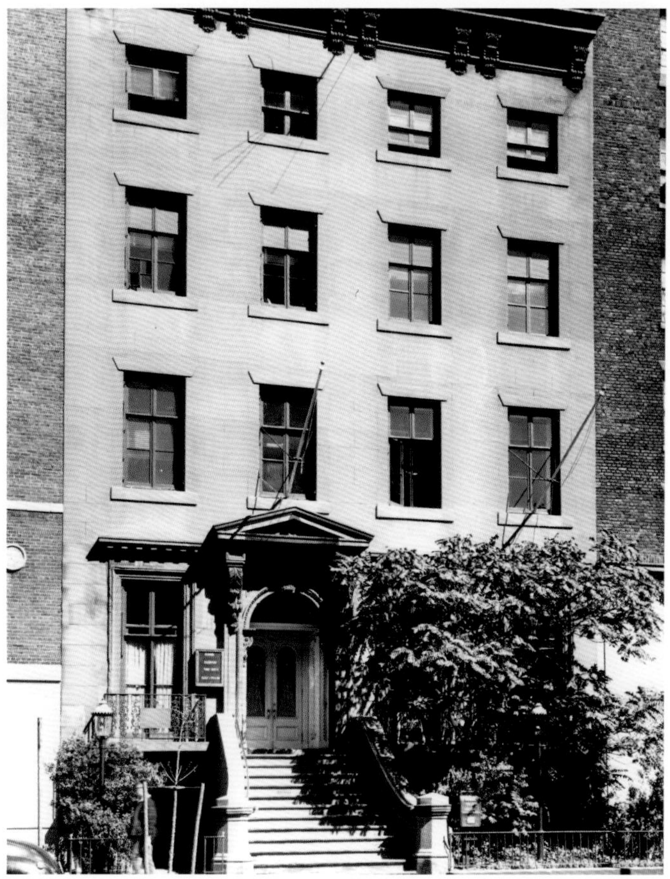

Figure 55 and 56.
Parlor, nd. (above).
Photo courtesy of Essential-Architecture.com.

Salmagundi Club at 47 Fifth Avenue, 1965, (right).
Collection of the Greenwich Village Society for Historic Preservation. Gift of NY Bound Bookshop, 996.001.021.

[33] William Klauer to Walter Ufer, 1919, KFPUND.

[34] Unidentified newspaper clipping in the Ufer Papers, UPUNDSG.

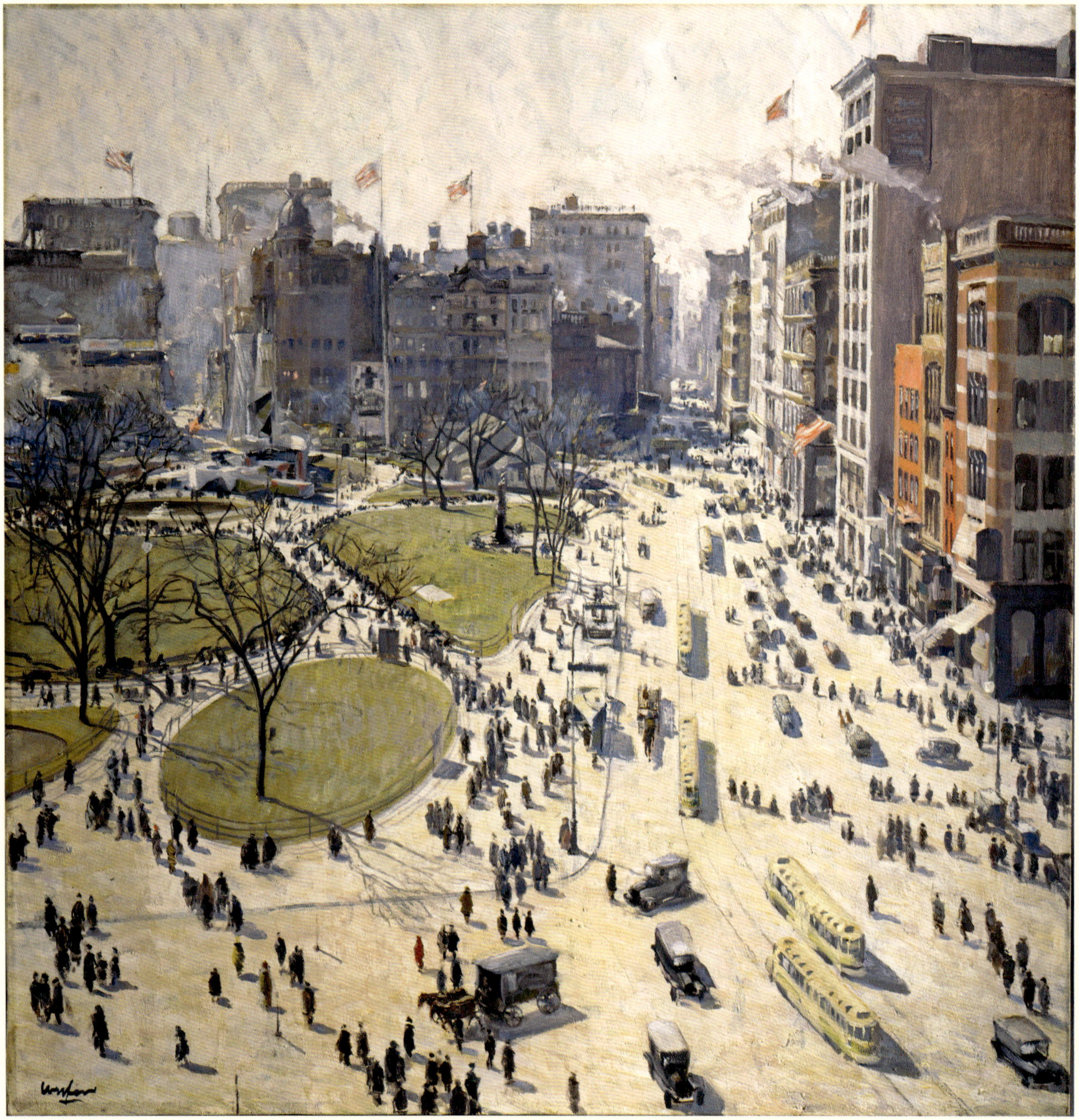

Figure 57. Walter Ufer. *Union Square: The Battery*, 1919. Oil on canvas, 30 x 30 inches. Collection The Snite Museum of Art, University of Notre Dame, Gift of the Klauer Family.

automobiles moving to and from their daily activities.[35] Ufer ushered the viewer's eye down an avenue framed by tall structures decorated with American flags while capturing the chill of a cold, wintry day in January.

Ufer sent the finished painting to Newcomb-Macklin Company for framing in early April. Mary finally saw the painting and described it as being "cold," giving one "the feeling of winter and of the ant

[35] Ufer first explored deep spatial accommodations for ant-size figures in *In Land of Mañana*, Collection Union League Club of Chicago.

hill life of New York. It is a picture that grows on one."[36] While Mary's analysis is sensitive and descriptive, her words betray a feeling of disappointment. Her husband had made a decision critical to his career and their life together. How much of a market would there be for New York street scenes created by an artist whose reputation was for paintings of life in and around Taos, New Mexico? Even more important was whether or not they could survive if her husband could only finish one painting in three months. It wasn't long before a disappointed Mary and Klauer knew Ufer was leaving New York.

Back in Iowa, a patient Klauer, after waiting nearly four months, was "...glad to know that the Corn Picture [*Indian Corn–Taos*] and *Going East* are finally coming to Dubuque. I received all the dumb pictures you sent me but am waiting for the real ones."[37] Once Klauer's collection of paintings by Ufer had grown, he became a serious collector and a patron who developed discriminating taste. Unlike so many private collectors, Klauer wasn't afraid of size—a significant percentage of Ufer's paintings measured 40 by 50 inches or 50 by 50 inches. Eventually, the purchase of so many large paintings did create a problem for Klauer as he ran out of wall space.

As he left New York, Ufer praised the city in a *Chicago Tribune* article, "Walter Ufer Likes New York." "There is only one art center in America," said Mr. Ufer yesterday. "It is New York. Compared to it, Chicago is crude, gross, ugly. When I think of eastern hospitality to art and artist, I shiver at Chicago's crudity, her grossness, her ugliness."[38] Not surprising, his thoughtless comments proved to be devastating to his career. George L. Scheins, an attorney and one of Ufer's patrons, wrote, "I am afraid the people of Chicago will not like very much your sentiments about their city..."[39]

The major reason for leaving New York was not finding subject matter that could sustain his career. In Chicago and Taos, he was well known, even celebrated. In New York, he was but one of thousands of artists who struggled and vied for attention. Furthermore, his potential buyers were looking for canvases that featured Taos Indians and horses.

Interestingly, Ufer followed up his critique of Chicago by comparing New York with Taos, and in a sense, justifying his departure from the Big Apple:

> *New York, though a very fine big city has not the attractions that a wild, but beautiful country like Taos has. Primitive, that is the word for Taos—New York is too large, too rushing, an immense Art Center, and is growing finer and bigger each day. I love to come to New York on a visit for a month or two, but after that the West —the Rocky Mountains, the gushing streams, the color in fact the life is calling out loud for me, and I can not wait till I see those beautiful peaks of the Sangre de Cristo Range again...Naturally a trip each year to New York...stimulates me and carries me through another long season, deciding to do better work. I do not know what I would do if we did not have New York, but I could not live there permanently...I have seen considerable of the world & I believe that I have chosen the places I like best.*[40]

Before returning to Taos, Ufer travelled to Chicago and painted several portraits, including two of Mary [fig. 58]. Financially distressed, he was in desperate need of selling some paintings. Even though his sales card reveals that he priced *Union Square: The Battery* at $1200, Ufer would eventually sell it for

36 Mary Ufer to Walter Ufer, 7 April 1919, UPUNDSG.
37 William Klauer to Walter Ufer, 4 April 1919, UPUNDSG.
38 Walter Ufer Likes New York," *Chicago Tribune*, 1919, UPUNDSG.
39 George L. Schein to Walter Ufer, 21 April 1919, UPUNDSG.
40 Good, "Walter Ufer," 168.

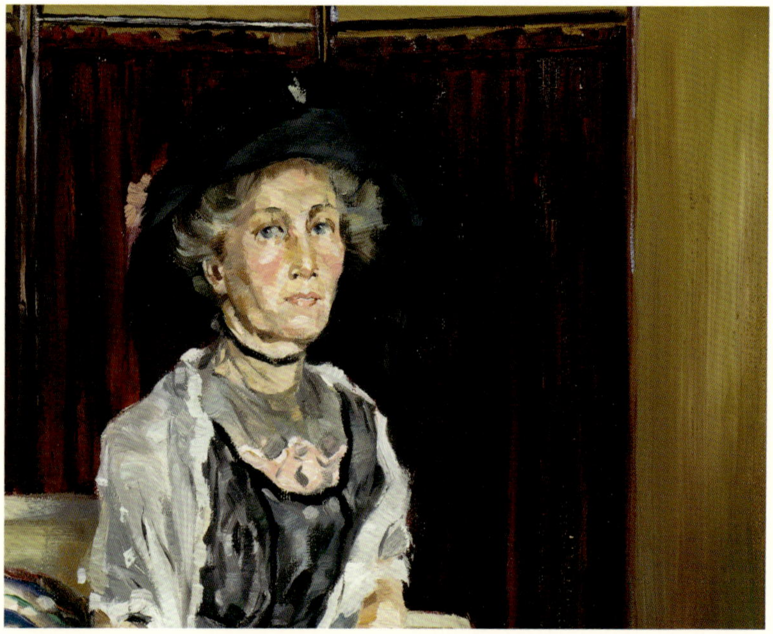

Figure 58.
Walter Ufer. *Portrait of Mary*, 1919.
Oil on canvas.
Lunder Research Center for the Taos Society of Artists, Couse Foundation, Taos, NM.
Gift of Charles S. Hayes.

$120 to Klauer. With studios in New York, Chicago and Taos, his expenses incurred between January and June 1919 left him looking for revenue to survive on when he returned home. Back in New Mexico, he had to make up for lost time, and once again, William Klauer would be his salvation.

THE DEATH OF PETER KLAUER

While Ufer prepared to leave New York, Klauer's father Peter was experiencing declining health. On July 8, 1919, Peter Klauer died, having established an impressive tradition. After working for other firms as an apprentice, Peter opened his own business, Peter Klauer Stove and Hardware. Within a quarter of a century, through judicious acquisitions, he expanded Klauer holdings until he, and his son, incorporated their firm as Klauer Manufacturing Company in 1904. By the time of Peter's death, the Klauers were contributors to a higher quality of life in Dubuque. In 1923, the Union Trust and Savings Bank wrote in memoriam:

> *Peter Klauer, one of the organizers of the Bank and for years one of its directors, was elected president of the Bank in January, 1899, and for twenty-one years remained in active direction of its affairs [sic]. A man of unusual force of character and high business integrity, eminently successful in business, a leader among men, he proved a tower of strength to the young institution, on which he left a lasting impress.*[41]

The tradition of philanthropy established by Peter would be carried on by his family—his son William and grandsons William J. and Walter J. Klauer. Carol and William J. Klauer gave birth to William, James, and Robert, and the Klauer family's role as philanthropists carries on. While the family is known for leadership in the corporate world, the more important role is the one they had and continue to play in Dubuque.

---

[41] "In Memoriam," *Union Trust and Savings Bank*, 1923, 20. KFPUND.

RETURN TO LAGUNA, 1919

Of the thirty-three paintings Ufer created and recorded on his sales cards in 1919, William Klauer purchased six. In fact, in an attempt to give Ufer financial stability, Klauer purchased two "lots" at $1200 each. *Union Square: The Battery* and *Their Audience–Laguna* [fig. 59] were included in the first lot. *Head of a Man with a Beard, Early Evening–Taos Panel, The Desert, Towards Evening* and *Canyon to Taos* were in the second. The sixth canvas *November Taos Canyon*, Klauer purchased for $117.

Their Audience–Laguna, sales card number 54 was his most important group portrait [fig. 59]. How Ufer was able to find time to paint *Their Audience–Laguna* remains a mystery. His sales cards, which are numbered chronologically, imply that he painted it in a few days because of the location of Laguna and the dates of the cards. It is a painting that would normally require weeks if not months. He painted the seven young Laguna women with a remarkable sensitivity. With his daring brushwork, reflecting his European training, he captured the personality of his sitters, who look out at the viewer, their audience.

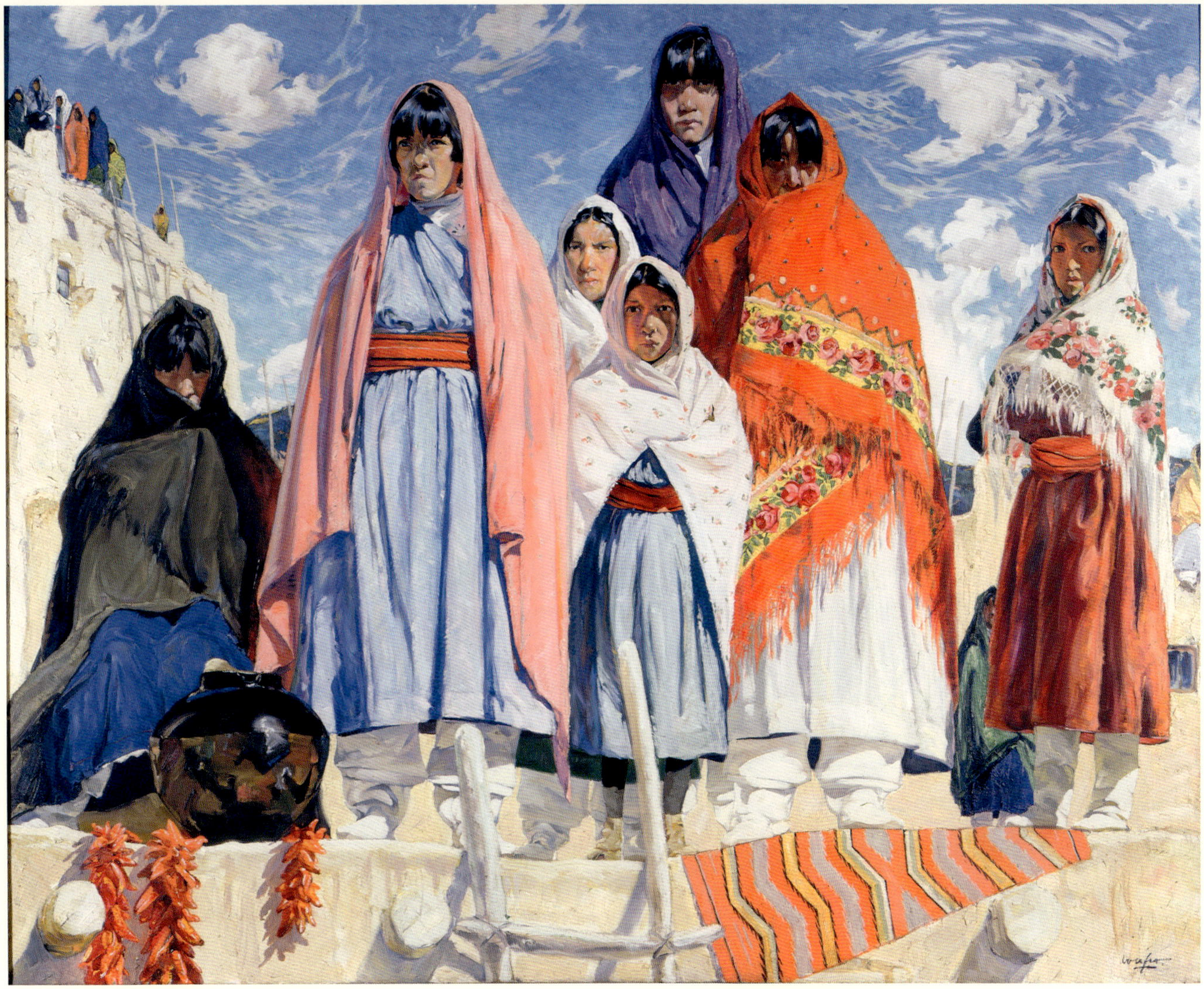

Figure 59. Walter Ufer. *Their Audience-Laguna,* 1919. Oil on canvas, 40 x 50 inches. Collection The Snite Museum of Art, University of Notre Dame. Gift of Klauer Family.

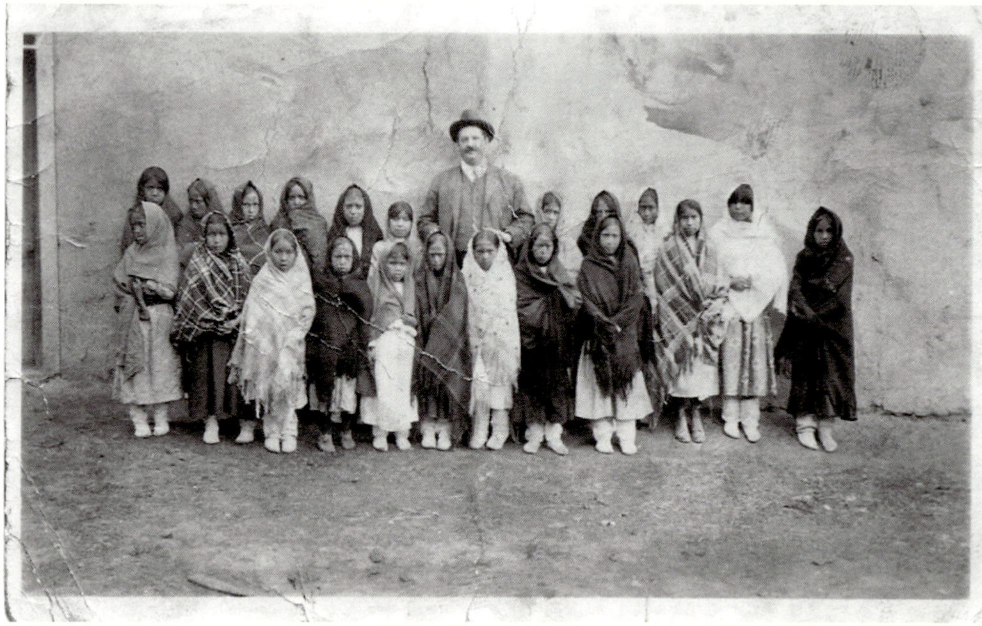

Figure 60. *William Klauer with Young Taos Women*.
Postcard courtesy Klauer Family Papers, University of Notre Dame Archives.

Ufer's continuing economic woes were recorded on his sales card for *Their Audience–Laguna*. Klauer acquired it in the "first lot for $1200." Ufer wrote, "that is how broke financially I was and am."[42] Klauer purchasing "lots" of paintings is yet another example of the patron coming to the aid of a financially distressed artist.

Their Audience–Laguna may be a rare instance where Klauer suggested a specific subject for Ufer to paint. A postal card in the Klauer Family Papers shows Klauer with a group of young Laguna Pueblo (or Taos) women dressed in their finest ceremonial costume [fig. 60]. It is possible Klauer asked Ufer to paint *Their Audience–Laguna*, partnering with him in the artistic process.

In September 1919 Klauer planned another trip to Taos. Even though Ufer needed more time at the easel to restock his inventory, he couldn't neglect his patron. He needed a fresh collection of paintings due to an upcoming four-person show in New York with Blumenschein, Higgins, and sculptor Phimister Proctor, and at least three juried shows. As usual Ufer responded, taking time from painting to make sure the cottage was accessible and ready for occupancy. Besides asking Ufer "to look up some good fishing country" as he would be bringing his friends, including Mr. Secrist. Klauer also wanted Brazelton to cut "several cords of wood before I get there, which will be about the 20th…"[43] Unfortunately, the road was in a state of disrepair, and the cost to fix it between $100 and $150. Klauer quickly telegrammed Ufer, authorizing the repair.[44]

As in December of 1918, it appears as though Klauer's 1919 visit was festive and financially rewarding for Ufer. On the anniversary of his December 1918 sale, Klauer had paid Ufer $2400, keeping the artist in business. With Klauer's support, Ufer was able to pay his framing and shipping bills for his New York four-person show.

---

[42] Ufer's sales card, #54. UPUNDSG.
[43] William Klauer to Walter Ufer, 30 September 1919, KFPUND.
[44] William Klauer to Walter Ufer, 30 September 1919, KFPUND

Chapter VII
Big-Game Hunting in Alaska, 1920

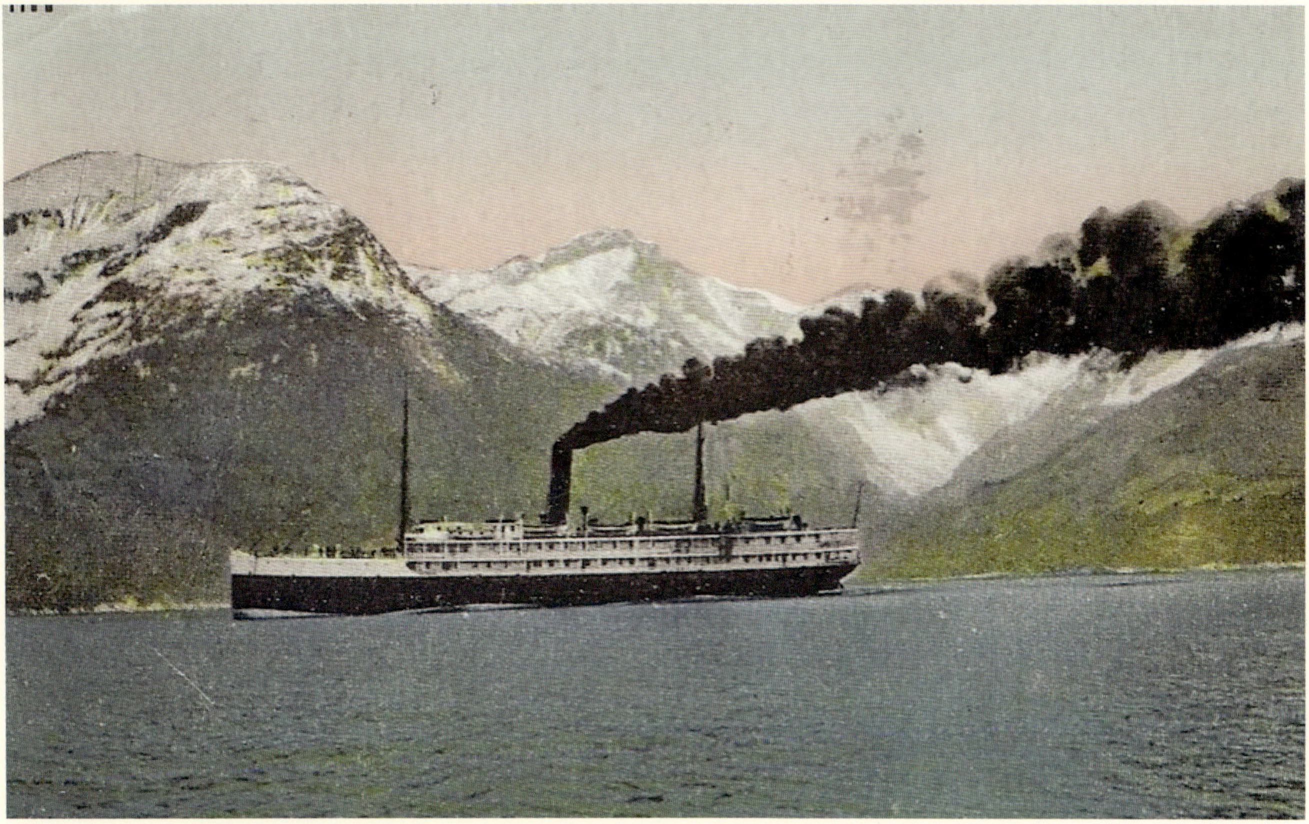

Figure 61. *Steamship 'Spokane.'* Postal card from Klauer to Ufer. 13 September 1920.
Postcard courtesy Ufer Papers, University of Notre Dame Archives, Gift of Stephen L. Good, Denver.

In 1920, Klauer spent August and September on a big game hunting trip in Alaska, "the farthest point travelled by white men." Hunting for moose, Klauer nearly lost his life. The party had seriously injured a moose three days earlier, and the animal was seeking revenge.[1]

> *Their outfit, secured at White Horse, comprised of twenty animals for pack and riding, and five attendants. Two hundred miles inland from White Horse, Alaska, the party guided by Native Indians, pitched camp for a night and on the following day set out for moose. They had not gone far when there burst through the brush in the rear of them a monster bull moose which attacked the party, killing one of the Indians, seriously injuring a white attendant, and attacking Mr. Klauer. The hunter had, however, time to prepare for the onslaught from having witnessed the approach, and he brought the big brute down with a shot between the eyes, just as the moose was lunging for him.*[2]

---

[1] Interview with Bill Klauer, April 2016.

[2] "Klauer Nearly Gored to Death," unidentified newspaper article in Klauer Family Papers, KFPUND.

Klauer documented the trip on a postal card to Ufer dated September 13, 1920 [fig. 61]. Klauer wrote: "Dear Ufer / Just returning from Alaskan hunting trip. You should see this scenery. Wonderful. / W.H.K."[3] While the note is short, he failed to mention his near-death experience. Furthermore, Klauer didn't mention the animals he bagged on the trip—moose, caribou, sheep, elk and deer.

Besides Klauer's note, the postal card described the amenities of the steamship "Spokane." The color image of the steel steamship with the spectacular landscape on the "Totem Pole Route" could only impress Ufer who enjoyed such luxury. Living accommodations on the 281-foot-long "Spokane" included a "social hall, large observation room, men's smoking room, bar, wireless telegraph…"[4] With a double bottom-water-tight bulkhead, the "Spokane" was built for safety and comfort for Klauer and the other 280 passengers.

Following his trip to Alaska, Klauer returned to Dubuque where he was once again faced with supporting his friend's activities and his problems with the Orchard property. Ufer had weathered a world in conflict with Klauer's support. In 1918 and 1919, Klauer had spent $4200 on sixteen of Ufer's paintings, enabling the artist to survive financially. In 1920, Ufer began a program of booking exhibitions wherever he felt he could make a sale. While Klauer would still acquire canvases, Ufer had to expand his base of financial support. Even though he continued to create important, prize-winning paintings, his over zealousness drove him to increase his productivity. One way to satisfy the demands of the market was to develop a series of themes he could repeat with relative ease. As he worked through the next decade, there was a tendency to create images that tended to be repetitive. For instance, he turned to the landscape and created images with or without figures.[5]

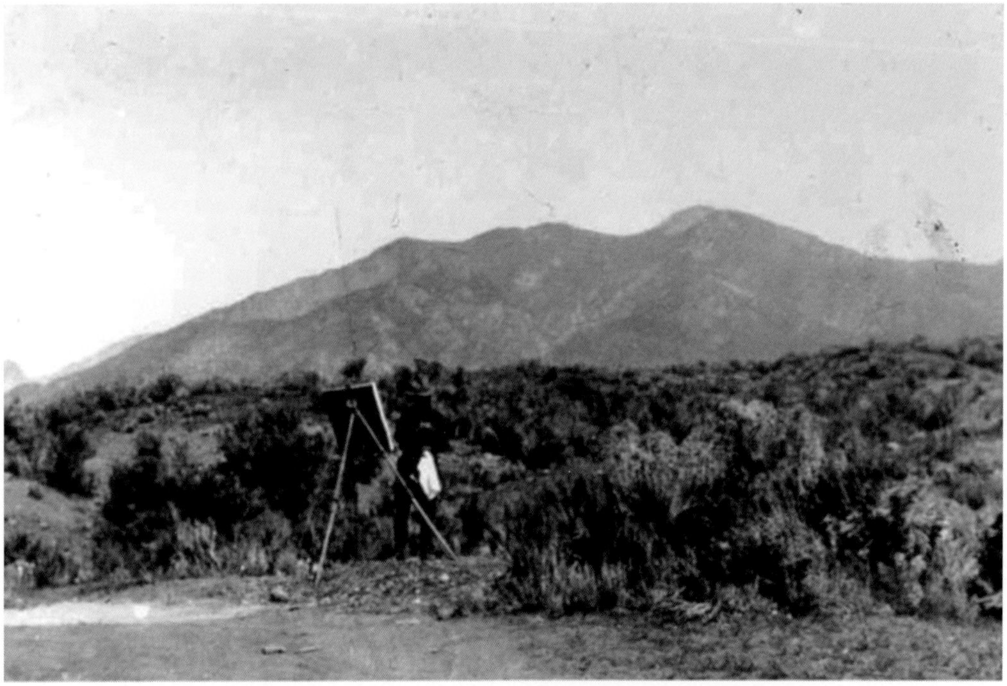

Figure 62. *Ufer Painting*.
Photo courtesy J. B. Speed Museum of Art, Louisville.

[3] William Klauer to Walter Ufer, 13 September 1920, UPUNDSG.
[4] Ibid.
[5] The paintings with figures often were of Jim Mirabel on horseback.

Chapter VIII
Modernism

UFER'S SELF-PORTRAITS, 1920

Before Ufer lapsed into convention, he created a small group of highly imaginative paintings that reflected his encounter with a style labeled "Modernism." The year 1920 was a period when Ufer balanced experimental with conventional compositions. Throughout his career, Ufer painted a number of self-portraits, and 1920 was no different. A few of his self-portraits were innovative and contrasted dramatically with his peer's self-images. They were no longer the pro forma portraits of Mary [fig. 58] and other Chicago notables that Ufer painted in 1919 and earlier.

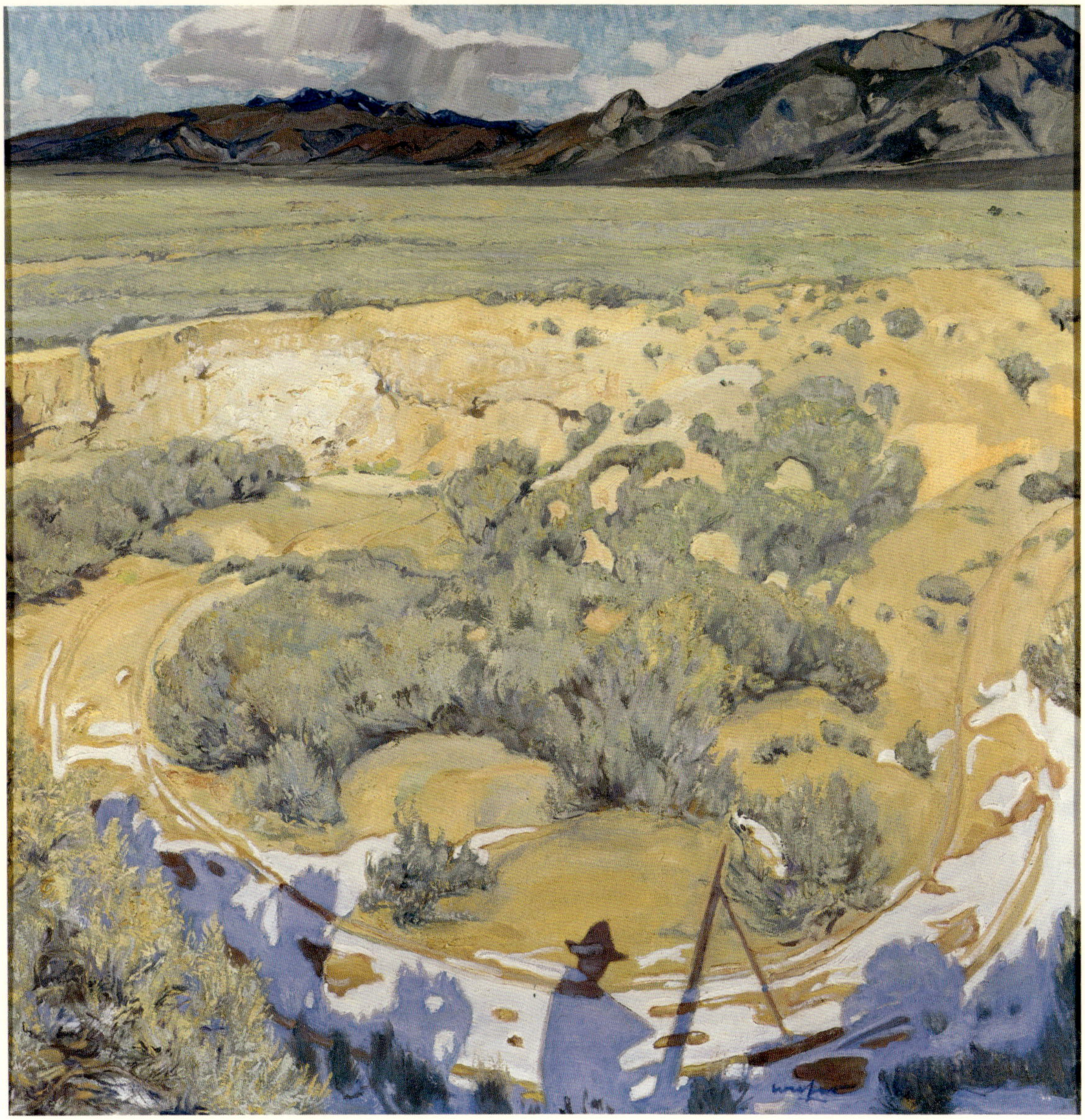

Figure 63. Walter Ufer. *Looking North*, 1920. Oil on canvas, 25 x 25 inches.
Collection The Snite Museum of Art, University of Notre Dame, Gift of the Klauer Family.

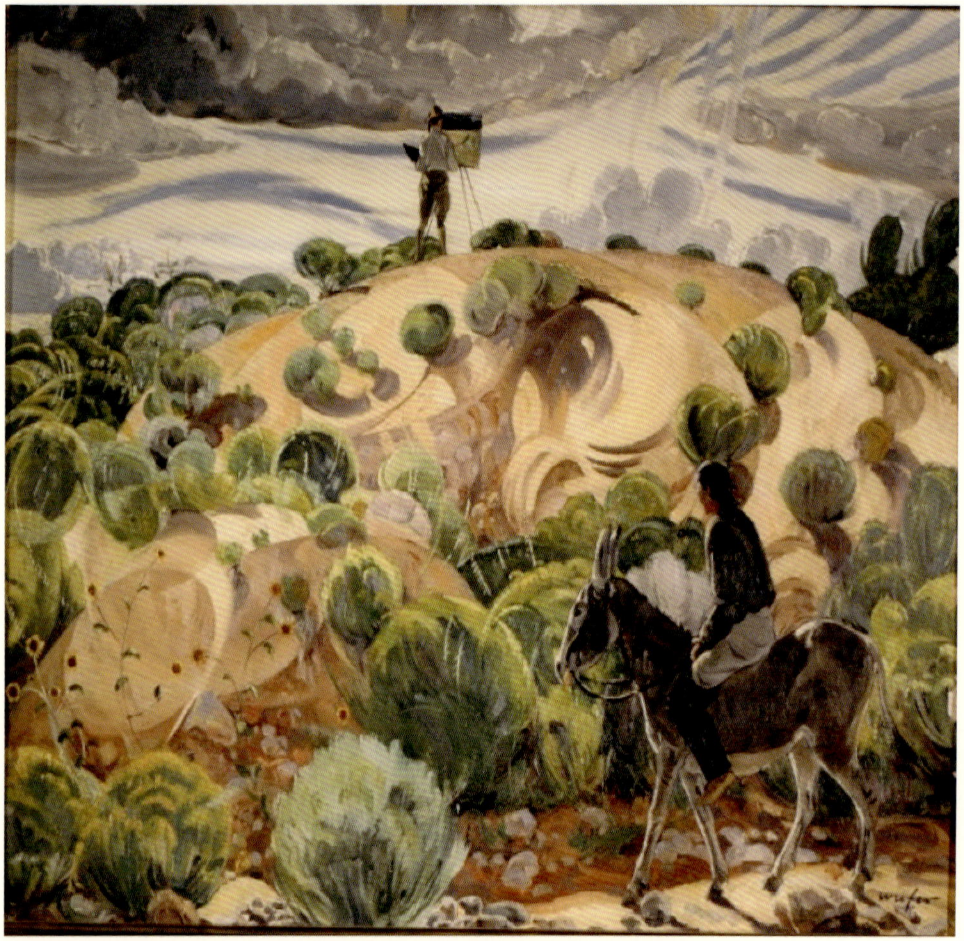

Figure 64. Walter Ufer. *The Artist*, 1920. Oil on canvas, 30 x 30 inches. Collection Klauer Manufacturing Company.

While some of his earlier self-portraits painted in Taos were straight forward bust views often silhouetted against an adobe wall, others demonstrate Ufer's capacity to explore contemporary styles of painting. Two of these self-portraits were acquired by Klauer. The first, *Looking North* [fig. 63], features a high horizon and a bird's-eye view showing the shadow of the artist standing at his easel on the arroyo floor below. Ufer energized the painted surface, stressing the circular patterns left by unmelted snow and passages of *chamisa* and *piñon*. The viewer, standing shoulder to shoulder with Ufer, experiences a grand New Mexico panorama. On a clear day in northern New Mexico one can easily see for miles.

The second self-portrait shows Ufer standing at the apex of a hill before his easel. Its title is possibly *The Artist* [fig. 64]. Jim Mirabel, seen at the foot of the hill, is riding his burrow and seemingly passing by as he observes the master at work. For Ufer, modernism came in different forms. In this unusual landscape, he has taken the abstractions seen in *Looking North* one step further. He reduced the elements of nature to the most basic swirling, simplified, organic shapes. *Chamisa* and *piñon* are seen as circular, curvilinear forms, organized according to some formula, likely following Jay Hambridge's revolutionary and very popular teachings in *Dynamic Symmetry in Composition.*[1] Even though Ufer created few paintings that were more abstract, after a short period of experimentation, he reverted back to his more conventional bust view self-portraits.

[1] Hambridge's theory of "dynamic symmetry" is a proportioning systems and natural design methodology that defines compositional rules.

UFER'S LANDSCAPES, 1920

In the early 1920s Klauer began to add landscapes to what had primarily been a collection of figurative paintings. *Foothills, Early January* [fig. 65] and *Among the Sage* [fig. 66] are pure landscapes that remained in Ufer's studio until their titles were transferred to Klauer in 1932.

Foothills, Early January is a symphony of shapes, colors and patches of light and an energized landscape seen under a typical Ufer impressionist-styled sky. Ufer modeled his sky by juxtaposing blue and white with short strokes of pigment. He enjoyed the opportunity to offer dramatic contrasts between the snow's brilliant highlights with deep shadows cast on the Picuris Mountain range. Most impressive is Ufer's use of blue to purple shadows that are found in so many of his winter paintings.

Among the Sage [fig. 66] was not one of Ufer's more inspired canvases. In a sense, he was simply painting what Mother Nature laid out before him that morning—a desert landscape featuring clumps of sage. In actuality, Ufer demonstrates that he has mastered painting desert fauna. Besides elevating sage to a position of significance, it gave him the opportunity to demonstrate his facility with the brush, applying generous amounts of pigment with the sureness and dexterity of a master.

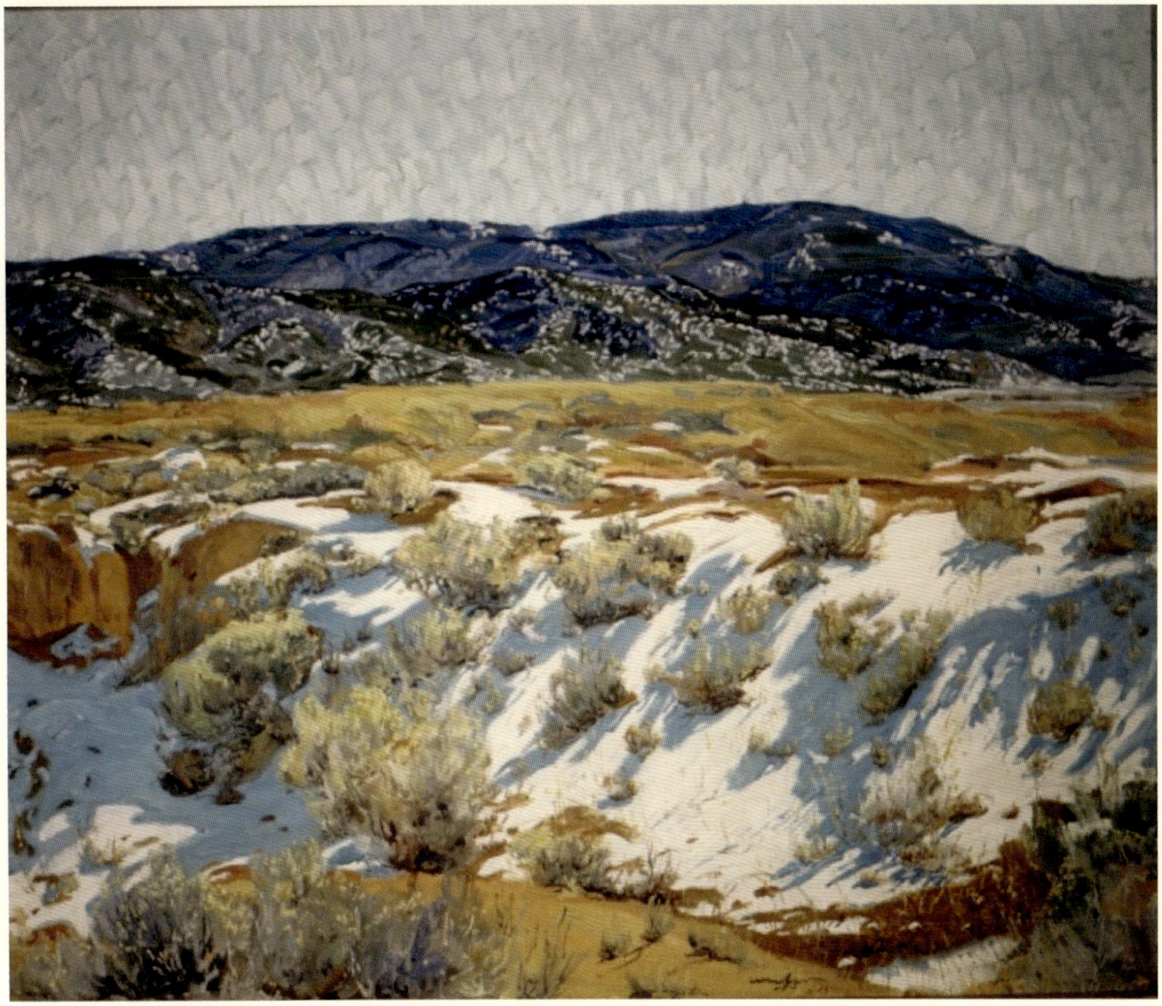

Figure 65. Walter Ufer. *Foothills, Early January*, 1920. Oil on canvas, 25 x 30 inches. Collection Klauer Manufacturing Company.

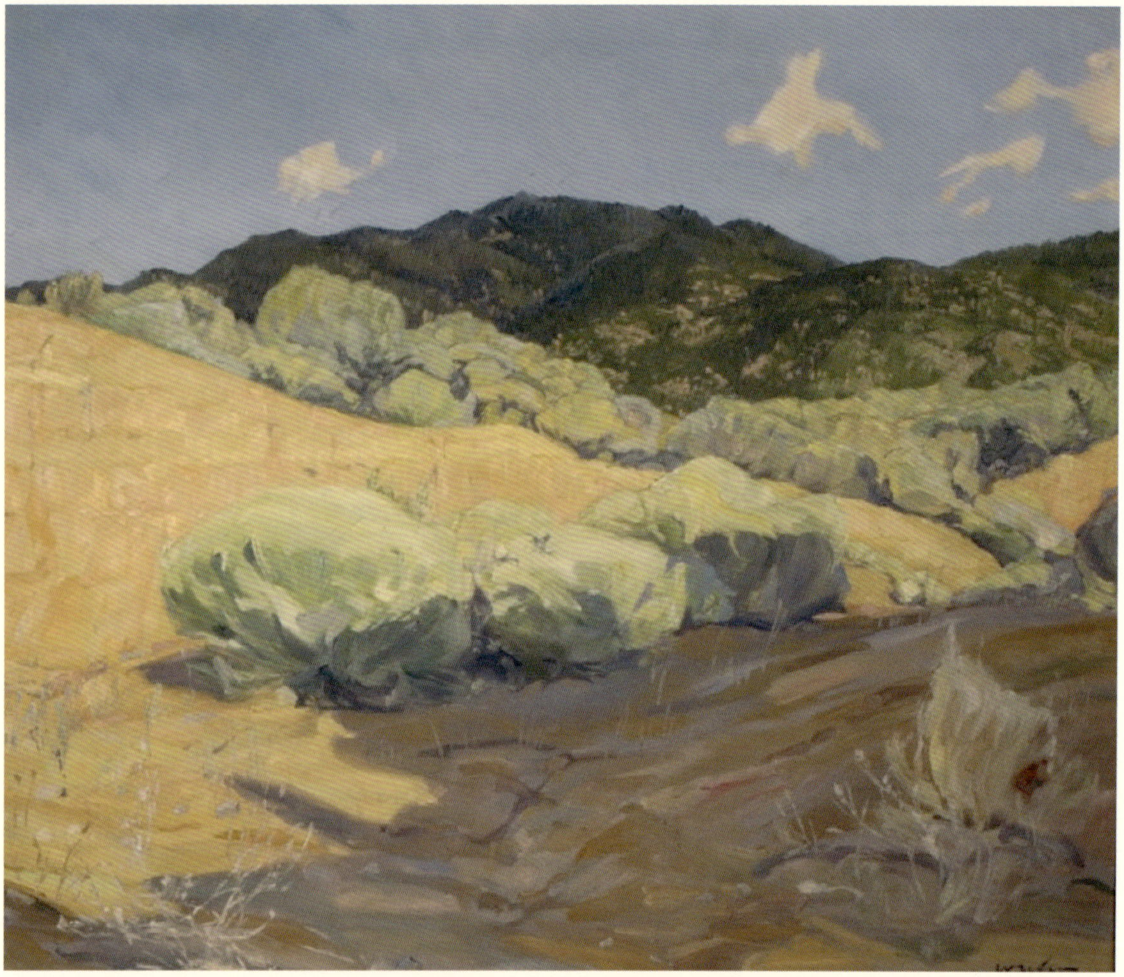

Figure 66. Walter Ufer. *Among the Sage*, 1920. Oil on canvas, 30 x 30 inches. Collection Klauer Manufacturing Company.

Ufer is not known as a painter of landscapes, but for years his friends told an amusing story about his painting in the out-of-doors. When Ufer painted a landscape, he would start by attaching the three legs of his easel to stakes driven into the ground. He would return the following day and reattach the easel's legs to the stakes. This would assure Ufer that he was painting the landscape from the same position and angle each time. Some of his friends, knowing of his procedure, decided to play a joke on the artist. What did they do? No, they didn't move his stakes. Instead, they dug up and moved some of the *chamisa*. This would have driven Ufer crazy—an artist who was unwavering about his approach to painting.

INSIDE LOOKING OUT

In 1920, Ufer won the bronze medal for his painting *Luzanna and Her Sisters* [fig. 68] in the Carnegie International in Pittsburgh. This bronze medal was an award Blumenschein and many of his peers considered to be the artist's most important. Soon after creating *Luzanna and Her Sisters*, Ufer painted *At the Window* [fig. 67], and his model was once again Luzanna Luhan.[2] *At the Window* offered Ufer another opportunity to pose his model in an interior setting while also demonstrating his skill at

[2] *Luzanna and Her Sisters* is now in the collection of the Baltimore Museum of Art and *At the Window*, formerly part of the Klauer Manufacturing Company Collection, is now in a private collection.

painting Anglo decorative objects—the high gloss vases, the reflective surfaces of an oil lamp with its melon-shaped shade, the intricate-patterned wall paper, as well as the lacy frills on the window's valance. From the darkened interior in *At the Window*, Ufer allowed the viewer to experience the intense New Mexico light and the majestic Sangre de Cristo Mountains. While this painting wasn't done in his studio, a space devoid of any superfluous decorations, it was done in one of the other rooms in the Ufer's rental property. *At the Window* stresses Luzanna's role as a housekeeper for Anglo employers. Her role can be contrasted with Jim Mirabal and his associate in the painting *In Taos* whose role could be either model or laborer. Once again, Ufer has made the viewer question the role of the figure—this time as model or housekeeper.

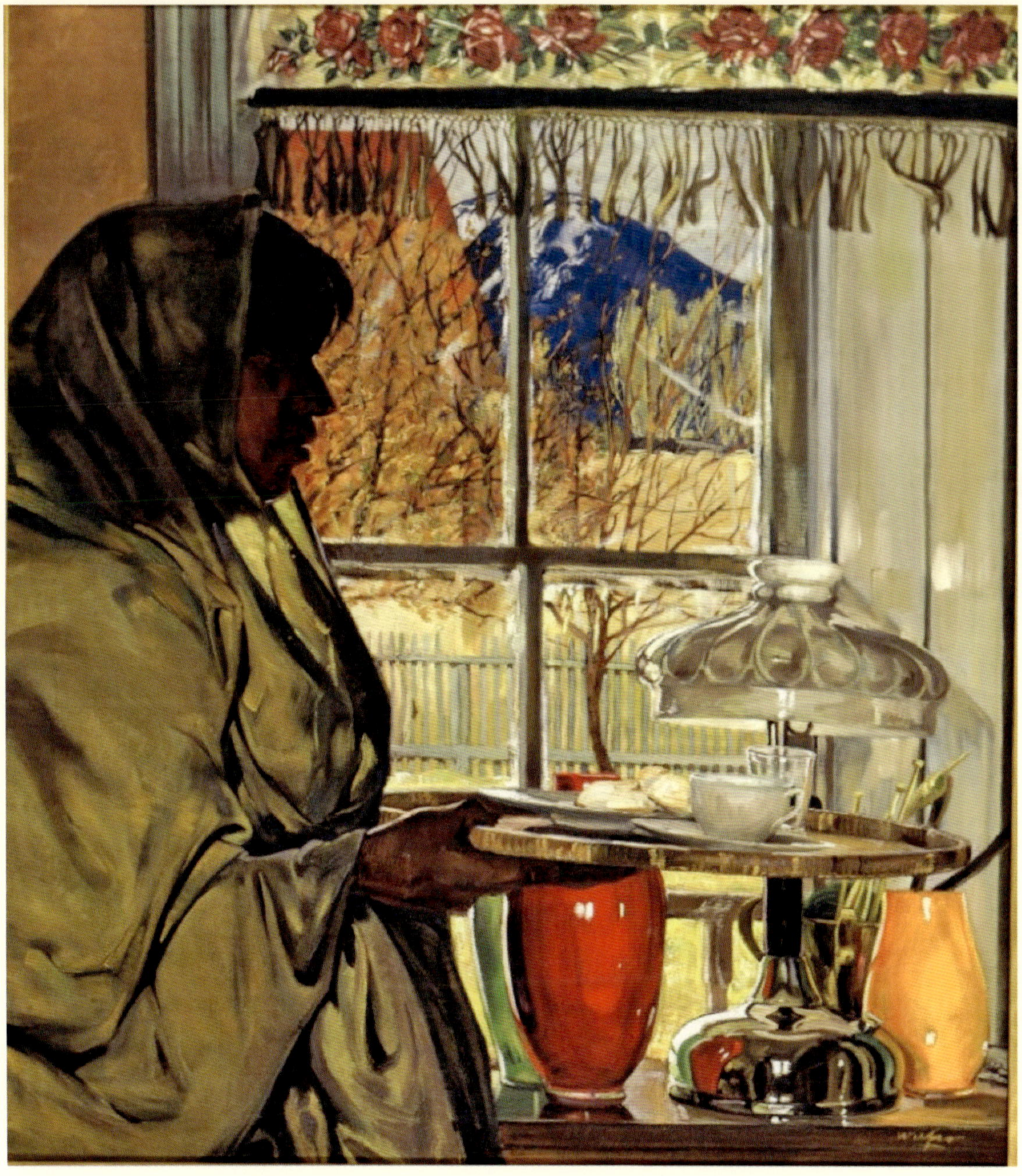

Figure 67. Walter Ufer. *At the Window*, c. 1920. Oil on canvas, 36 x 30 inches. Photo courtesy J.N. Bartfield Galleries, NYC. (former Klauer Family Collection)

By the time Klauer accepted title to *At the Window*, it had been unveiled in at least ten venues, including The Art Institute of Chicago, National Academy of Design, Buffalo Academy, and Milwaukee Art Institute, among others. Ufer also included it in the 1922-23 Circuit Exhibition of the Taos Society of Artists and his personal exhibit circuit in 1925. On June 16, 1927, Klauer wrote to Ufer expressing his pleasure of finally receiving the painting; however, he seemed to regret that he had been asked to hang it "in one of the large rooms in the Chicago Club when the new structure is completed."[3] It wasn't uncommon for Klauer to be compelled to enjoy paintings he purchased in places other than his home. In a sense, while Klauer held title to a painting, he was also the curator, registrar, and shipper because of the many venues the painting was committed to by Ufer.

In 1920, Ufer, Blumenschein, and Higgins enjoyed a second traveling show that opened in New York's Milch Galleries.[4] Several paintings bore the Klauer provenance—notably *Friends*, *Their Audience–Laguna*, *Acequia Madre*, *In Taos*, *Taos in Snow*, *The Foothills*, and *Early January*. From that time on, Ufer borrowed paintings from Klauer for his exhibitions, which almost made the loaning of the works a full-time job for Klauer. With his annual hunting trips, running Klauer Manufacturing Company, and taking the appropriate actions to see if the paintings he owned arrived at the venues Ufer committed them to, Klauer led a full and complicated life. Whenever Ufer couldn't muster sufficient paintings for a show, he would borrow works from Klauer. When Klauer purchased groups of paintings from the artist, he often had to wait months, or even years, before he could install them in his home. *Indian Corn–Taos*, which was purchased in 1918, was not hung in Dubuque until a decade later.

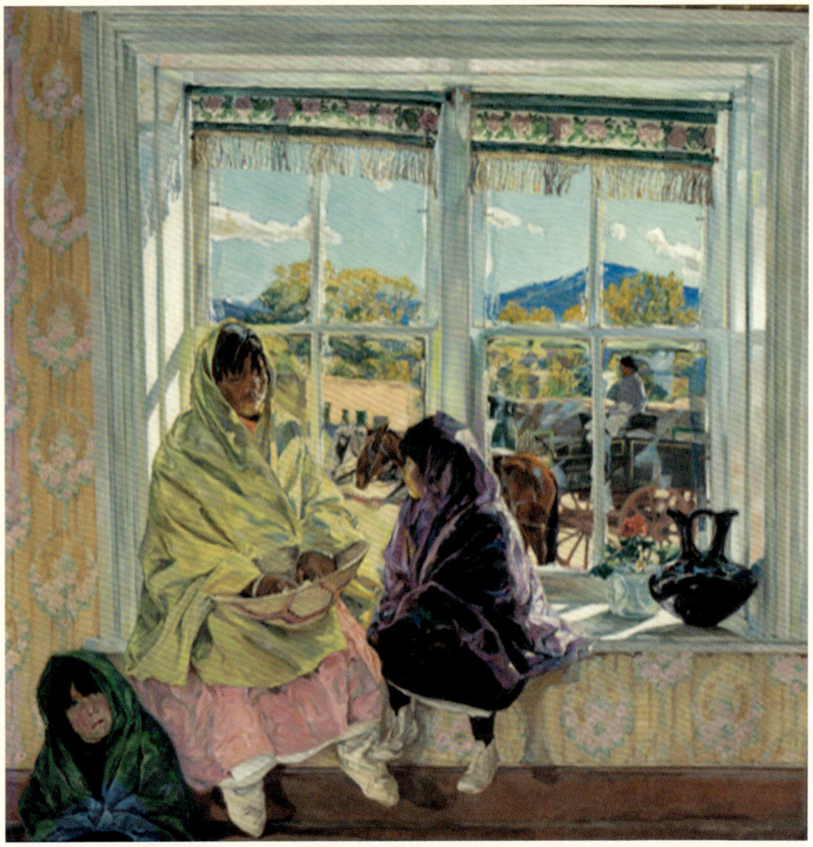

Figure 68.
Walter Ufer. *Luzanna [Lousuanna Lujan] and Her Sisters*, 1920.
Oil on canvas, 50 x 50 inches.
Collection Baltimore Museum of Art.
Gift of the Friends of Art,
BMA 1931.5.1.

[3] William Klauer to Walter Ufer, 16 June 1927, UPUNDSG.

[4] Phimester Procter's sculpture was not included in the second show of paintings by Ufer, Higgins, and Blumenschein.

Chapter IX
The Final Flowering, 1922-23

Scholars Stephen L. Good, Thomas Smith, along with this and other writers, consider the period of 1917 through 1922 to be the high point of Ufer's career. During this relatively short period of time, Ufer created a remarkable body of paintings, a large percentage that would bear the William Henry Klauer provenance. While Klauer's collection grew after 1922, most of the paintings that entered his collection were the result of the artist defaulting on his loans. Ufer, not Klauer, usually selected those paintings accepted in lieu of payment. The patron eventually tried to exchange paintings for ones that better suited his needs.

Several paintings created during 1922 and 1923 eventually bore the ownership of Klauer. These included *Homeward Bound*, *My Studio Courtyard* [fig. 69], *Where the Desert Meets the Mountains* [fig. 71], *The Watcher* [fig. 70], *September Morning* [fig. 44], *Talpa* [fig. 73], *Builders of the Desert* [fig. 74], and *Western Rain* [fig. 72]. According to Ufer's sales card, *Homeward Bound* was included in the "2nd lot for $1200." Several of the pictures were reproduced in Rose V. S. Berry's article "Walter Ufer in One–Man Show" for The American Magazine of Art.[1] Berry was a dedicated supporter of Ufer, her words having a profound influence on potential buyers.

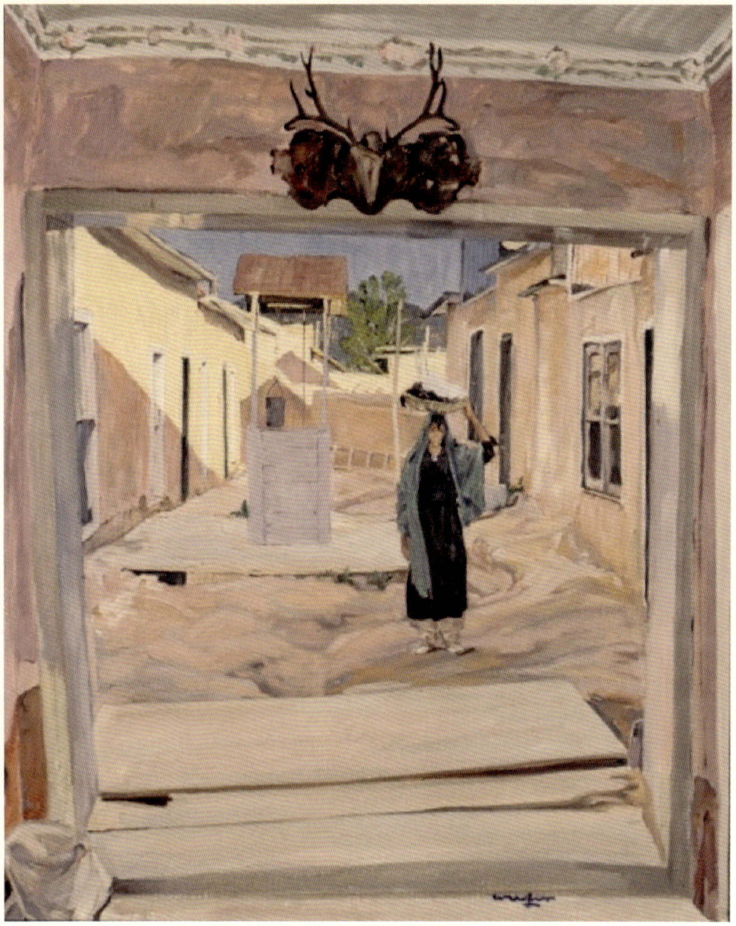

Figure 69.
Walter Ufer.
My Studio Courtyard, 1922.
Oil on canvas, 30 x 25 inches.
Collection Klauer Manufacturing Company.

[1] Rose V. S. Berry, "Walter Ufer in One–Man Show," *The American Magazine of Art*. Vol. XIII, no. 12, 1922, 507-11.

In terms of subject matter, Ufer's paintings in 1922 and 1923 are characterized by their diversity. On days when he didn't want to load up his Buick and drive east past the Mabel Dodge Luhan compound or south to Talpa, he could paint in the courtyard outside his studio. *My Studio Courtyard* [fig. 69] shows modernist stylistic tendencies and invites the viewer to look into the alley from his studio. The door's frame serves like a proscenium opening on a stage. At the top Ufer included a medium-size deer's rack, a detail that would have appealed to Klauer. Jim Mirabal's daughter is located to the left center of the composition, and she stands before a Spanish well balancing a black-ware pot on her head. The backyard of several peoples' homes was a subject that attracted Ufer. He paid the same reverence to his alley that he would a church courtyard.

In the 1920s, Ufer painted a series of paintings depicting a young man astride a burro. The finest of the group is *The Watcher* [fig. 70]. One of the interesting aspects of the work is the uncertainty of what the youthful rustic is watching—a second burro or perhaps a herd of sheep not seen on the canvas. Essentially, Ufer made a study and explored the dramatic visual effects of the intense sunlight that illuminated desert outcroppings. The work is punctuated with flowering *chamisa* and the Picuris Mountains, which are silhouetted against a pointillist, blue sky with a scattering of white, airy clouds.

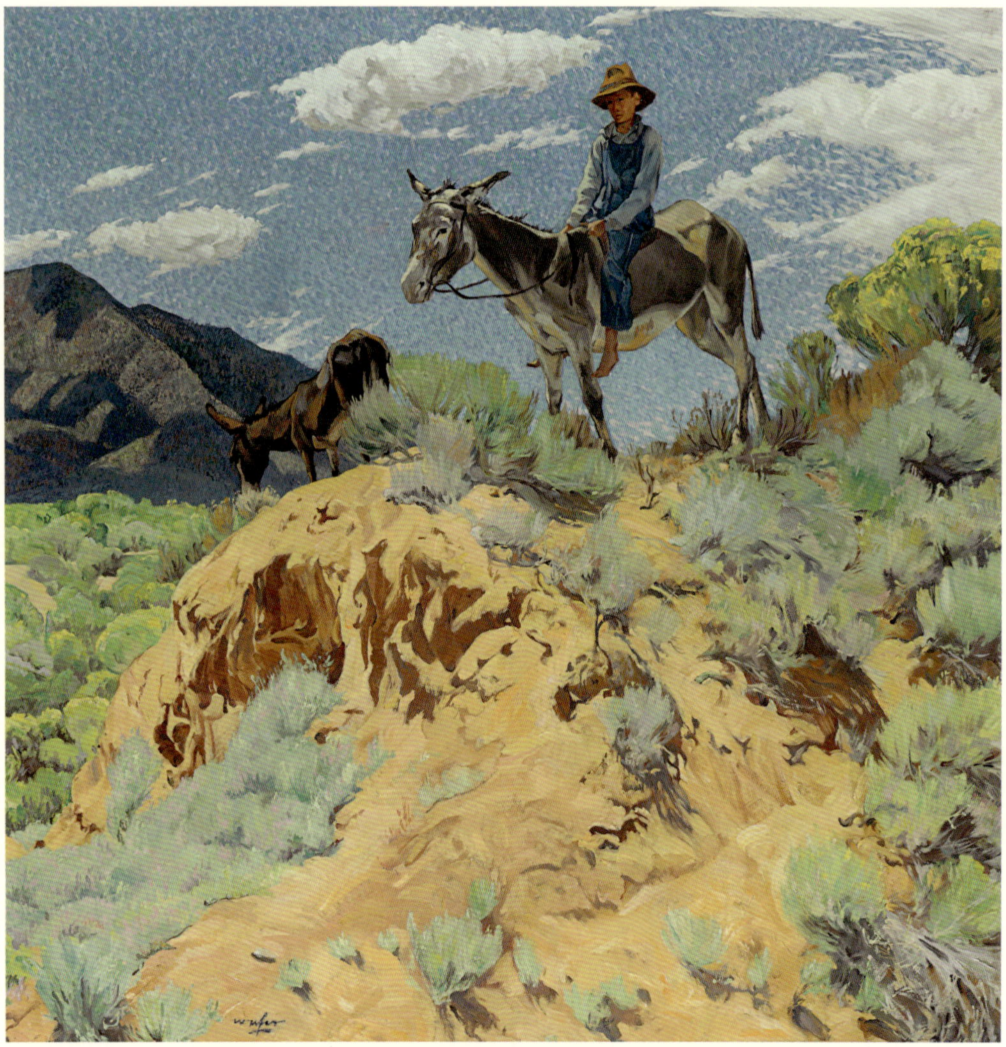

Figure 70. Walter Ufer. *The Watcher*, 1922. Oil on canvas, 36 x 30 inches. Blake Hotel Collection, Taos, New Mexico. (former Klauer Family Collection)

THE DESERT STORM

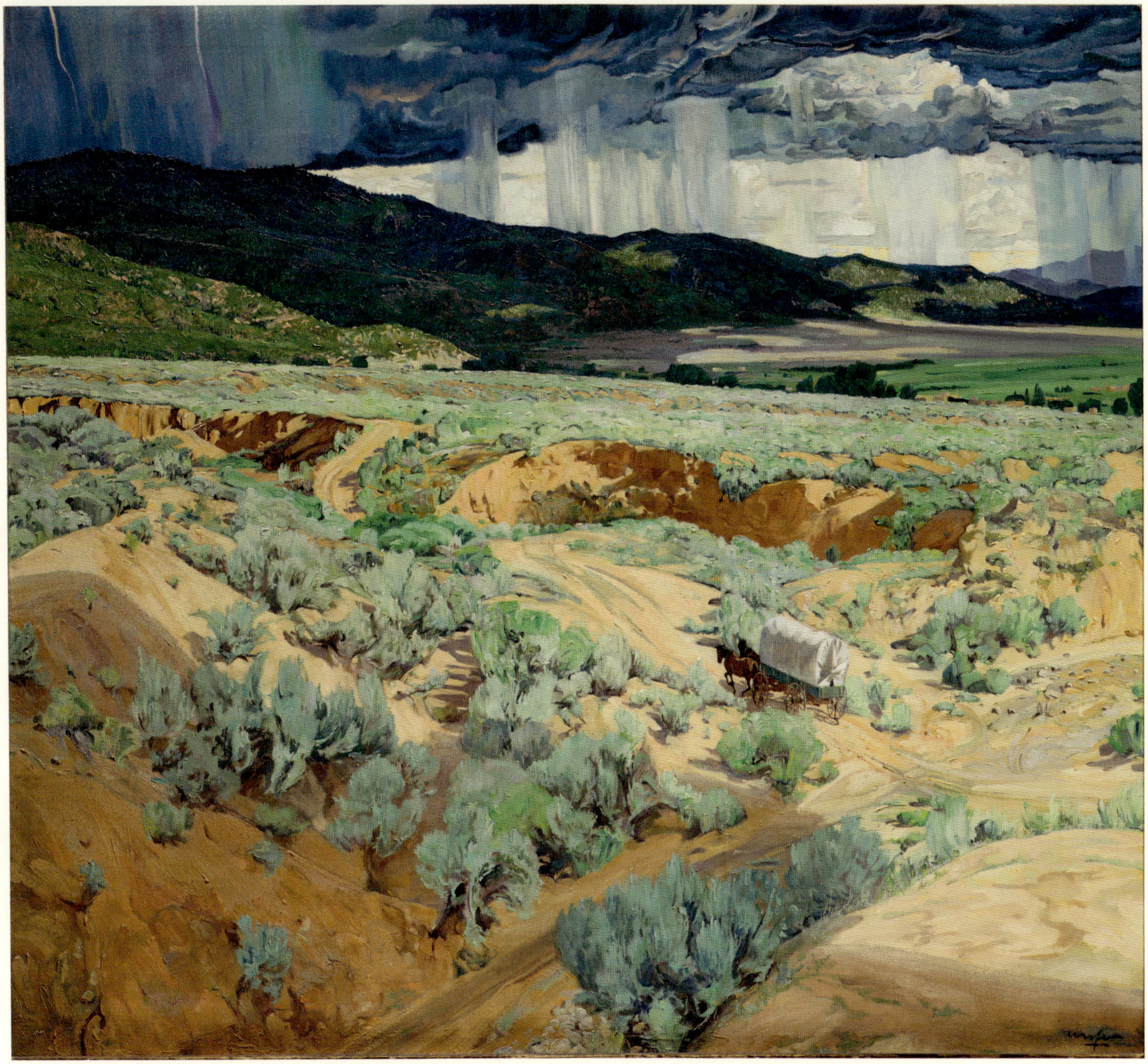

Figure 71. Walter Ufer. *Where Desert and Mountain Meet*
(alternate title *Where the Desert Meets the Mountains*), 1922. Oil on canvas, 30 x 30 inches.
Courtesy of American Museum of Western Art—The Anschutz Collection. (former Klauer Family Collection)

Ufer's stunning storm scenes are among the finest created by any member of the Taos Society of Artists and are the highlights of the Klauer collection. Northern New Mexico is known for its afternoon torrential downpours, pictured in *Where the Desert Meets the Mountains* [fig. 71]. One of the most romantic of Ufer's canvases, it is a classic example of man's eternal struggle with the forces of Mother Nature. Soon to experience what is referred to as "walking rain," the wagon heads north—its eventual destination unknown. Charles Eldredge wrote, "the small wagon, lost amidst the rolling emptiness, seems unlikely ever to attain its destination."[2] Man finds himself in an ominous landscape. He must move fast

[2] Charles C. Eldredge, "The Faraway Nearby: New Mexico and the Modern Landscape" in *Art in New Mexico, 1900-1945: Paths to Taos and Santa Fe.* (New York: Abbeville Press, 1986), 173.

in order to beat the storm that already attacks the Picuris Mountains. Often overlooked are the shadows casting darkness over the lower left quadrant of the composition. The waggoneer is trapped with nowhere to go. He must follow a rutted trail and gambles that the trail and storm will not converge. For if they become one, the arroyos will flood in death-threatening torrents.

Ufer employed a bird's-eye view and created a zigzag pattern of light through the use of contrasting areas—brightly illuminated sections alternating with deeply shadowed areas. Ufer highlighted the covered wagon, loaded down with cargo and pulled by lumbering horses, carving its way through the arroyo. He asks the viewer if man will survive the battle of Mother Nature in conflict.

Talpa, painted in 1923 [fig. 73], depicts another scene a few miles north of Taos, where a storm is about to strike. The storm, once again a torrential down pour, is seen as it 'walks' through the distant mountain range, menacingly advancing towards the quiet settlement. The peaceful home will soon be the victim of an onslaught of what could become a violent storm. In *Western Rain* [fig. 72], Jim Mirabal rushes with his two animals as he attempts to beat the storm.

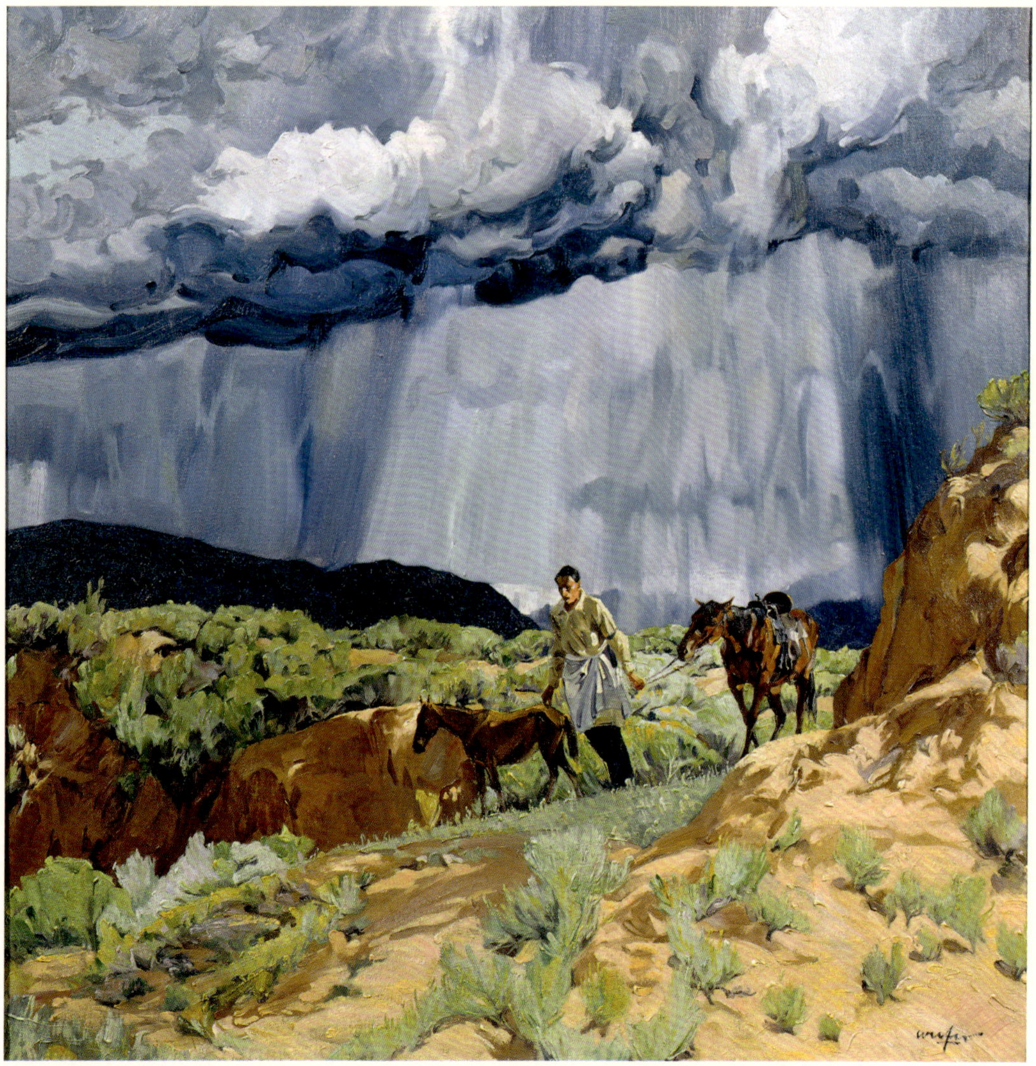

Figure 72. Walter Ufer. *Western Rain*, 1922. Oil on canvas, 30 x 30 inches. Location Unknown. (former Klauer Family Collection)

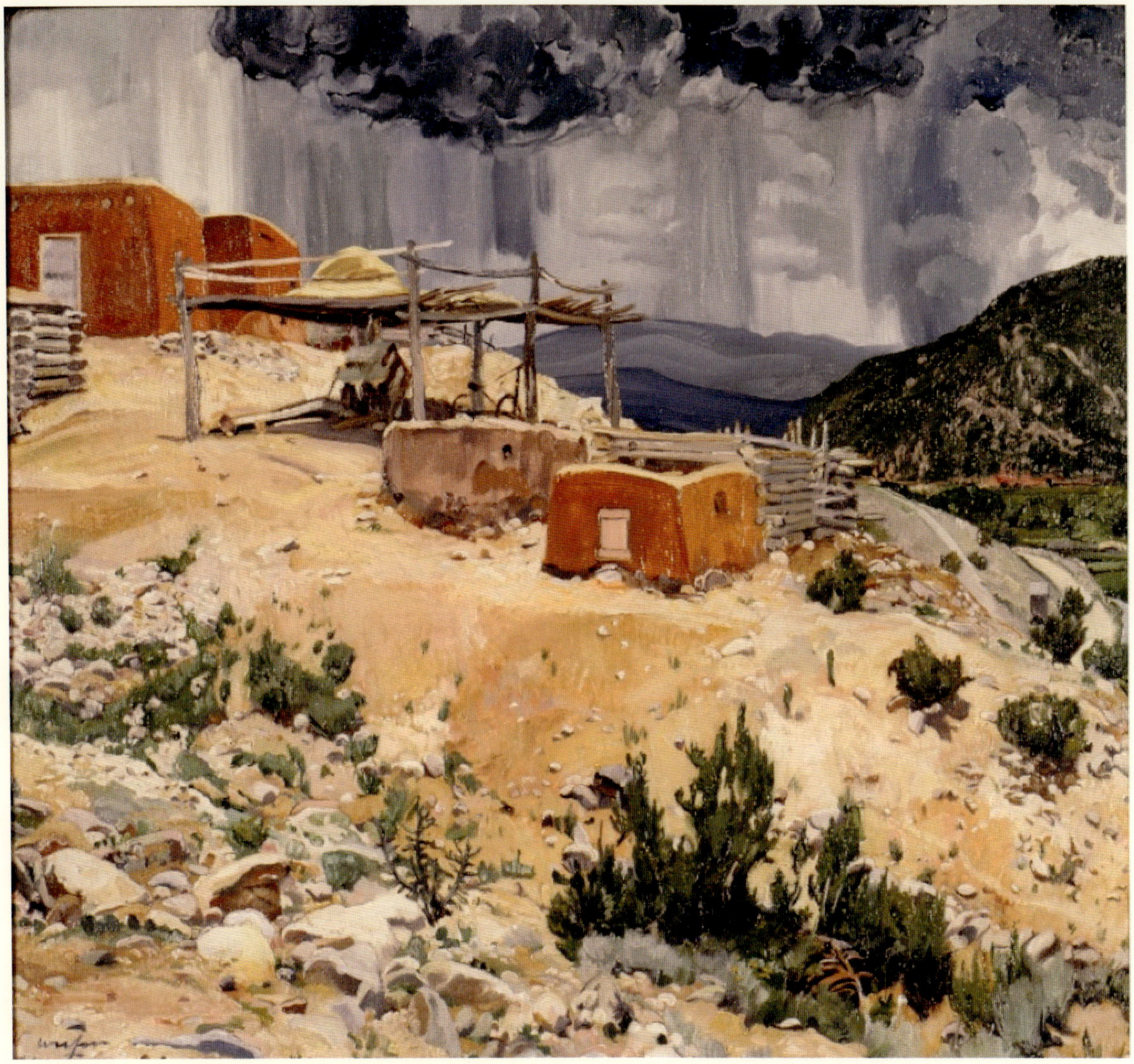

Figure 73. Walter Ufer. *Talpa*, 1923. Oil on canvas, 24 x 27 inches. Collection Klauer Manufacturing Company.

BUILDERS OF THE DESERT

Builders of the Desert [fig. 74] places the viewer in one of Ufer's favored painting sites—Mabel Dodge Luhan's property, which was on the border of Pueblo land. In 1923 Mabel married Taos Indian Tony Luhan and began to build their home, Los Gallos. Mabel, in her book *Edge of Taos Desert*, wrote about her "delight" in being "with these workmen," watching the process of creating adobe bricks for her Los Gallos home. She stated: "...there was no indignity in raising a house, and nothing sordid in either the materials or in their use of them." She spoke of their reverence for the mud which was earth, something living and precious to be handled with understanding and care." For the laborer, it "was a noble occupation, that required mixing wheat straw" with mud, "thoughtfully layering them in rows to dry," before "fitting them carefully "upon each other with the rich dark mud between that will turn as hard as stone..." Mabel concluded, "...all of it is sacred matter, for the wonder of the creation is in it, the wonder of transformation which always seems of greatest significance to Indians."[3]

[3] Luhan, *Edge of Taos Desert*, 292.

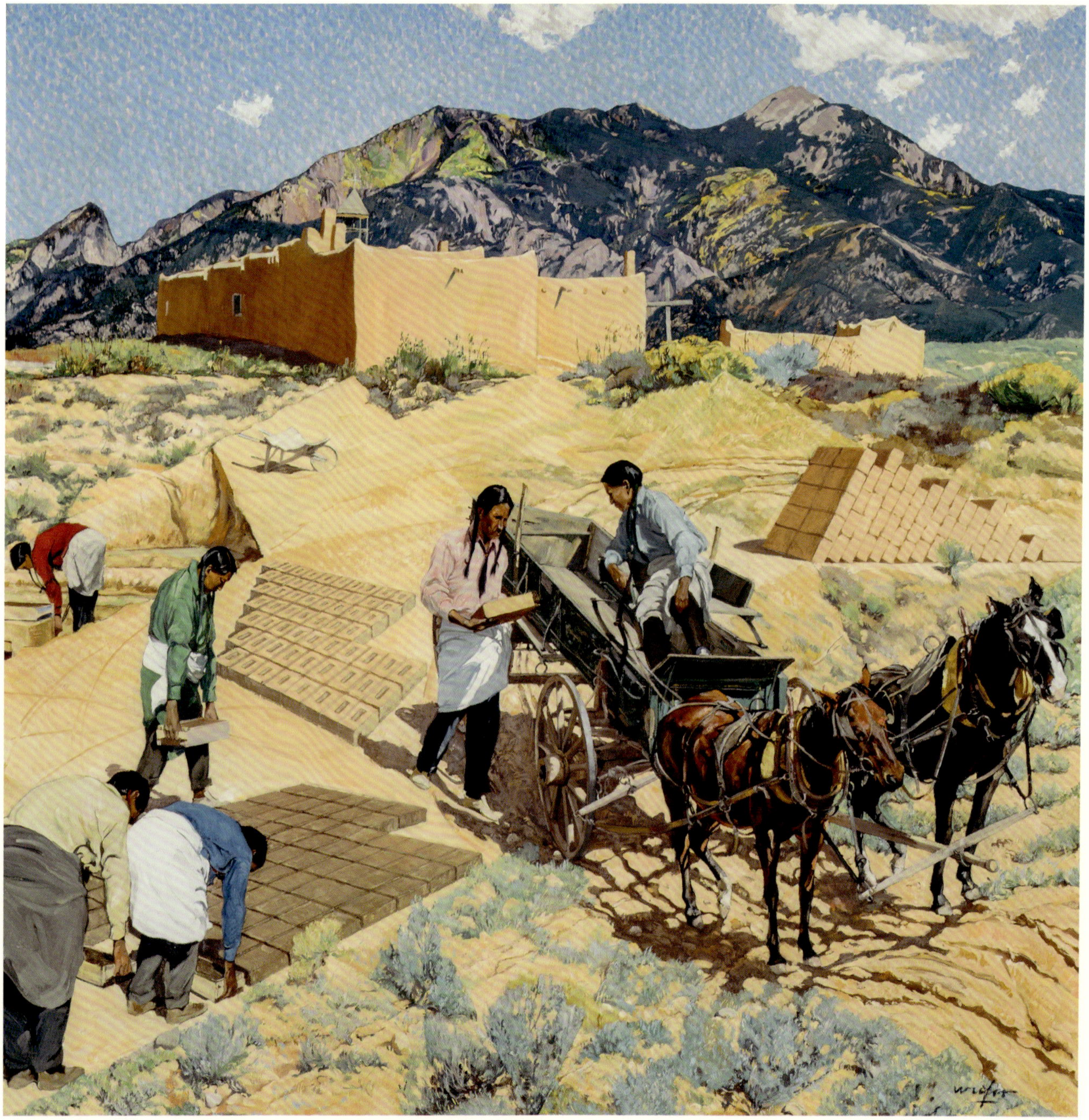

Figure 74. Walter Ufer. *Builders of the Desert*, 1923. Oil on canvas laid down on aluminum. Image 50 1/8 x 50 1/8 inches. Terra Foundation for American Art, Daniel J. Terra Collection, 1992.174. (former Klauer Family Collection)

Even though Walter Ufer didn't enjoy a particularly warm relationship with Mabel Dodge Luhan, her words offer a good description of this painting. Ufer tried in vain, to endear himself to Mabel's most famous guest, the British literary giant, D. H. Lawrence. Ufer frequently offered to drive Lawrence around Taos—in order to bring attention to himself and make him feel important in his association with Lawrence. In the background of Ufer's painting is La Morada de la Nuestra Senora de Guadalupe (also known as Taos Morada) and the Sangre de Cristo Mountains. A large, white cross can be seen at the entrance to the penitente morada.

In November 1923, Klauer made his annual trip to Taos and asked Ufer to make arrangements "to have a car get us at Santa Fe as soon as we reach there."[4] The stove had also been stolen from the cottage, and Klauer suggested that one of the artists might have had it "in their possession." As always, Klauer was concerned about the condition of the road leading to his cottage. Klauer continued, "Also, please ask Earl whether the road from his place to the cottage can be used. If not, the new road that has gone through might ought to land within a short distance of us."[5] During this trip, Klauer saw *Builders of the Desert*, a painting he considered among the artist's finest. On February 26, 1924, Ufer offered the painting to Klauer who "wanted to buy it. Are you in earnest? The painting is listed at $5000. Please let me know."[6] There is no evidence that Klauer ever responded.

Builders of the Desert enjoyed exposure in at least ten significant exhibitions, including The Art Institute of Chicago (1924), Pennsylvania Academy of The Fine Arts (1924), and National Academy of Design (1925). In fact, Ufer eventually sent the canvas to at least twenty-one venues. Ufer never forgot Klauer's comments, and four years later, owing his very survival to his friend, he sent the painting to Dubuque as a gift.

---

[4] William Klauer to Walter Ufer,13 November 1923, KFPUND. Klauer was probably referring to Long John Dunn.
[5] Ibid.
[6] Walter Ufer to William Klauer, 26 February 1924, UPUNDSG.

Chapter X
Klauer and the Dubuque Art Association

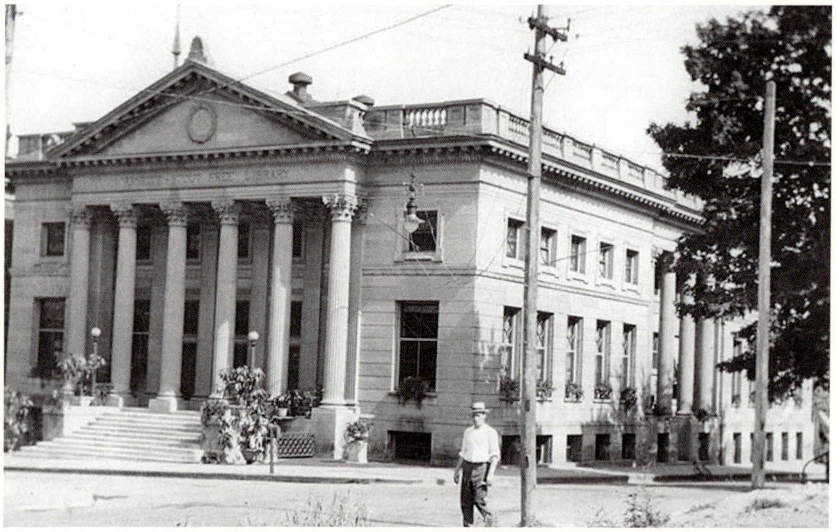

Figure 75.
Reverend H. J. Loemker.
Carnegie Stout Public Library, Dubuque, Iowa, 1915-17.
Rev. H.J. Loemker Collection,
Loras College,
Center for Dubuque History.

Klauer was instrumental in bringing exhibitions to the Dubuque Art Association during the 1920s, largely because of his support of Walter Ufer, Victor Higgins and E. Martin Hennings. Even though Ufer asked Klauer about having a show in Dubuque in 1917, it wasn't until 1922 that Klauer and the Dubuque Art Association arranged a solo show for Ufer in the Art Room of the Carnegie-Free Library [fig. 75].

Following in his father Peter's footsteps, Klauer acted as an intermediary between artist and the Dubuque Art Association. In fact, several of his activities would suggest that he was a curator, art association director, and dealer rather than a simple patron. Highly respected in the Dubuque community, he played an active role in influencing exhibitions to be seen in Dubuque. Besides the several paintings he had acquired for his personal collection, he sold some to others. In a January 24, 1923 letter to Ufer he enclosed a check for a painting he had sold to Mr. Coates and his sister called *His Pack*. Klauer boasted, "When she came to my office it didn't take her more than five minutes to decide that she wanted the picture. So, you see there are some people in Dubuque who appreciate good things."[1]

Besides *His Pack*, Klauer had recommended the sale of *In Taos* [fig. 53] to the Dubuque Art Association. Ufer's sale of *In Taos* was incredibly important to Klauer. Ufer had little respect for Dubuque and felt that the community was not sophisticated enough to pay the price of one of his paintings. Klauer, whose pride in Dubuque could not be challenged, made it possible for the Art Association to own a significant Ufer. Fortunately, in 1923, Mary Lull, the wife of a physician, donated $5000 for the acquisition of art. Some of her gift was to acquire an important portfolio of photographs of Native Americans by Edward Sheriff Curtis and paintings by Grant Woods.[2] The Dubuque Art Association was able to purchase Ufer's *In Taos*, but only after Klauer saved it for them by purchasing it and removing it

[1] William Klauer to Walter Ufer, 24 January 1923, KFPUND; on his sales card, Ufer listed the painting for $900.

[2] "Dubuque Museum of Art," *Encyclopedia Dubuque*, accessed July 5, 2018 http://www.encyclopediadubuque.org/index.php?title=DUBUQUE_MUSEUM_OF_ART.

from the market. While the painting would have sold for $1500, Ufer gave Klauer a special price of $500. Klauer eventually sold it to the Association for $600.00, an action which irritated Ufer. With that sale, Klauer wrote, "...you ought to be pretty well satisfied with your trip to Dubuque. If you can do as well in other cities where you exhibited, as you did in Dubuque, in proportion to the size of the town, you will sell $10,000 worth of pictures."[3]

SOLO EXHIBITIONS FOR UFER (1923) AND HIGGINS (1925)

It seemed that Klauer couldn't do enough for Ufer. The exhibition was typical of Ufer's "circuit exhibitions," small in size, containing shop-worn pictures salted with but a few, fresh-off the-easel quality examples. Of the seven canvases Ufer exhibited, *In the Mojave Desert* (1915) and *American Desert–San Juan* (1916) proved to be of little interest to his followers, while *In Taos* (1918) and *Hunger* (1919), priced at $5000, were important paintings. Other paintings in the show were *Plaza de Taos, Ranchos Church*, and *September Morn* [fig. 44]. While none of the paintings sold during the exhibition, all but *Hunger*, at some time would bear the Klauer provenance. Today, *September Morn* remains in the Klauer Manufacturing Company Collection.

In 1925 and 1926, Ufer again tried to book another Dubuque Art Association solo show. Because of the small size and poor quality of some of the paintings in his 1923 exhibit, Klauer was less than enthusiastic about a repeat performance. Even though Klauer had promoted Ufer's art and was responsible for two sales, the exhibition failed to live up to expectations. In addition, Ufer failed to show gratitude and only offered criticism to his patron. Ufer's 1923 exhibition would be his last one in Dubuque.

Despite Ufer's disappointing exhibition in 1923, Klauer looked to bring another exhibition of Southwest art to the Dubuque Art Association, this time featuring the paintings of Victor Higgins. Higgins was booking as many solo exhibitions as possible in the hopes of creating a steady stream of income. Dubuque had already proved to be a good venue for Southwest painting. By 1924, Higgins and Klauer were enjoying a close relationship. Klauer personally owned *New Mexico Dooryard* [fig. 41] by Higgins, and he thought the artist should be represented in the Association's collection.

Even though Ufer's exhibition sold but two paintings in Dubuque, Higgins recognized that with Klauer in his corner there was potential for a successful show. Higgins also realized that Klauer would likely purchase at least a painting or two, whether or not there were other buyers. Klauer wrote to Higgins on March 28, 1924, the first in a series of letters attempting to secure an April opening. Klauer stated they were "all set for it here and would advise that you send your pictures as soon as the Washington Exhibition (at the Corcoran Gallery) is over. Possibly you could send them on April 22 and they would get here on the 24th. We could run the exhibit from the 24th of April to the first of May. You would have plenty of time to get to Indianapolis at the Pettis Gallery."[4]

Higgins was running exhibitions from one venue to the next with little time between each. It is amazing how much work they put into a show that would be seen for no more than seven days. However, Klauer felt it would give the Art Association a good chance to select a painting and "we can use our influence to select one of yours when the time comes."[5] Klauer concluded, "Please do not disappoint me.

[3] William Klauer to Walter Ufer, 24 January 1923,. KFPUND.
[4] William Klauer to Victor Higgins, 24 March 1924, KFPUND.
[5] William Klauer to Victor Higgins, 28 March 1924, KFPUND.

I am very anxious to have this go through because I think you will not be disappointed with the interest taken in your pictures in Dubuque."[6]

Even with Klauer's input the exhibition failed to materialize for April 1924. In an undated letter from Kate Van Duzee to Higgins, she rescheduled the exhibition for January 1925 after consulting with Klauer and others.[7] "Mr. Klauer says he is writing you. The Art Association would pay the express on the pictures one way and see to packing them for shipment from here."[8] Klauer wrote to Higgins on December 26, 1924, "I understand that you are going to bring your exhibit to Dubuque early in January, around January 12. I am trying to arrange matters so that I can get you here at that time."[9]

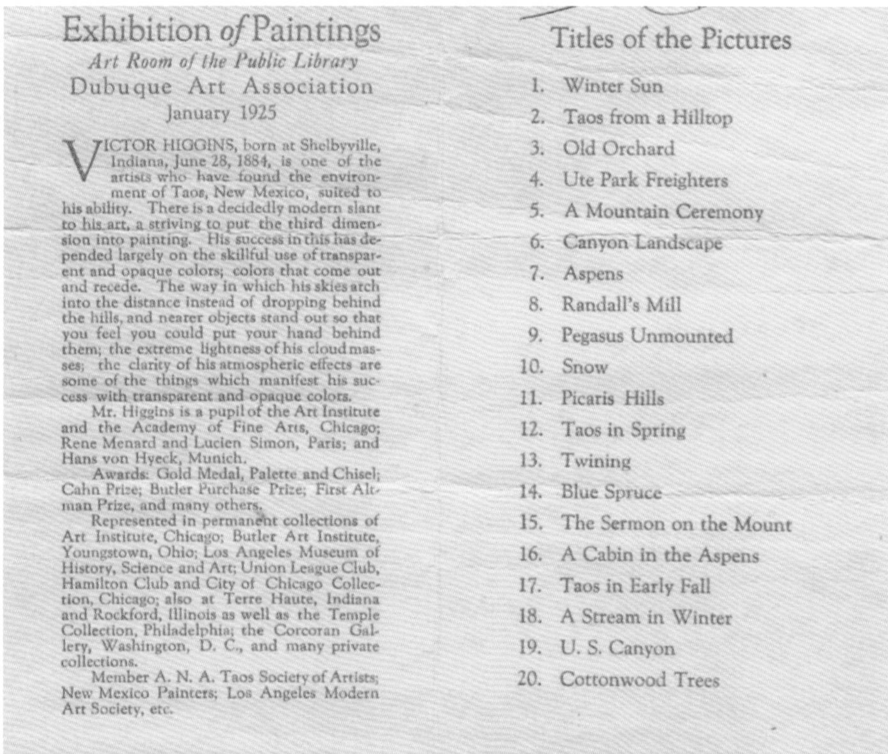

Exhibition *of* Paintings

Art Room of the Public Library

Dubuque Art Association

January 1925

VICTOR HIGGINS, born at Shelbyville, Indiana, June 28, 1884, is one of the artists who have found the environment of Taos, New Mexico, suited to his ability. There is a decidedly modern slant to his art, a striving to put the third dimension into painting. His success in this has depended largely on the skillful use of transparent and opaque colors; colors that come out and recede. The way in which his skies arch into the distance instead of dropping behind the hills, and nearer objects stand out so that you feel you could put your hand behind them; the extreme lightness of his cloud masses; the clarity of his atmospheric effects are some of the things which manifest his success with transparent and opaque colors.

Mr. Higgins is a pupil of the Art Institute and the Academy of Fine Arts, Chicago; Rene Menard and Lucien Simon, Paris; and Hans von Hyeck, Munich.

Awards: Gold Medal, Palette and Chisel; Cahn Prize; Butler Purchase Prize; First Altman Prize, and many others.

Represented in permanent collections of Art Institute, Chicago; Butler Art Institute, Youngstown, Ohio; Los Angeles Museum of History, Science and Art; Union League Club, Hamilton Club and City of Chicago Collection, Chicago; also at Terre Haute, Indiana and Rockford, Illinois as well as the Temple Collection, Philadelphia; the Corcoran Gallery, Washington, D. C., and many private collections.

Member A. N. A. Taos Society of Artists; New Mexico Painters; Los Angeles Modern Art Society, etc.

Titles of the Pictures

1. Winter Sun
2. Taos from a Hilltop
3. Old Orchard
4. Ute Park Freighters
5. A Mountain Ceremony
6. Canyon Landscape
7. Aspens
8. Randall's Mill
9. Pegasus Unmounted
10. Snow
11. Picaris Hills
12. Taos in Spring
13. Twining
14. Blue Spruce
15. The Sermon on the Mount
16. A Cabin in the Aspens
17. Taos in Early Fall
18. A Stream in Winter
19. U. S. Canyon
20. Cottonwood Trees

Figure 76. Brochure for Higgins's Solo Exhibition in 1925, Dubuque Art Association. Brochure courtesy Sara Parsons Mack, Santa Fe.

The long awaited *Exhibition of Paintings by Victor Higgins* opened on January 12, 1925 [fig. 76]. Higgins managed to assemble twenty paintings that had been created in the early 1920s. By the time the show closed and Higgins and Klauer had finalized their transactions, including his earlier purchase *New Mexico Dooryard*, the collector owned five paintings. In addition to cash, Higgins also received binoculars and a shotgun as part of the transaction. In 1925 Klauer purchased *Taos in Early Fall* [fig. 79], *Stream in Winter* [fig. 6], *U. S. Canyon* [figs. 2 and 80] and *Cottonwoods* [fig. 81]. Interestingly, while the patron hung paintings by Ufer, Hennings, and Phillips in the Klauer Manufacturing Company factory, Klauer hung all five Higgins paintings in his home. The Dubuque Art Association, however, failed to acquire a painting from the exhibition.

---

6 Ibid.

7 Kate Van Duzee was the secretary and founder of the Dubuque Art Association.

8 Kate Van Duzee to Victor Higgins, KFPUND.

9 William Klauer to Victor Higgins, 26 December 1924, KFPUND.

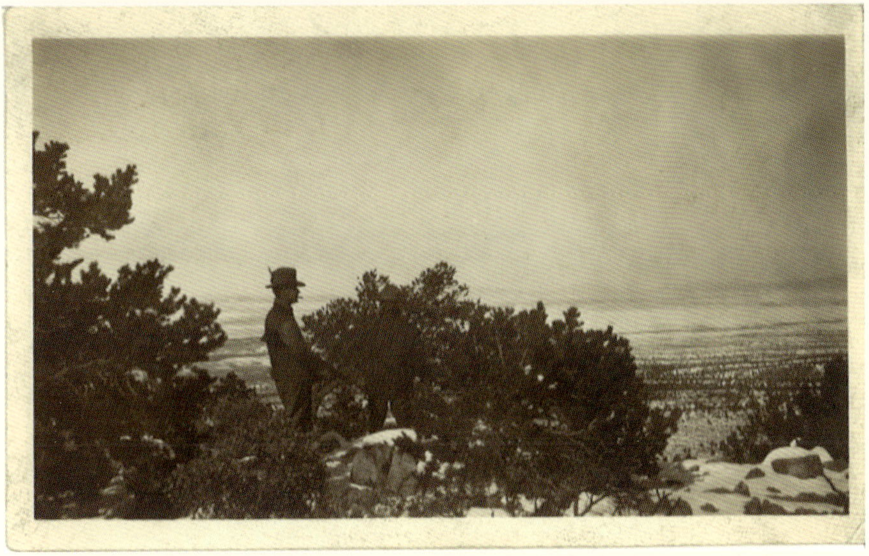

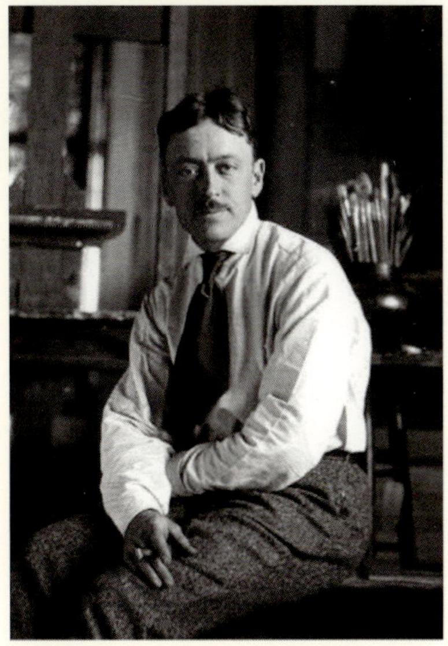

Figure 77 and 78. *Victor Higgins Hunting* (left), c. 1925. Klauer Family Papers, University of Notre Dame Archives. *Victor Higgins* (right). c. 1920s. Photo courtesy Robert L. Parsons Fine Art.

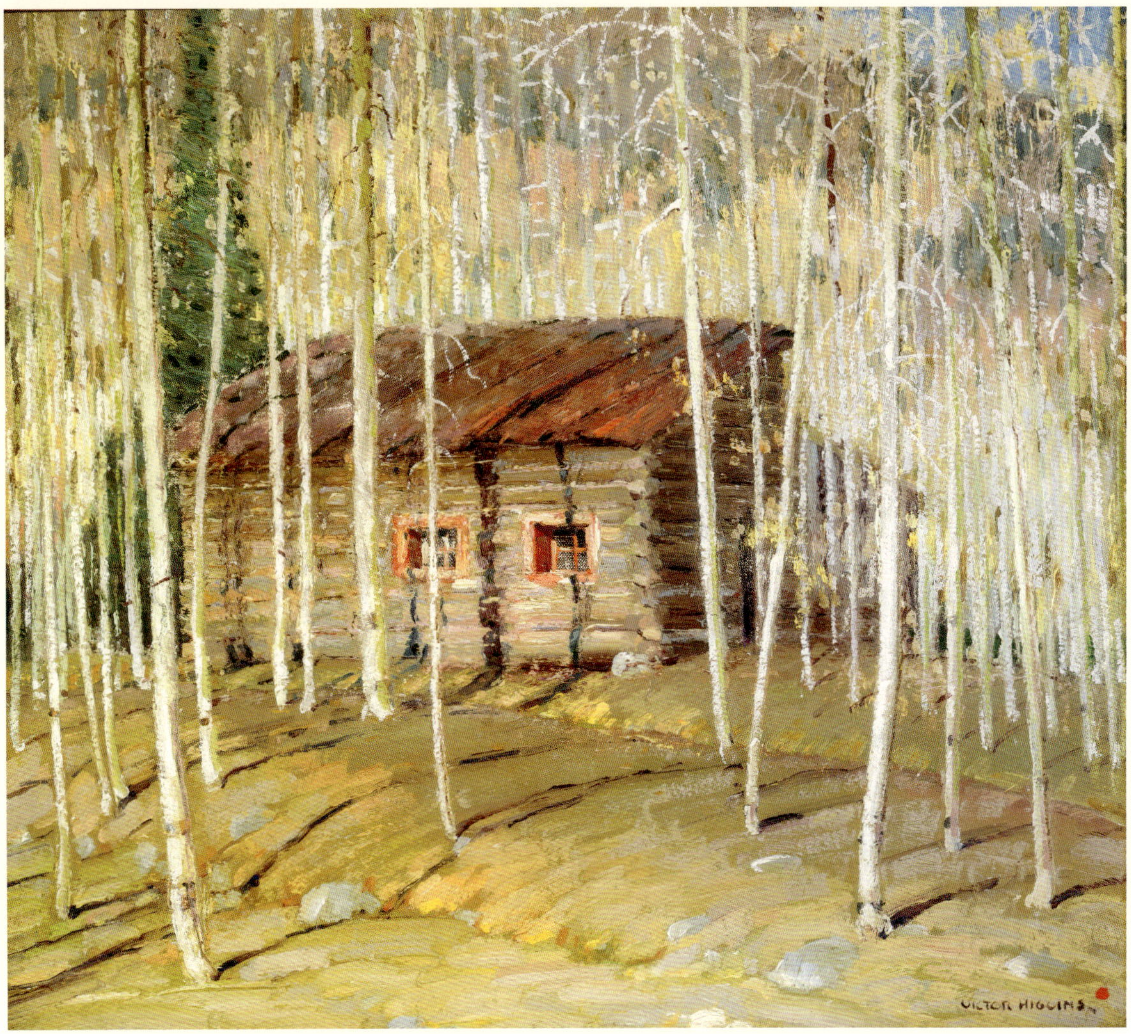

Figure 79. Victor Higgins. *Taos in Early Fall*, c. 1924. Oil on canvas, 22 x 26 inches. Collection Klauer Manufacturing Company.

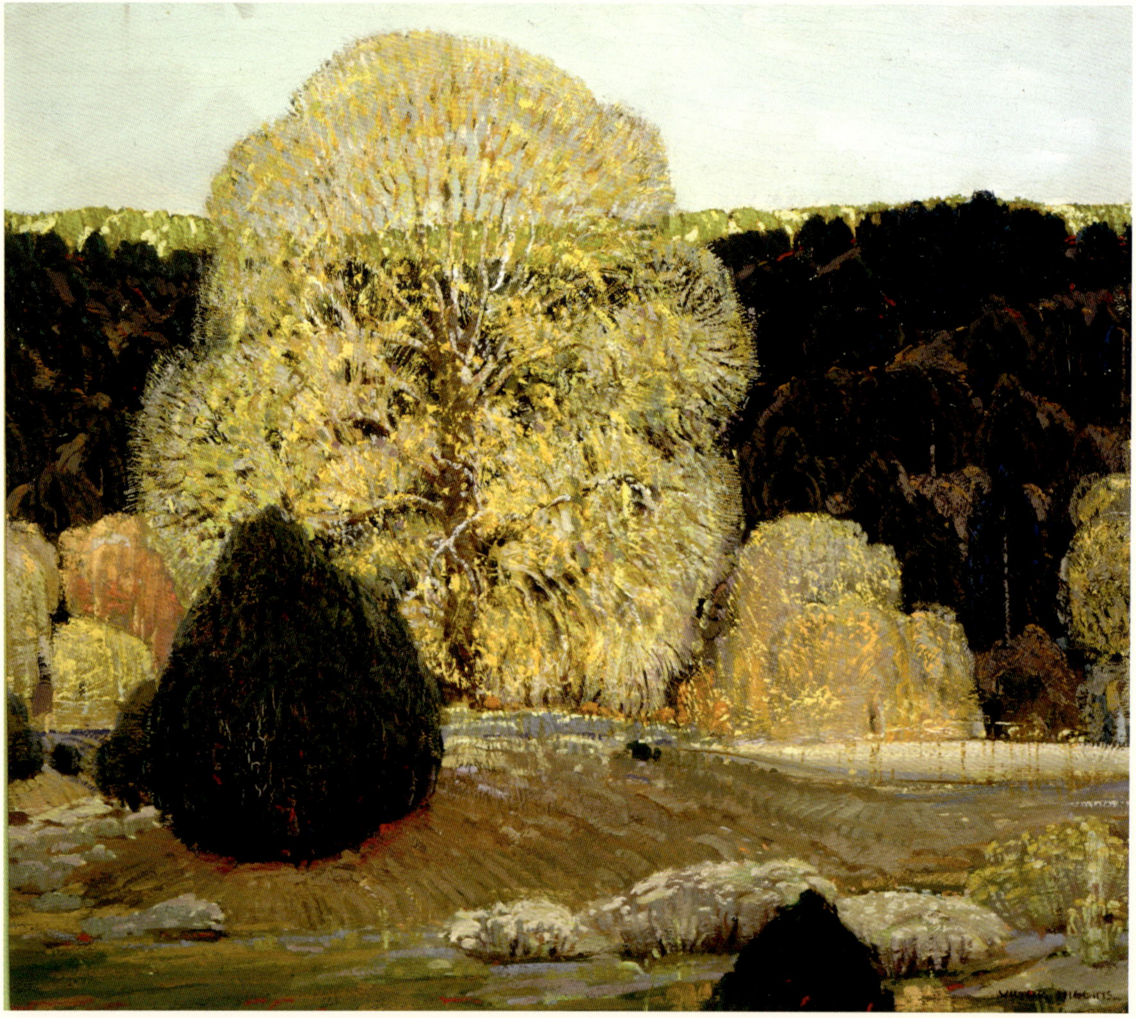

Figure 80. Victor Higgins. *U.S. Canyon*, before 1925. Oil on canvas, 22 x 26 inches.
Collection Klauer Manufacturing Company.

Taos in Early Fall [fig. 79] is but one of several paintings created by Higgins of the deserted gold mining camp at Twining, New Mexico. Mabel Dodge Luhan described the camp as being a "long, empty, white frame hotel and several log cabins."[10] To get there, the artist would have to go, "nine miles up the winding and twisting rough road, across nine rickety bridges, over the ice-cold mountain stream, into the high altitude of aspens and pine trees..."[11] Higgins, who was considered a loner, welcomed the solitude while painting a camp whose only occupants were "large pack rats with angora tails, chipmunks and squirrels" that ran from one cabin to another.[12]

The most important canvas of the four in Klauer's collection at that time was an 18-by-18-inch oil sketch titled *A Stream in Winter* [fig. 6]. William Klauer acquired what was likely a study for *Reflected Light*, a 52 ¼-by-56 ¼-inch masterpiece that Higgins exhibited in the *34th Annual Exhibition of Paintings and Sculpture* at The Art Institute of Chicago.[13] Both the small oil sketch and the painting are

[10] Luhan. *Edge of Taos Desert*, 236-237.
[11] Ibid, 236.
[12] Ibid, 236-237.
[13] Another version exists in the private collection of Mr. and Mrs. Michael Frost, New York.

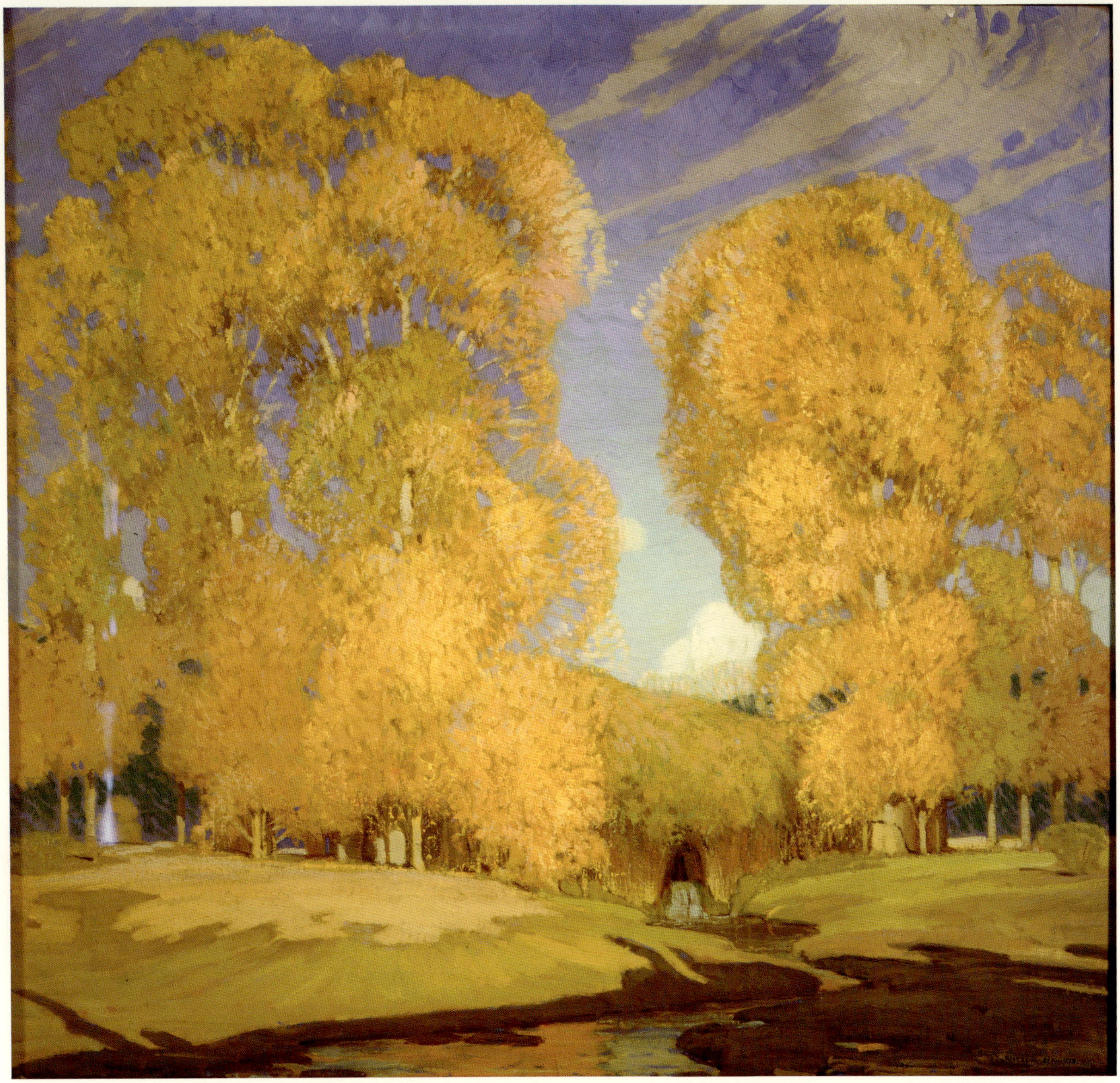

Figure 81. Victor Higgins. *Cottonwoods*, before 1925. Oil on canvas, 34 x 36 inches. Collection Klauer Manufacturing Company.

elegant essays in pattern, color and brushwork. The brook glistens with reflections from the icy snows camouflaging the meandering stream's movement through the banks of snow and *piñon*.

With *U. S. Canyon* [fig. 80] Higgins created a feathery, fan-like cottonwood, the reigning king of the New Mexico landscape. Each layer of pigment works in harmony, whether it was applied in a buttery consistency or dragged and scrubbed to a dry thinness. In *Cottonwoods* [fig. 81] Higgins demonstrated his fascination for meandering streams—this one fed by a small waterfall moving gently between the stands of trees. The golden cottonwoods stand in majesty, making it easy to understand why Higgins was called "a painter's painter."

E. MARTIN HENNINGS AND WILLIAM KLAUER, 1926

In 1926, at the same time that he was working with Ufer and Higgins, Klauer began supporting E. Martin Hennings. Hennings, along with Catharine Carter Critcher, became the tenth and eleventh members of the Taos Society of Artists in 1924.[14] Klauer's patronage of Hennings began before the artist became a member. As early as January 20, 1920, Carter Harrison wrote to Klauer about a "Gloucester picture by Hennings you [Klauer] subscribed for at $75."[15] He continued, "As for Hennings' picture, I would advise you to pick a fine little landscape, 25/30, which he has in the Penna [Academy of the] Fine Arts show at Philadelphia, but he wants $125 for it. If you don't want to go beyond $75, he has several of the same size in his studio, as well as a lot of 12/14 he asks $25 for."[16] Harrison continued a practice that he introduced a dozen years earlier. One of his major motivations in acquiring paintings was to buy as cheaply as possible. Klauer, on the other hand, paid his artists a price commensurate with the quality of their paintings.

The self-centered Harrison invited Klauer to come to Chicago and "go over to the Institute with Uncle [Otto] Demme to see a portrait Hennings painted of me in my fighting togs—some class to it believe me!"[17] Hennings had painted Harrison dressed as a member of the American Red Cross. "Hennings is coming fast—we want to get up a 'skindicate' and send him to Taos this coming summer."[18] The use of the word "skindicate," instead of syndicate, says volumes about Harrison's respect for Hennings.

Klauer apparently owned paintings by Hennings and Higgins as well as Ufer as early as 1922. He used this point on September 12 of that year when he was concerned about the quality of the paintings Ufer was sending him. He wanted higher quality paintings, "something that is worthy of the name *Ufer*." He goes on to say, "there are Higgins's and Hennings' pictures in my office. Do you want yours to take third place? If not, send something respectable and let me know what to do with the stuff you sent me."[19]

Four years later, as he had with Ufer on repeated occasions, Klauer responded to Hennings's financial needs. During a 1924 exhibit, Hennings had met and fallen in love with Helen Otte, a beautiful young woman who was assistant art buyer for Marshall Field and Company. Two years later, on July 20, they married and left for a sixteen-month honeymoon and painting trip through France and Spanish Morocco.

Hennings invited Klauer to his studio to raise money for their trip. After the visit, Hennings wrote to Klauer, "I am taking the liberty of sending you four small paintings and trust all of them will find an owner, if not just return them at your convenience."[20] Titles of the four paintings were *Grazing in the Canyon*, *Golden Cottonwoods*, *Setting Suns Last Rays* and *Distant Downpour*. Klauer, anxious to help, also told Hennings of two other potential buyers.

Intent on making as many sales as possible, Hennings had also spoken to their mutual friend Oscar Mayer. Mayer advised Hennings to give Klauer a discount on his pictures, a suggestion the artist was more than happy to accommodate. For the pictures Hennings sent a few weeks earlier, he reduced the price from $275 to $250. He also offered two 30-by-30-inch canvases "which I showed you in the studio, two

[14] In 1926, Kenneth Adams became the 12th and final member of the Taos Society of Artists.

[15] Carter H. Harrison to William Klauer, 20 January 1920, KFPUND.

[16] Ibid.

[17] Ibid.

[18] Ibid.

[19] William Klauer to Walter Ufer, 12 September 1922, KFPUND.

[20] E. Martin Hennings to William Klauer, 17 May 1926, KFPUND.

of my very best. I will take off $150 making the price $600. I've a couple nice frames for them and they look fine."[21] Hennings also reminded Klauer that he hadn't given him the names of the potential buyers.

With two weeks to go before his trip, a persistent Hennings again approached Klauer, being "keenly interested in raising a little more money before starting out..."[22] If Klauer would return to his studio, Hennings would show him 30-by-30-inch paintings that he would lower the price to $250, and the four smaller ones that Klauer already had for $200. With Klauer's financial assistance, Hennings would be in better shape and was all "set for matrimony."[23] He again voiced his appreciation if Klauer could put him "in touch with the two gentlemen of whom you spoke when you were here."[24]

Klauer's sponsorship of Hennings was not a new experience as he had already funded Ufer's trip to New York City in 1918. On July 16, 1926, Klauer sent a check for $500 for two 30-by-30-inch canvases—*Taos in Winter* [fig. 83] and *Silver and Gold* [fig. 1]. With these funds, the Hennings began their marathon, sixteen-month "honeymoon."[25] Unlike Ufer, who finished but one painting in New York City in three months, Hennings filled crates with canvases as he toured Europe, painting virtually everything that excited him.

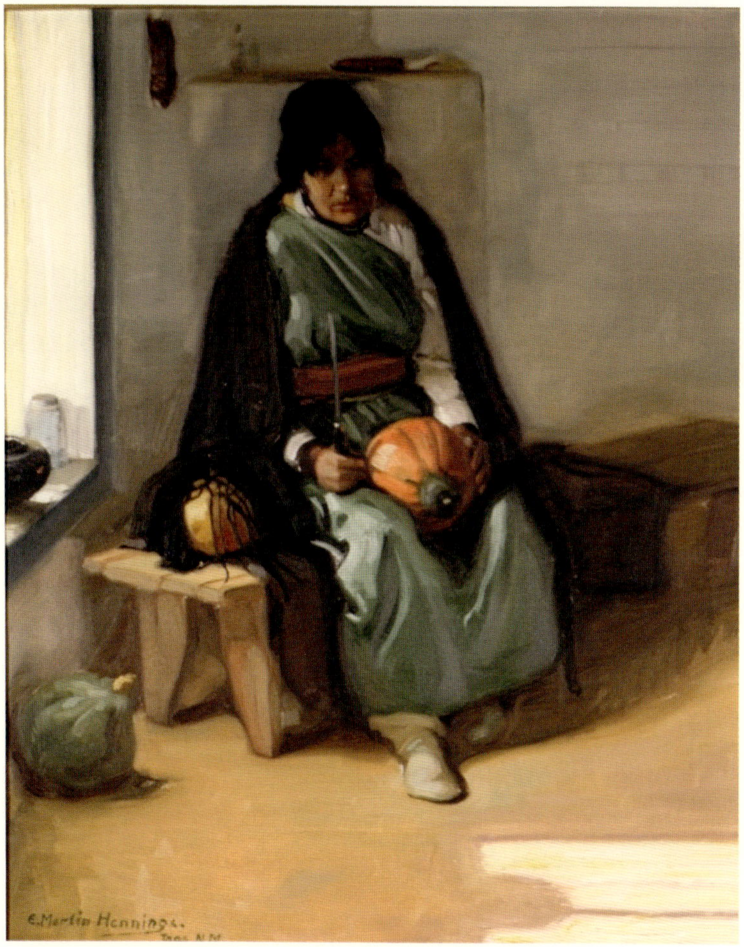

Figure 82.
E. Martin Hennings.
Indian Holding a Gourd, 1917.
Oil on canvas, 21 1/2 x 14 7/8 inches.
Collection Klauer Manufacturing Company.

[21] E. Martin Hennings to William Klauer, 7 June 1926, KFPUND.
[22] E. Martin Hennings to William Klauer, 5 July 1926, KFPUND.
[23] Ibid.
[24] Ibid.
[25] Robert Rankin White, "E. Martin Hennings," in Laura M. Bickerstaff, *Pioneer Artists of Taos,* revised and expanded (Denver: Old West Publishing Company, 1983), 200-202.

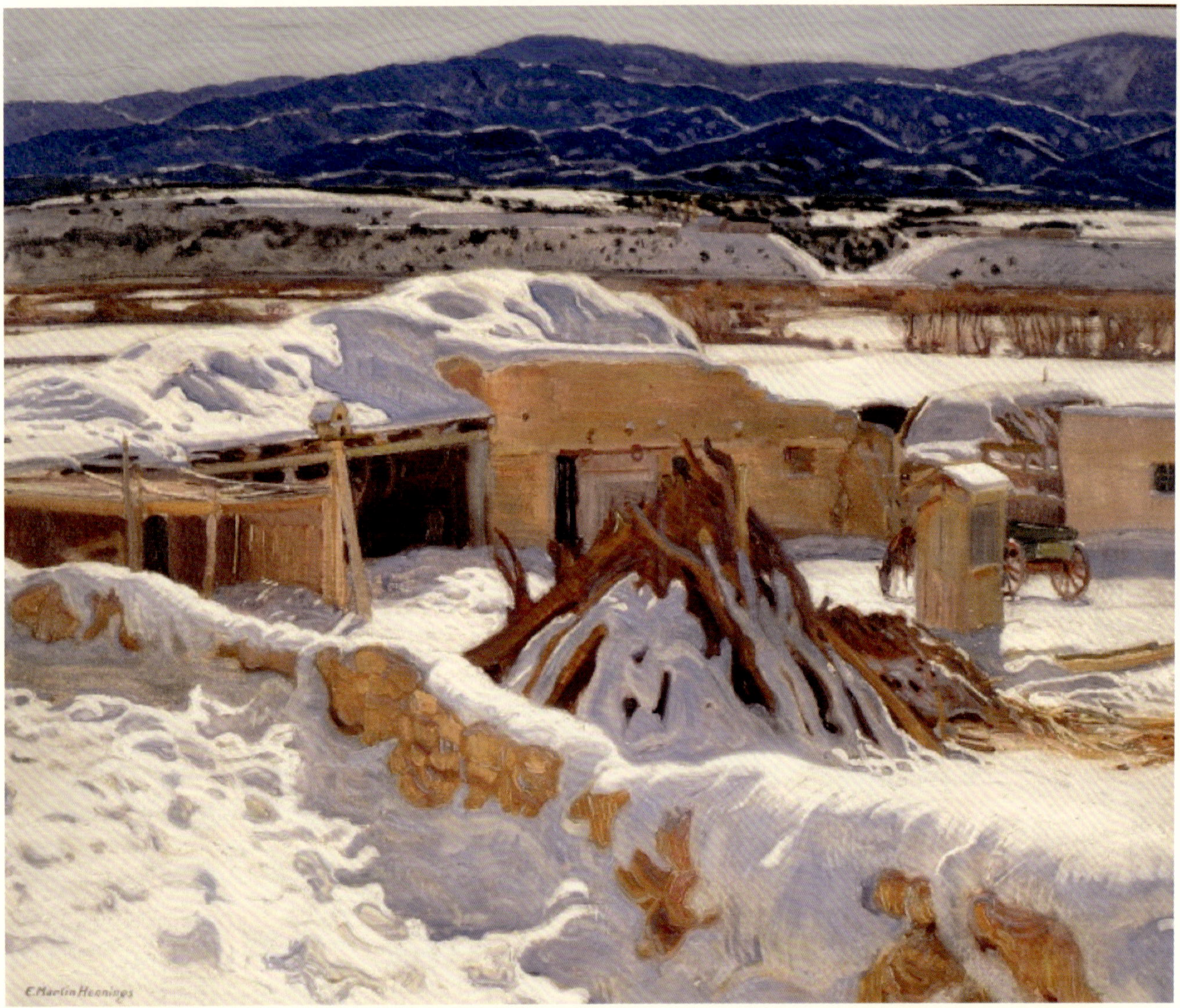

Figure 83. E. Martin Hennings. *Taos in Winter*, before 1926. Oil on canvas, 30 x 30 inches. Collection of Matthew and Joyce Walsh, Chicago. (former Klauer Family Collection)

The Hennings paintings in Klauer's collection offer an excellent overview of the artist's work in Taos. *Indian Girl with a Gourd* [fig. 82] is a remarkable effort he finished a few weeks after his arrival in Taos in July of 1917. In November 1917, Hennings was invited to exhibit in the grand inaugural opening of the Museum of Fine Arts in Santa Fe. One of his paintings shown was *Taos Indian* featuring the same Taos woman seen in Klauer's *Indian Woman with a Gourd.*[26] The painting in the Klauer collection depicts a woman, seated by a window, experiencing a private moment, and wearing a green costume, cutting a melon.

Taos in Winter [fig. 83] is a handsome winter scene, showing a fresh blanket of heavy snow with distinctive blue shadows. The barnyard is filled with wonderful sculptures that man and Mother Nature partnered in creating—adobe structures, a crumbling wall, stacks of wood and a variety of earth outcroppings all wrapped in thick blankets of soft snow. This is but one of multiple versions of the snow-covered barnyard that Hennings painted.

[26] *Taos Indian* is in a private collection.

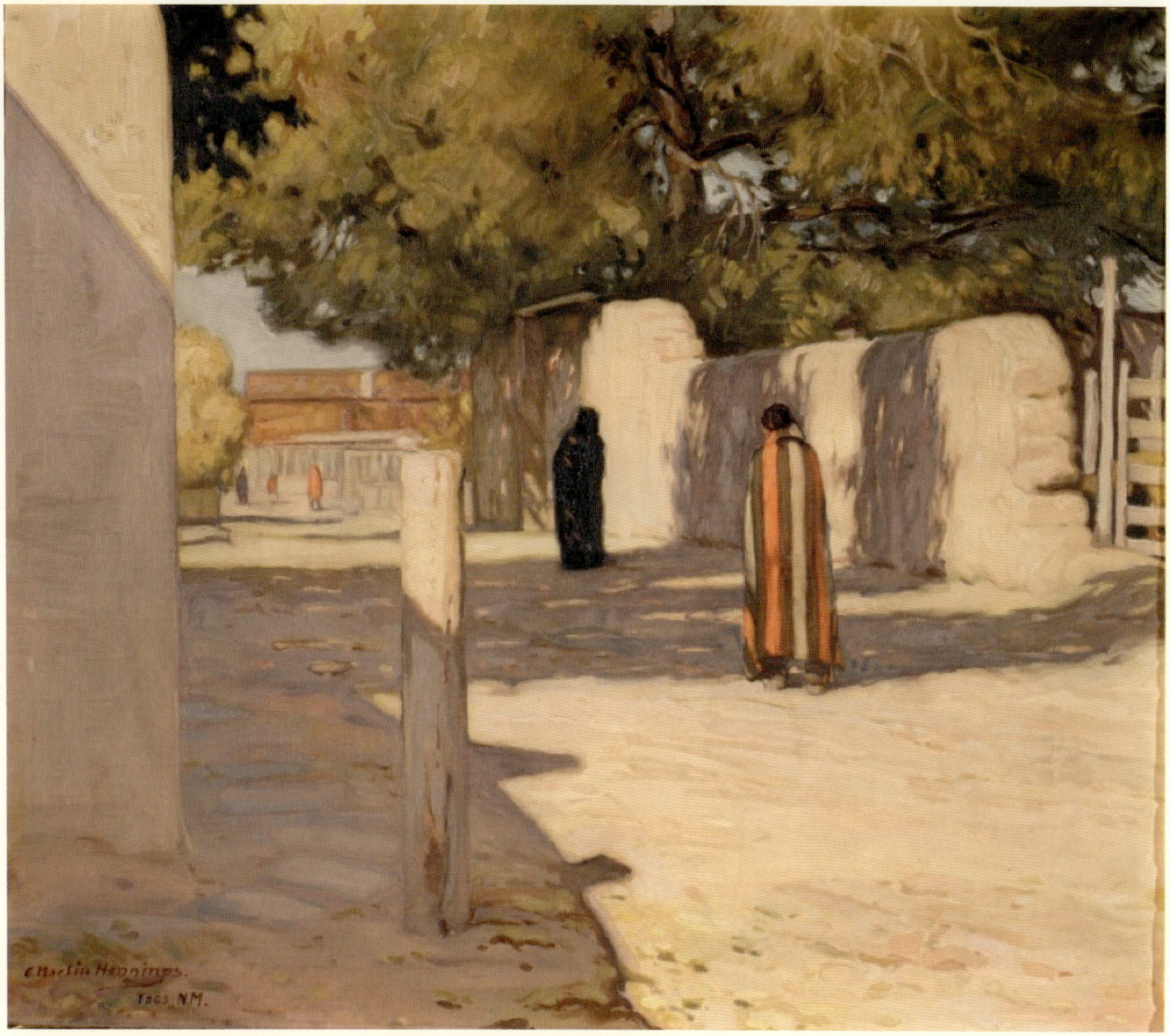

Figure 84. E. Martin Hennings. *Untitled (Street Scene-Taos)*, before 1926. Oil on canvas, 25 x 30 inches. Collection Klauer Manufacturing Company.

A theme favored by Hennings was the Taos Indian walking or riding on horseback, slowly winding his way through the slender shafts of an aspen grove [fig. 1; frontispiece]. Both Hennings and Higgins popularized paintings of aspens. The basic difference in approach was Hennings's inclusion of human figures and animals. Higgins customarily painted aspens nestling a solitary fir tree, confined to or surrounding a cabin [see fig. 79]. Hennings's *Silver and Gold* features the arabesques of white-barked aspens so densely compacted in a shallow picture plane, that it is virtually impossible for the red-cloaked hunter with his bow to make his way through the forest. Klauer likely selected the painting because of its subject—an Indian hunting.

In *Untitled (Street Scene–Taos)* [fig. 84], Hennings depicted two Taos Indians clad in handsome robes, strolling between heavy adobe walls and under a massive, hovering cottonwood. Hennings effectively captured the feeling of a hot summer day. Judging by the shadows, it is about four o'clock in the afternoon. The Taos Indians seem unaware of the artist who has set up his easel to capture them enjoying a quiet afternoon.

As late as July of 1930, Klauer was still interested in acquiring additional paintings by Hennings. The artist responded by sending three "worth a total of $300…"[27] Somehow the paintings became lost between Taos and Dubuque, and Hennings and Klauer agreed on a "settlement" of $300. Hennings also hoped that he could receive a check from Klauer "this summer."[28] Klauer, in his last letter to Hennings, wrote on August 4, expressing regrets over the lost paintings and enclosed a check for $300."[29] What became of these paintings remains a mystery as there is no evidence that Klauer ever received them.

BERT GEER PHILLIPS AND WILLIAM KLAUER

Trail Through the Aspens [fig. 85] is the only painting Klauer purchased from his old friend Bert Geer Phillips, who was considered the "welcome wagon" for Taos. Few Anglos came to Taos without meeting Phillips. The artist was one of the founding members of the Taos Society of Artists, and Klauer had known him since 1914. In 1915, Carter Harrison spoke of Phillip's friendship with William Klauer. In fact, the friendship between the two was the reason Carter Harrison did not include Klauer in the original art syndicate he had organized.

It is remarkable how Phillips was able to capture the magic of October with the golden glow of aspens. While Phillips was primarily known for his paintings of the Taos Indian, Klauer decided on adding another pure landscape to his collection. *Trail Through the Aspens* complemented the four Higgins landscapes that Klauer purchased from his Dubuque Art Association solo exhibition.

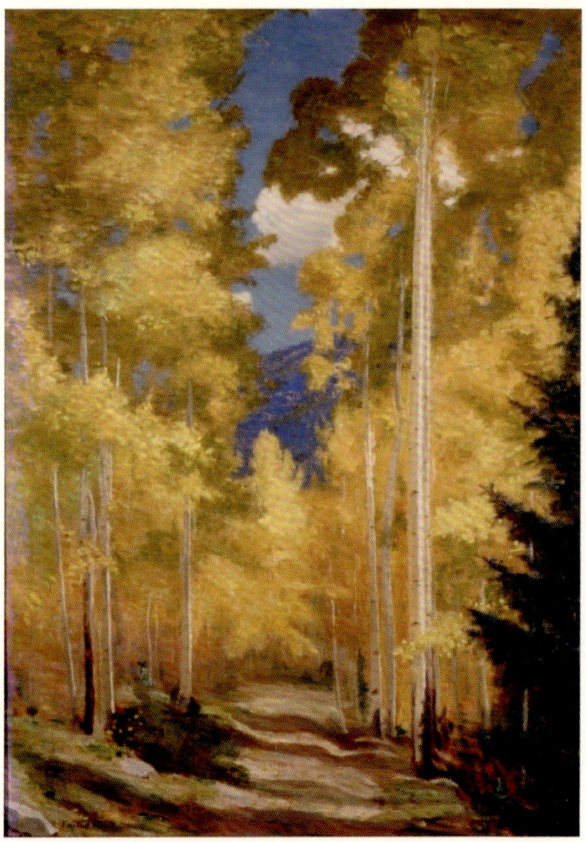

Figure 85.
Bert Phillips. *Trail Through the Aspens*, c. 1920s.
Oil on canvas, 39 x 29 inches.
Collection Klauer Manufacturing Company.

[27] E. Martin Hennings to William Klauer, 29 July 1930, KFPUND
[28] Ibid.
[29] William Klauer to E. Martin Hennings, 4 August 1930, KFPUND.

Chapter XI
The Downward Spiral, 1924-1927

UNION TRUST & SAVINGS BANK LIFELINE

By 1924 Ufer had grown accustomed to living high, and his affluent lifestyle necessitated that he sell more paintings. As a temporary solution to his problem of needing cash to operate on, he took a second loan from the Union Trust & Savings Bank for $3380. As usual, the support of William Klauer was critical to Ufer's receiving the loan. As he had with earlier loans, Ufer used most of his inventory of paintings as collateral—basically placing a lifetime of work in the hands of Union Trust & Savings Bank and William Klauer. From the early 1920s to the 1930s, Ufer lived under incredible pressure as he struggled to satisfy the holders of his notes. The quality of his production, as well as exhibitions, began to suffer. To make matters worse, his anxiety to make sales made him often offer his paintings at dramatically reduced prices.

On August 14, 1924, N. C. Gindorff, cashier of the Union Trust & Savings Bank, wrote to Klauer requesting that a new note, for the same amount as the original April note of $3380 be created. This required Ufer to update his list of paintings being used as collateral and increased the overall value of the loan to $8675.[1] For the next half dozen years, Ufer attempted to reduce the principal of the loan only to request to have its terms extended. On several occasions when he was about to retire his indebtedness to the bank, he would find that he had to extend the loan. Even when he had a good cash flow and a respectable balance in his checkbook, he was only able to pay the interest on his loan. Fortunately, the influential William Klauer remained in Ufer's corner and covered his shortfalls. On several occasions Ufer was once again compelled to use paintings to satisfy his creditors. In addition to personal loans from Klauer, Ufer's brother Otto, his insurance agent, and even his wife Mary, lent him money. He needed funds to pay home and studio rentals, insurance policies, as well as to pay off other debts. Living on credit, by 1928 his debts had grown to an astronomical total of over $8000.[2]

While Ufer struggled to pay off his loan to Klauer and the Union Trust & Savings Bank, the lenders grew increasingly concerned about the location of the paintings being used as collateral. Ufer's dealers, Erwin Barrie and John E. D. Trask, held several of the paintings. To make matters worse, by 1924 both dealers had changed their places of business. Trask had left New York to become the director at the Milwaukee Art Institute, and in 1923, Erwin Barrie left Chicago to accept the directorship of Grand Central Art Galleries in New York. Once Trask moved to Milwaukee, he was no longer as effective as Ufer's dealer. It was difficult to feel comfortable with the paintings as collateral if they were hard to locate. On August 27, Ufer assured Klauer and the Bank that their collateral was secure. Because of exhibitions, paintings held on approval by potential buyers, and other factors, his work was "bound to shift its locality from time to time, in order to sell them."[3]

Ufer kidded himself as he was convinced that his situation would improve. He also continued offering excuse after excuse when failing to live up to his commitments. Ufer claimed he "had been busy

[1] N. C. Gindorff to William Klauer, 14 August 1924, UPUNDSG.

[2] $8000 in 1928 would be equal to $117,760 in 2019.

[3] Walter Ufer to William Klauer, 27 and 29 August 1924, UPUNDSG.

entertaining more people this year with excellent prospects for the future..." Still trying to sell himself, he stated "I am very busy—I am painting hard, doing big things..."[4]

By November, Klauer, in an attempt to help Ufer, was still trying to secure paintings to sell in Dubuque. Not learning from previous mistakes, Ufer cast dispersions on the people of Dubuque just as he had in Chicago and New York in 1919. "I doubt very much that the people of Dubuque [are] sufficiently educated artistically to understand good work and pay the price for it. I can no longer sell at the price that I sold one in Dubuque—through your efforts and not mine."[5] Ufer was referring to *His Pack*, sold to Mr. Coates.

On November 27, 1924, Ufer sent his 1915 painting, *Taos in Snow* [fig. 39], to Klauer "... in part payment of what I owe you."[6] He also sent four other paintings from Milch Galleries, and one, *Homeward Bound*, from Aurora, Illinois. This meant that Klauer received six works in 1924.[7] In a letter to N. C. Gindorff, Ufer stated that the six paintings were for "a private debt in part" and he wasn't "to pay 20% to you for gifts to him [Klauer].[8] Klauer, further clarifying the transaction, wrote to Gindorff, "For your information, Ufer owed me a number of pictures and I paid him Twelve Hundred Dollars in cash for a number of pictures which he delayed sending for two years."[9]

In August, *El Palacio* reported that Ufer had "remodeled a chapel recently acquired at Taos into a commodious studio."[10] Writing to Klauer, Ufer stated, "everything is going fine here. I am hard at work. I have enlarged some—I have a 42 x 17' studio opposite my home." Klauer and his friends were coming to Taos and he offered, "...stay in my guest house. You need not stay in the hotel. I have better beds than they have."[11] This statement suggests that Klauer did not always stay in his cottage when he visited Taos. Staying at a hotel would have been a matter of convenience, particularly if Klauer only spent a few days and did not want to go to the trouble of opening up the cottage.

During 1925 Ufer sent paintings to seventeen exhibitions, a remarkable number of venues for any artist or museum with a full-time staff. For several of the exhibitions, which he continued to call "my circuit," he showed between six and eleven paintings. Two paintings that he sent to several sites were *At the Window* [fig. 64] and *The Builders of the Desert* [fig. 74], canvases that would eventually enter the Klauer collection.

Another subject Ufer enjoyed creating in the 1920s can be seen in *Waiting for the Gates to Open* [fig. 86], painted in 1925. He had found a market for the pictures of horses he rented when painting Jim Mirabal working as a freighter. Ufer also painted the horses grazing in the fields, tied up to hitching rails or, in this instance, waiting for the gate to open at day's end. The horse located at the apex of Ufer's compositional triangle and nearest the gate, still bears Mirabal's saddle. While Ufer is seldom praised for his paintings of horses, it was a key component in many of his successful compositions. More often than not, Ufer positioned the horse with its backside facing the viewer.

---

[4] Walter Ufer to William Klauer, 29 August 1924, UPUNDSG.
[5] Ibid.
[6] Walter Ufer to William Klauer, 27 November 1924, UPUNDSG.
[7] Ibid.
[8] Walter Ufer to N. C. Gindorff, 8 December 1924, UPUNDSG.
[9] William Klauer to N. C. Gindorff. 16 December 1924, UPUNDSG.
[10] *El Palacio*, 1 August 1925, Vol. XIX, nos. 2-3, 42.
[11] Walter Ufer to William Klauer, August 1925, UPUNDSG.

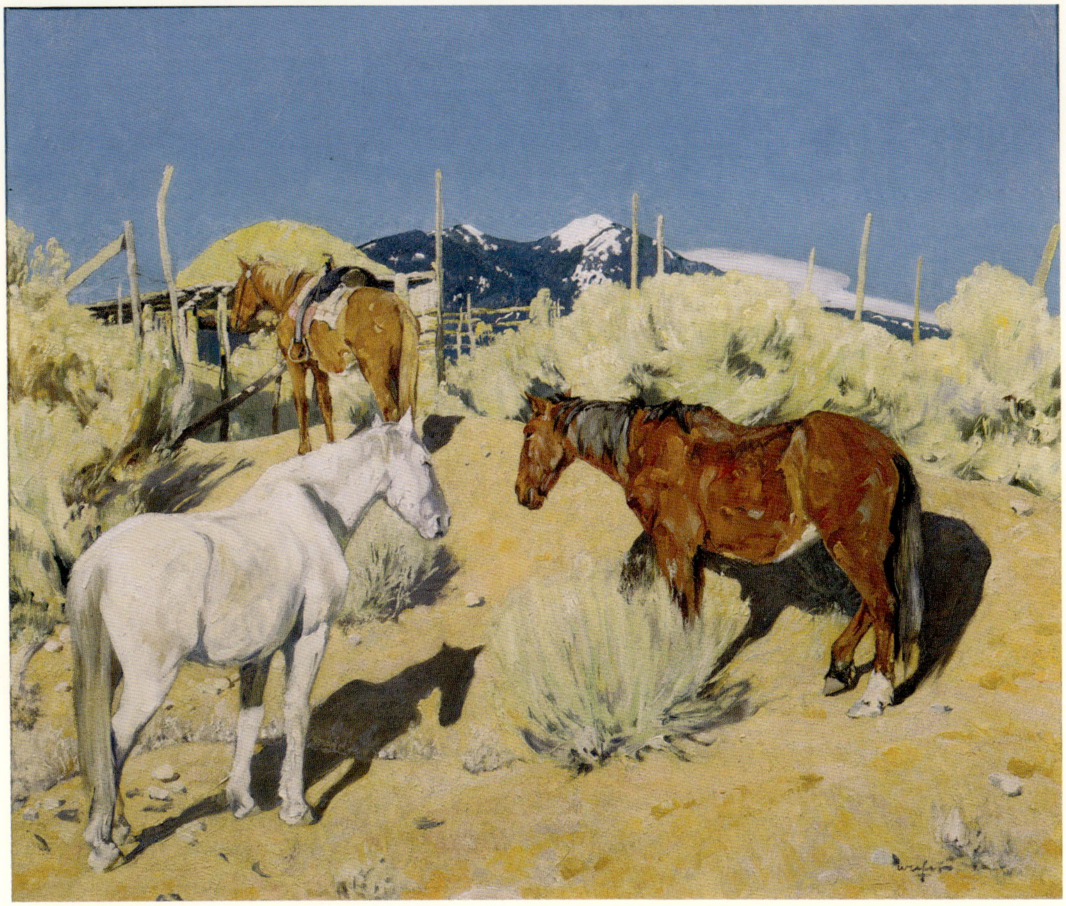

Figure 86. Walter Ufer. *Waiting for the Gates to Open*, 1925. Oil on canvas, 25 x 30 inches. Location unknown. (former Klauer Family Collection)

Waiting for the Gate to Open remained in Ufer's studio until March 1932 when Ufer had it shipped to Dubuque. It had been included as collateral for a $5000 loan after the Union Trust & Savings Bank closed and Klauer assumed the note. Interestingly, Ufer initially priced the canvas at $500 from 1925 through 1932, but by June 19, 1934, a month after he took his last drink, it was priced at $1500 on a list appended to a letter from Mary Ufer to Klauer.[12] *Waiting for the Gate to Open* was one of nine paintings sent from the Stendahl Galleries in Los Angeles, Grand Central Art Galleries in New York, and an unidentified location in Iowa, to Klauer.

UFER DECLARES HIS INDEPENDENCE, 1927

Following a successful solo exhibition in 1926 at The Art Institute of Chicago and the sale of several paintings, including *His Wealth* to The Metropolitan Museum of Art, Ufer was able to send Gindorff a check in March for $565. He boastfully reported he had reduced his indebtedness to $1925.[13] Now Ufer believed he was free of the pressure of his many loans; however, he continued to function under the pressure of meeting financial obligations while maintaining an opulent social life—one that he could ill afford in Chicago or New York.

[12] Mary Ufer to William Klauer, 19 June 1934, KFPUND.

[13] Walter Ufer to N. C. Gindorff, 22 March 1926, UPUNDSG.

From 1927 on, even though Ufer believed he had declared his independence, he turned more and more to Klauer for financial assistance. His loans and sales kept Ufer in business and allowed the artist to continue his practice of creating and marketing paintings. It also allowed him to maintain an active social life, with sessions in bars, dining rooms, and living rooms with potential buyers. With the dissolution of the Taos Society of Artists and The New Mexico Painters in 1927.[14] Ufer had to rethink his patronage system. Erwin Barrie at Grand Central Art Galleries had satisfied some of Ufer's needs while Klauer assumed the onus of the burden. Without Klauer, Ufer's downward spiral would have been catastrophic. His patronage allowed for some bright, although not brilliant, moments.

After 1927, Ufer no longer felt the need to be part of any formal organization in order to succeed. The essential role of his previous organizations was to sell paintings through annual circuit exhibitions, keeping his art before the public. Even though he had exhibited in the TSA shows for more than a decade, TSA minutes reveal that he only sold four paintings. He had sold none through The New Mexico Painters. Neither Victor Higgins nor E. Martin Hennings ever made a sale through the two organizations. Ufer, writing to Ernest Blumenschein, declared that he will "continue to stay out of their exhibitions [The New Mexico Painters]—also the Taos Society of Artists." Ufer no longer spoke of a great art movement, only running his "own one-man shows throughout the country."[15] Prophetically, Ufer told Blumenschein "when the time comes where they want me no longer probably I will be gone, and I should worry."[16]

After 1927, Ufer had to rely on his own resources to maintain his good standing in New York City and Chicago. It was New York City that eventually allowed Ufer to pay off his debt to the Union Trust & Savings Bank. On April 21, 1927, Ufer wrote to Gindorff advising that he had sold four large paintings, netting him $6000, to "one of our prominent collectors in the East..." He would be "in a position to pay my debts in full."[17] In fact, his ledger indicates that Ufer netted $9870 for the months of April and May. When he received his check from Grand Central, he immediately retired his note with Union Trust & Savings Bank.

Six days later, in a move uncharacteristic of Ufer, the artist again wrote to Gindorff, "as soon as you see W. H. Klauer please tell him I will be sending him a large 50" x 50" canvas (*Builders of the Desert*) that he liked in Taos—as a Gift."[18] Two weeks later, Ufer wrote to Klauer, announcing that he had instructed Newcomb-Macklin Company, "to ship to you *The Builders of the Desert* 50" x 50" as I want to make a present to you of this painting which you admired so much when you saw it in Taos the year it was painted. You asked for it then in 1923 and stated that you wanted that painting."[19] Ufer also took the opportunity to have Gindorff tell Klauer that he would be "in a position to pay my debt to Mr. W. H. Klauer in full."[20]

A relieved Klauer, expressing his pride in the artist, stated that he was pleased to have been able to give Ufer assistance in the past and would "take care of Ufer's affairs with the Bank."[21] Klauer praised Ufer, because "of a feeling of relief on my part..., ...it shows me that you have reached the point of success and

---

[14] Ufer, Higgins, and Ernest Blumenschein, with other New Mexico painters, created the organization in 1923. It proved to be in direct competition with the Taos Society of Artists.

[15] Ibid.

[16] Ibid.

[17] Ibid.

[18] Walter Ufer to N. C. Gindorff, 27 April 1927, KFPUND.

[19] Walter Ufer to William Klauer, KFPUND.

[20] Walter Ufer to William Klauer, 11 May 1927, UPUNDSG.

[21] William Klauer to Walter Ufer, 20 May 1927, UPUNDSG.

that you are now on your way to do bigger things."[22] There can be little question that Ufer had achieved, in his and Klauer's mind, a level of accomplishment long struggled for.

Even though Ufer's relationship with Klauer seemed to be running smoothly, rough moments soon followed. Ufer had admired a cedar cabinet in Klauer's "room in the Old Bismarck Hotel…" and the patron made the mistake of promising he would order one for the artist.[23] In May, Ufer sent Klauer two more paintings, *Angling* and *September Morning* [fig. 44] and in June, three "30 x 36 as a trade, and 2 – 25 x 30 for the Chicago Club for Klauer's suite."[24]

Unfortunately, the wardrobe had to be fabricated, which caused an impatient Ufer to write, "send the cedar wardrobe as soon as you can—I need it much."[25] Finally, after several demanding, rude letters, the wardrobe arrived, unfinished and bearing a cash-on-delivery charge of $16.59.[26] In a gesture typical of Ufer, he claimed that in their previous transactions, the sender always paid the shipping charges. He demanded, "so bring up the cheque."[27] Ufer was also upset that the wardrobe wasn't finished—a simple matter of applying stain or oil to its surface. Even though Klauer was responding to Walter's request for the wardrobe, and he willingly paid for its construction, Ufer turned the patron's kind gesture of a gift into a confrontational matter. No matter how much Klauer supported Ufer, the artist failed to show his appreciation. Why Klauer didn't terminate their relationship is open to speculation since most patrons would not have tolerated Ufer's actions.

In June, Klauer announced that he planned on being in Taos, and "he wished to spend a few days together."[28] During previous years, Ufer was more than happy to spend time with Klauer and usually welcomed the opportunity to enjoy the good life—socializing with Klauer and his friends. He enjoyed the great meals, alcohol, fishing, hunting, and camaraderie that made Klauer's visits special, but, this year, the artist had more commitments than he was capable of accommodating. He found himself experiencing unbelievable pressures. If he accepted Klauer's invitation to meet at the cottage, Ufer would have to spend too much valuable time preparing for and enjoying his patron's visit.

Klauer must have found Ufer's response to his invitation surprising, if not shocking. "Glad to see you in Taos, but as to staying with you for a few days is hardly possible because I am right on my work, and I must work hard for the Carnegie Institution, and my show in New York City for 1928." He also needed three large paintings for Pittsburgh by September. He went on to say, "I know you will excuse me."[29] In November, as Klauer's arrival date drew nearer, Ufer again addressed his concerns. "I will be glad to see you—but Klauer, as much as I like you, please let me stay with my work, and that I [don't] go to your cottage in the mountains. My show in New York City demands that I—make good—I am working hard to accomplish that. I will see you in town at the Hotel, but that must be all."[30] Being a figurative painter, there weren't appropriate subjects in and around Klauer's cottage to serve as subjects for his exhibitions.

Ufer's reference to Klauer's cottage is the last to be found in the artist's and patron's archives. According to Klauer's son, his father's cottage was stolen. Klauer returned to Taos, only to discover that

---

[22] Ibid.
[23] Walter Ufer to William Klauer, 25 May 1927, UPUNDSG.
[24] Ibid.
[25] Walter Ufer to William Klauer, 9 November 1927, KFPUND.
[26] Walter Ufer to William Klauer, 30 December 1927, KFPUND.
[27] Ibid.
[28] William Klauer to Walter Ufer, 20 June 1927, UPUNDSG.
[29] Walter Ufer to William Klauer, 20 June 1927, UPUNDSG.
[30] Walter Ufer to William Klauer, 3 November 1927, UPUNDSG.

his cottage had "disappeared"—logs, windows, roofing, and even the furniture. All that remained was the footprint where the cottage once stood and a pair of metal ceiling tiles stamped "Klauer Manufacturing Company." As the cottage was well known, it would have been easy prey for vandals. Stealing the cabin log by log did not happen overnight. It would have taken a team of workers a great deal of time.[31] The absence of notices of Klauer's visits to Taos in *Taos Valley News* after 1927 suggests the cottage had been taken in 1928 or 1929. Klauer never rebuilt his Taos cottage. Fortunately, Carter Harrison's photographs, the ceiling tiles, and the colorful reports of those who enjoyed being guests of Klauer, survive. Whenever Klauer's friends visited Taos, and despite Ufer's tight schedule, the patron wrote, asking the artist to "show his friends same courtesies —it will be highly appreciated."[32] Obviously Ufer was a critical figure when Klauer and his friends came to Taos, whether they stayed in the cottage or a Taos hotel.

Sales began to improve for Ufer in 1927. His records indicate that he found a new market for the period of 1927 through 1929. Besides sending paintings to the Grand Central Art Galleries and Macbeth Gallery on consignment, they began buying his canvases outright. By then, both galleries were aware of Ufer's alcoholism and how it was affecting his ability to create paintings that would interest customers. His paintings began to be repetitive, and their quality was uneven. The galleries also found that his mid-size paintings were the most saleable. Interestingly, large-scale paintings remained in Ufer's inventory if they weren't acquired by a public museum or Klauer.[33] Klauer also recognized the seriousness of Ufer's situation and acted accordingly. If Ufer couldn't make payment on his note, the bank would be forced to relieve the debt by transferring titles of his paintings being held as collateral. Klauer and the commercial galleries did all they could to make certain that Ufer's prices didn't fall.

Ufer's cost of doing business was also escalating at an alarming rate. Even though the cost of living in Taos was low, he had amassed huge expenses on the road. From January through March 1928, his ledger entries show expenses totaling over $4000. In Taos, rentals on a house, studio and garage were $25. In Chicago, hotels alone averaged $90 monthly. Ufer's expenses also included Mary's travel expenses, huge insurance premiums, and railway charges to and from Chicago and New York. Accounting for every expense and income, his journal entries included entertainment for business, travel, lodging, numerous memberships to arts organizations and subscriptions to periodicals, groceries (including alcohol), and drugstore (slot machines and punch boards). The more he earned, the more he spent. He was completely out of control. From Chicago, Ufer boasted to Kenneth Adams in Taos:

> *I live high and the costs are such. This hotel since Dec. 1st has cost me a barrel full. But even so—with a high-class hotel as an address it may pay big in the end. However, I am paying off debts and besides gaining new clients.*[34]

Even though there is no record of how much time he spent with Klauer during the patron's 1927 visit, a dedicated Ufer was able to finish the pictures he needed for juried shows. By budgeting his time, Ufer created three or four large-scale, impressive canvases including *My Studio Entrance* [fig. 88] and *Thanksgiving Time* [fig. 87]. Their creation marks his last period of spirited activity. Even though he still

---

[31] Interview by Dean Porter with William J. Klauer, Dubuque, December 1995.

[32] William Klauer to Walter Ufer, 7 November 1927, UPUNDSG.

[33] In fact, some of the most important large-scale paintings by Taos artists often remained in their studios, usually selling very late in their careers or by their heirs. Most big city dwellers could not accommodate, nor were anxious to acquire the more expensive, large-scale pictures. The price of large-scale paintings was often beyond the reach of most collectors.

[34] Walter Ufer to Kenneth Adams, 18 March 1927, Walter Ufer Papers, Forrest Fenn, Santa Fe.

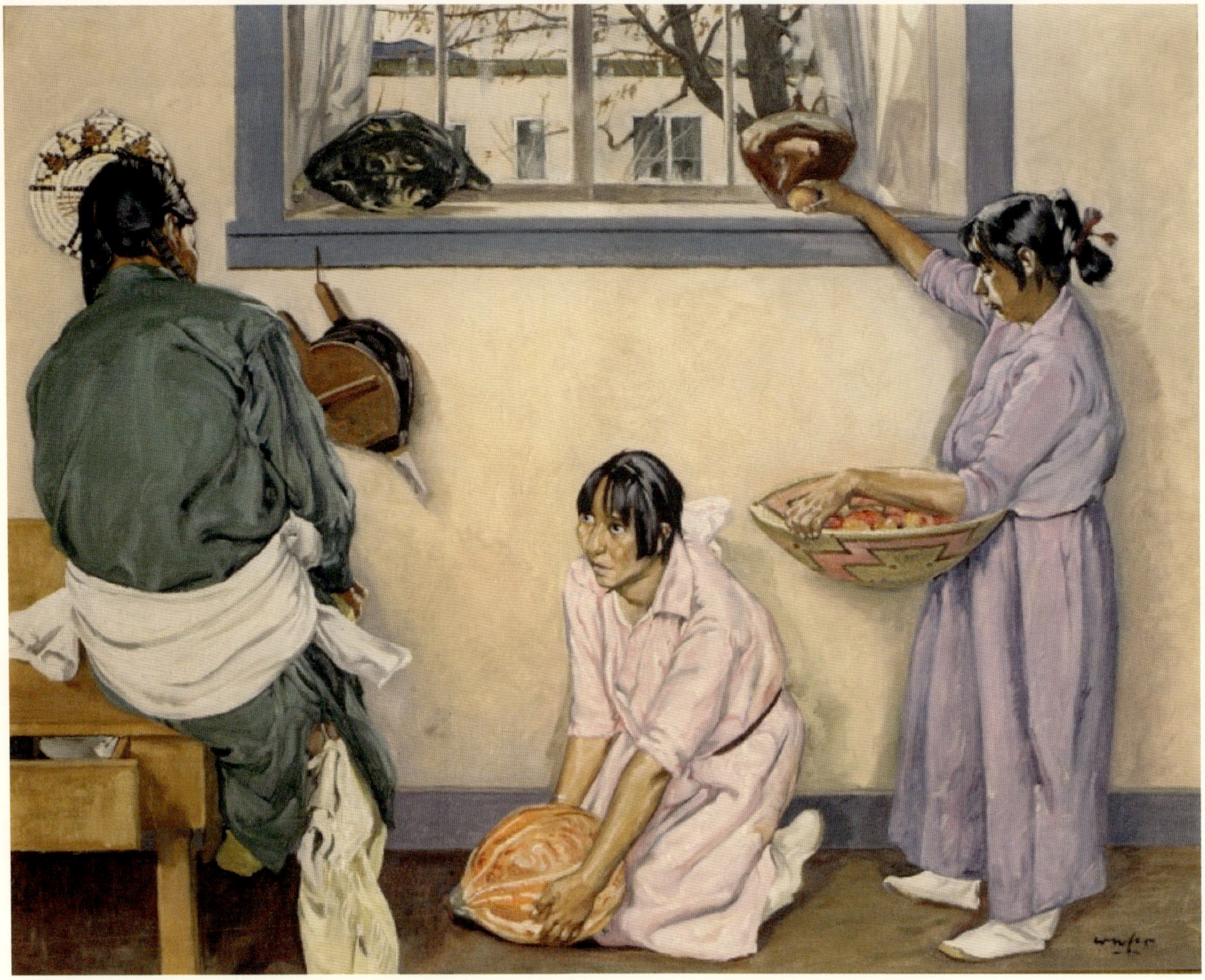

Figure 87. Walter Ufer. *Thanksgiving Time*, 1927. Oil on canvas, 40 x 50 inches. Collection Klauer Manufacturing Company.

had a good reputation, and the future, in his eyes, reflected some promise, his lifestyle was destroying his health and ability to produce quality pictures. It was only when he remained sober that he managed to paint a few, competent paintings.

MY STUDIO ENTRANCE, 1927

In 1927, the horse, this time casting long, afternoon shadows, was again the focal point for Ufer's painting *My Studio Entrance* [fig. 88a; cover]. When painting for juried exhibitions, he managed to create images of some quality. With the horse as the principal figure in the composition, he displayed his mastery of painting the animal. By his own admission, most collectors interested in acquiring one of his paintings looked for a horse.

My Studio Entrance is a rare, Taos garden scene for Ufer. While Ufer never painted a pure still-life, on this occasion he included a generous section of his garden. It served as a handsome setting for the all-too-familiar white horse and Jim Mirabal, wearing his rose-colored shirt and seen entering Ufer's studio. To the left, Mirabal's daughter waits patiently and admires the garden. Even though Ufer priced

My Studio Entrance at $2500, it remained unsold. A tour de force, *My Studio Entrance* would eventually find its way to Klauer's living room [fig. 88b].

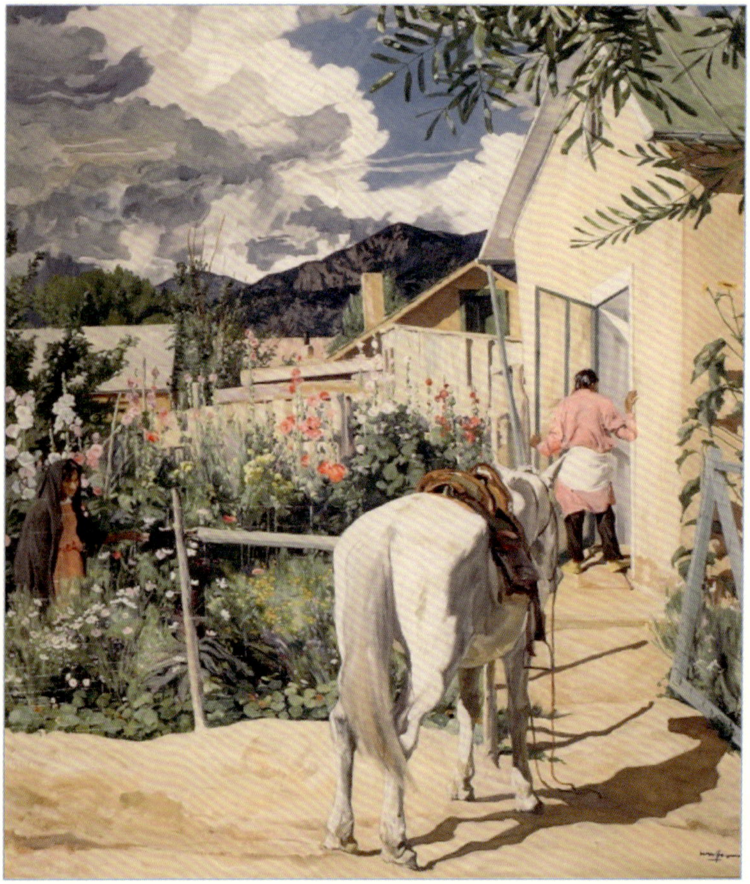

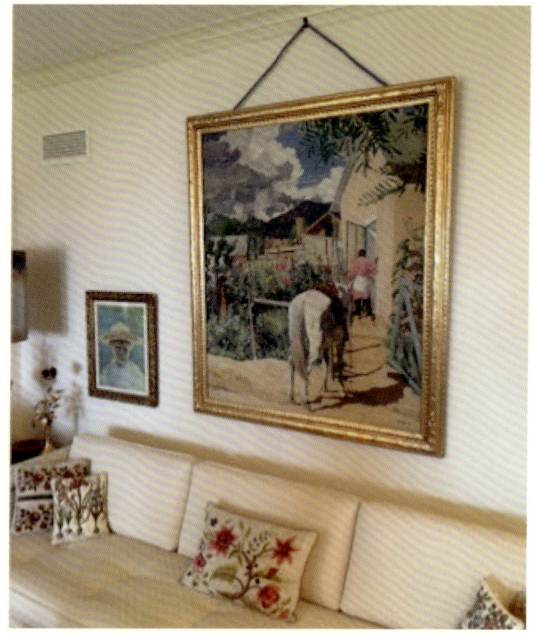

Figure 88a. Walter Ufer.
My Studio Entrance, 1927 (left).
Oil on canvas, 50 x 40 inches.
Collection Klauer Manufacturing Company.

Figure 88b. Walter Ufer's *My Studio Entrance* hanging in the family's living room (right).

In that same year, Ufer brought Jim Mirabal and his daughters to his studio and painted *Thanksgiving Time* [fig. 87]. Ufer painted *Friends–Laguna Pueblo* [fig. 47] a decade earlier, and it depicted a rare scene of simple life in Laguna. In both that painting and *Thanksgiving Time,* Ufer painted Cistercian interiors. As Mabel Luhan wrote, "Indian houses are empty..." She claimed God said "Indians cannot have things white people have things, but God give [sic] the Indians just what grows on the Mountain."[35] Ufer's *Thanksgiving Time* shows Jim seated on a table while one daughter kneels on the floor holding a cabbage and a second young woman holds a basket of apples as she places one on the window ledge. The artist achieved a compositional unity by compressing the figures actions in a narrow space. He silhouetted them against the dun colored adobe wall and violated the shallow space by seating Jim, with his back to the viewer, on the edge of a projecting table. Ufer also employed a slightly elevated bird's-eye view by slanting the floor, tabletop and window ledge. The window, which looks out onto neighboring adobes, also provides the viewer some spatial relief.

[35] Luhan, *Edge of Taos Desert*, 197.

Chapter XII
The Depression

Throughout 1928 and well into 1929, Ufer continued his one-man shows; however, he was again facing financial problems and mounting debts resulting from his extravagant lifestyle. Amazingly, as soon as his debts were paid off, he lapsed back into his old habits of spending more than he earned. As before, his ledger continued to show large sums being spent on travel, hotels (like the Bismarck), the Salmagundi Club, food (alcohol), drugstore (slot machines), and more. One entry for clothing was over $400.[1] Ufer continued to believe that he would be able to satisfy his creditors with his next sale. What he didn't anticipate was the Great Depression.

When the stockmarket crashed on October 29, 1929 and ushered in the Great Depression in America, it had a devastating effect on the country. Not even the remote community of Taos would be immune to the aftermath. While Ufer had achieved some degree of financial stability in 1927, by 1929, he in conjunction with Grand Central Art Galleries, was planning a trip to Houston and other venues to raise much needed funds. As in 1918, Ufer found that his market in Taos had dried up. The number of visitors to Taos had declined, and those who did come were not in the habit of, much less in the mood for, buying art or anything considered unessential. Ufer saw little promise for future sales in Taos.

Rejecting Mary's repeated suggestions to move to Chicago, Ufer was in need of finding another market. For nearly a decade, he had been considering Texas, and even California, as potential venues. Ufer's greatest problem, however, remained his addiction to alcohol. His brother-in-law, Ditlev Frederiksen, wrote to Mary on May 28, 1929, that he was "sorry that Walter is still drinking more than he should. I thought he was getting close to the danger line when we were in Chicago, and was thinking that when he got back to Taos he would be all right again."[2] When it came to his drinking problem and his indebtedness to William Klauer and others, Ufer continued to kid himself—always believing he could resolve his problems—tomorrow. Unfortunately for Ufer, tomorrow was slow in coming. Alcoholism continued its strangle hold on him, and it would be four more years before Ufer would find the strength to make one, last heroic effort to save himself.

By October of 1929, Ufer had finalized his plans for the extended trip to Houston, but as usual, he found himself in a financial bind. Although he professed to Klauer that he was not broke, he owed his patron $500 and several other venders money for supplies and services. Furthermore, Ufer confessed that he "was working hard as usual," but he had not "sold any [paintings] in Taos this year." When he sold a painting, "payment came in too slow and in small amount that does not often reach."[3]

This time, however, Ufer did not return to his well-proven tactic of selling a group of paintings to Klauer in order to afford the trip. If he did, Klauer probably turned him down. By 1929 Klauer had more canvases by the artist than any collector needed. It also did not help that by this time Ufer had an inflated notion of what his paintings were worth. Ufer's only choice was to approach Klauer and the Bank, "I have

[1] $400 in 1928 would be equal to $5888 in 2019.

[2] Ditlev Frederiksen to Mary Ufer, 28 May 1929, UPUNDSG.

[3] Walter Ufer to William Klauer, 13 October 1929, KFPUND.

to refinance myself again and I want to come back to you again. I would like to have you lend me $5000 and on the same basis as before—only I am sure that I can pay it in full much earlier than before."[4]

Ufer's letter must have been a big surprise to Klauer. Two years earlier Ufer had paid off his notes and his future looked promising. In fact, according to a letter between the two, Klauer believed Ufer should be building "a castle of your own from your own income."[5] Klauer's son was also building him a home, a mansion at 700 West 7th Street in Dubuque. At the same time, Blumenschein, Joseph Fleck, E. Martin Hennings, Irving Couse, Nicolai Fechin, and several other Taos artists had made their commitment to Taos by building new or modifying existing homes and taking up residence year-round. Taos finally had electricity, running water and a modern sanitary system. Walter Ufer was not in this same position. He had driven his wife from town. He couldn't give her a future. He had flushed Mary's dream of a home and life together, down drains and slot machines, literally and figuratively.

How could Klauer react to Ufer's request to borrow yet more money—this time for $5000?[6] How could he approach the bank with another request, particularly when Ufer had so much difficulty paying earlier loans off in a timely manner? How could the bank make another loan at a time the world was facing the worse depression in history? How much could Klauer's friendship with Ufer withstand? It would never be more severely tested than with the events which followed between October 1929 and Ufer's death on August 2, 1936.

Each time Ufer wrote to Klauer requesting more funds, he was forced to commit additional paintings as collateral. A typical transaction saw Ufer sending four paintings to retire the outstanding $500 debt to Klauer. In October, Ufer promised Klauer "some paintings from New York" that would "be good ones."[7] Unlike early transactions, when Ufer pressed Klauer to accept paintings that didn't interest him, the patron was more selective. Klauer finally settled on *Talpa* [fig. 73], *Evening Rays, Looking North* [fig. 63] and *Thanksgiving Time* [fig. 87], paintings Ufer valued for about $4000.[8]

Even though Klauer had his own financial concerns and rushed to Chicago "on account of the terrible condition of situation," he could not let his friend down. Klauer instructed Ufer to send his "old chattel mortgage immediately." Ufer had sent the document on two earlier occasions. Again, the Union Trust & Savings Bank and Klauer were willing to take yet another chance on the artist.[9] Beginning in January 1930, Ufer opened his tour in Houston, followed by a schedule far more ambitious than he had proposed to Klauer.[10]

FINAL LOAN AND EXHIBITION TOUR, 1930

On November 11, 1929, Klauer reported to Ufer that, after using "a lot of pressure," he had secured from the bank $3000 of the $5000 requested. As soon as Ufer signed the "two notes and the mortgage," Klauer committed to sending a personal check for the additional $2000. Unbelievably, even after Klauer assured Ufer that he would receive the full $5000, a desperate Walter wrote by return mail,

---

[4] Ibid.

[5] Walter Ufer to William Klauer, 16 October 1929, KFPUND.

[6] $5000 in 1930 would be equal to $75,363 in 2019.

[7] Walter Ufer to William Klauer, Western Union Telegram, 18 October 1929, KFPUND.

[8] Ufer priced *Talpa* at $1300, and *Evening Rays* and *Looking North* at $800. While there is no record for *Thanksgiving Time*, an estimate of about $2000 seems reasonable.

[9] William Klauer to Walter Ufer, 1 November 1929, KFPUND.

[10] Walter Ufer to William Klauer, November 1929, KFPUND.

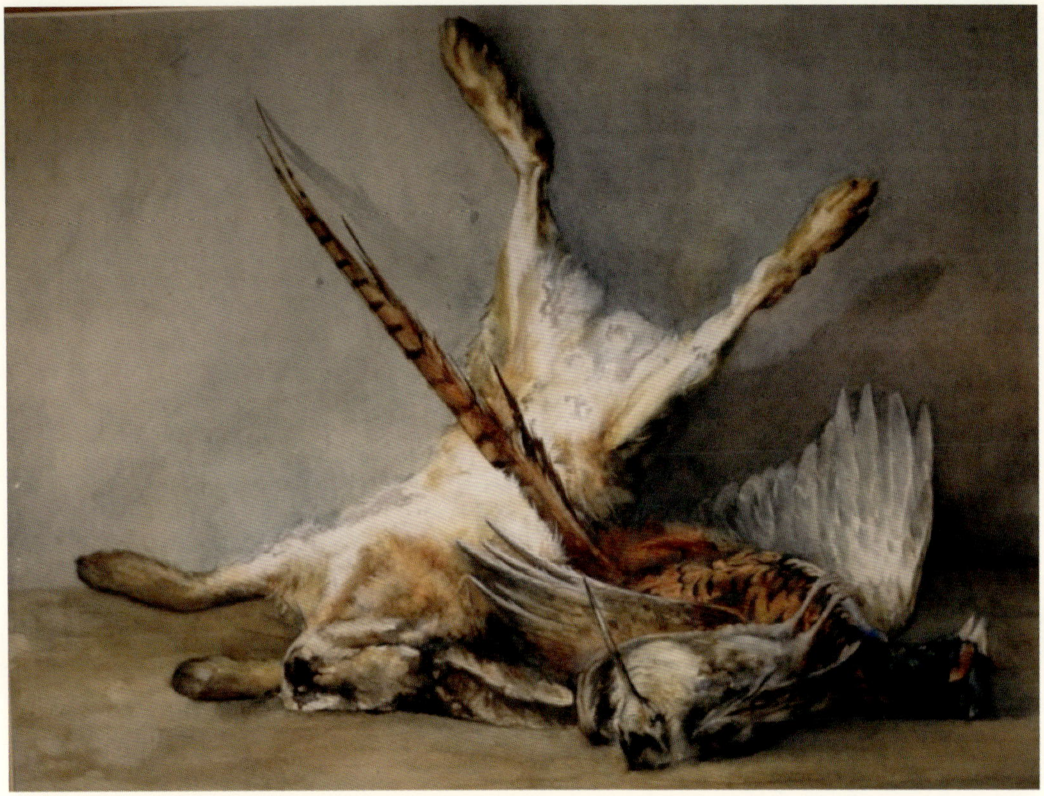

Figure 90. Walter Ufer. *Rabbit, Pheasant and Woodcock*, 1896. Watercolor on paper mounted on board, 18 x 22 inches. Collection Klauer Manufacturing Company.

"just on account of the Stock Market which is bad & the people who generally put their extra money in Art Objects, and have not been buying much this year—I need that extra $2000 much. Please do this, I have had to ask for credit this summer for Frames, Express, Etc., and these people are now asking for their money."[11]

Working on credit, Ufer had already committed a significant percentage of the $5000 he had requested. To show Klauer his appreciation, Ufer gave his patron another painting—*Rabbit, Pheasant and Woodcock* [fig. 90], a watercolor he had created in Europe nearly thirty-five years earlier. Even though it is tempting to minimize the artistic value of the gift because of its nineteenth-century style and subject matter, it was appropriate for the avid fisherman and hunter. Ufer must have believed that Klauer would be able to find a suitable spot in his home or cottage for a painting that illustrated the fruits of his hobbies.

Despite the modest travel itinerary Ufer proposed to Klauer in his letters at the end of 1929, entries in his ledger described a far more ambitious trip. Between January and September of 1930 his travels saw him in Houston, San Antonio, Chicago, New York, Washington, D.C., back to Chicago, and returning to New York for June, July, August, and part of September before returning to Taos. Other than the Houston Museum of Fine Arts, there is no record that he had other exhibitions during this eight-month period.[12]

[11] Walter Ufer to William Klauer, 15 November 1929, UPUNDSG.

[12] William Klauer to Walter Ufer, 15 November 1929. KFPUND. According to Ufer's ledger entries, he received $1000 on October 23 and $2000 in December from Klauer. The remaining $2000 does not appear in the ledger.

On the surface, it appears as though Ufer was experiencing a last hurrah. Even though he stayed at the finest hotels, the total cost being $967.34, his ledger for 1930 shows that he sold nine paintings for a total of $7,725.[13] The Houston Museum of Fine Arts purchased a portrait of Jim Mirabal for $2500 and Erwin Barrie and Grand Central Art Galleries continued strong support of Ufer, selling paintings for $1750.

In all likelihood, by the time Ufer returned to Taos, he had spent all or most of the $5000 loan from Klauer and Union Trust & Savings Bank. After 1930, there would be no more major sales or large-scale loans from Dubuque. From that point, Ufer joined the way of life of Higgins and other poverty-stricken Taos artists. He would live on the few dollars he earned from teaching young students and sporadic sales from the Work Progress Administration in 1934 as well as the munificence of William Klauer.

THE KLAUERS AND THE JULIEN HOTEL

While Ufer was experiencing what turned out to be his "grand finale"—a desperate attempt to save himself, the Klauers were taking advantage of the Great Depression. In addition to building a home, they took occupancy of Mather Cottage on Grand Island, Michigan, and added the Julien Hotel [fig. 91] to their portfolio, thus saving it from bankruptcy. Once a magnificent hotel, the Julien had been reduced to a state of ruin due to mismanagement and fraud. Over the next three decades the Klauers returned it to a state of luxury, making it the place for travelers to stay in the city. Because of their purchase, they also brought ownership of the hotel back to Dubuque. The purchase "diversified Klauers" investments away from manufacturing.

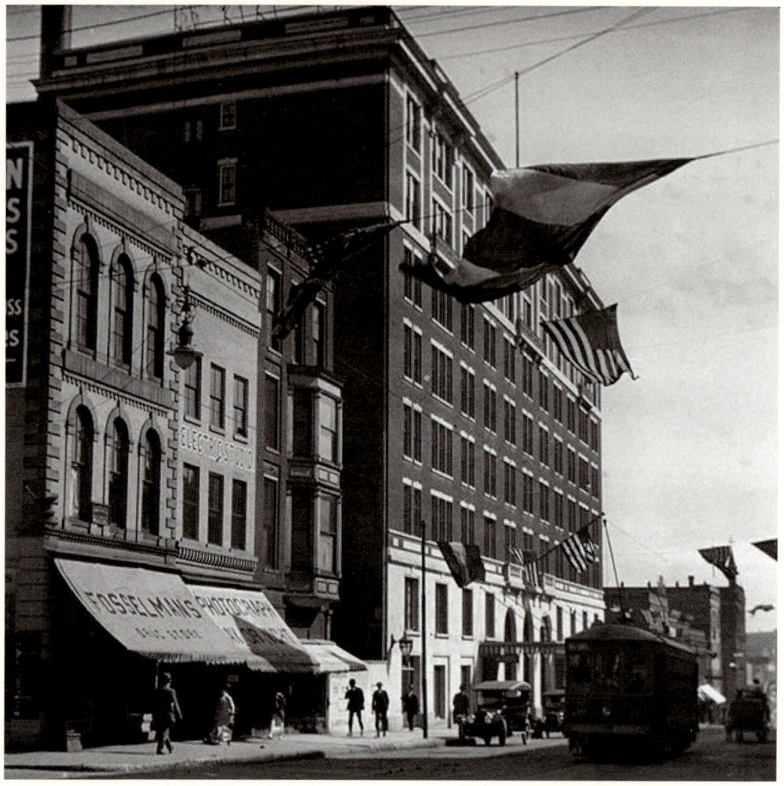

Figure 91.
Rev. H. J. Loemker. *The Hotel Julien and Fosselman's Drugstore*, 1915.
Glass plate.
Rev. H.J. Loemker Collection,
Loras College,
Center for Dubuque History.

[13] Walter Ufer's Ledger of Income and Expenses, 1926-1931. UPUNDSG.

Historically, the Julien Hotel was an integral part of the fabric of Dubuque's history. It was built in 1839 and called the Waples House after a wealthy Dubuque merchant. In 1854, it was enlarged, remodeled, and renamed Julien Hotel after the community's founder Julien Dubuque. After a devastating fire in 1913, it was reopened in 1915, and after years of a sordid history, purchased by the Klauers in 1930. Over the years the hotel had hosted famous guests, notably Abraham Lincoln, "Buffalo Bill" Cody, and Mark Twain—even the notorious Al Capone.[14] The Klauers maintained ownership of the hotel until 1962 when it was sold. By then, the hotel's reputation had been returned to its former greatness.

Most important, however, the Klauers established two rooms where Ufer's paintings could be seen. Klauer's collection of Ufer paintings would increase dramatically in numbers during the 1930s. Klauer's son, William J. Klauer became the hotel's manager and assisted his father in attempting to sell some of the artist's paintings. While no records have survived documenting sales, the Klauers made an exerted effort to liquidate the large inventory that had been accumulated in Dubuque. Between 1932 and 1934, more than a dozen paintings changed title from the artist to his patron. With father and son selling paintings, and with a clientele wealthy enough to purchase art, Ufer couldn't ask for better representation.

BILL KLAUER BUILDS A HOME FOR HIS FATHER

The Klauers needed a retreat to replace their stolen Taos cottage, so the family had begun taking annual trips to Grand Island, Michigan. At the same time, Bill Klauer began building a home for his father on 500 West 7th Street [fig. 92]. Located on the highest bluff and overlooking downtown Dubuque, the stately home was a handsome environment for paintings by Ufer, Higgins, Hennings, Blumenschein, and the other American artists Klauer had been purchasing from Grand Central Art Galleries since 1923. They would be joined with over a thousand German steins collected by William's brother, Alphonse Klauer [fig. 93] as well as a fabulous Tiffany lamp [fig. 94] and other fine decorative arts. The Klauer home became a veritable museum.

Klauer's biggest problem was hanging and rehanging paintings as Ufer needed them for exhibitions. A large wall in the home's living room was the wall where the Klauers hung their favorite paintings by Ufer. The study was the room where Klauer hung his paintings by Victor Higgins.

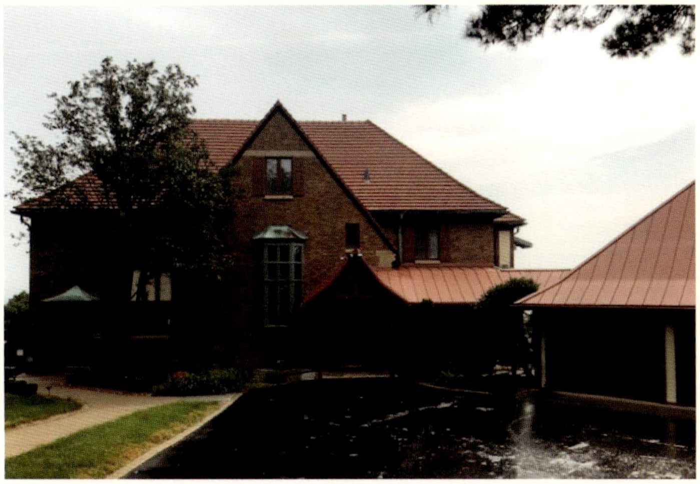

Figure 92.
The Klauer Home, Dubuque. Photo courtesy of the author and Michael Wright.

[14] "Julien Hotel," *Encyclopedia Dubuque*, accessed July 1, 2018. http://www.encyclopediadubuque.org/index.php?title=HOTEL_JULIEN_DUBUQUE

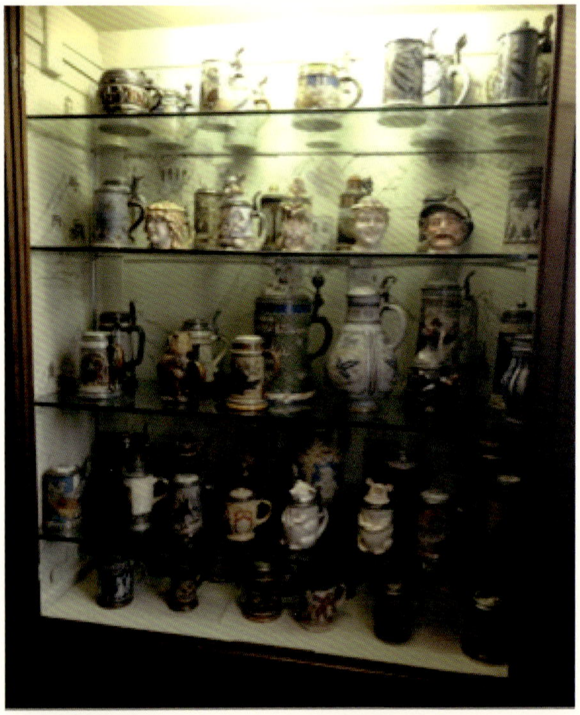

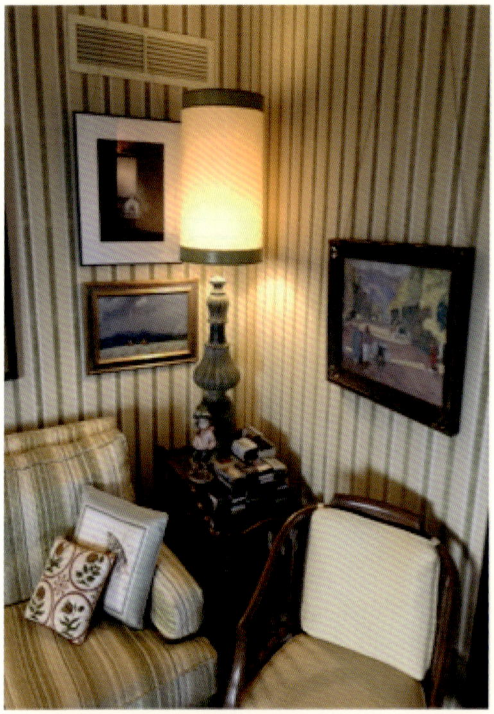

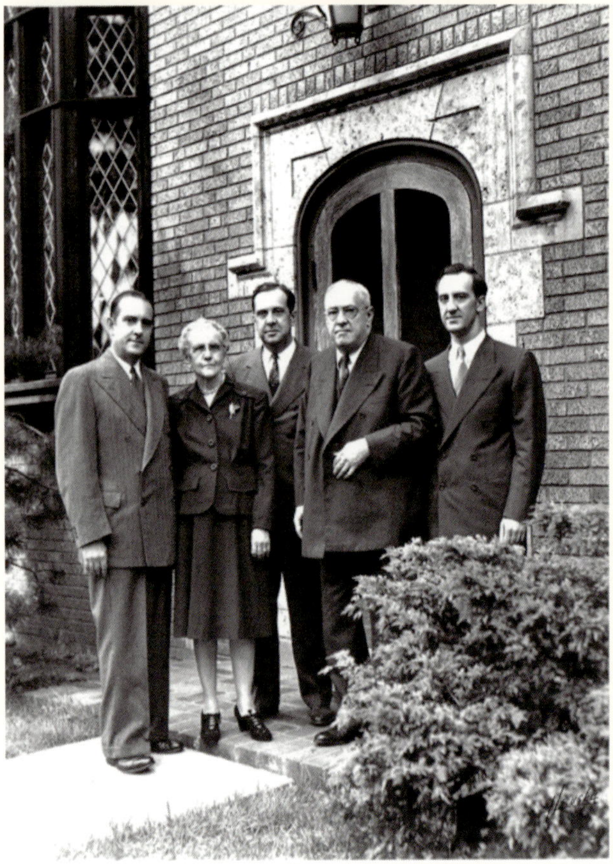

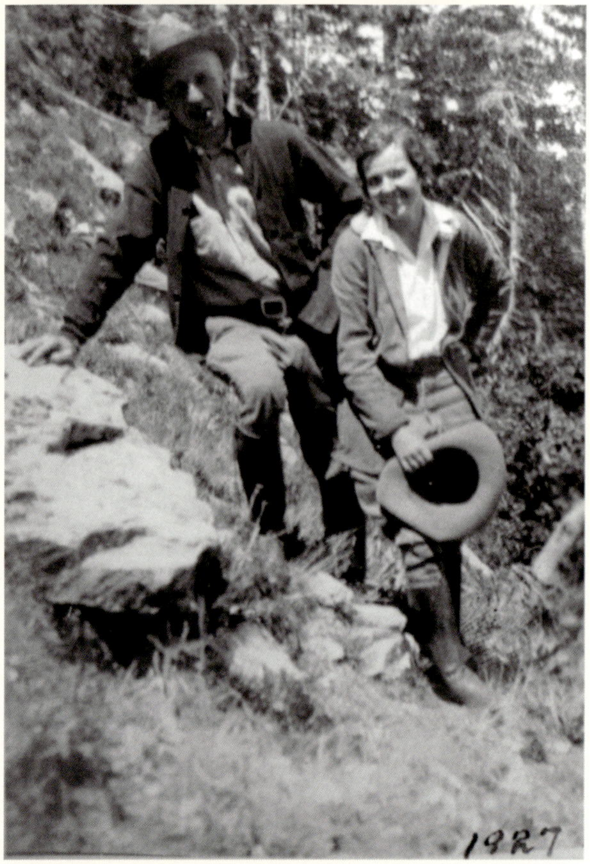

Figures 93 and 94. The Klauer Family's collection of German steins (top left) and paintings by Hennings and Blumenschein (top right).

Figure 95. *Members of the Klauer Family*, 1940s. [left to right: Alphonse Klauer, Mrs. Klauer, Walter J. Klauer, William H. Klauer, and William J. Klauer] (bottom left). Photo courtesy Klauer Family.

Figure 96. *Dorothy and John Brandenberg*, 1927 (bottom right). Photo courtesy Mrs. Dorothy Brenner.

THE BRANDENBURGS VISIT WILLIAM KLAUER

From his first appearance in Taos, Klauer had developed a large group of friends. Besides the artists and other Taos notables in the business world, he befriended a young lawyer and his bride —Jack and Dorothy Brandenburg [fig. 96]. Dorothy was the daughter of Oscar Berninghaus, one of the founding members of the Taos Society of Artists. When the couple married in 1927, they received two gifts from Victor Higgins, a small oil sketch for a painting now hanging in the Amarillo Public Library, and the shotgun Higgins had received in partial payment for a painting from William Klauer.[15]

Dorothy remembered Klauer fondly, "Oh, Bill Klauer. He was really a character. He'd come out to Taos every once in a while. When he bought all that land out here…Floyd Butler was the attorney. Bill would always call Floyd and say that he was coming and he'd say, 'Floyd, get plenty of groceries in the house because I want to cook.' He was a great cook." According to Barbara Brenner, Klauer and Butler may have shopped for groceries at Sisneros. "So Klauer would go to Margaret and Floyd's house and he'd cook up all this meal and he'd say…Now, Margaret and Floyd, go invite some of your friends to come over and we will have tuna with a lot of drink on the side. He loved his drink."[16]

It wasn't unusual for Klauer's Taos friends to visit him in Dubuque. Dorothy spoke of a wonderful visit that she and Jack had in Klauer's home on West 7th Street [fig. 92]. After Klauer's son built the home for his father, the Brandenburgs, joined by the Butlers, traveled north on "a little football trip." In Dubuque, they visited the Klauers and stayed at the Julien Hotel. When Klauer came to pick the four of them up to take out to dinner, he said, "By the way, I hope you like your accommodations at the hotel." We responded, "Oh yes we like them just fine." He then asked what rooms they were in. "So, we described the two rooms."[17] Apparently the rooms were not acceptable to Klauer, and he had them moved to the Presidential Suite. By the time they got back from dinner, the hotel staff had all their clothes hung up just the way they were before—their toothbrushes out and their beds turned down.

After dinner, everyone went back to Klauer's house because they had to see his liquor cellar.[18] Dorothy described the cellar in great detail. "I've been down in it and Bill picked one bottle out, and he blew the dust off of it and gave Margaret and me each a pint bottle of the finest bourbon. He got it all during the Prohibition when they had to get rid of this warehouse. So, he bought the liquor and converted the whole basement…here it was…it was big. The whole thing just lined with bottles. And they had been there awhile because you had to blow the dust off them. It made it a little attractive."[19] Besides the rows of bottles, there were also several boxes of uncorked liquors stacked in the room [fig. 97].

While Dorothy didn't speak about it, she would have seen the Taos Room [fig. 98] that Klauer incorporated into his new home. Klauer was so fascinated by the art, architecture and culture of Northern New Mexico that he went a step further than hanging paintings by Ufer, Higgins and Hennings. When the

---

[15] The Brandenburg's' friendship with Klauer began in the late 1920s and is well documented in the author's interview with Dorothy and her daughter Barbara Brenner (October 12, 1994). Dorothy, in her early 90s, recalled life in Taos in exacting detail. I am only sorry that I couldn't have written Dorothy Brandenburg's Taos as the picture she painted made us feel like we were riding horseback down Pueblo Road, our animal kicking up dust. She had an excellent grasp of the various personalities that brought life to the "mud town.'"Certainly, her acquaintance with William Klauer merits a chapter.

[16] Dorothy Brandenburg and Barbara Brenner interview with Dean A. Porter and Teresa Hayes Ebie, 12 October 1994. Porter Archives, Couse/Sharp Foundation Archives, Taos.

[17] Ibid.

[18] In the early 1990s, Klauer's son invited the author to the Klauer home to see paintings and the family's legendary liquor cellar.

[19] Dorothy Brandenburg and Barbara Brenner interview with Dean A. Porter and Teresa Hayes Ebie, 12 October 1994. Porter Archives, Couse/Sharp Foundation Archives, Taos.

Klauers built their new home, they included an adobe room complete with *vigas*, *hornos* (fireplace), white painted walls, and a tiled floor carpeted with an Indian rug making one feel like they had been transported back to Taos, New Mexico.

Dorothy recalled one humorous story that merits mentioning. It was a trip Bill made with "a great friend who was a director on the Santa Fe Railroad"—possibly William Haskell Simpson, General Advertising Manager and a major patron of Taos artists. The two had gotten together in the Blackstone Hotel in Chicago. Klauer intended on spending only two nights in Chicago before returning to Dubuque, when on the spur of a moment, they decided to go to Taos. "...so, they got on the train and both got drunk and went to sleep. And instead of getting off to go to Santa Fe, they went all the way to California. They had to turn around and come back, and by that time they'd sobered up and came up to Taos."[20]

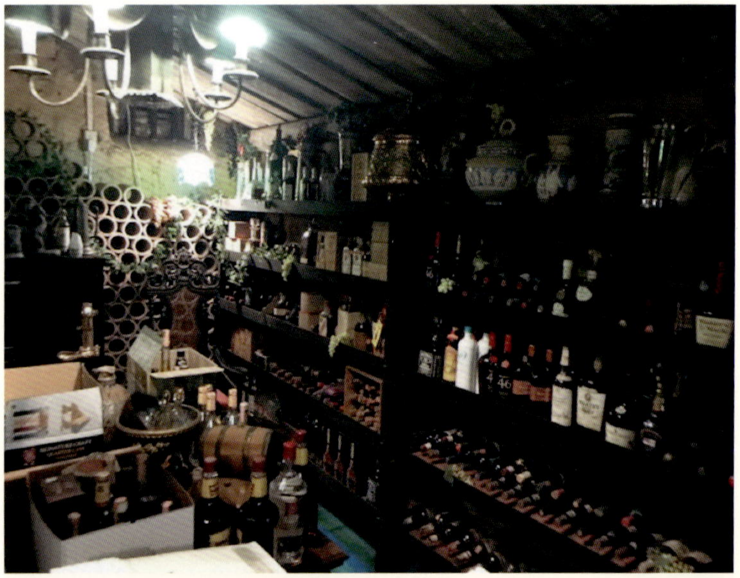

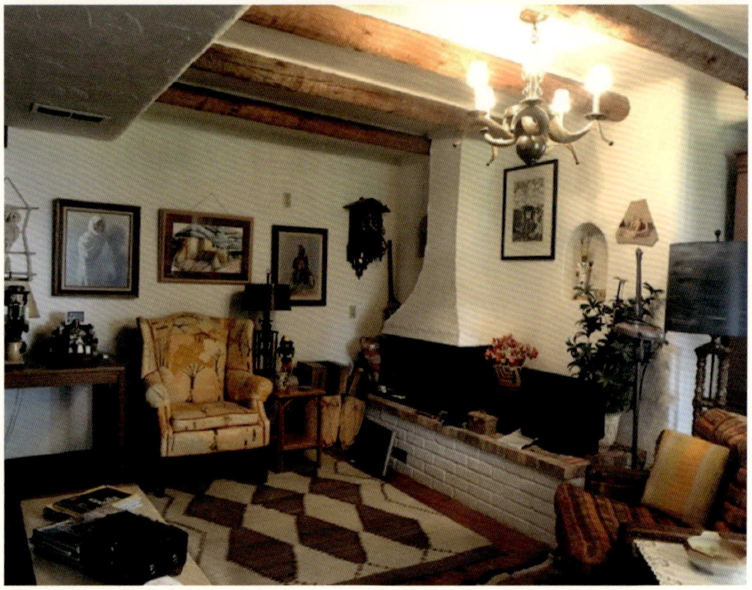

Figures 97 and 98.
The Klauer Wine Cellar (top) and *Taos Room, Klauer Home, Dubuque* (bottom).
Photos courtesy of the author.

[20] Ibid.

THE MATHER-KLAUER LODGE, GRAND ISLAND, MICHIGAN

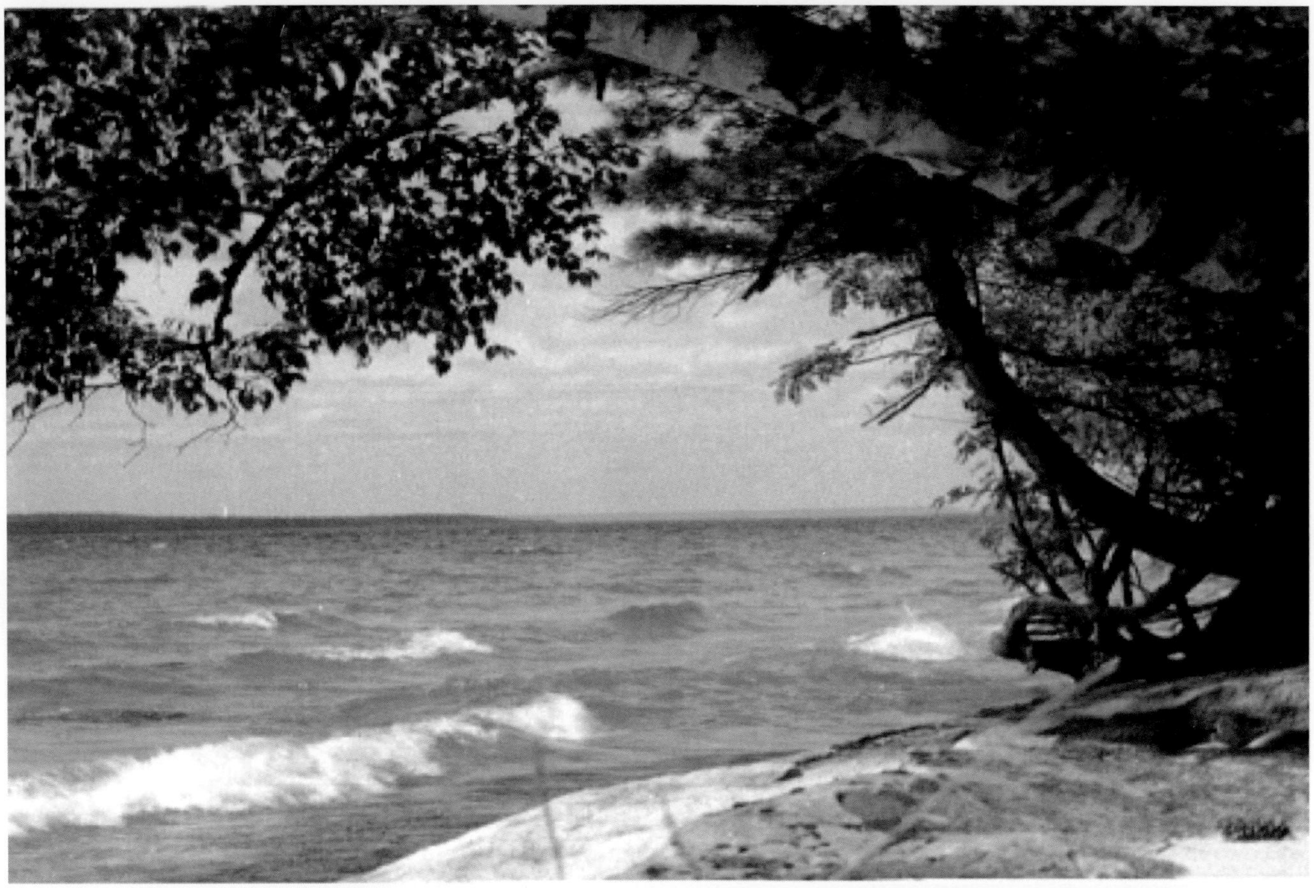

Figure 99. *Grand Island, Michigan*. Photo courtesy Klauer Family.

For over fifteen years, William Klauer travelled over 1100 miles to reach his cottage located south of Taos, New Mexico. Even before his cottage was stolen, Klauer and family members had been visiting Grand Island, Michigan, approximately 400 miles from Dubuque. Grand Island satisfied the family's (his sons Walter J. and William J. inclusive) need to live on a relatively untamed, remote island. Grand Island was located a boat ride away from Munising, Michigan, on Lake Superior, and was relatively easy to reach from Dubuque, but only after riding on several forms of transportation. Like Taos, Grand Island had a long history; among its earlier inhabitants was the Ojibwa culture. As with Taos, Mother Nature had blessed Grand Island with a scenic landscape—13,500 acres of dense woodland, thirty-five miles of shoreline, several lakes, and breath-taking views.

Like his Taos cottage, Grand Island became a vital part of Klauer family life. It was remote yet close enough for Klauer to spend several months there annually. Prior to Klauer's first visits to the Island, owner William Gwinn Mather, an important Midwestern industrialist and President of the Cleveland Cliffs Iron Company (CCI), "had taken steps to preserve the island's beauty and natural state [fig. 99]." The company had purchased much of Grand Island from Abraham Williams in 1901 for the sum of $93,701.61, with the intention of developing "a vacation and hunting paradise" for "the hunting pleasure of company executives and their guests."[21] Mather fenced off the northern portion of the island for

[21] "The Mather-Klauer Lodge Grand Island Heritage Research and Interpretive Center," material provided by Klauer Family.

imported animals like elk, antelope and caribou. According to Klauer's son, John Rush, who worked for Land and Real Estate, introduced his father to Mather.

Abraham Williams was the first American to take up permanent residence on the island, and he farmed the land and built several structures, including a sawmill, cabins, a blacksmith's shop and a trading post. As Grand Island was heavily forested with hardwood, Williams financed his operations by selling it to passing ships. When Mather acquired Williams's home, he had it saved and it became part "of a hotel in the Mather resort area."

In 1901, Mather constructed what is known today as the Mather-Klauer Lodge [fig. 100].[22] The lodge was "originally built as a personal cottage for Mather. The original lodge, built by George Leiphart, featured a significant addition in 1911, designed by the Marquette-based architectural firm of Charlton and Kuenzli. The Mather-Klauer Lodge was described as a 'primitive but comfortable,' six-bedroom cottage."[23]

Grand Island proved to be an ideal retreat for William Klauer from the beginning. According to Klauer's son, the family purchased Mather Lodge about 1930 after staying in cabins and the Old Lighthouse, located on the East Channel of the Island during their earlier retreats to the island. After building his New Mexico cottage, Klauer knew what was required for him to be happy on Grand Island.[24]

When Klauer traveled to Grand Island, he had a "faithful companion" in Frank Wild, a person dedicated to his every need. As Klauer's son stated, "he [Wild] was a personal helper, cook, housekeeper, handyman. He was everything. Without him my dad could never have spent the days, weeks, and months

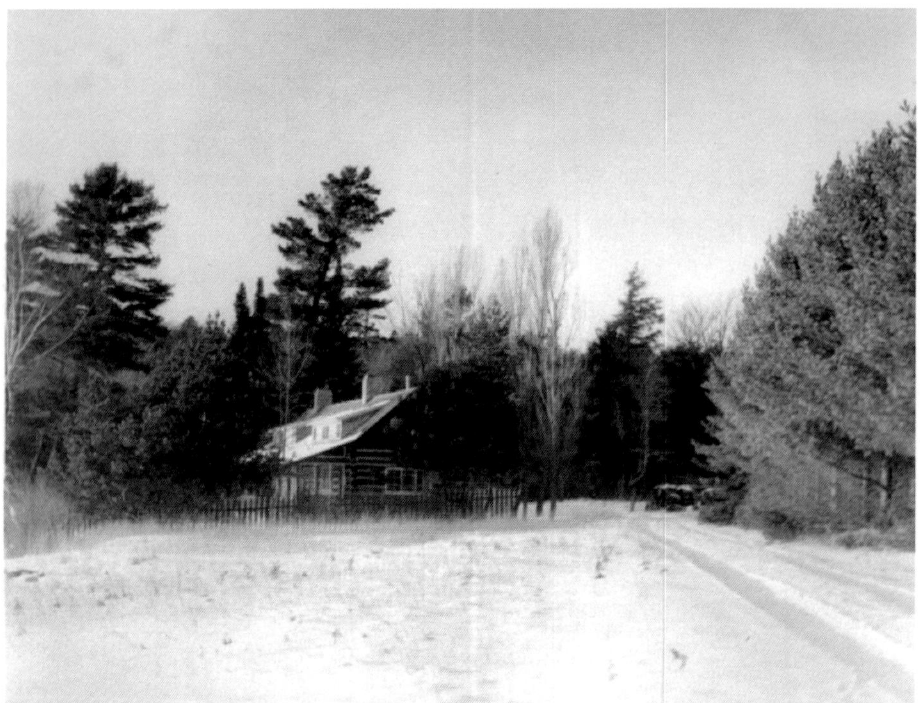

Figure 100.
Mather-Klauer Lodge,
Grand Island, Michigan.
Photo courtesy Klauer Family.

[22] Ibid.
[23] Ibid.
[24] Ibid.

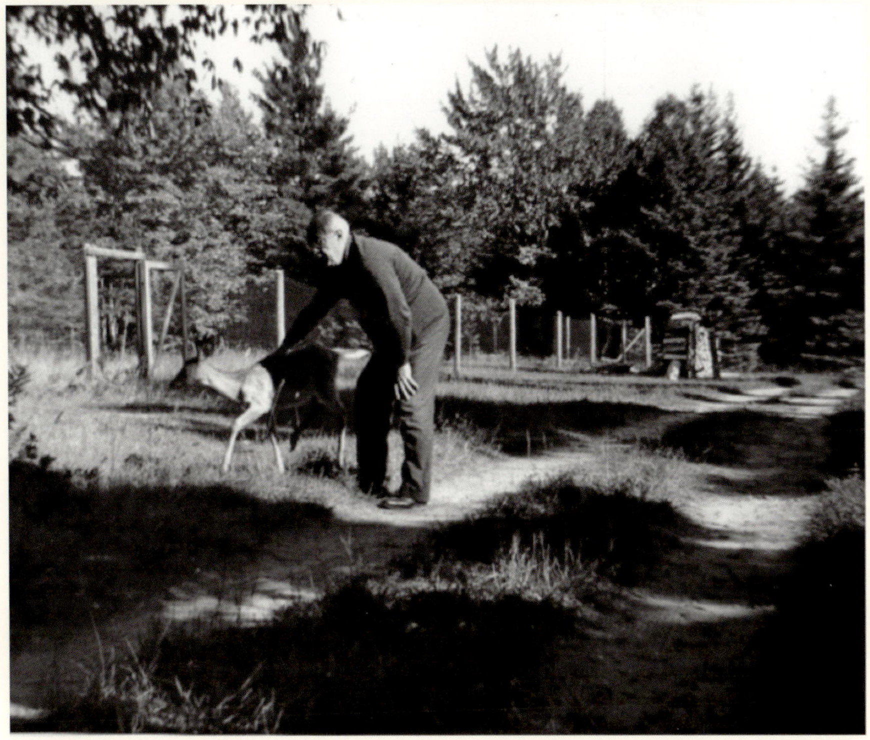

Figure 101.
William H. Klauer Enjoying Grand Island 'Neighbors.'
Photo courtesy Klauer Family.

he spent up there." During his later years, the senior Klauer had a heart problem and a weakness in his legs. "He could walk, but he tired easily."[25] While Ufer was Klauer's "man" when he was at the Taos cottage, Wild was his right-hand man for the Grand Island cottage. In a sense, Frank Wild served Klauer in the same way that Ufer served his patron in Taos.

His son recalled walking around the island with his father. "My dad was a hunter. I was a hunter, but it was such a joy to walk around and see the deer [fig. 101]. There were so many deer on Grand Island you couldn't believe. Many a day I would walk around with a gun and never would even point it at a deer." [26]

The records show that after occupying the lodge "seasonally," Klauer had alterations and additions made to accommodate his lifestyle. The family occupied the lodge until William's death in 1952. At that time, they simply walked away from the lodge. According to Bill Klauer, it remained in the possession of caretaker John Lezotte, and his wife Nona and their family until 2012.[27]

The lodge was well-used during Klauer's lifetime. Like Taos, he would invite friends from all walks of life...a former mayor of the second largest city in America, the chief operating officer of a major meat packing firm, the head of a hotel, a state senator, former syndicate members, lawyers, a banking officer from Taos, food critic (Duncan Hinds), nationally known artists, and anyone Klauer chose to invite to his table [fig. 102]. "Louis Murphy, the U. S. Senator from Iowa, was a frequent visitor at Dad's cottage."[28] Sessions with Klauer were always joyous affairs. Everyone welcomed an invitation.

---

[25] William J. Klauer interview with Dean Porter, 1993.

[26] Ibid.

[27] Bill Klauer interview with Dean Porter, 2017.

[28] Ibid.

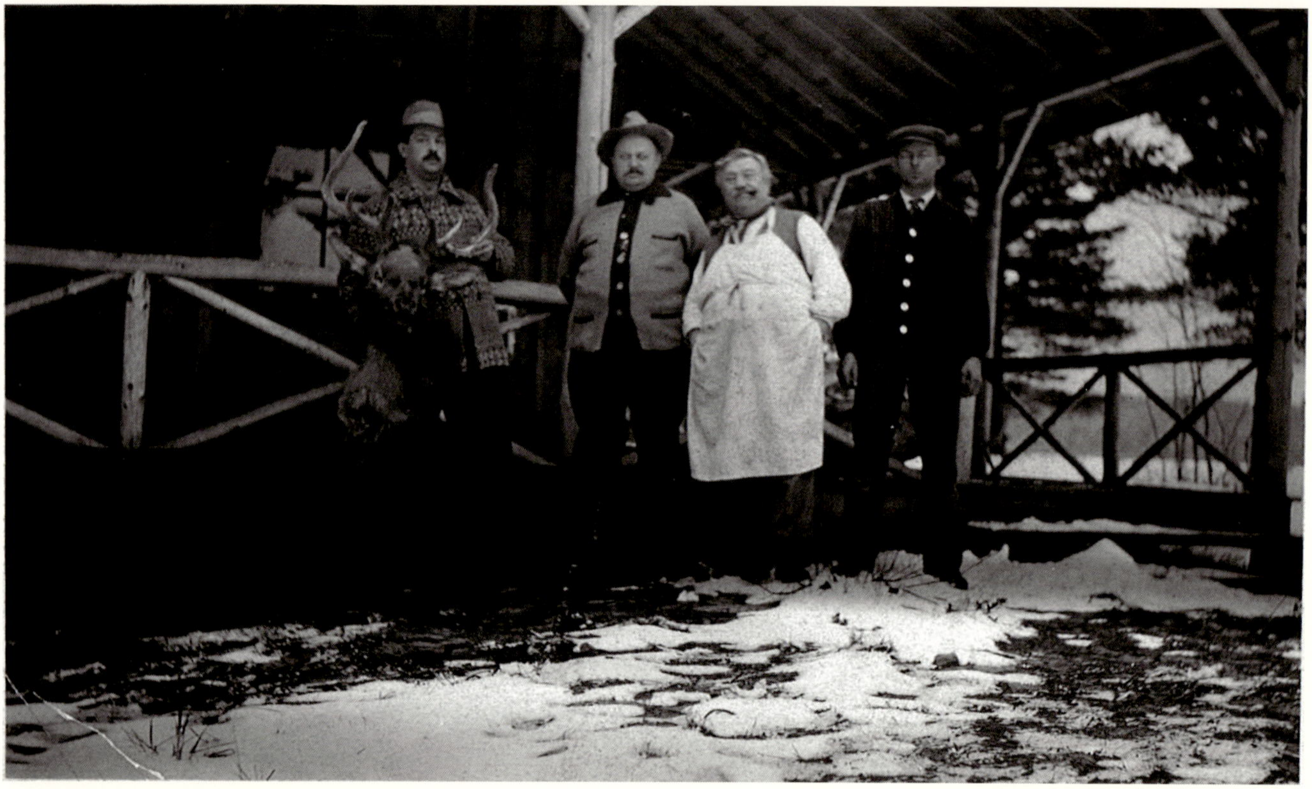

Figure 102. *Otto Demme and William Klauer with Friends.*
Photo courtesy of University of Notre Dame Archives, Klauer Family Papers.

This undated photograph shows Klauer with friends as well former syndicate member Otto Demme, who proudly displays a large rack of an animal he bagged as well as a chef (probably Frank Wild) wearing a white apron.

Klauer was a "jolly person who loved his friends." In his rotundity, he projected quite an image as he bellowed, "Hi ya. Nice that you could come up. Join us for a few days or whatever."[29] He enjoyed having his friends show up in numbers, those with and without invitations. No one was asked or wanted to leave.

Klauer spent week after week in his cottage. He usually arrived in November, staying two to three months—maybe longer. He would return to Dubuque to take care of business. Following his return, he stayed home until business necessitated a trip to Chicago, or until the approach of hunting season, or the urge to return to Grand Island. He was absent so many months from Klauer Manufacturing Company, one might question how the company was so successful. For over 140 years, Klauer Manufacturing Company prospered because of the dedication of every family member—father, sons, grandsons. At least one family member always remained at home running the business.

On Grand Island, Frank Wild knew where to find fresh vegetables, white fish or trout. Frank's friend, John Lezotte, knew all the fishing boats and who owned them. He would buy the catch of the day when the vessels passed by the island. Klauer designated a day each week to shop in Munising. They would take their "old jalopy of a car to the point," where a flag was hung indicating they wanted to be picked up. Within a half an hour or so, a boat would stop and pick them up, taking them to the Michigan

[29] William J. Klauer interview with Dean Porter, KFPUND. The Klauer Family is currently funding the restoration of the Mather/Klauer Cottage.

shoreline where they boarded their Dubuque car and motored to Munising to fill their mile-long shopping list. "Then a stop at the ice house to get 100 pounds of ice. We had a huge freezer. Old time ice and salt, loaded with meats of every description."[30] Of course, Klauer could also count on his good friend Oscar Mayer to send meat such as a deer, sausages, sturgeon, a Westphalian style ham, and more. Klauer and his guests were always treated to the finest of meals—always a feast.

Eventually Klauer acquired a fifty-foot boat, equipped with two fishing seats, a Mathews Twin Screw, a central cabin and sleeping quarters for six or more.[31] It was named "The Snogo" after a snow remover Klauer Manufacturing Company developed in 1925. It could take people to the mainland or on fishing trips around the "beautiful Picture Rocks' near Munising."[32] They had a captain who lived on the boat, mooring it wherever convenient. In the winter, the boat went into "hibernation," moving to Florida where Klauer's son Walter "used it to entertain."[33]

When Klauer wasn't entertaining his friends, Frank chauffeured him so he could visit others who lived on the Island. One of the neighbors was the Beich family who were makers of the famous candies. "Seems like, even though our cottage was somewhat remote, you could expect anyone to drop in for a visit, John Lezotte, John Bush (Cleveland Cliffs land agent), neighbors, the lighthouse keeper with semi-weekly visits, or Old Jim the next door neighbor who was very elderly and lived alone but appreciated a good meal, friends from home or anywhere."[34]

In the first decade of the twentieth century, Carter Harrison was the magnet that attracted artists and friends to New Mexico. Following the dissolution of the syndicate, Klauer assumed the role of bringing artists and friends to his cottages—first in Taos and then Grand Island. In fact, Klauer made the Mather-Klauer cottage available to his friends even when he wasn't there to serve as host.

Grand Island was ideal for those who enjoyed hunting and consuming good food and drink. As there was no electricity, the cottage's freezer was filled with the fruits of the hunt, the catch of the day, the shipment of meat from Oscar Mayer, and, of course, ice. Weekly trips to Munising, Michigan, with a shopping list were intended to keep the freezer crammed with food. For William Klauer and his friends, there would never be enough food for the ten to fifteen visitors who vacationed and hunted with Klauer.

The Mather-Klauer Cottage was key to the lasting friendships of Klauer, Oscar Mayer, Carter Harrison, Otto Demme and others who had enjoyed close relationships since the early teens. During World War II, Klauer and his friends spent long periods of time on Grand Island hunting. A series of letters between Klauer and Oscar Mayer document the continuing relationship between the former members of Harrison's syndicate.

On December 1, 1942, Mayer wrote to Klauer, describing a hunting trip he, Carter Harrison and his son, took on Grand Island. Despite a huge snowstorm, the Harrison's and Mayer's hunt was not hampered. Mayer wrote, "I will say for seasons there have been five deer on the island, there are now six. We got two nice bucks weighing 160 and 175 pounds. My license I took the liberty of hanging on to your buck which will be shipped to you by John Lezotte," and "I wish to thank you for the kind offering

---

[30] Ibid.
[31] Ibid.
[32] Ibid.
[33] Ibid.
[34] Ibid.

of your nice lodge." Unfortunately, the buck never reached Klauer.[35] The Klauer-Mayer close friendship continued, usually featuring gifts of meat, "a hunk of venison and a few sausages...sturgeon, ham and a few pounds of sausage," shipped to Munising.[36]

On December 9, 1944, Oscar wrote to "Billy," after having returned to Grand Island Lodge "with the Harrisons." Oscar complained, "bucks were few. Of course, I hadn't fired a shot in the last five years now—yet I enjoy the Island and the evening sittings, and, of course, the talk by the Harrisons."[37] A few days later Mayer wrote another letter, this time to "Bilenski." Mayer was sending by express "a saddle from Carter and a piece of a deer leg from our buck. Am also sending a few varieties of sausage which accept with my compliments."[38]

William Henry Klauer continued to spend months, entertaining friends on Grand Island until his death in 1952. Oscar wrote to Bill on Grand Island in September 1947. As usual he sent meat, in this instance a ham. Mayer had spoken to "King John Bush," who had reported that Klauer was "looking well and very fit."[39] A year later, Congressman Charles E. Potter, wrote to Klauer, "the high-light of our recent

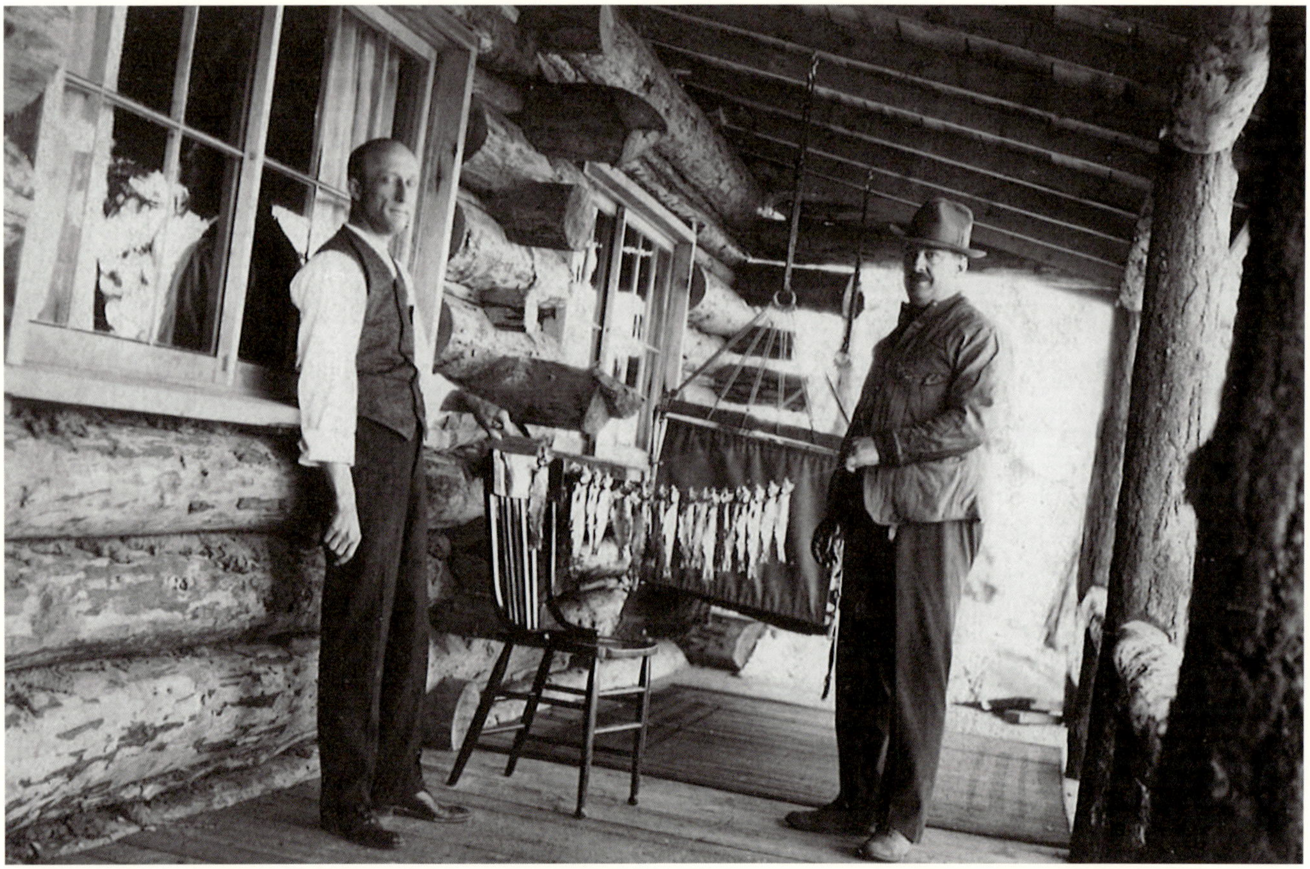

Figure 103. *Bert Barker (left) and William Klauer (right).*
Photo courtesy of University of Notre Dame Archives, Klauer Family Papers.

[35] Oscar Mayer to William Klauer, 1 December 1942, KFPUND.
[36] Oscar Mayer to William Klauer, 2 August 1943, KFPUND.
[37] Oscar Mayer to William Klauer, 9 December 1944, KFPUND.
[38] Oscar Mayer to William Klauer, 13 December 1944, KFPUND.
[39] Oscar Mayer to William Klauer, 3 September 1947, KFPUND.

visit to the Upper Peninsula was the evening that the Senator and his wife and Mrs. Potter and myself spent as your guests."[40]

When William Henry Klauer died in 1952, the family left Grand Island, not to return until 2018. Today, however, that involvement has been revived. In 2001, individuals representing Illinois State University and Hiawatha National Forest initiated the Grand Island Archaeology Research Project. At the center of the project is the rehabilitation of the Mather-Klauer Lodge, turning it "into a working museum that will house archaeologists and students whose goal is to investigate the specific activities of the people who lived on and used the resources of the land.[41] The Klauer family, as they have with other educational institutions in Dubuque and Taos, have taken a leading role in supporting a project that will benefit thousands of students and other visitors to Grand Island.

THE FREIGHTER

After eight months on the road, Ufer returned to Taos in September 1930. As happens with so many artists after a long lull in their career, he returned to his once successful subject matter that offered little challenge. Even though critics had grown sensitized to his themes of the twenties, he needed to create paintings that his followers, including private collectors and jurors, would accept. He had explored subjects like Jim Mirabal as musician, fisherman, model, and gardener repeatedly, but it was Jim working as freighter that seemed to appeal to him most. He painted the theme of Mirabal as a transporter of goods with astonishing frequency.

In 1930, he painted two "freighter" canvases, *The Southwest* [fig. 104] and *Greasewood and Sage* [fig. 106], that would eventually bear the Klauer provenance. Measuring 40-by-50-inches, *The Southwest* was created for juried exhibitions while *Greasewood and Sage*, a 25-by-30-inch canvas was for the private sector. *Greasewood and Sage* was the artist's final 5-by-8-inch card documenting the sale of a painting. It appears as though Ufer, who had maintained such impeccable records, had lost interest as his sales declined. In actuality, Ufer created few, if any, new paintings from 1931 through April 1934.

His trip behind him, he immediately went to work stretching a large canvas. He loaded up his Reo, and leading several horses, drove with Jim Mirabal to his favorite painting spot behind the Mabel Dodge Luhan compound. After staking out the legs of his easel and attaching a cloth over the verso of the canvas to prevent light penetration through, he began to paint.

After he roughed in the composition with a number six, hard lead pencil, he reinforced the design with a turpentine diluted permanent blue pigment. Once it dried, he erased the graphite. He worked from the top to the bottom, dividing the canvas into three sections. Jim can be seen in the foreground, wearing a bright yellow shirt, sitting sidesaddle and riding a brown horse in an arroyo. Following Jim is the familiar white horse loaded with cargo while a brown horse trails behind. On the ledge of the arroyo, Ufer painted two more horses, silhouetting them against the Picuris Mountains and a cloud-filled sky.

[40] Charles E. Potter to William H. Klauer, 25 August 1948, KFPUND.

[41] "Grand Island Archaeology Program," Illinois State University, accessed October 15, 2018, https://about.illinoisstate.edu/jmskibo/Pages/Grand-Island.aspx#top

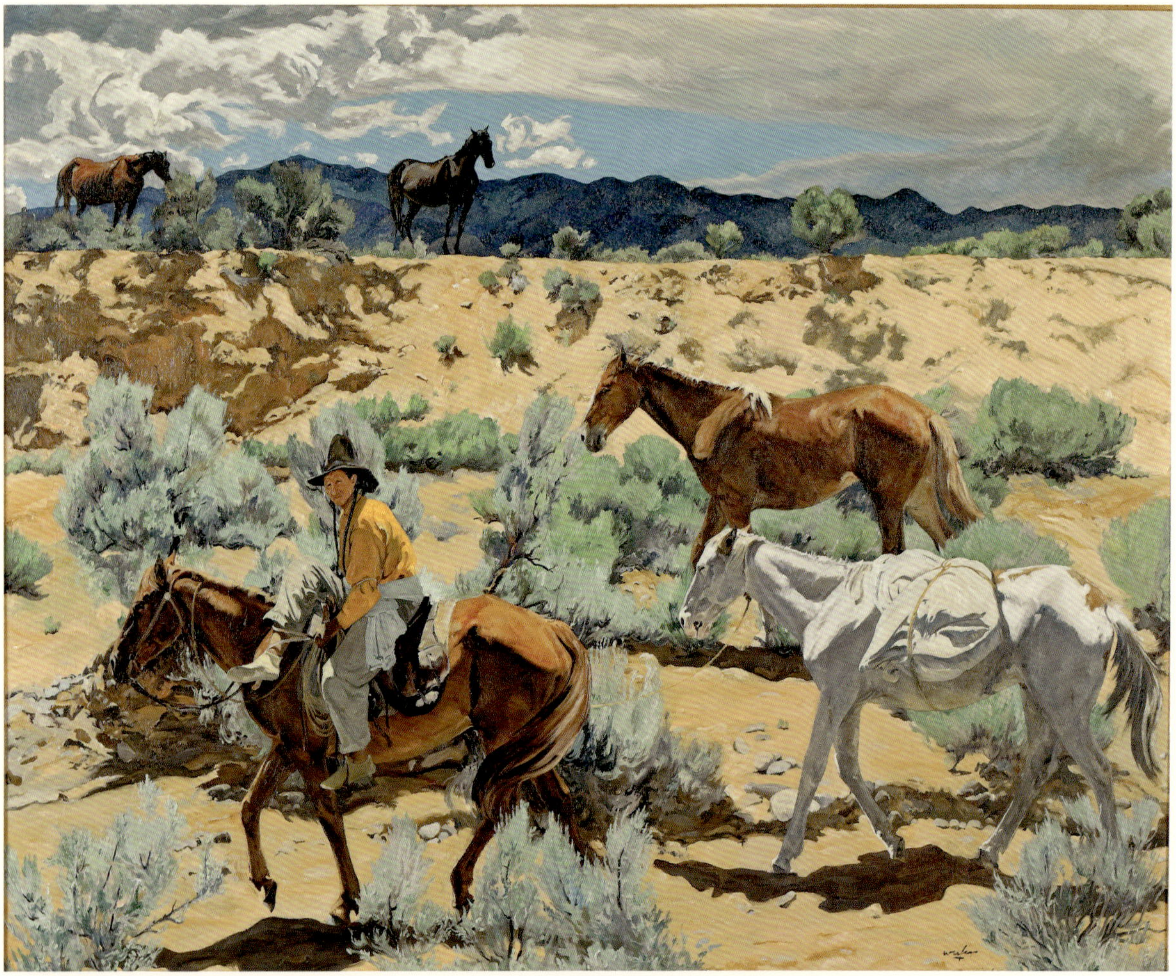

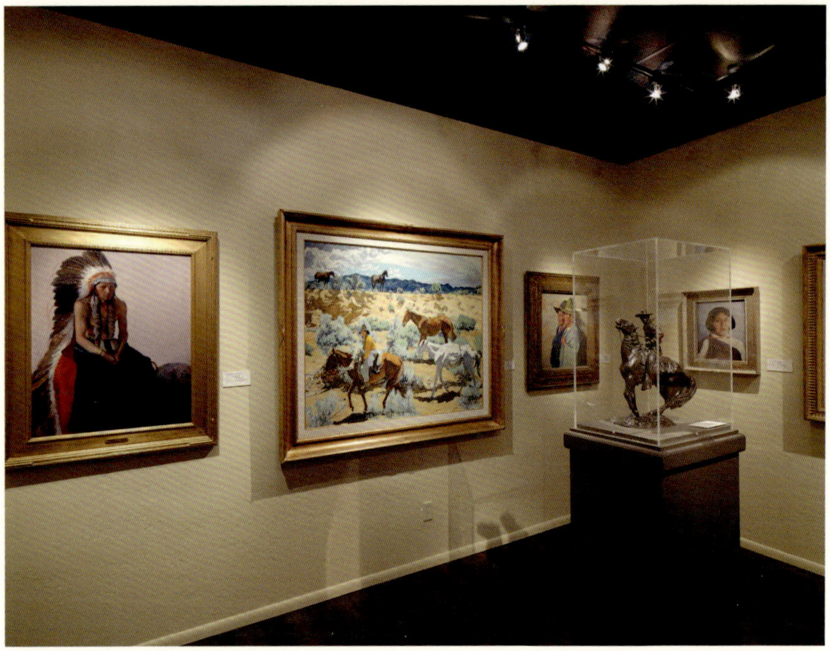

Figures 104 and 105. Walter Ufer. *The Southwest*, 1930 (top). Oil on canvas, 40 x 50 inches. Collection Desert Caballeros Western Museum, Wickenburg, Arizona. (former Klauer Family Collection) Walter Ufer's *The Southwest* hanging in museum (bottom), photo © Wayne Norton.

To Ufer's delight, the painting was accepted in juried exhibitions in the Corcoran Gallery of Art, Washington, D. C., the National Academy of Design, and a solo exhibition, *Walter Ufer: Paintings of the West*, at the Babcock Art Galleries in New York.

The smaller *Greasewood and Sage* lacks the ambition of *The Southwest.* Jim made yet another trip to the all too familiar arroyo. It appears as though Ufer wanted to create another painting to bolster up his shrinking inventory. Unfortunately, he lacked the passion necessary to create a painting of the quality evident in *The Southwest.* While Ufer was making some sales in 1930, letters to Klauer indicate that he was having difficulty paying the interest on his loan, much less the principal. According to a telegram sent to Klauer, Ufer was incurring heavy expenses due to his wife's accident.[42] Mary had been hit by a yellow cab and suffered serious, expensive injuries. Walter was able to get the hospital to accept a painting in partial payment of her expenses. Klauer also responded by recommending the bank extend Ufer's note for another six months. Frustrated by last-minute panic requests, Klauer exhorted Ufer to write him in the future before the note's next expiration date.[43] By December, Ufer's note came due, and again he couldn't make the payment. As before, Klauer interceded, instructing Ufer to send "a number of pictures" to Dubuque. Klauer felt Ufer had "too many paintings." Klauer would "pay off $500" of Ufer's note when it came due and would send the artist $500. He also assured Ufer that the paintings "would never get on the market."[44]

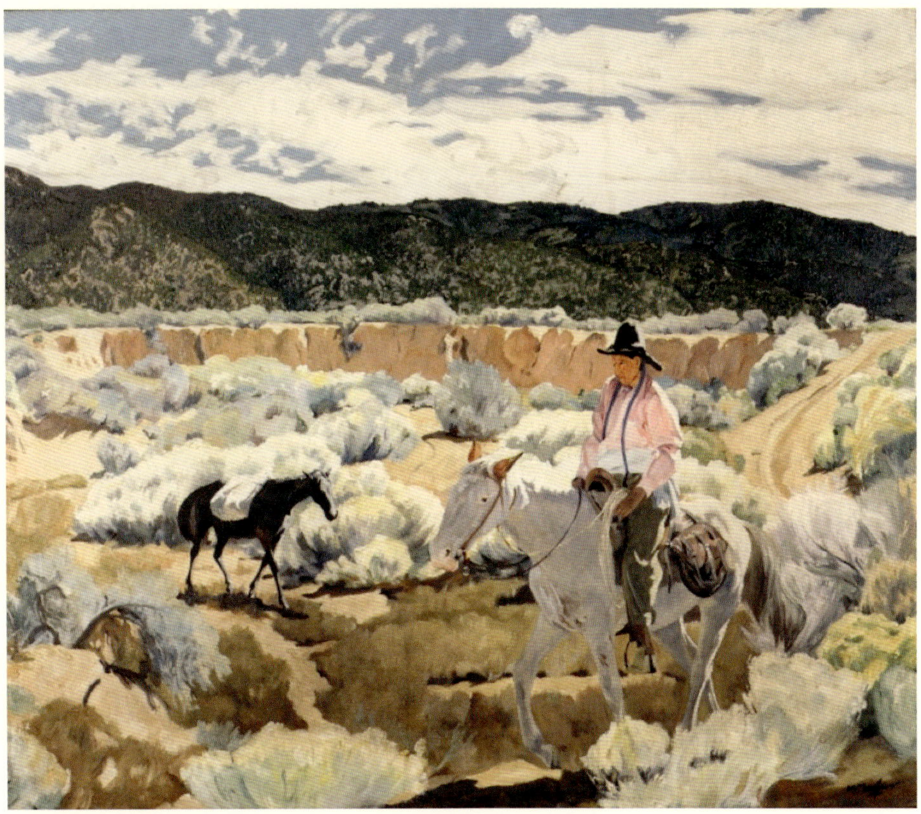

Figure 106. *Greasewood and Sage,* 1930. Oil on canvas, 25 x 30 inches.
Collection Klauer Manufacturing Company.

[42] WIFE'S ACCIDENT, NEW YORK SO KINDLY ASK YOU RENEW IT FOR SIX MONTHS STOP LETTER TO YOU GIVING FULL REASONS UNDER WAY, Western Union telegram, Walter Ufer to William Klauer, 10 June 1930, UPUNDSG.

[43] William Klauer to Walter Ufer, 14 June 1930, UPUNDSG.

[44] William Klauer to Walter Ufer, 24 December 1930, UPUNDSG.

WILLIAM KLAUER AND WALTER UFER: THE FINAL YEARS, 1931-1936

Ufer created *Reflections* [fig. 107] in 1931. It was one of his last portraits of his friend Jim. No artist ever knew his or her model better. Jim sat for fifteen years, developing a close, personal relationship with the artist. This was especially true during the Depression when Ufer seldom had the money to pay his friend. Yet a faithful Jim stuck with Walter through thick and thin, continuing to serve as the artist's model, gardener, handyman and friend. Jim referred to Ufer as his "brother," while Taosenos called him "Ufer's Jim."

Ufer's portrait speaks eloquently about their relationship. In this painting, artist and model, seeking a private moment, have climbed to the roof of an adobe. Ufer posed Jim in a state of relaxation. By the early 1930s, Jim had sat as quietly as possible for thousands of hours. He had learned how to manage what is one of a model's most difficult of jobs—sitting without moving. *Reflections* must be seen in a different light than Ufer's earlier portraits of Jim. The painting is autobiographical, focusing on the history the two shared. Even though Ufer's ability as a painter had been effaced by drink, he was capable of capturing times when the two experienced prosperity, as well as the present, when they helplessly watched *their* world collapse.

Jim Mirabal's once beautifully chiseled facial features appear bloated and almost boneless. Ufer's treatment of Jim's clothing, refined a few years earlier, is now missing. A weightless Jim hovers above, rather than sitting upon, the low adobe wall. The glazed look on the Indian's face also suggests that their drinking sessions were having an adverse effect on Jim as well.

After finishing *Reflections*, Ufer shipped the painting to Phoenix for a group exhibition. Sadly, an art critic panned the painting. The reviewer wrote, "*Reflections* lacks a solidity in the wall and building. Frankly, I cannot see that the arbitrary placing of light and shadows adds anything to this picture."[45] Ufer was responsible for organizing the exhibition and must have felt devastated when reading the critique of what was a painting fresh off his easel. After the Phoenix show, when he needed additional paintings as collateral, Ufer sent it to Dubuque where it joined the Klauer collection.

From 1931 until his death, Ufer seldom left Taos. Fragmentary records indicate that he was in New York and Chicago for the month of May, staying at the Salmagundi Club and the New Bismarck Hotel, respectively. A Western Union telegram to Klauer in 1932 indicates that he spent the week of March 13 in Denver.

Unable to paint and to protect paintings already collateralized, Ufer had additional canvases shipped to Dubuque. Galleries were having no luck making sales, a plight Ufer expressed in a letter to Klauer. Klauer had agreed to "pay off $500 providing you [Ufer] would send me a good number of pictures." Klauer's letter suggested that Ufer had sold some paintings and hadn't paid the bank the twenty percent of the list price. "The bank as well as the bank examiners want to know whether you have sold any of these pictures [those held for collateral] and if you have, why haven't you not made any returns for them."[46] On June 22, Ufer reported possible sales to Iowa State University and New Mexico State University. He then confessed "when my agent comes in July to take me to Oklahoma I will find out just

[45] "Many Artists of Phoenix Colony Find Taos Exhibition Interesting," Unidentified Phoenix newspaper in the Ila McAfee Scrapbooks (3), The Couse-Sharp Foundation Archives, Taos.

[46] William Klauer to Walter Ufer, 16 June 1931, UPUNDSG.

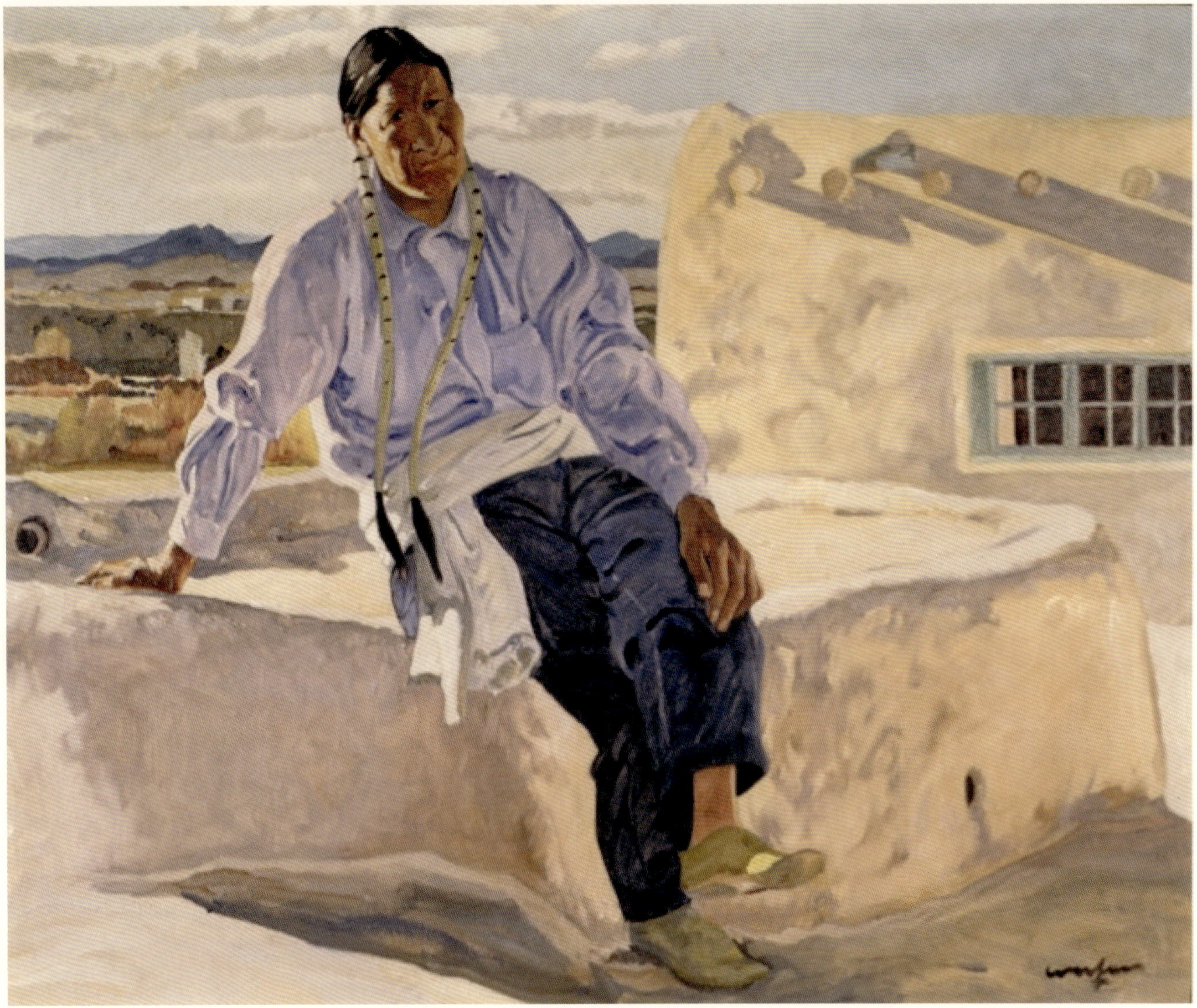

Figure 107. Walter Ufer. *Reflections*, c. 1931. Oil on canvas, 20 x 25 inches.
Collection Klauer Manufacturing Company.

what he has sold of mine—I do not know at present."[47] Ufer tried to explain his way out of the situation, "I have let him have nothing but old canvases so far—none that I nor Barrie [Grand Central Art Galleries] could do anything with."[48]

From June 1931 to the beginning of 1932, Ufer had at least fifteen paintings shipped from several commercial galleries to Dubuque. While in title, they were still owned by Ufer and could be released when he resolved his indebtedness to the bank and Klauer. The paintings were being removed from the market. While Klauer continued to believe that Ufer was able to replenish his inventory, he failed to understand the degree of the artist's incapacitation—it was impossible for Ufer to paint.

For several months in 1931, Klauer waited for paintings Ufer had promised. Several paintings were tied up in exhibitions and commercial galleries from New York to Los Angeles. He was having a solo show at the Currier Museum and asked Klauer to wait until the exhibition closed. Finally, on June 13,

[47] Walter Ufer to William Klauer, 22 June 1931, UPUNDSG
[48] Ibid.

Ufer sent a list of seventy-two paintings valued at $65,430, and on July 2, W. S. Budworth & Son wired Klauer, advising eight framed paintings in two crates were being shipped. Klauer received *Man with an Olla, Mi Casa, Winter in New Mexico, My Model at Rest, The Artist* [fig.], *Acequia Madre* [fig.], *My Studio Courtyard* [fig.], and *A Yearling.*[49] Unfortunately, Klauer wasn't satisfied with all that Ufer sent as they failed to "answer my [his] purpose..." *Taos in Snow* and *Mi Casa* were acceptable, but not the others. Rather than simply accepting paintings that Ufer selected, Klauer was increasingly concerned that his collection wouldn't be of the same quality as the earlier paintings *he* had purchased. Because his acquisitions made in the teens were of such consummate quality, he was attempting to add quality to quality. By the early 1930s, the number of desirable paintings by Ufer had been dramatically reduced, making it more difficult for Klauer to make judicious selections. Klauer wanted smaller pictures and stated, "they need not be portraits because I know you get more for portrait pictures than the others."[50]

THE FALL, 1932

Ufer's financial situation took a turn for the worse in 1932. During the first three months of the year, Ufer made request after request for funding programs that he could not support. He continued his habit of committing himself to exhibitions that he knew he wasn't able to accommodate without Klauer's financial assistance as well as loans of the patron's paintings.

In a January 23 letter to Klauer, he again expressed need for a personal loan—this one for $500. "I truly need it. The money coming to me, I cannot collect. They cannot pay at the present time. The people I owe are begging for it, but I have nothing to pay with."[51] Any hope for help was dashed when Klauer advised Ufer about the financial conditions in Dubuque. The bank had to close "on account of a run" and there was a very strong possibility that "the loans will be called very soon. That will put us all in a bad way." Klauer also warned that Ufer would have to send more pictures "to keep the loan going, otherwise they may have to collect it. These pictures would be held in trust for you until the Bank's situation cleared." Klauer closed by telling Ufer that it was impossible for him to send money "as funds are all tied up here."[52]

On February 12, Klauer wrote, "send all the pictures you can and I will have them insured and store them." Recognizing that the quality of his friend's paintings varied, he instructed Ufer to "send some of the better pictures."[53] Klauer had watched the prices of paintings by American artists, noting that even the most celebrated plummeted during the Depression. Paintings that had been valued at a couple thousand were failing to sell at a few hundred dollars. He had to protect the Bank as well as his interest in Ufer's paintings.

Following Klauer's instructions, Ufer had two groups of paintings sent from Stendahl Galleries. The first group contained *Taos Loma* [fig. 45; $800], *Western Rain* [fig. 72; $1000], and *My Studio Entrance* [fig. 88; $2500]; and the second group consisted of *Where Desert and Mountain Meet* [fig. 71]; *The Watcher* [fig. 70; $1500], and *End of a Perfect Day* [$600]. As Ufer only had "$125 at present in my bank," he asked Klauer to pay the freight.[54]

---

49 W. S. Budworth & Son to William Klauer, 2 July 1931, KFPUND
50 William Klauer to Walter Ufer, 13 July 1931, KFPUND.
51 Walter Ufer to William Klauer, 23 January 1932, UPUNDSG.
52 William Klauer to Walter Ufer, 2 February 1932, UPUNDSG.
53 William Klauer to Walter Ufer, 12 February 1932, UPUNDSG.
54 Walter Ufer to William Klauer, 15 February 1932, UPUNDSG.

Even though Ufer had six paintings sent to Dubuque, the Bank required more. Klauer advised Ufer to send more as the Bank had "the power to file on these pictures [those covered by the mortgage still under Ufer's control] and pick them up wherever they are."[55] Klauer felt "it would be a great sacrifice if any of your [Ufer's] pictures were thrown on the market now, they would bring very little money."[56]

A February 19, 1932 letter to Klauer illustrates the absurdity of Ufer's requests. In an attempt to impress Klauer he listed the forthcoming shows that he was committed to—the Moore Galleries, Huntington Hotel in Pasadena, and Stendahl Galleries, Los Angeles. He needed three large paintings by March 1 for the American Exhibit at the Carnegie Institute; one painting for the National Academy of Design; paintings for six exhibitions in Texas and Oklahoma booked by a traveling agent; and "other smaller shows follow."[57] By 1932, there was little hope that he could accommodate any of these shows, if it meant sending recent paintings. He would have to borrow paintings from Klauer.

Ufer reminded Klauer that he had sent six paintings valued at $8200 "at your list price. Please remember that I cannot break any contracts—I would never get an exhibition again."[58] Ufer continued to burden Klauer with his poor planning. No matter how much Klauer helped him, Ufer refused to accept responsibility for his actions. Each letter pleaded a new cause…exhibitions he committed to, life insurance, rent, food, bad debts, and so on. Despite Ufer's claims, there is no evidence that he submitted paintings to juried exhibitions from 1931 through 1934.

By March 18, Ufer again arranged to have additional paintings sent to Dubuque. From Phoenix he sent *Desert Grey Day* [$375]; and *Reflections* [fig. 107; $400]; from Los Angeles, *Among the Sage* [fig. 66; $450]; *Foothills-Early January* [fig. 65; $500]; *A June Storm* [$500]; and from Iowa City, *Across the Arroyo*, and *Waiting for the Gate to Open* [fig. 86; $500]. Ufer was also going to have the Grand Central Art Galleries send *An October Breeze* [$500] and *The Southwest* [fig. 104; $2500] to Klauer.[59] With an aggravate value of $5,225, combined with the six paintings valued at $7200 sent a few weeks earlier, Ufer had sent paintings valued at $13,425 to Dubuque.

Dubuque became the place to go if buyers were interested in seeing paintings by the artist after 1930. By then, William Klauer either owned or controlled a significant number of the artist's paintings. Most importantly, they were quality paintings. Visitors to Dubuque could see Ufer's paintings in the Art Room and Harbor Gallery in the Julien Hotel, which attracted a class of visitors who could afford Ufer's paintings, even during the Depression.

By June 1932, Ufer again asked for a $500 loan as he was "completely broke, and do not know what to do, or how to work. I am in distress—absolutely so."[60] Klauer quickly responded. He also had problems and found that it wasn't "quite possible to give you help at the present time." Again, Klauer left the door open with the phrase "at the present time."[61]

In letters dating the second half of 1932 and all of 1933, Ufer continued to burden Klauer with his problems, sometimes physical, but always financial. In June, Klauer had to take over Ufer's account

[55] William Klauer to Walter Ufer, 16 February 1932, KFPUND.
[56] Ibid.
[57] Walter Ufer to William Klauer, 19 February 1932, UPUNDSG.
[58] Ibid.
[59] Walter Ufer to William Klauer, 18 March 1982, UPUNDSG.
[60] Walter Ufer to William Klauer, 20 June 1932, UPUNDSG.
[61] William Klauer to Walter Ufer. 23 June 1932. UPUNDSG.

as “the Bank refused to carry it any longer.”[62] Ufer gave Klauer permission to sell his paintings, sending a percentage of the selling price to him. Klauer advised Ufer to put his “rock bottom prices” on his paintings, hoping that he could “dispose of a few for you.”[63] A few days later, Ufer gave Klauer permission to offer his paintings at a fifty percent discount. “When you make a sale please let me have some of the money as I need it badly.”[64] In December, Ufer’s letters didn’t change. He urged Klauer “...to put me back into some money. It is going hard with me and I do not know how I can pull through...”[65]

Finally, in 1932, Ufer experienced a bright, albeit brief, moment when Erwin Barrie, in charge of selecting paintings by American artists for the Venice Biennial international exhibition, included the artist’s *Thanksgiving Time*. Ufer’s inability to create quality, large-scale paintings caused Barrie to turn to Klauer. The loan brought prestige to Ufer, as he was one of fifteen American artists whose paintings were selected.

TAOS SOCIETY OF ARTISTS: THE LAST SITTING, 1932

During the summer of 1932, ten members of the Taos Society of Artists [fig. 108] gathered in the garden of Irving Couse to be photographed by C. E. Lord. By then Julius Rolshoven had died (1930) and Catharine Carter Critcher hadn’t returned to Taos for several years. Within four years, Dunton, Couse and Ufer would also be dead.

Throughout 1933 Klauer continued to keep Ufer afloat while maintaining a fair market value for his paintings. The economic outlook for artists remained unchanged. Even though Ufer had paintings available for purchase in Taos, Dubuque, Los Angeles, and New York, there were few, if any, potential buyers even after the asking price for the paintings had been dramatically reduced. Klauer also felt he had to guard against too many bargain sales or the value of his investments, like the stock market, would also experience a dramatic crash.

On March 3, 1933, Klauer reported that the pictures being held in Dubuque were “subject to the note of the Union Trust & Savings Bank, plus interest.”[66] According to Klauer, the Bank had “decided to foreclose and sell the pictures at public sale. That would have meant a great loss and would have disposed of all of your pictures. If they had not brought a sufficient amount, the Bank would have attached your other pictures. I stopped this by putting up a bond, so you will not need to write the Union Trust & Savings Bank Receiver on this subject. They are safe here but cannot be moved.”[67]

Again Klauer reminded Ufer that if he could raise money and retire his note, the paintings being held in Dubuque would be “expressed to you immediately.”[68] Klauer wasn’t opposed to selling them at reduced prices because he recognized that Ufer’s paintings would not bring pre-Depression prices. Klauer was a realist, having been in New York where the galleries were “selling pictures by some of the best artists for $100 each, with frames.”[69] He asked Ufer to tell him what his “bottom prices are” as he might

[62] Ibid.
[63] Ibid.
[64] Walter Ufer to William Klauer, 26 June 1932, UPUNDSG.
[65] Walter Ufer to William Klauer, 7 December 1932, UPUNDSG.
[66] William Klauer to Walter Ufer, 3 March 1933, KFPUND.
[67] Ibid.
[68] Ibid.
[69] Ibid.

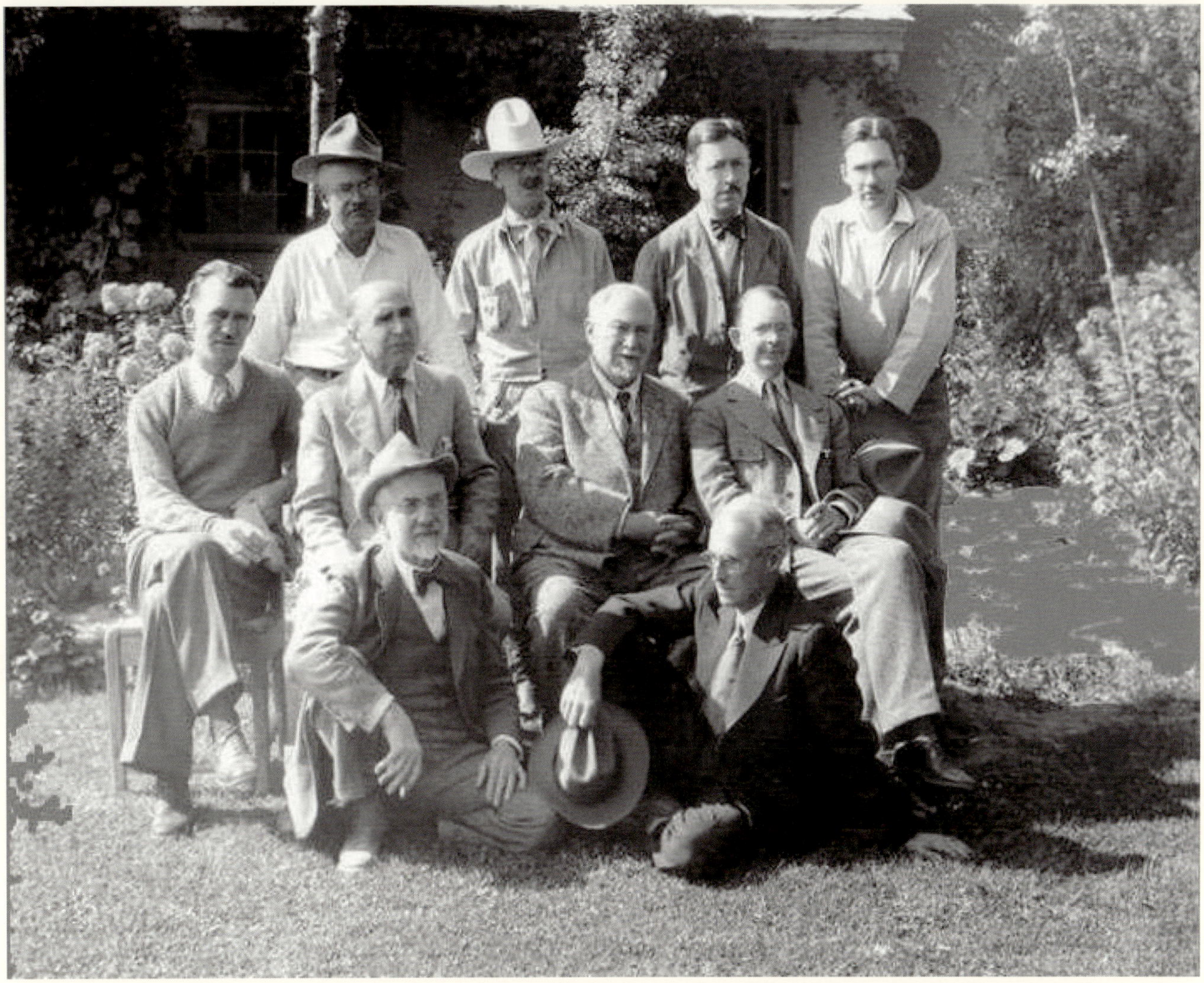

Figure 108. C. E. Lord. *Former Members of the Taos Society of Artists in the Courtyard of Irving Couse's Home*, 1932. Back row: Ufer, Dunton, Higgins, Adams. Seated: Hennings, Phillips, Couse, Berninghaus. Front Row: Sharp, Blumenschein. Photo Courtesy Couse/Sharp Foundation Archives, Taos.

"be able to sell some and turn about twenty percent of the sales price to you."[70] Even though Klauer was making every effort to help Ufer, he could offer little hope as "conditions are worse now than ever were before. Money is being hoarded but nothing is being bought, even by people who have a lot of it."[71] Ufer responded by recommending that Klauer sell his paintings for half price, and "of the money you take two-thirds and let me have the other one-third so that I can live."[72] Ufer concluded by asking Klauer to do what he could. "I want to pay my debt to you—I want my pictures back—and I want your friendship."[73]

Klauer thought he had found at least a temporary solution to Ufer's problem by May 1933. He had shown Ufer's paintings to a "visitor from St. Paul" who "became very much interested." The party was typical of so many who looked to make a deal, taking advantage of those who were facing financial ruin. Klauer reported that he "made an offer to enter into the partnership of these pictures should they be acquired from you on the basis of $5000. He would pay me $2500 and I would pay you the difference

[70] Ibid.

[71] Ibid.

[72] Walter Ufer to William Klauer, 13 March 1933, KFPUND.

[73] Ibid.

of what you owed and $5000."[74] Klauer thought Ufer had quite a few other paintings "and no doubt were doing some painting now and that the number of pictures you had, would be too large to place on the market."[75] Klauer continued to believe that Ufer was actively painting. Klauer's prospect also claimed that the buyer would never sell the paintings and "these pictures would not compete with you in any way."[76] Klauer expected to be in Taos "next week" allowing Ufer to consider the proposal.[77]

Ufer wasted little time responding to Klauer's promising letter. On May 28, he wrote and asked Klauer to send "about $2000 in advance on this deal. It would help me to pay life insurance for the favor of my wife, and other things. I am really hard hit."[78] Ufer stated the check would be "a blessing to me." "Bill—you have no idea how you have helped me if you can send the $2000 in advance."[79] Even when he didn't have funds to cover basic necessities, he continued to seek funds to cover insurance premiums.

On June 7, a frantic Ufer sent a Western Union telegram, imploring Klauer to "telegraph First State Bank Taos New Mexico about five hundred dollars immediately in my favor they threaten to sell me out for back taxes I beg you to do this."[80] On June 9, Ufer applied yet more pressure, telling Klauer that he was suffering from pleurisy, a very painful sickness. He continued to ask Klauer to send him "$500 in advance." He closed: "P. S. Dr. Martin asked if I was spitting blood—I am not—but the pain is hell!"[81] On the same day Ufer wrote a second letter, again stressing graphically his "hard case of Pleurisy." He also asked Klauer for time, and he would write again "to get ourselves straightened out."[82]

When Ufer pleaded to Klauer for more money, he never once spoke of Mary and her life as a pauper. While working at any job that would earn her a few dollars, she frequently had to survive on a meal or two a day. She slept wherever she was, with a friend or relative, while being in desperate need of medical and dental care. In all the letters between them, never once did Ufer offer Mary any feeling of hope.

The only relief Klauer had from Ufer's pressure came in the 1930s when he vacationed at Grand Island. Upon returning to Dubuque, he knew he would be faced with several letters of woe. No matter how many times he "bailed" Ufer out, there was always the next mail delivery from his desperate, alcoholic friend.

On June 14, Ufer's hopes were dashed when he learned that Klauer's St. Paul friend had decided to invest his money "in some stocks he doesn't want to budge."[83] Furthermore, even if Klauer's client was willing to purchase some paintings, the client had "proposed that he would have his choice of all the pictures," and that would leave Klauer "with a lot of undesirable ones. If he is going to try to hog it, I will of course have to refuse his proposition."[84]

Realizing that he was holding too many paintings that were not marketable, Klauer proposed an exchange with Ufer. "We could exchange six or seven of the pictures here now, for some that you have

[74] William Klauer to Walter Ufer, 24 May 1933, KFPUND.
[75] Ibid.
[76] Ibid.
[77] This is the last reference to Klauer's visiting Taos in the Ufer and Klauer Archives.
[78] Walter Ufer to William Klauer, 28 March 1933, KFPUND.
[79] Ibid.
[80] Walter Ufer to William Klauer, Western Union Telegram, 7 June 1933, KFPUND.
[81] Walter Ufer to William Klauer, 9 June 1933, KFPUND.
[82] Ibid.
[83] William Klauer to Walter Ufer, 14 June 1933, KFPUND.
[84] Ibid.

down East, but I do not have an accurate list of those that you still have. Perhaps you can give it to me and we can make some exchange that will be satisfactory."[85] Ufer wasn't pleased that Klauer wanted to exchange some pictures. Ever since working with the syndicate, he wanted to be involved in the decision of assigning paintings. Klauer, recognizing Ufer's pride, made his recommendation easier to accept when he included a check for $100, "to apply as an additional loan upon your pictures."[86]

As soon as Ufer received the check, he asked for another $100. Still suffering from pleurisy, Ufer claimed he was "so weak that I [he] can hardly write this letter." Ufer was facing eviction, as he was "5 months in arrears" with his rent. If Ufer didn't pay up, he would be thrown out on July 1. Ufer reasoned that he could help out his landlord with nine children with the additional $100 check.[87] On July 5, Ufer asks for yet one more check, this one for $200, again "to cover premium of one of my insurance policies."[88] And, finally, on July 11, he wrote a short note, " I have written you about June 21st and telegraphed you later—please send me some money—I am broke."[89]

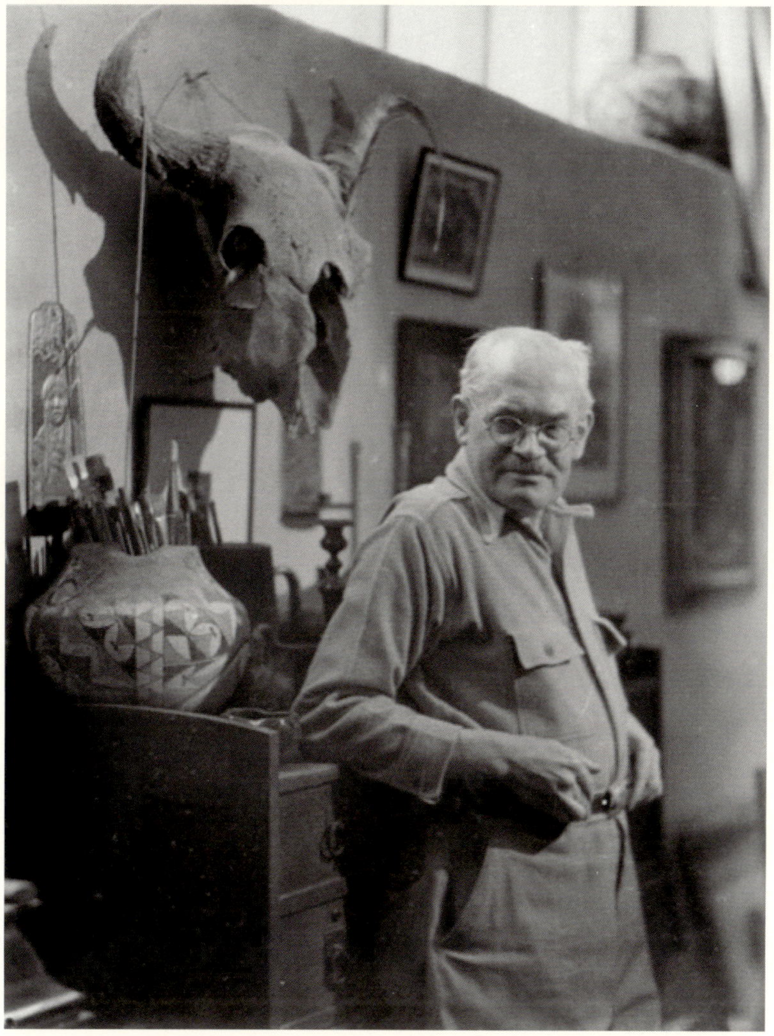

Figure 109.
Will Connell.
Walter Ufer in his Studio, Taos, New Mexico, 1932.
Courtesy Palace of Governors Photo Archives (NMHM/DCA), 042910.

---

[85] Ibid.
[86] Ibid.
[87] Walter Ufer to William Klauer, 21 June 1933, UPUNDSG.
[88] Walter Ufer to William Klauer, Western Union Telegram, 5 July 1933, KFPUND.
[89] Walter Ufer to William Klauer, 11 July 1933, UPUNDSG.

Chapter XIII
Resurrection and Death, 1934-1936

The year 1934 began on a familiar note with the Ufers still struggling to raise money—Mary on the road and Walter in Taos. While Ufer's health was precarious at best, Mary attempted to take care of business from New York, Chicago, Minneapolis, and anywhere else her jobs took her. Walter had basically forced her to remain away from Taos. When she managed to save enough money, she would return to Taos to get some rest and to work in their garden. Even though her "visit"' was only for a month or two, Ufer constantly complained that she upset his routines. He was happy to live as a bachelor—without having to contend with a wife.

Unaware of her husband's financial arrangements, Mary's letters to Klauer grew in frequency. On February 19, Mary wrote about "a group of Walter's pictures" Klauer was holding "as security on a loan which Walter has procured from you." She asked Klauer to send her "a statement as to what extent we are indebted to you."[1] She finally learned that her husband owed more than $3500. In her letters to Klauer, Mary reported "Walter had "completely broken down" and that "Doc" Martin wrote her "it might be too late if he was not immediately placed in a hospital."[2] His health had deteriorated to the point where there were serious concerns about how long he could survive if drastic action wasn't taken. It had become "a matter of life and death saving Walter's life."[3]

The commercial galleries were forced to sell paintings for a fraction of their worth if they had a prospect. Klauer wrote that Macbeth Galleries had sent him a list of Walter's paintings that were "being sold at $100 apiece." "Macbeth wanted me to send some of them but I did not give permission to do so."[4] Even at low prices, the galleries couldn't sell Ufer's pictures. The principle advantage of Klauer holding the bulk of paintings was that they were secure and wouldn't be liquidated at bargain basement prices.

KEELEY CURE, 1934

Recognizing Ufer's need of immediate, life-saving treatment in a sanitarium, his fellow artists came to his rescue in April 1934. Artists from Grand Central Art Galleries raised funds, and an old Chicago friend, Gustave Baumann [fig. 110], drove Ufer to Pueblo, Colorado, to take the Keeley Cure.[5] The *Taos Valley News* announced, "Ufer goes to hospital in Pueblo, Colorado."[6]

Sadly, the trip had tragic consequences. On the way to Pueblo, Baumann's automobile struck a young boy in Costilla, Colorado, who eventually succumbed to his injuries. Even though Ufer was able

---

[1] Mary Ufer to William Klauer, 19 February 1934, KFPUND.

[2] Mary Ufer to William Klauer, 8 March 1934, KFPUND.

[3] Mary Ufer to William Klauer, 1 March 1934, KFPUND.

[4] William Klauer to Walter Ufer, 19 June 1934, KFPUND.

[5] The Keeley Cure was invented by Leslie Enraught Keeley, M. D. (1836-1900). The program basically consisted of having the patient drink as much alcohol as he could imbibe. This was followed by four injections of dichloride of gold daily (The Gold Cure) plus other tonics. Despite being criticized by many in the medical profession, for nearly 85 years it had a commendable rate of success.

[6] *Taos Valley News*, 1 March 1934.

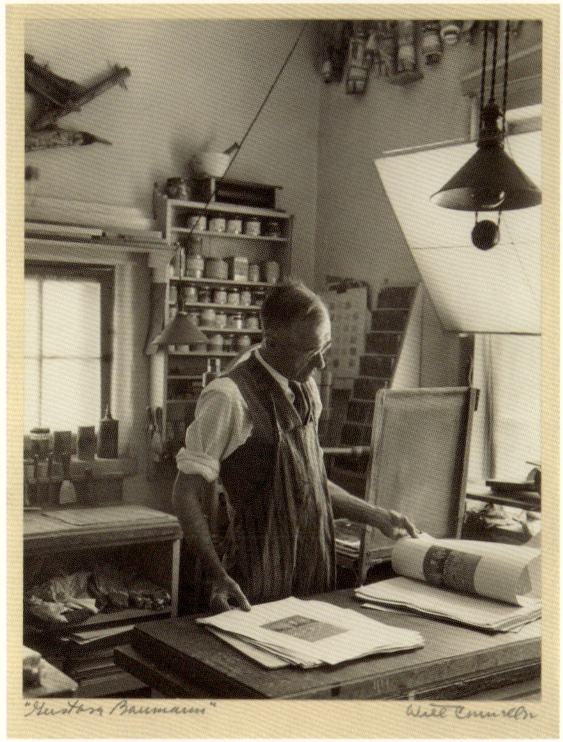

Figure 110.
Will Connell, *Gustave Baumann*, 1932.
Black and white photograph, 20 x 16."
Collection of the Harwood Museum of Art, Taos, NM.

to return to his easel to create a few paintings of quality, both Ufer and Baumann would be haunted by the memory of the awful tragedy.

With Walter on the road to recovery, Mary, on April 29, in an attempt to clarify issues of ownership, sent Klauer a list of paintings she needed photographs of: *Western Rain* [fig. 72], *The Southwest* [fig. 104], *Across the Arroyo, Among the Sage* [fig. 60], *My Studio Courtyard* [fig. 69], and *Desert Gray Day*. At the time of Ufer's death, these paintings all bore the Klauer ownership. In fact, on May 16, 1934, Grand Central Art Galleries provided a list of fifteen paintings in their possession with an aggregate value of $28,800.[7] On May 24, Mary telegrammed Klauer, "Walter reported much better."[8] In June, Mary announced that Walter was "back on the job again." Klauer responded: "From the text of your note and the handwriting, I think you are getting along fine and I sincerely trust that I am not mistaken."[9] After so many letters of impending doom, Klauer welcomed any positive news from Taos.

Despite giving up alcohol, however, Ufer's financial situation remained unchanged. In his continuing attempt to save the artist, Klauer offered a program that would retire the artist's indebtedness to John McDonald (a Bank associate who had a $500 credit with Ufer) and himself, while offering some money to survive on. Klauer wrote:

> *The question is, have you more pictures to sell and are you willing to part with those in my possession? If you are, I will pay you the difference between what you owe and $5000 but the McDonald matter will have to be included because he can attach these pictures at any time. I can send you $500 now and the remainder [$400] within a very short time. If you decide to do this, let me know immediately.*[10]

[7] Grand Central Art Galleries, 16 May 1934, KFPUND.
[8] Mary Ufer to William Klauer, Western Union Telegram, 29 May 1934, KFPUND.
[9] William Klauer to Walter Ufer, 19 June 1934, UPUNDSG.
[10] William Klauer to Walter Ufer, 19 June 1934, UPUNDSG.

Ufer agreed with the proposal and wrote to Klauer asking for the money while requesting the loan of large paintings for exhibitions he was committed to. Finally, after what was probably an extended trip to Grand Island, Klauer sent a check for $500 and stated "which leaves about $400 and that includes the amount you owe John McDonald." Klauer cautioned "to go slow with this money because it will be sometime before pictures can be disposed of at any reasonable price. Make this go as far as you can."[11]

BOB ABBOTT AND ASSISTANT, 1935

In a letter to Klauer on November 12, Ufer made his earliest reference to the painting *Bob Abbott and His Assistant* [fig. 111] a work that he labored over and was proud of. He planned to show the canvas in the National Academy or Corcoran exhibitions. He also mentioned that he might have to "draw" a painting from Klauer for a show in Los Angeles.[12] By November, he had spent the $500 Klauer had sent him in September and asked for the $400 balance. On December 5, after a lengthy trip to Grand Island, Klauer sent Ufer the final check, concluding their agreement.[13]

Even though Ufer continued feeling the financial stress that most artists working in Taos experienced, his situation was not as dire as expressed in letters to Mary and Klauer. Despite being opposed to working for the federal government, he finally conceded, accepting funds for paintings he was incapable of creating. Despite the Depression, young artists continued knocking on his studio door, convincing Walter to teach them. Regina Tatum Cooke, who studied with Ufer during the summers between 1934 and 1936, paid him "$36 a month."[14]

Furthermore, in 1935, Ufer made at least three sales. His recovery was remarkable, particularly when examining *Bob Abbott and His Assistant*, *Lonesome Song* [fig. 112], and *The Entertainer*—the latter was sold for $350 in June 1935 to Dr. E. O. Holland, the President of Washington State University. He also sold an oil, the title unknown, to a friend of his insurance agent, Samuel Lustgarten, netting him $750. This sale was recorded in letters from Lustgarten and others who had seen and admired it. He also copied a group of 8-by-10-inch portraits that earned him a few hundred dollars.

Yet, he failed to mention any of this income in his letters to Klauer or Mary. If he would have reported these sales, he would have to send money to Mary, who was on the road and struggling to survive. She was slowly starving, and as mentioned earlier usually living on the generosity of relatives (in Minneapolis) and friends (in Chicago). She didn't have funds to return to Taos, and even if she did, she would have to contend with what was an uncomfortable situation. If Ufer shared any good news of sales, he couldn't continue pleas for financial assistance. It is no surprise that by 1934, Klauer was completely frustrated with their nineteen-year relationship.

While no letters have survived documenting Klauer's interest in the painting, on November 12, 1934, Ufer once again requested money from Klauer. "It costs lots of money to paint."[15] At the time of his request, Ufer also mentioned working on his 50-by-50-inch canvas. Creating the last of his major, large-scale paintings, Ufer deviated from the formulaic. The painting is a symbol of Ufer's physical as well as artistic recovery. To create his masterpiece, during a particularly cold winter, Ufer labored over every

---

[11] William Klauer to Walter Ufer, 22 September 1934, KFPUND.
[12] Walter Ufer to William Klauer, 12 November 1934, KFPUND.
[13] William Klauer to Walter Ufer, 5 December 1934, KFPUND.
[14] Mary Carroll Nelson, *The Legendary Artists of Taos* (New York: Watson-Guptill Publications, 1980), 80.
[15] Walter Ufer to William Klauer, 12 November 1934, KFPUND.

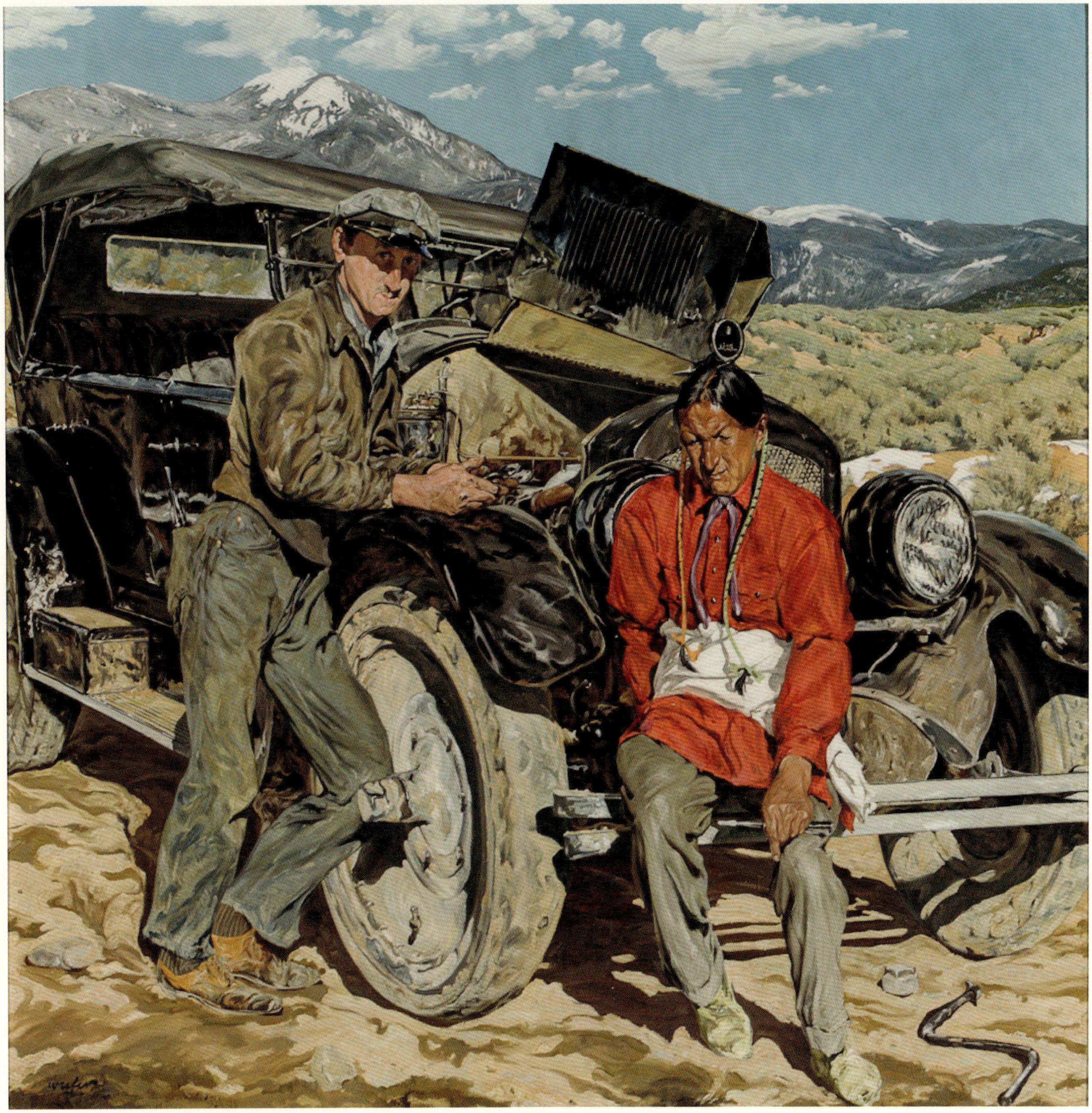

Figure 111. Walter Ufer. *Bob Abbott and His Assistant*, 1935. Oil on canvas, 50 1/4 x 50 1/2 inches. Collection of the Speed Art Museum, Louisville, Kentucky. Bequest of Mrs. Walter Ufer, 1947.13.

aspect of the painting. In fact, it would be difficult to determine which elements were more important to Ufer—his friends, the automobile, or the landscape.

The painting shows Bob Abbott and Jim Mirabal pausing from their work. The broken down automobile may be seen as symbolic of Ufer's health situation. The mechanic, who was owner of Abbott Motor Company, looks back toward the viewer quizzically while a dejected Jim, wearing his brilliant red shirt, casts his eyes downward. Both seem to be asking Ufer if the Reo is really worth repairing again. Together they had worked on the broken-down artist's car many times. They seem to be wondering if Ufer would sustain his recovery or slip back into "disrepair" as an alcoholic.

As early as January 2, 1935, while the painting was still in the works, Ufer began sending letters to prospective buyers. He wrote to Carter Harrison, the first letter in years. "You may believe me, I have not slumped any this season. The one I am finishing now, a 50-by-50-inch canvas, will be the best one I ever did. My only worry is that my money runs out before I finish. It costs to paint. I am happy though I am terribly broke. I love this painting."[16]

He finally finished the painting and was successful exhibiting it in the Corcoran, The Art Institute of Chicago, the Texas Centennial Exposition in Dallas, and the National Academy of Design. While the painting brought him satisfaction, Ufer could not find a buyer in Carter Harrison, William Klauer, or Oscar Mayer, II. His biggest disappointment, however, came when Robert B. Harshe, Director of The Art Institute of Chicago and Advisory Director of the Texas Centennial Exposition in Dallas, approached Ufer about borrowing a painting for the exposition. While Walter was enthusiastic about lending his most recent masterwork, Harshe was more interested in *Luzanna and Her Sisters* [fig. 68], his prizewinner hanging in the Baltimore Museum of Art. A clumsy Harshe reasoned that the committee wasn't "in touch with some of your more recent work." He continued, only making matters worse, when he wrote, "We could use *Bob Abbott and His Assistant* but perhaps you have other works that you would rather be represented by."[17]

Ufer's final attempt to sell *Bob Abbott and His Assistant* was written to Oscar Mayer, II on June 8, 1936. His father already owned several paintings by Ufer and Hennings, undoubtedly the reason why he responded, "I regret that economic conditions with me are still such that I have no funds from which to satisfy my artistic instincts and so cannot consider buying any paintings."[18] Despite Ufer's several letters and the painting's impressive track record in exhibitions, Mary anticipated its failure to sell when she saw it at Grand Central Art Galleries in June 1935. Even though she thought the painting "splendid," Mary predicted, "But Walter, no capitalist will buy it, of that I am sure."[19]

RETURN TO THE NATIONAL SCENE, 1935

After finishing *Bob Abbott and His Assistant*, Ufer experienced a brief period of inspired productivity. Having regained his confidence, he began creating paintings that would find a market. Besides *The Entertainer* that he sold to Dr. Holland, he sent a list to Holland with a description of three other paintings, fresh off the easel, that were remarkable in their quality. Based on these, it is obvious that Ufer had experienced a "resurrection," following his victory over the demons of alcoholism. The unfailing support of William Klauer had enabled Ufer to perform a miracle and enter into a period of productivity and a personal "rebirth."

Following the sale to Holland, and believing the market would again support pre-Depression prices, Ufer attempted to revert back to his earlier price structure. He also returned to an earlier theme with *Lonesome Song* [fig. 112], a painting showing Jim playing a flute. As with *Bob Abbott and His Assistant*, Ufer made a major effort to create a masterpiece that harkened back to his earlier situational scenes. While it was a successful effort, Ufer offered *Lonesome Song* to Klauer for $1500. He wrote, "believing that I still have a clientele that is willing to pay for what they get, and where my reputation has not faltered any, I am asking my price of $1500 for it. I consider this an excellent price for my work. Will

[16] Walter Ufer to Carter Harrison, 2 January 1935, Newberry Library Archives, Chicago.
[17] Robert Harshe to Walter Ufer, 30 December 1935, UPUNDSG.
[18] Oscar Mayer Jr. to Walter Ufer, June 8 1936, UPUNDSG.
[19] Mary Ufer to Walter Ufer, 10 June 1915, UPUNDSG.

you write me, and I hope favorably?" Ufer described the painting as "representing a full-length figure sitting against an adobe wall and playing a flute."[20]

No evidence has survived indicating whether or not Klauer ever responded. Even if he did, it seems unlikely that he would have been interested, certainly not at the $1500 price.[21] Apparently, Ufer failed to learn a lesson from his sale to Dr. Holland. *The Entertainer* was a fine painting, probably higher in quality than *Lonesome Song*, but his pricing was unrealistic. Moreover, by 1936, Klauer had a superb collection of Ufer's paintings, knowing no equals. It was still the Depression, and despite his recent success, Ufer failed to understand the world in which he was living.

Ufer's May 31 letter to William Klauer was the last communication between the two. Ufer continued painting and teaching a student or two, but the fire and restless energy that characterized his work during his greatest period of activity was lacking. From April 1934 until his August 2, 1936 death, he went through the motions of being an artist. In twenty-five months, he finished between eight and ten paintings, one 50 by 50 inches, two or three 30 by 25 inches, and the rest 10 ½ by 12 ½ inches.

While it seems he was physically incapable of creating more paintings, he did spend a great deal of time working with the American Artists Congress as well as on political causes. Besides his frequent letters to Klauer and some women friends, he wrote almost daily to Mary.

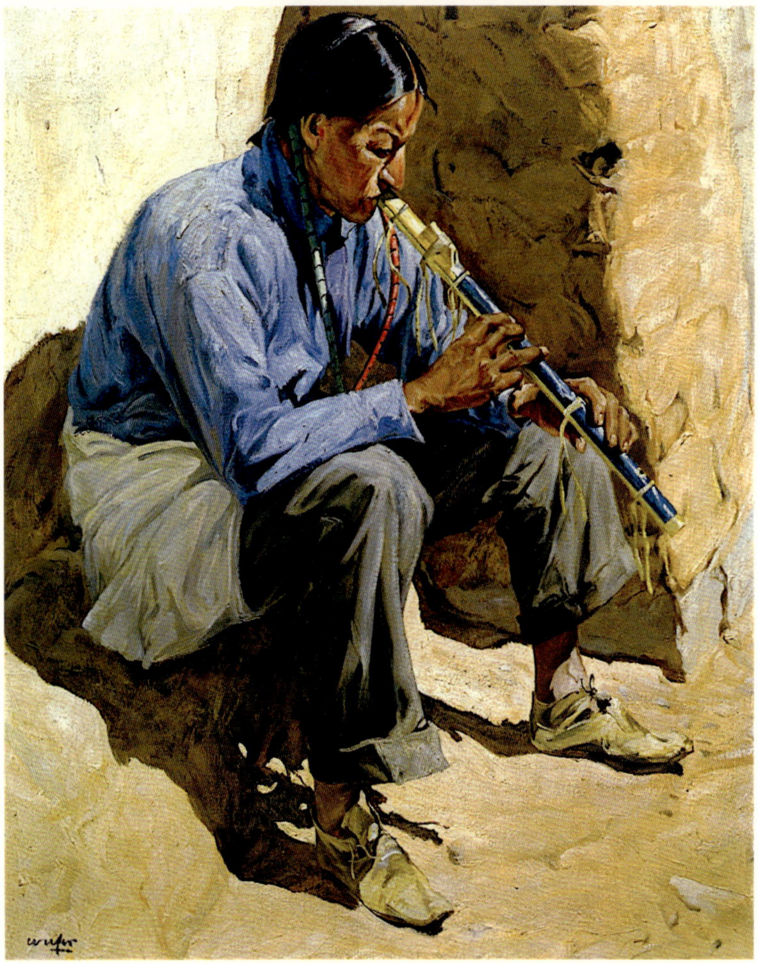

Figure 112.
Walter Ufer, *Lonesome Song*, 1936.
Oil on canvas, 30 x 30 inches.
Private Collection.
Photo courtesy Gerald Peters Gallery,
Santa Fe, New Mexico.

[20] Walter Ufer to William Klauer, 31 May 1936, KFPUND.
[21] $1500 would be $17,848 in 2017 dollars.

UFER'S UNTIMELY DEATH, 1936

By June of 1936, Ufer knew that he was going to spend the remainder of his life by himself. Mary wrote, "you love Taos and I hate it. Black is white, and white is black and two and two make five: that is Walter Ufer's logic."[22] Mary's biggest problem with Taos was its sluggish life style in contrast with "the tremendous fastness with which events are moving in the rest of the world; we have no time to lose."[23] Mary's statement could not have been more prophetic.

Ufer's work as an artist and representative to the American Artists Congress ended abruptly when, on July 29, his appendix ruptured. Ufer was loaded into E. Martin Hennings's automobile and rushed to St. Vincent's Hospital in Santa Fe. They reported that he cursed every time the car hit a bump all the way to Santa Fe. After unsuccessful surgery the next day, and despite fighting a courageous battle, he succumbed to peritonitis on August 2, 1936.

After Mary returned to Taos, Ufer's friends held a memorial service in his Des Georges Lane studio on August 10. Following the service, Bob Abbott and Jim Mirabal scattered his ashes from the bank of Los Cruces arroyo—over the land that he loved so much.[24] While records have not survived documenting his financial status at the time of his death, we can be certain that he left Mary impoverished. Years after his death Grand Central Art Galleries was still trying to sell Walter's work for Mary [fig. 58]. Ironically, his last masterpiece, *Bob Abbott and His Assistant* [fig. 111], remained unsold in 1947. On her deathbed, Mary bequeathed the painting, along with a 1912 Munich self-portrait, to the Speed Art Museum in Louisville, Kentucky.

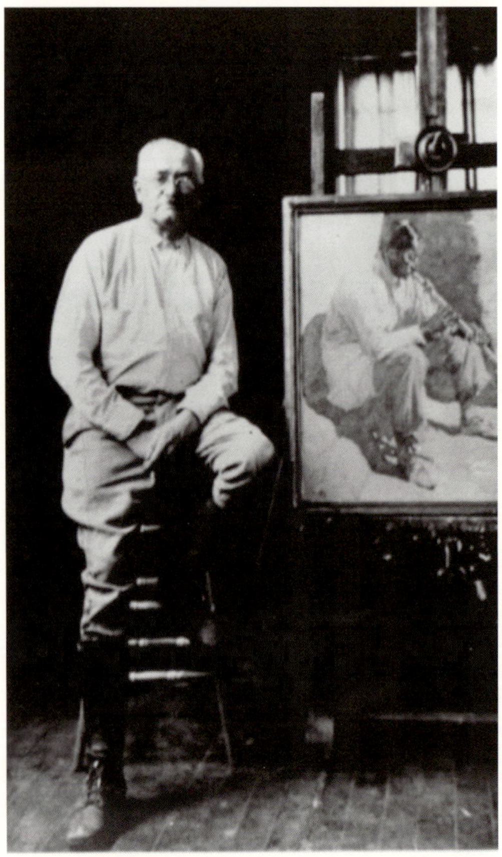

Figure 113.
Photograph of Walter Ufer with *Lonesome Song*, 1936.
Courtesy of the Speed Art Museum, Louisville, Kentucky.

---

[22] Mary Ufer to Walter Ufer, 15 June 1936, UPUNDSG.
[23] Ibid.
[24] Moore, "That Man Out There in the Mountains," 144.

Chapter XIV
William Klauer and Grand Central Art Galleries, 1923-1941

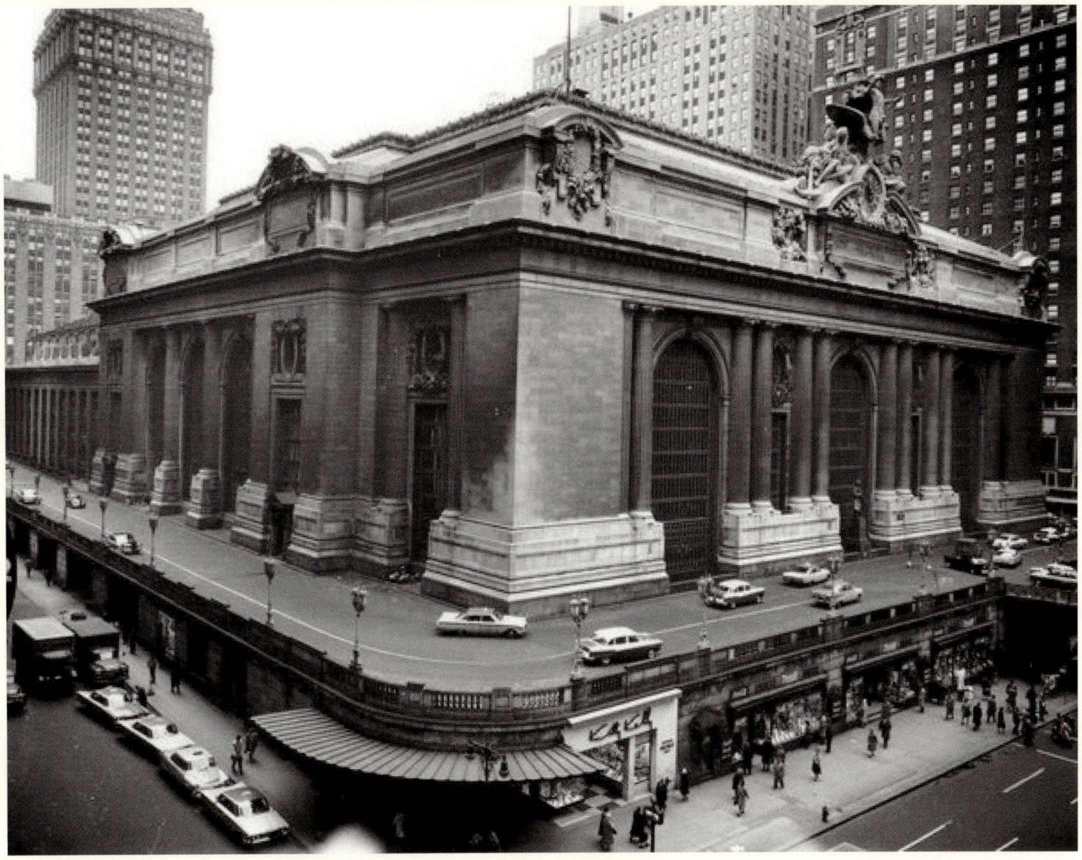

Figure 114. Grand Central Station in the 1950s, from "The History of Grand Central Station, in Photos" *The Atlantic Wire*. Image from the Associated Press.

William Klauer became a founding member of Grand Central Art Galleries [figs. 114 and 117] in 1923. It opened in New York as a co-op under the direction of Erwin S. Barrie. According to gallery records,

> *It is proposed to form an association composed of Painters, Sculptors and Laymen to establish a large sales gallery where these artists can have the opportunity to keep their work on constant exhibition and where the public can become familiar not along with those struggling for recognition. It is believed that the public will patronize a permanent exhibition run exclusively in the interest of the artist.*[1]

Grand Central advocated the creation of a national organization that represented "a group of our best painters and sculptors on one hand and laymen on the other." The organization also recognized that all

---

[1] *Grand Central Art Galleries Yearbook*, 1926.

"lay members" were "picture collectors." The membership was either officers or directors of principal museums of art—men and women whose influence is of greatest importance to any effort in this direction."[2]

Klauer, as a "lay member" sent $600 checks annually until 1934, when Barrie lowered the annual fee to $350 because of the Depression. The annual fee enabled Klauer to participate in a drawing for a painting. Before making his choices, Klauer often asked Ufer for his advice. On August 20, 1925, Ufer responded by putting "them according to their reputations..." He felt that Klauer could "not make a mistake by choosing according to the list."[3] Ultimately, however, paintings Klauer wanted had to still be available when his number was drawn.

William Klauer showed amazing patience with Erwin Barrie and Grand Central over the years. He maintained his membership even though he was often disappointed with the selections available to him. In 1924, he drew a painting by Oliver Dennett Grover that, according to Victor Higgins, Klauer didn't like. In the 1925 drawing, Klauer selected a typical seascape by Frederick Waugh [fig. 115], but once again wasn't happy with his selection. Barrie had a stock of marine paintings by Waugh and offered Klauer alternatives, and in 1926, the dealer asked the dissatisfied collector to "return whichever one of the Waugh marines you have decided not to keep."[4]

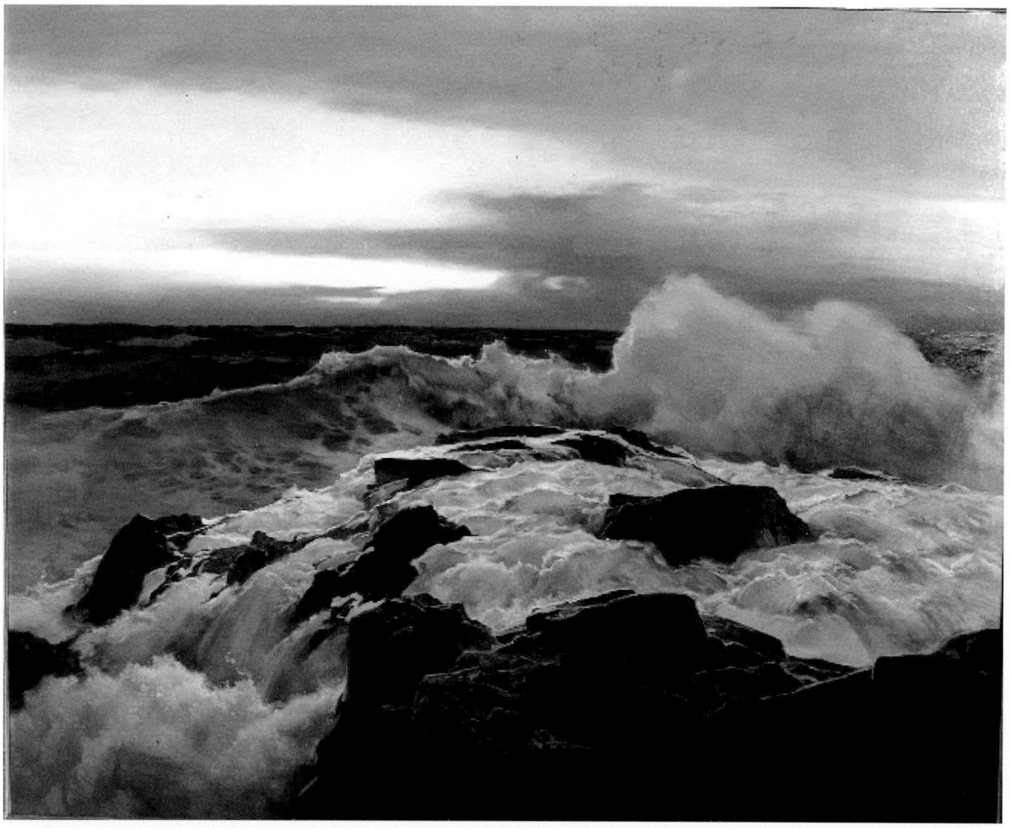

Figure 115. Frederick Waugh. *Grey Dawn*, c. 1930. Oil on canvas. Colletion The Snite Museum of Art, University of Notre Dame, Gift of Mr. Walter Klauer, 1962.027.

[2] Ibid.

[3] Walter Ufer to William Klauer, 20 August 1925, UPUNDSG.

[4] Erwin S. Barrie to William Klauer, 16 February 1926, KFPUND.

1927 EXHIBITION FOR DUBUQUE ART ASSOCIATION

In 1927, Klauer worked on an exhibition of American paintings from Grand Central Art Galleries for the Dubuque Art Association. After lengthy negotiations with his friend Erwin Barrie and Grand Central, the Dubuque Art Association hosted a show of American paintings. In appreciation, Kate Van Duzee expressed her thanks to Klauer "for the role he played in securing the January exhibition. I know you can best select what is good and secure it."[5]

The fee for the exhibition was $100. Barrie sent a representative from Grand Central hoping to make a sale. While no record of sales exist, Klauer likely made a purchase or two. In the Klauer Manufacturing Company collection there are several American paintings that were not created by members of the Taos Society of Artists. Notable are canvases by Frederick Waugh and Frederick Carl Frieske [fig. 116]. Klauer may have made one or more purchases to avoid embarrassment for the city and the Dubuque Art Association. By the mid-1920s, William Henry Klauer was a major patron, supporting artists in Taos, the Grand Central Art Galleries and Dubuque.

In the 1927 drawing, Klauer drew the chance to sit for a portrait by Randall Davey.[6] On September 12, 1930, Klauer wrote to Barrie about how, "in the past, I have been a bit unfortunate in the drawings and still have coming a portrait from Randall Davey. You remember I selected his subscription to paint a portrait of me and I fear now that I shall never be able to get that portrait from him because he is a traveler and cannot be located when one is ready for a sitting."[7] Ten years later, after repeated letters from Klauer, the Klauer/Davey "contract" was still unsettled. Barrie blamed Klauer for not bringing up the matter sooner, and in 1937, declared "I am afraid it would be hard to get Randall Davey to do anything now."[8]

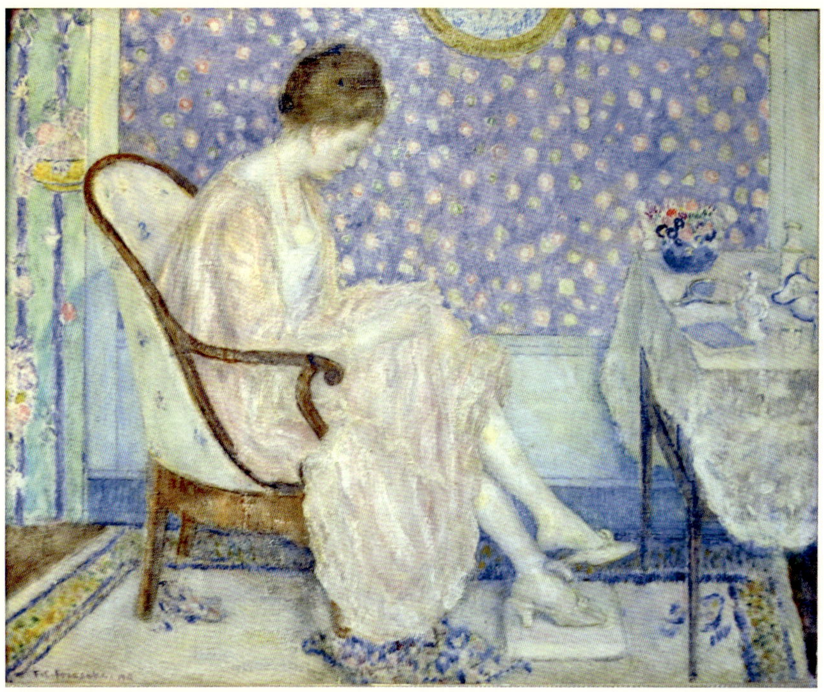

Figure 116.
Frederick Carl Frieske
The Torn Dress, c. 1930.
Oil on canvas.
Collection Klauer Manufacturing Company.

[5] Kate Van Duzee to William Klauer, undated, 1927, KFPUND.
[6] Ibid.
[7] William Klauer to Erwin S. Barrie, 12 September 1930, KFPUND.
[8] Erwin S. Barrie to William Klauer, 27 July 1937, KFPUND.

From 1931 until Ufer's death, Klauer continued to renew his membership. In 1933, Barrie praised Klauer, saying "you have been one of our lay members who made the establishing of these Galleries possible."[9] Barrie, always the salesman, reasoned, "this is a philanthropy that returns to you a picture worth much more than you paid for it."[10] However, according to Klauer's accounting, the value of the paintings he was stuck with was far less than what he paid. Yet, Barrie continued to play the role of salesman, telling the patron that for $350, Klauer was eligible for paintings, including an Ufer, "worth from $600 to $1500 each."[11] By 1933, Klauer was painfully aware that paintings by Ufer and his peers were not selling at any price. The country was mired deeply in the Great Depression.

Needing to retain Klauer's membership, Barrie finally offered possible solutions, the final one on October 5 1937 stated,

> *I am shipping to you the Waugh painting size 40" x 50" with the understanding that it will settle the Lay Membership for which you never received any award, and with the understanding that you will send us your check for $1050. It is further understood that by so doing you will be entitled to participate in the Lay Membership Drawing for 1937, 1938 and 1939 without any further payment of any kind. It is also understood that if the painting I send you does not please you, we will exchange it for one that does.*[12]

When Klauer sent the check for $1050 on October 16, it appears that Klauer was more interested in seeing the survival of Grand Central Art Galleries than owning more paintings that he had little need for.

INTERNATIONAL BIENNIAL ART EXHIBITION

In 1938, Erwin Barrie was appointed Director of the American Section of the Fine Arts for the International Biennial Art Exhibition in Venice, Italy. He was responsible for assembling and shipping a collection of paintings from New York on April 9 of that year. On March 2, he contacted Klauer and requested the loan of five of Ufer's largest and most important pictures.[13] According to Barrie, "a feature will be a group of Western subjects by Messrs. Ufer, Blumenschein, Randall Davey, and others, selected for their American content which will represent the Indian life of the Southwest."[14] Five of Ufer's early paintings were among the sixty-four paintings chosen and were from Klauer's collection. Barrie wrote,

> *I would like very much to honor our old friend Walter Ufer, whom you know I really brought out some twenty-five years ago, by giving him an entire wall in the United States Galleries—that is I would like to hang five of his largest and most important pictures. The big one, say about 40/50 or larger for a center and a pair as nearly as large for the ends and then two somewhat smaller, say about the size 25/30 to hang on either side of the center picture.*[15]

Barrie thought Ufer was a great painter and realized Klauer owned "the best of his work."[16] Klauer agreed to the loan even though there was considerable risk lending paintings to Europe in the late 1930s. As he didn't have time to prepare them for shipping, he asked Barrie to have them "washed" as they had

[9] Erwin S. Barrie to William Klauer, 2 March 1933, KFPUND.
[10] Ibid.
[11] Erwin S. Barrie to William Klauer, 20 June 1933, KFPUND.
[12] Erwin S. Barrie to William Klauer, 5 October 1937, KFPUND.
[13] Erwin S. Barrie to William Klauer, 2 March 1938, KFPUND.
[14] Erwin S. Barrie, *Venice Biennial International Exhibition*, 1938. Exhibition brochure.
[15] Erwin S. Barrie to William Klauer, 2 March 1938, KFPUND.
[16] Ibid.

been in Klauer's office and "had accumulated considerable dust."[17] Klauer's penchant for smoking Cuban cigars would have also caused further conservation problems. While no list of the paintings sent exists, three would most certainly have been *Going East*, *Indian Corn–Taos* and *Their Audience–Laguna*. Interestingly, Barrie told Klauer "Walter would cuss me out and tell me how rotten the rest of the pictures were…"[18]

Following the Venice show, Klauer asked Barrie to return the five paintings as soon as he was through with them. Klauer, continuing his role as Ufer's curator, stated, "I have been flooded with requests to let these pass on to other exhibits and don't feel like I want to go to the trouble."[19] Barrie responded, "the American section this year was considered by the foreign critics the best that has ever been sent to Venice."[20]

At the conclusion of the show, Barrie was interested in showing Ufer's paintings in Grand Central Art Galleries for two or three weeks. "If we should get any inquiries on these would you be interested in selling them? If so, at what price?"[21] It cannot be determined whether or not Klauer was interested. His letter to Barrie dated December 6, 1938 is missing. On December 12, 1938, Barrie announced that he would return the Ufer paintings next week. "They have attracted a great deal of attention and I am glad that you did this for Walter."[22]

On December 7, 1941, the Japanese attacked Pearl Harbor, and the country directed its efforts and resources to victories in Europe and the Pacific. The Klauer Manufacturing Company retooled and produced ventilators to be used in munition factories in Florida.[23] It would be five years before America would again experience peace.

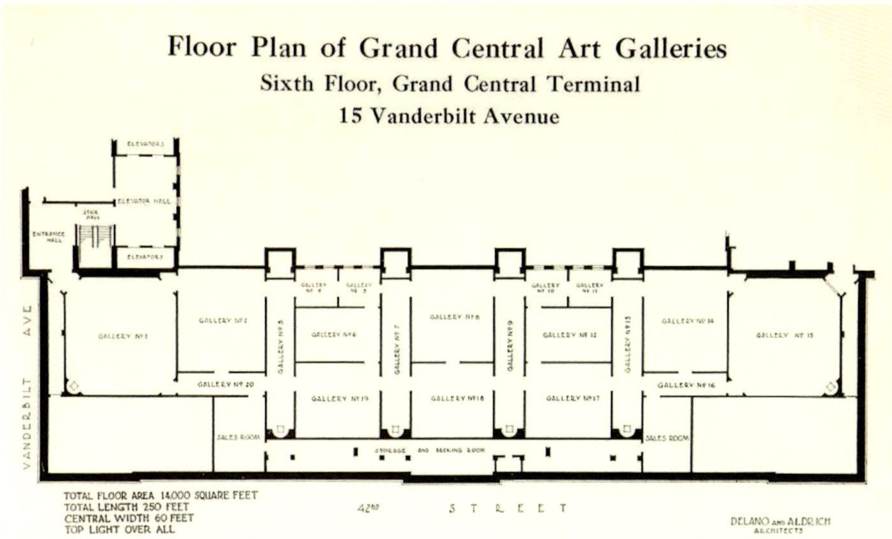

Figure 117.
Floor plan of the Grand Central Art Galleries, New York, New York, from the Galleries' 1923 opening exhibition catalog.

[17] William Klauer to Erwin S. Barrie, 23 March 1938, KFPUND.
[18] Erwin S. Barrie to William Klauer, 1 June 1938, KFPUND.
[19] William Klauer to Erwin Barrie, 6 December 1938, KFPUND.
[20] Erwin S. Barrie to William Klauer, 29 October 1938, KFPUND.
[21] Ibid.
[22] Erwin S. Barrie to William Klauer, 12 December 1938, KFPUND.
[23] William Klauer interview with Dean Porter, 14 August 2018, Dubuque.

Chapter XV
William Klauer After Walter Ufer's Death

With Ufer's death, William Klauer's role as a patron of artists came to an end. His involvement with Ufer's art, however, was another chapter yet to be written. While the exact number of Ufer paintings owned by Klauer at the time of the artist's death is unknown, it is evident that a major collection of paintings was in the hands of the Dubuque patron.

Having a large number of Ufer paintings—certainly more than he needed—Klauer explored ways to reduce the size of his collection. On May 25, 1937, he wrote E. C. Babcock in New York. Babcock Galleries, founded in 1852, was the oldest commercial gallery specializing in American art at that time. Babcock had also hosted solo shows of Ufer's paintings in 1928 and 1931. Klauer, aware of Babcock's track record, stated, "I have quite a collection of Ufers and if you wish will send you a list of them."[1]

By June, Babcock and Klauer were exchanging letters, discussing the possibility of staging a one-man show. Babcock wrote, "I had hoped that Mrs. Ufer would arrange a memorial exhibition of his work as he surely deserves it." He proposed that Klauer's group of paintings "might be made the nucleus of such a showing if the estate have not enough to make one."[2] Unfortunately, no record has surfaced listing paintings remaining in Ufer's estate.[3]

In July, Klauer advised Babcock that all of his Ufers weren't in his home, but he would prepare a list "with the sizes as near as possible."[4] Klauer's letter seems to project a sense of urgency. "From my friends in Taos, I understand that Mrs. Ufer had disposed of quite a few pictures before Walter died and when he died she had very few good ones to dispose of."[5]

Mary had lived in poverty for so long it is not surprising if she did try to liquidate as many of Walter's paintings as possible. Unfortunately, even if there was a record of sales, such a liquidation would have only amounted to a few dollars. While Mary continued to work with Barrie and Grand Central Art Galleries, she received little, if any funds from the sale of Walter's paintings.[6]

---

[1] William Klauer to E. C. Babcock, 25 May 1937, KFPUND.

[2] E. C. Babcock to William Klauer, 9 June 1937, KFPUND.

[3] No will was found in Ufer's papers.

[4] William Klauer to Babcock, 1 July 1937, KFPUND.

[5] Ibid. It seems unlikely that Mary was able to dispose of her husband's paintings "before he died." The word "disposed" could also suggest that Mary gave away some of Walter's work. It would be difficult because she remained on the road when he died.

[6] Mary did work for the Work Progress Administration for $77 per month and received Social Security. However, having little interest in remaining in Taos after Walter's death, Mary eventually took up permanent residence in New York's Hotel Albert in 1937. At that time she lost her WPA position, which had been funded through New Mexico.

Chapter XVI
Klauers' Gifts to the University of Notre Dame

During the Klauer's ownership of the Julien Hotel from 1930 until 1962, it prospered and became an important venue for Dubuque social events. It also served as an exhibition space for paintings by Ufer, which were displayed in the hotel's Art Room and Harbor Gallery.

In 1962, sons Walter J. and William J. Klauer [fig.] decided to sell the hotel. With the loss of space to display the Ufer paintings, the Klauers needed to find a suitable place that would share the paintings with the public. The brothers, in an act of munificence, donated nineteen Ufer paintings to the University of Notre Dame's Art Gallery. Walter was a graduate of the University of Notre Dame, and the Klauers, devout Catholics, were dedicated to the university. Besides the donation of Ufer paintings, the family donated the paintings *Nor'easter* and *Grey Dawn* by Frederick Waugh, *Glorious Tomorrow* by Hosep Pushman, and a watercolor by Alexander Wyant.

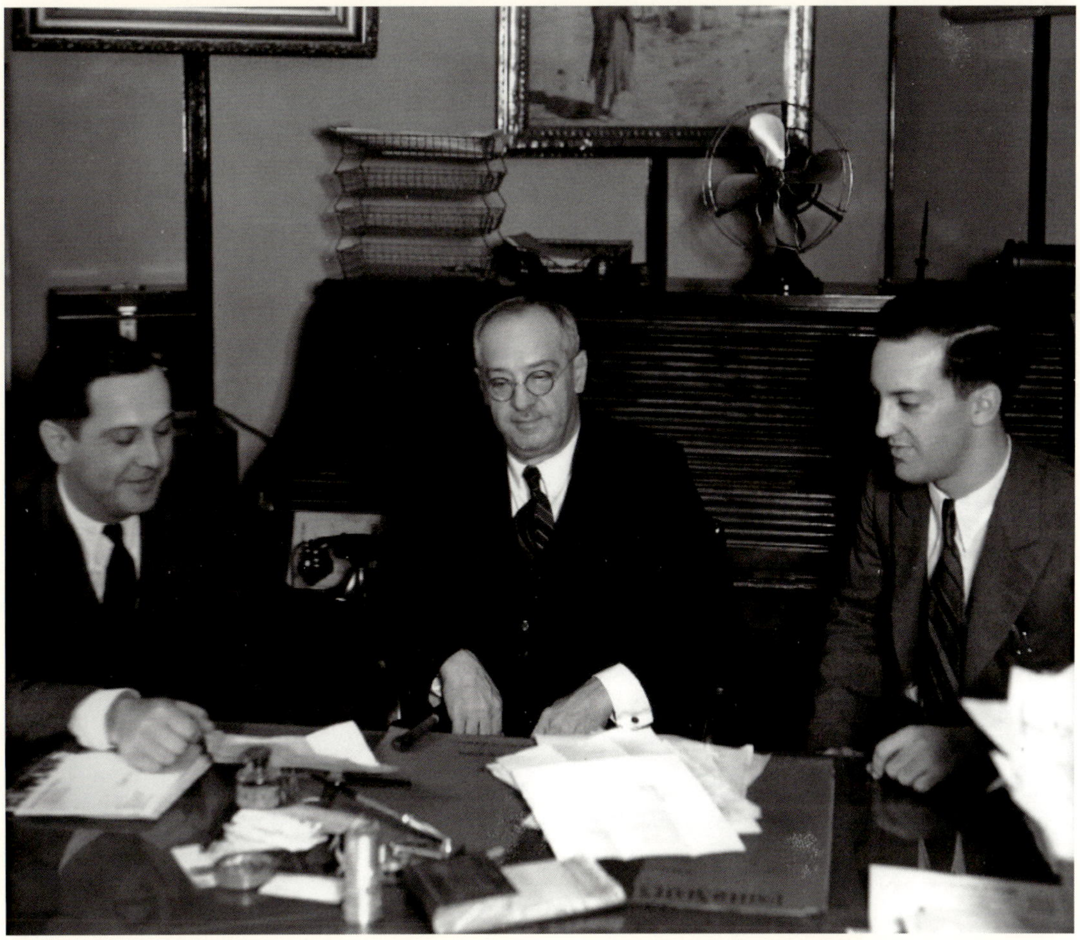

Figure 118. *William Henry Klauer with his Sons Walter J. and William J. Klauer.* Photo courtesy Klauer Family Papers, University of Notre Dame Archives.

While the Klauer's generous donation became common knowledge in the art world, the family also gave one of the most important gifts to the university—a revolutionary 400-horsepower rotary plow, called Snogo [fig. 119], "capable of removing 2,400 tons of snow per hour."[1] By the 1950s, the family had developed close relationships with three members of Notre Dame's Congregation of Holy Cross, Reverends Jerome J. Wilson, Theodore M. Hesburgh and Edmund P. Joyce. Faced with the problem of placing the collection, Bill Klauer called Father Wilson, who enthusiastically accepted the gift.

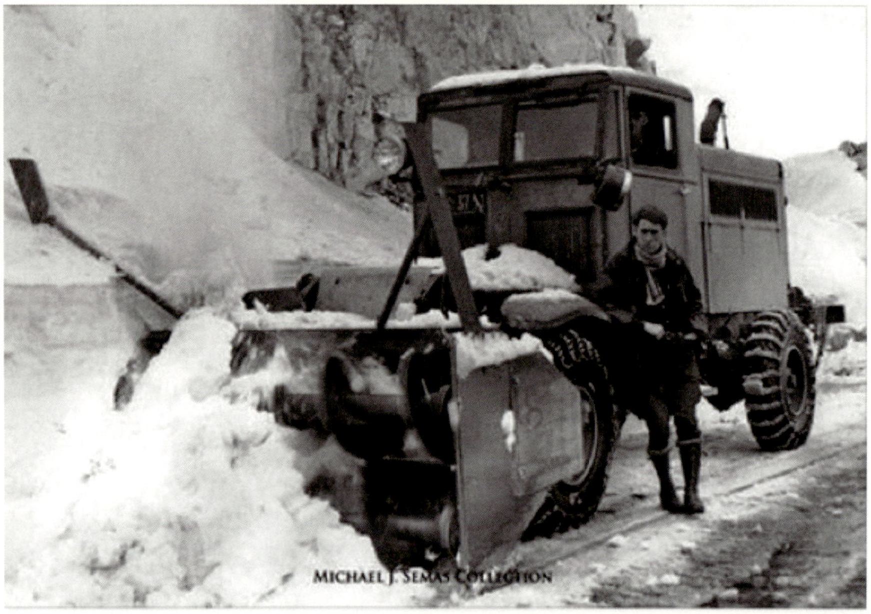

Figure 119.
A Snogo Created by Klauer Manufacturing Company.
Photo courtesy
Klauer Manufacturing Company
[Michael J. Semas Collection]

In 1968, Father Hesburgh approved the creation of an Advisory Council for the Art Gallery. Director, Reverend Anthony J. Lauck, attracted a membership of distinction that included some of America's most important collectors and museum professionals. During the initial meeting, the Advisory Council quality rated the entire collection of paintings. The Council's chief purpose was to upgrade the Art Gallery's permanent collection. After studying the Ufer collection, they felt that a Midwestern museum had little need for nineteen paintings by a Southwestern artist. Feeling that the paintings should be exhibited rather than remain in storage, the Council recommended the deaccession of all but two of the Ufers. Proceeds realized from the deaccessioning would enable the Art Gallery to add much-needed works of art while narrowing obvious gaps in the collection.

Father Wilson contacted William J. Klauer, requesting approval of the plan. Father Wilson wrote, "I am writing this letter, Bill, to see if you have any objections to the University selling some of the Ufer paintings..." Parroting the Advisory Council's recommendation, "the reason for selling is the fact that our Art Gallery is so in need of having examples of works of many artists and, therefore, with limited storage facilities, it is difficult to have so many paintings by one artist."[2] Father Wilson also stressed that if the family had any objections, "we will forget the matter at once."[3]

[1] "Klauer Manufacturing Company," *Encyclopedia Dubuque*, accessed July 9, 2018 http://www.encyclopediadubuque.org/index.php?title=KLAUER_MANUFACTURING_COMPANY

[2] Rev. Jerome J. Wilson, C. S. C. to William J. Klauer, 12 December 1968, KFPUND.

[3] Ibid.

Bill Klauer's response was not surprising:

> *In regard to the Ufer paintings–I certainly concur with your thinking that you have an abundance of the works of one artist. The paintings are yours, to do as you see fit. I surely want no strings attached to this gift.*[4]

Dorothy and Jack Brandenburg knew of Notre Dame's collection of Ufer paintings through their long-standing friendship with the Klauers. Dorothy also was serving on the Board of Directors of the Harwood Museum (University of New Mexico) in Taos. The museum was looking for a painting by Ufer. Jack wrote, "a painting [by Ufer] here may I say, has a very respectable home."[5]

With the Brandenburg request, Klauer asked Father Wilson and the University of Notre Dame to donate a Ufer to the Harwood:

> *I am not in a position to give them one. It seems they are difficult to obtain and since Ufer was one of the founders of the artist colony, they would love one, as a gift of course. If you would care to deplete your holdings by one, I would consider it a great gesture. Again, this would be your decision, so if it sounds unreasonable, forget it.*[6]

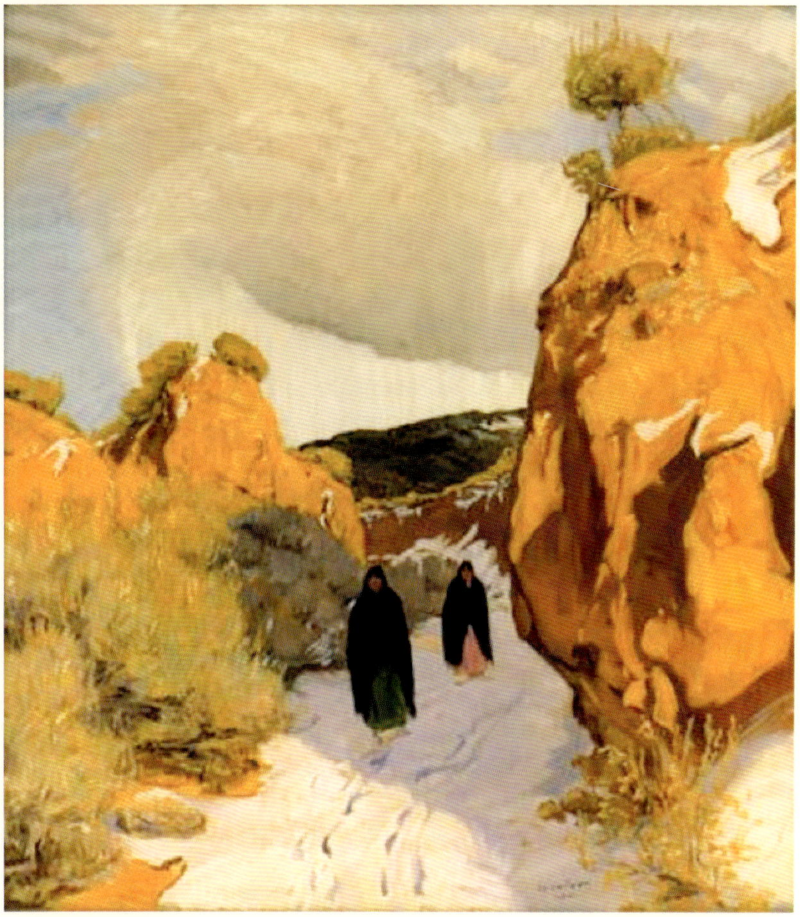

Figure 120.
Walter Ufer. *Winter in Taos*, 1920.
Oil on canvas, 18 x 18 inches.
Collection Harwood Museum of Art, Taos, New Mexico.
Gift of the Klauer Family and the University of Notre Dame.

[4] William J. Klauer to Rev. Jerome J. Wilson, C. S. C., 27 December 1968.
[5] Jack B. Brandenburg to William J. Klauer, 4 February 1969.
[6] William J. Klauer to Rev. Jerome J. Wilson, C. S. C., 27 December 1968

Today, *Winter in Taos* [fig. 120] hangs on the walls of the Harwood Museum, with a label that reads "Gift of the Klauer Family and the University of Notre Dame." This was to be the first of many acts of generosity that the Klauer family made to Taos, New Mexico.

Ufer was always proud of having his paintings in numerous museums—from the East to West coasts. Today, several of the Ufers from the Klauer's collection are hanging in museums and other public buildings across America. Since the Klauer Ufers left Notre Dame in 1969, the paintings have been enjoyed by audiences during several major exhibitions on Ufer and the Taos Society of Artists.[7] In 1970, the Phoenix Art Museum hosted the artist's first retrospective. In 1983, Christie's in Houston auctioned twelve of the Klauer's Ufer paintings. Two of the paintings set records for paintings by a Taos Society of Artists member. In 1999, 2016, and 2018, Klauer's Ufer paintings were featured in three major exhibitions organized by The Snite Museum of Art (University of Notre Dame, Indiana) [fig. 128], the National Cowboy and Western Heritage Museum (Oklahoma City, Oklahoma), and the Denver Art Museum (Denver, Colorado). The impact of the Klauer family's patronage cannot be over estimated.

The Ufer exchange program launched an important period of collecting art at Notre Dame. Ten years after the Ufer exchange, The Snite Museum of Art opened. Visitors to the new museum witnessed the importance of that exchange. The objects bearing the Klauer credit line were highlights in the museum's eighteenth- and nineteenth-century galleries. Objects received through the Ufer exchange played a significant role in elevating Notre Dame's art museum from one of little consequence to one of the top ten university museums in North America.

The Klauer family's patronage to Notre Dame's art museum has proven to be invaluable, yesterday and today. In 1995, the family donated the Klauer Family Papers, documents that have proven to be critical to a scholar studying Ufer's career and his relationship with William Henry Klauer. A year later, Bill Klauer once again called me and announced "if you come back, I have some more 'junk' for you." Bill had visited the attic of the family home and made some exciting discoveries. He found Ufer's *Union Square: The Battery* [fig. 57], along with a small seascape by Frederick Waugh, a watercolor by Alexander Wyant, and a group of Carter H. Harrison's sepia-tone photographs [figs. 24 and 37], that the family donated to The Snite Museum of Art.

---

[7] Paintings once owned by Klauer and the University of Notre Dame are on permanent view in the Desert Caballeros Western Art Museum (Wickenburg, Arizona), The Anschutz Collection (Denver, Colorado), the Fred Jones, Jr. Museum of Art, University of Oklahoma (Norman, Oklahoma), Terra Museum for American Art Collection at the Art Institute of Chicago (Chicago, Illinois), and The Snite Museum of Art, University of Notre Dame (Notre Dame, Indiana).

Chapter XVII
The Klauers, Patrons of Taos

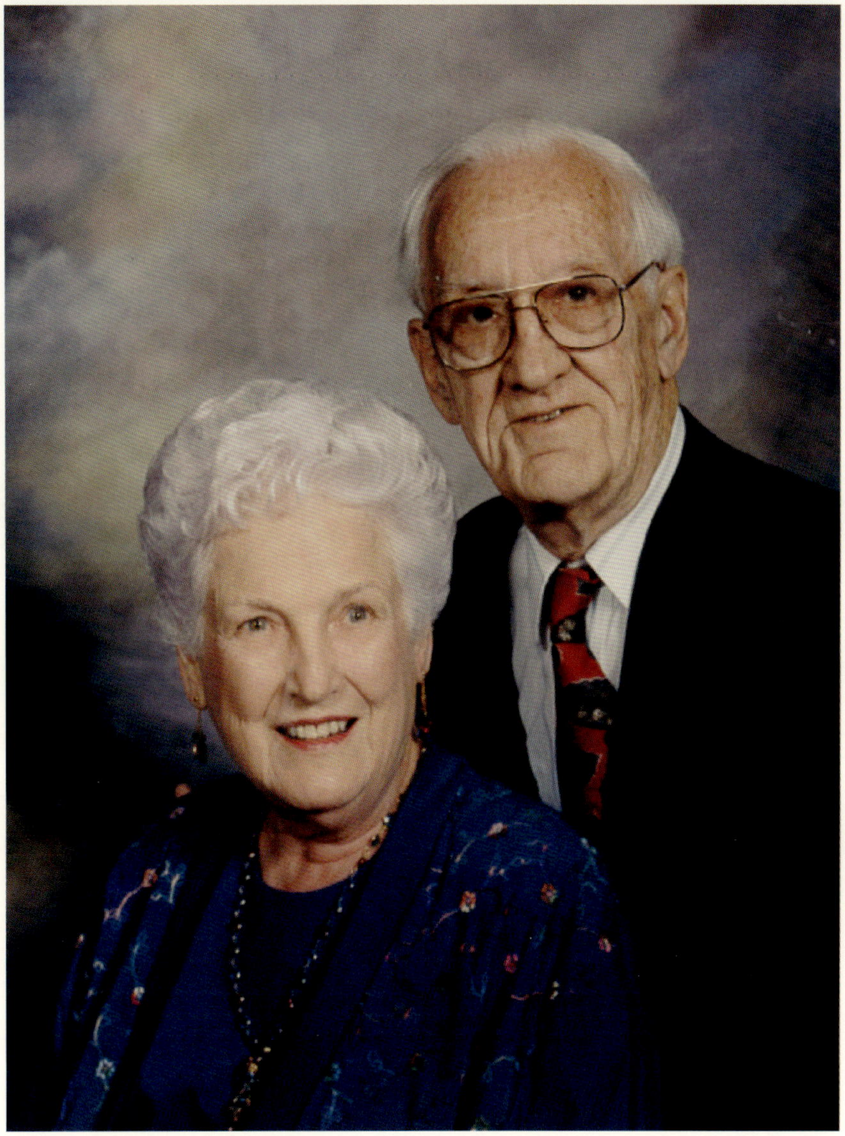

Figure 121. *Carol and William J. Klauer*, 1990s.
Photo courtesy Klauer Family.

KLAUER'S TAOS CAMPUS, 2001

The Klauer family returned to Taos in the 1990s and became important patrons of the community. They gifted over eighty acres of the property that William H. Klauer purchased in 1914 and established Taos's Klauer Campus for the University of New Mexico [fig. 122]. Since that gift, the campus has shown remarkable expansion, offering educational opportunities to the youth of northern New Mexico.

Taos is traditionally celebrated for its fine art and history museums and artists' homes. With the Klauer Campus joining programs offered by the University of New Mexico, Southern Methodist

University, Oklahoma State University, and other universities, the community offers educational opportunities unequalled by any other community with a population of 10,000 or less. The Sangre de Cristo Mountains and the intense light combined with the sense of history combine to make the educational experience unique.

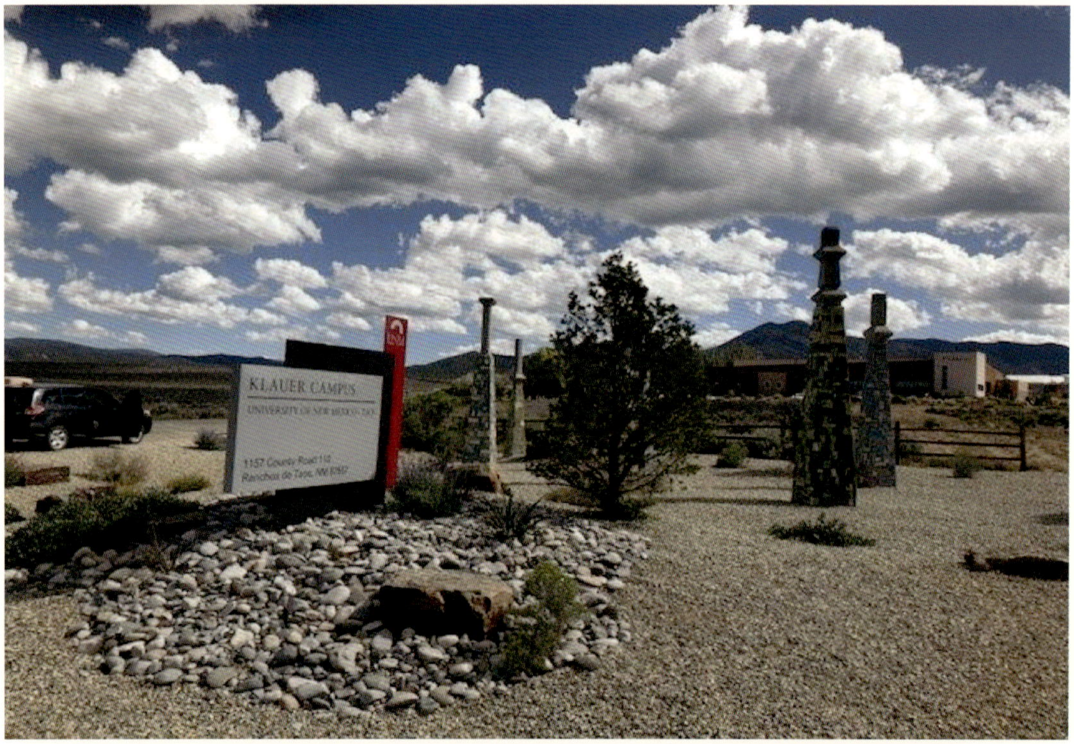

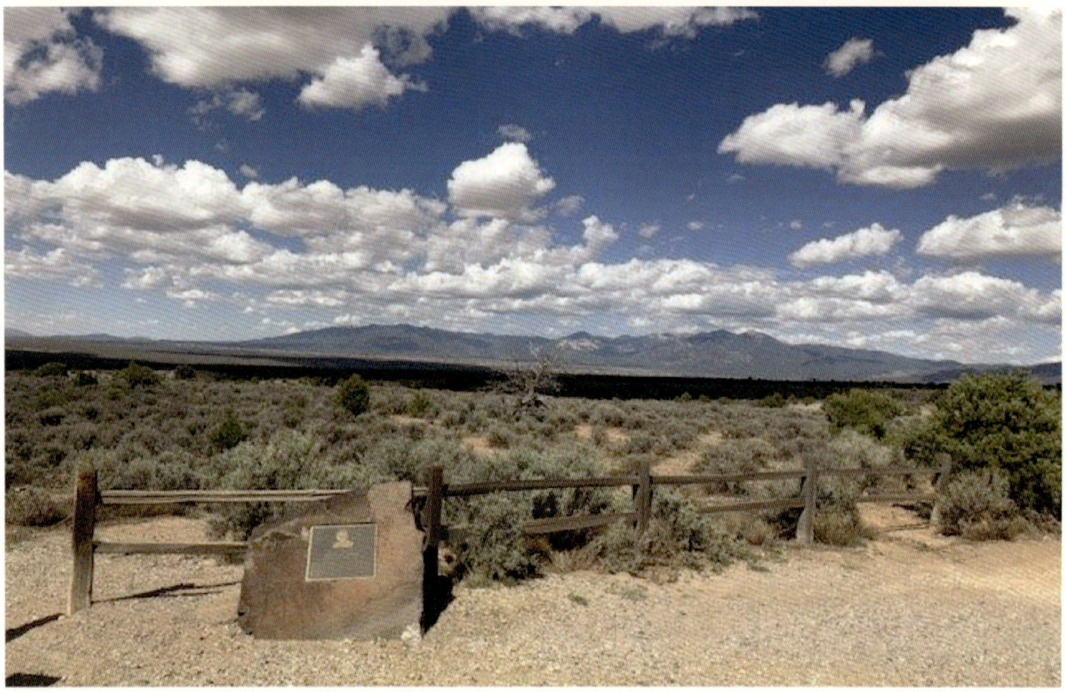

Figures 122 and 123. *Klauer Campus, University of New Mexico* (top) and *Taos Valley Overlook* (bottom). Photos courtesy of the author and Skip Miller.

For the ground-breaking ceremonies, the town, led by Mayor Fred Peralta, came out in huge numbers. The Klauers, led by Carol and William, and joined by sons William, James and Robert, daughter-in-laws Nancy and Judy, and their families, were celebrated in City Hall. Speeches by Peralta and the Klauers were followed by ceremonial dances performed by Taos Indians creating a moving, emotional event.

BILL KLAUER'S LAST DREAM: TAOS VALLEY OVERLOOK, 2001

On February 2, 2001, William J. ("Bill") Klauer passed away, but not before he knew a long-standing dream would become a reality. The Klauers had owned several thousand acres of prime land a few miles south of Taos—much of it for nearly a century. For years Bill and his family were strong advocates for shielding the property from commercial development, making a heroic effort to preserve the scenic view forever.

Two months after his death, on March 31, 2001, Klauer Manufacturing Company transferred Taos Valley Overlook to the U. S. Bureau of Land Management. This donation assured the Klauer family, who had maintained the property in pristine condition, that the property and view would be safe from man's commercial structures [fig. 123].

Taos Valley Overlook is a wonderful place where travelers who are emerging from Horseshoe Curve are afforded a breath-taking, awe-inspiring view of the Rio Grande Gorge and the Sangre de Cristo Mountains. There are few views more spectacular in America. Taos Valley Overlook offers an unbelievable view of the panoramic landscape that only God could carve and illuminate.

William Henry Klauer had passed on to his son Bill, a strong love for Taos and its people and the surrounding land. Bill and his wife Carol believed in preserving, untouched, what God had created. In June, Carol and four generations of Klauers, "gathered with Taos-area friends for a celebration to remember Bill Klauer and to commemorate the completion of the first phase of the Taos Valley Overlook project."[1]

To commemorate the Klauers' gift, a plaque was installed which reads:

The Klauer family of Dubuque, Iowa, stewards of the Taos Valley Overlook since 1920, transferred ownership of this property to the U. S. Bureau of Land Management on March 31, 2001, with the help of the Trust for Public Land and the Taos Land Trust. All who travel this route and cherish this vista are deeply grateful to the Klauer family for preserving this viewshed for future generations. The residents of Taos are blessed with W. J. Klauer's dream to save this land—his view of 'heaven on earth'—as he receives his eternal reward in Heaven above.[2]

For all that knew Bill Klauer, he was a kind gentleman who loved his city and visits to Taos. His philanthropy to Dubuque, its colleges, the Church, and any organization in need is legendary. Most importantly, he was a family man—deeply devoted to Carol and their family. Sister Catherine Dunn, President of Clarke College, called him an incredible human being who never knew a stranger. The world is better, Dubuque is better, because Bill Klauer lived here.[3]

---

[1] "Taos Land Trust Remembers Bill Klauer Sr." in *The Taos Land Trust Newsletter*, Fall 2001, no. 13, 8.

[2] Ibid, 5.

[3] Ibid.

THE KLAUERS AND THE LUNDER RESEARCH CENTER, 2018

The Klauer family munificence continues today when in September 2018, they agreed to donate Walter Ufer's *Taos in Snow* [fig. 39] to The Couse Foundation's forthcoming Lunder Research Center for the Taos Society of Artists (TSA) [fig. 124]. The Couse Foundation recently acquired the former home of Joseph Henry Sharp, the Cincinnati artist who was a founding member of the TSA. Paula and Peter Lunder [fig. 125] donated $600,000 for naming rights to the center, which is scheduled to open in 2022. The Klauer family's generosity has contributed significantly to the future of the research center. They have allowed the author to donate a copy of Klauer Family Papers and his library to the center. The donated Ufer painting will be installed in the Center's Porter Exhibition Gallery. This is the second Taos painting by Ufer that the Klauer family has donated to a Taos museum. The Klauer family's gift of the family's archives was another significant contribution to the Couse Foundation's collection. They join Virginia Couse Leavitt's gift of her grandfather's exhaustive collection of art and archival documents (including over 10,000 photographs and glass plates of Taos Indians). The Klauer gifts are among the first to be donated to what will be the Lunder Research Center for the Taos Society of Artists.

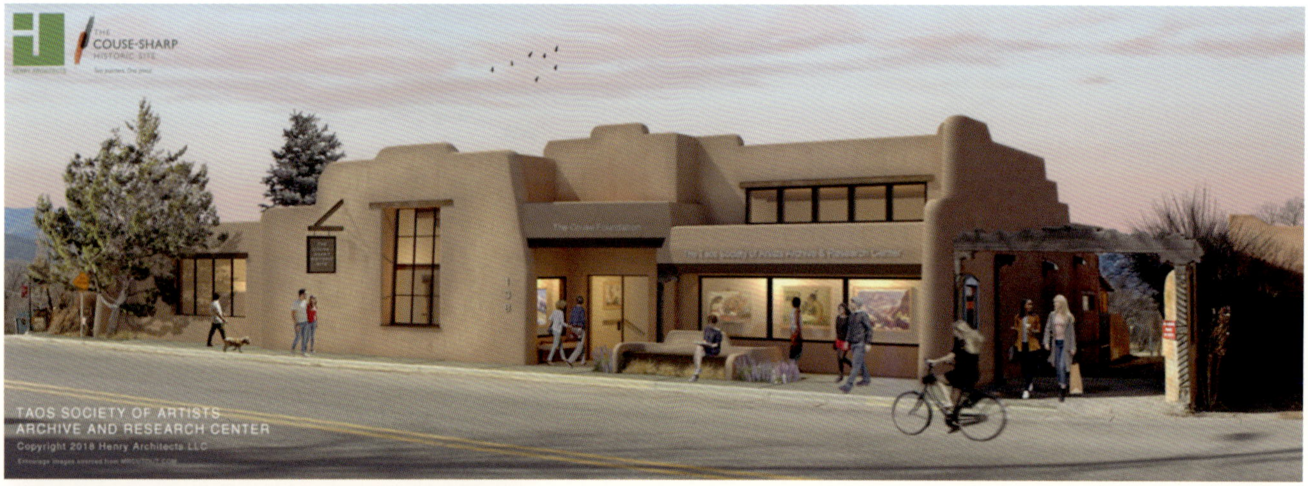

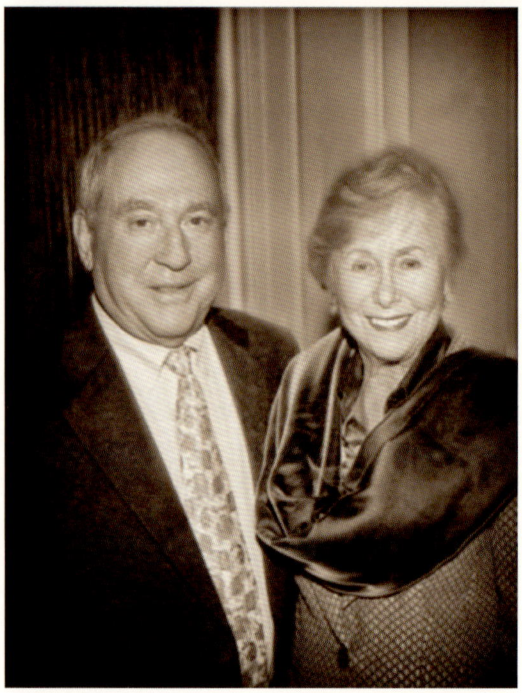

Figure 124 and 125. *The Lunder Research Center for the Taos Society of Artists, The Couse Foundation.* Taos, New Mexico (top) and Peter and Paula Lunder (left).

Conclusion

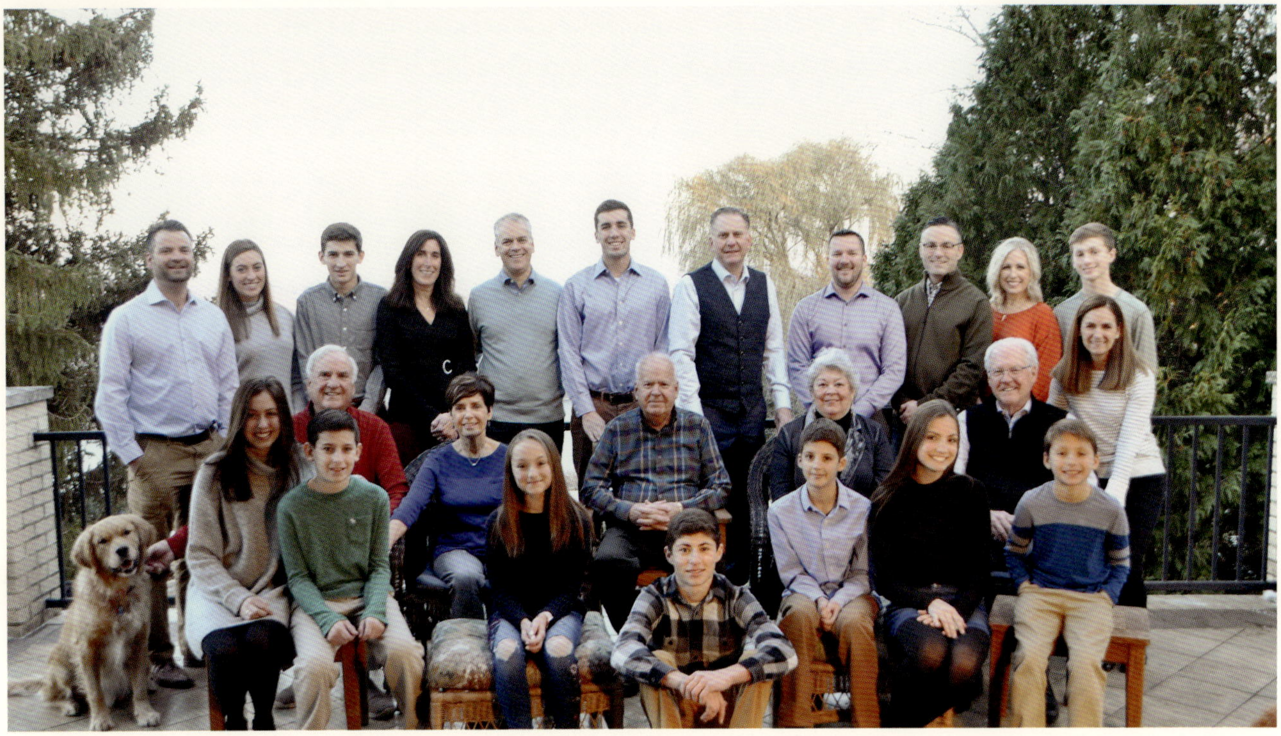

Figure 126. *The Klauer Family*, 2018. Photo Courtesy of the Klauer Family.

In the world of American art, William Henry Klauer, son of Peter Klauer, is well known for his patronage of Walter Ufer and other members of the Taos Society of Artists. To many aficionados of Taos art, he is considered to be Taos's most important patron. However, he is but one member of Peter's extended family who has made a difference in the world surrounding them. From the beginning Peter gave birth to a tradition of remarkable patronage—not by a single individual—but by family. Patronage has always been a family affair. For more than a century the Klauers have been one of the most generous families in Dubuque, actively supporting the Catholic Church, educational institutions like Loras College, University of Dubuque, Clarke College, the Dubuque Art Association, and other institutions and programs. A few years prior to William J. Klauer's death, Dubuque was running its annual United Way Campaign. When it appeared that campaign would fail to meet its goal, he wrote a check for $100,000. Like his father, grandfather, brother, and sons, he couldn't let this or any other important Dubuque fundraising effort fail.

Because of the family's century-long history with Taos, it is not surprising that their support has extended to the Klauer Campus, Armory, Taos Valley Overlook, and Couse Foundation's Lunder Research Center for the Taos Society of Artists. While it is tempting to give credit to William Klauer and several Klauer men for patronage to the University of Notre Dame, Carol Klauer's role in the family's munificence cannot be overlooked. While Bill was given a honorary doctorate by Loras College, Carol was honored by Clarke College. She also received an award as an outstanding philanthropist from the Eastern Iowa Chapter of National Society of Fundraisers. The Indiana Province of the Congregation of Holy Cross, the governing body of the University of Notre Dame, also honored Carol.

This study is only the first chapter of Peter Klauer's extended family's patronage. The baton of patronage has been handed down generation after generation. The Klauer family remains today exceptional humanitarians whose lives and acts of generosity thrive. Hopefully, a student studying on the Taos Klauer Campus or at one of the several Dubuque educational institutions will accept the charge of writing the next chapter on the Klauers' patronage.

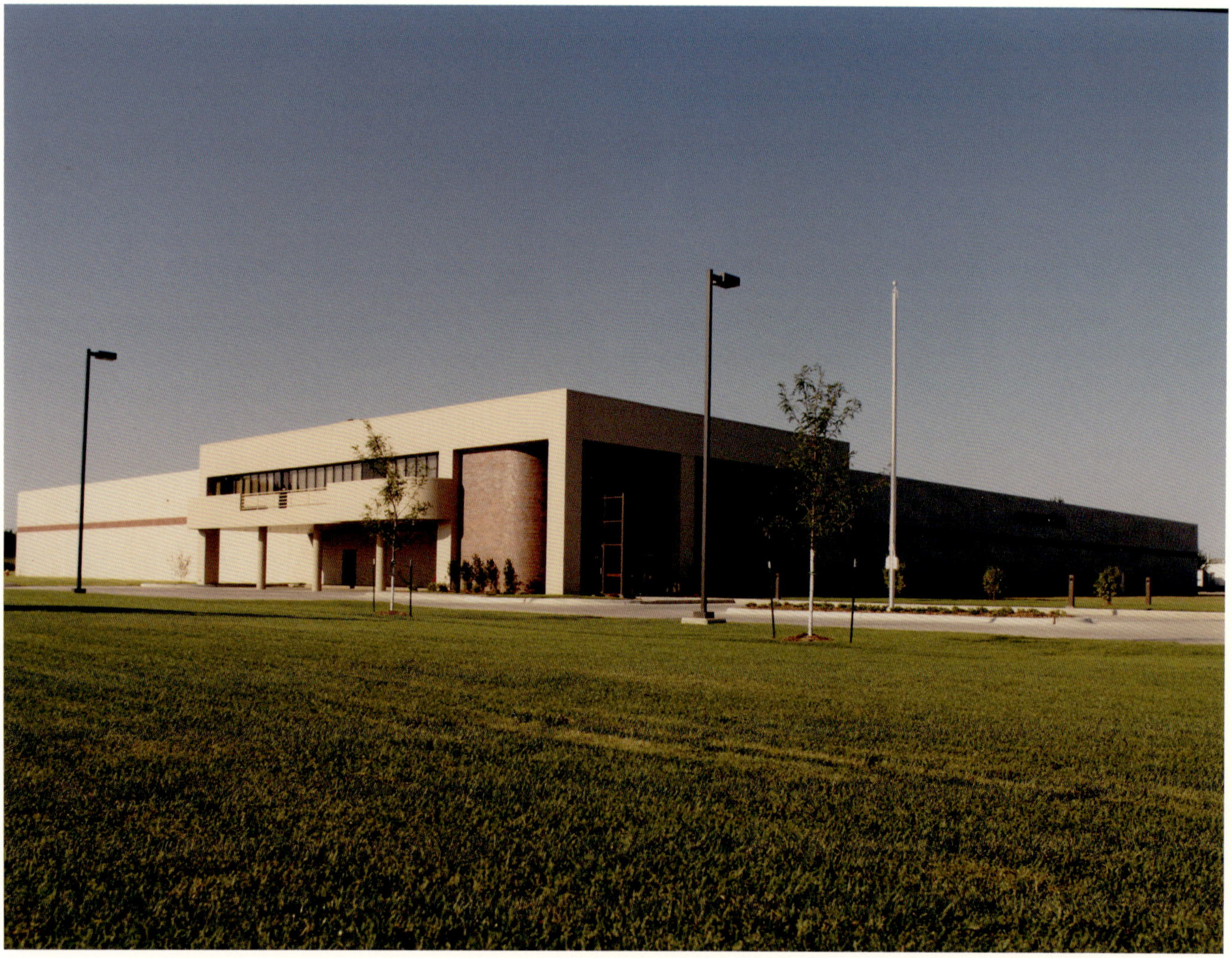

Figure 127. *The Klauer Manufacturing Company*, 2018. Photo courtesy Klauer Manufacturing Company.

Acknowledgments

It is with much pleasure that I express my appreciation to all who have made this publication possible. The acknowledgments are the final and most rewarding experience in writing a book. It is the one last opportunity to give credit to everyone who has shared in the rewarding experience of sharing knowledge. My gravest fear is that I will forget someone who deserves mention.

This book began when Stephen L. Good of Denver and William J. Klauer of Dubuque placed two sets of archives in my care for the University of Notre Dame Archives. It is almost impossible to thank them properly for providing me with materials that have shaped me as a scholar for more than a quarter of a century. It is with much gratitude that I thank them for having confidence in me to accept rare archival material to be used in lectures, exhibitions, catalogues, and finally, *The Klauer Family of Dubuque, Iowa, A Story of Patronage*. My heartfelt thanks to Steve, and Carol and William J. Klauer, and their sons, Bill, Jim and Bob.

When I made my initial trip to Taos, New Mexico in 1974, I had no idea that one day I would write a book on the Klauer family. Soon after arriving, however, I knew I would spend the rest of my life as a scholar and museum director researching those artists whose work inspired the *New York Times* to call Taos "The Provincetown of the West." I worked in partnership with so many people who were anxious to join me. From my early meetings with Sara Parsons Mack, Victor Higgins's first wife, to Helen Hennings, E. Martin Hennings's wife, to Dorothy Brandenberg and Barbara Brenner, Oscar Berninghaus's daughter and granddaughter, and Virginia Couse Leavitt, Irving Couse's granddaughter, I learned that they were the most important patrons of the artists we so admire. They recalled in exacting detail life in Taos for over three-quarters of a century. I only wish I had spent more time with these wonderful women. A book should and will be written on them.

In 1986, I attended the second annual board meeting of the Southwest Art History Council. I soon had a battery of friends—in particular Teresa Hayes Ebie, Suzanne Campbell, Robert White, David Witt, and others, who contributed significantly, and unselfishly, to my research for this and other publications bearing my name. As early as 1991, I promised Mike Leslie, retired curator of the Eiteljorg Museum, that I would curate a Walter Ufer exhibition for him. Twenty-three years later, Mike and I opened *Walter Ufer: Rise, Fall, Resurrection* at the National Cowboy and Western Heritage Museum in Oklahoma City, Oklahoma. These exhibitions and catalogues, and the teams that worked with me, formed the foundation for *The Klauer Family of Dubuque, Iowa: A Story of Patronage*.

I am forever indebted to the Klauer family, in particular for their friendship and for allowing me to write about their family. My meetings with Bill and his sons were enjoyable and fascinating. Little did I realize when I first started the project, the extent of the family's munificence and how many lives the family has and continues to affect. While I knew of William Henry Klauer's patronage of Walter Ufer and his peers, I didn't fully realize how much the family had touched the lives of people and institutions from Dubuque to Taos to Grand Island to the University of Notre Dame.

Fortunately, I spent my entire professional career at the University of Notre Dame (1966-2001), my first twenty years when Reverend Theodore M. Hesburgh, C.S.C. was president. In my forthcoming book on the history of Notre Dame's art museums, I called him "The Medici of Notre Dame." He always supported me and the time I spent working on subjects relating to Taos, New Mexico. In a very real way, with this book, I am able to keep yet one more of several promises I made to him over the years. I, like so many, was fortunate to know the man affectionately called "Father Ted."

While I conducted my research, Notre Dame students played a significant roll. I was assisted by two former Notre Dame students, John "Jay" Anderson and Steve Moriarty, who photographed paintings bearing the Klauer provenance. I was blessed to be assisted with graduate interns, Michael Baechler, Christine Fowler Shearer, and Brigitte Foley. I also want to extend a very special thank you to Julie Tressel of Klauer Manufacturing Company who was of invaluable assistance throughout the project.

My sincere thanks to the many collectors and museums that owned paintings bearing the Klauer provenance, and who allowed their paintings to be reproduced. Their names are included with the entries for the paintings illustrated. Special thanks goes to J. Matthew Thomas, collections manager at the Harwood Museum of Art; Mary Ann Igna, curator at the Desert Caballeros Western Art Museum; Victoria Perdomo, registrar at The Snite Museum of Art; Claire Mosier, museum librarian and historian and Darlene Dueck, curator at the American Museum of Western Art—The Anschutz Collection; Davison Koenig, director and Regina Scherffius, program manger at The Couse Foundation; Catherine Ricciardelli, director, registration and Shari Felty, assistant registrar at the Terra Foundation for American Art; Laura Bryan, curatorial projects manager and Lisa Parrott Rolfe, registar at The Speed Art Museum; Hadley Jerman, Eugene B. Adkins Curator and Selena Capraro, registrar at the Fred Jones Jr. Museum of Art, University of Oklahoma; William Kevin Cawley, senior archivist and curator of manuscripts at the University of Notre Dame Archives; Daniel Kosharek, photo curator at Palace of the Governors Photo Archives, New Mexico History Museum; and Colleen Hollister, image services and rights coordinator the Baltimore Museum of Art .

My thanks to Michael Frost of New York's J. N. Bartfield Gallery. Mike has handled so many of the Ufers that bear the Klauer provenance and was instrumental in making sure that we had permission to illustrate these paintings in our text. Ashley Rolshoven and her father Robert Parsons of Robert L. Parsons Fine Art Taos, Richard Lampert and David Clemmer of the Zaplin Lampert Gallery, Santa Fe; and Gerald Peters and Ana Archuleta of Gerald Peters Gallery, Santa Fe, and Steve Rose and Joshua Garcia, Blake Hotel Collection, Taos Ski Valley, were all instrumental in securing permission to reproduce one of Walter Ufer's prize paintings. Working with Mike Rink, Rob Crippin and the staff of Rink Printing has been a rewarding experience. They have exhibited an inordinate patience of which I am extremely grateful.

I am particularly appreciative of Mike Gibson and Tim Olson of the Loras College Center for Dubuque History. Their willingness to assist our search for images relevant to the Klauer story is particularly helpful. While I would welcome the opportunity to spend a week in Dubuque reviewing the 30,000 images they are responsible for, it was not possible. Loras College should take pride with this invaluable collection and those individuals who effectively facilitated our search.

Two people merit special mention—Christine Fowler Shearer, Ph.D. and Michael Wright. Even after Christine worked as my intern at The Snite Museum of Art (1994-1996), she was willing to step up as the project director for this book. She accepted multiple roles: general editor, photo permission registration, layout designer, and more. Besides securing permission for the images reproduced, she became the final word on what and how these words would appear to you.

Michael Wright, another Notre Dame alumnus, also willingly joined me in the creation of this book. Like Christine, Michael accepted several challenges. Importantly he served as a sounding board, as idea after idea was explored. Unable to drive, I rode with Michael, and we discussed the project on long trips to Dubuque. The Klauers, like me, knew that Michael would be a key player in finishing this publication. For the multiple roles Michael has played, and, most of all, for his friendship, I offer my heartfelt thanks.

My final thanks go to my family, my daughters Kellie and Tracie, and most importantly Carol, my bride of 55 years. They have had to listen to me about my research on the Klauers for over two decades, and finally, Carol volunteered to spend our "vacation" in Taos reading and editing the manuscript. Before we went to press, Carol edited the manuscript three more times. After I married Carol in 1963, she typed and edited my master's thesis and doctoral dissertation—flawlessly. Some 45 years later, Carol proves the old adage—"behind every good man is a better woman."

To Carol and Christine and the team, I offer my heartfelt thanks.

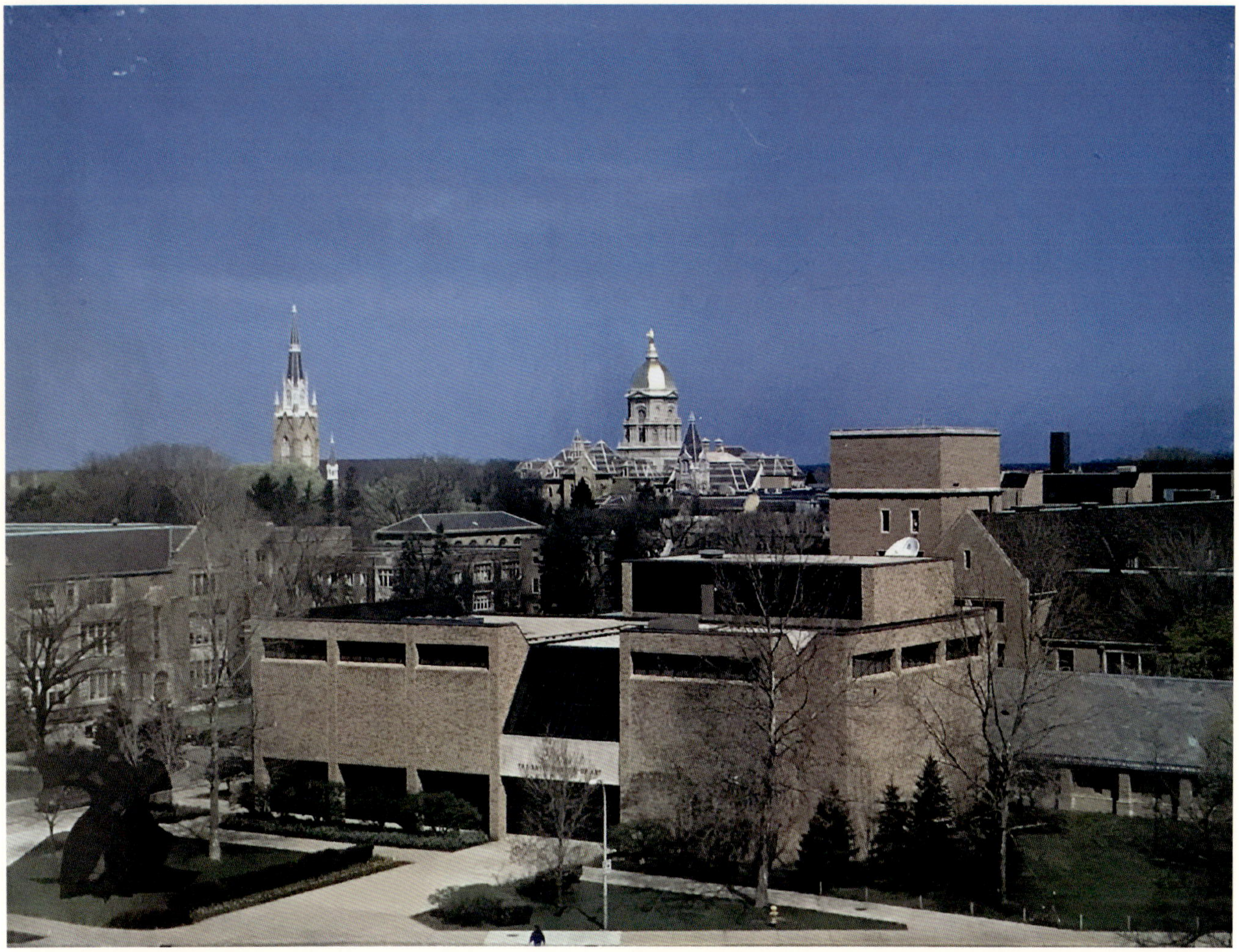

Figure 128. Steve Moriarity, *The Snite Museum of Art, University of Notre Dame, Indiana*. Photo courtesy of the author.

Selected Sources

"Artists as Influenza Nurses," *El Palacio*, 16 November 1918, vol. V, no. 17, 277.

"Artist Colony Corner," *Taos Valley News*, 17 March 1928; 2 March 1929.

Berry, Rose S. V., "Walter Ufer in One-Man Show," *American Magazine of Art*,13 December 1922, XIII, no. 12, 507-514.

—. "Walter Ufer and Some of His Gold Medal Pictures," *Art and Archaeology*, July-August 1923, XVI, nos. 1 and 2, 66-74.

Bickerstaff, Laura M., ed. *Pioneer Artists of Taos*, 2nd edition. Denver: Old West Publishing Company, 1983.

Boeller, Susan. "Two Americans in Munich," in *A Place in the Sun: The Southwest Paintings of Walter Ufer and E. Martin Hennings*. Norman: University of Oklahoma Press in Cooperation with the Denver Art Museum, 2016, 7-27.

Booth, Anne Lisle. "Two Moods of a Forceful Artist," *Fine Arts Journal*, vol. 34, May 1916, 221-226.

—. "The Santa Fe Art Colony, Walter Ufer," *El Palacio*, 3 August 1916, 79.

Broder, Patricia Janis. *Taos: A Painter's Dream*. Boston: New York Graphic Society, 1980.

Catalogue of Special Exhibitions: Paintings by Three Artists of the Taos Group: Ernest L. Blumenschein, A. N. A., Victor Higgins and Walter Ufer. The Buffalo Fine Arts Academy Albright Art Gallery, Buffalo, New York. 14 September-3 October 1920. Courtesy Michael Frost J. N. Bartfield Gallery, New York City.

Coke, Van Deren. *Taos and Santa Fe: The Artist's Environment, 1882-1942*. Albuquerque: University of New Mexico Press, 1963.

"Condition of Walter Ufer Improved," *Taos Valley News*, 30 July 1936.

"Costilla Boy Hit by Baumann Dies March 5," *Taos Valley News*, 15 March 1934.

Eldredge, Charles C. "The Faraway Nearby: New Mexico and the Modern Landscape," in *Art in New Mexico, 1900-1945 Paths to Taos and Santa Fe*. New York: Abbeville Press, 1986, 147-180.

Emken, Tyler. "Family Gift Support Illinois State's Anthropology Research" in *News Illinois State University*, March 8, 2018.

Fox, Steve. "Pesky Named for Arts Patron," Klauer Family Papers, University of Notre Dame Archives.

Good, Stephen L. "Walter Ufer: Munich to Taos, 1913-1918," in *Pioneer Artists of Taos*. 2nd ed. Denver: Old West Publishing Company, 1985, 113-173..

—. "Seven Paintings by Walter Ufer," *Artists of the Rockies and the Golden West*. Winter, 1984, XI, 1, 46-57.

Hassrick, Peter H. "Taos and the Art of E. Martin Hennings," in *A Place in the Sun: The Southwest Paintings of Walter Ufer and E. Martin Hennings*. Norman: University of Oklahoma Press in Cooperation with the Denver Art Museum, 2016, 93-124.

Henderson, Rose. "Taos Indians in Art," *Taos Valley News*, 22 June 1922.

Keegan, Marcia. *The Taos-People and the Sacred Blue Lake.* Santa Fe: Clear Lake Publishers, 1991.

Keeley, J. "Real American Art—At Last!" *Chicago Sunday Herald*, Part Five, no page. Victor Higgins Papers, University of Notre Dame Archives.

Lewis, Lloyd D. "News and Views in the World of Art, Some Glimpses of Walter Ufer, Chicago's Biggest Figure in Art Today," *Chicago Herald Examiner*, 3 February 1917. Ufer Papers, University of Notre Dame Archives, Stephen L. Good.

Luhan, Mabel Dodge. *Edge of Taos Desert*, 3rd ed. Albuquerque: University of New Mexico Press, 1991.

McWhorter, Karen Brooks. "The Country He Loved Best," in *A Place in the Sun: The Southwest Paintings of Walter Ufer and E. Martin Hennings.* Norman: University of Oklahoma Press in Cooperation with the Denver Art Museum, 2016, 77-92.

Moore, James C. "That Man Out There in the Mountains," in *A Place in the Sun: The Southwest Paintings of Walter Ufer and E. Martin Hennings.* Norman: University of Oklahoma Press in Cooperation with the Denver Art Museum, 2016, 143-167.

Nelson, Mary Carroll. *The Legendary Artists of Taos.* New York: Watson-Guptill Publications, 1980.

Pickard, John. *Report of the Capitol Decoration Commission, 1917-1928.* Columbia, Missouri: Capitol Decoration Commission. 1928.

Porter, Dean A., Ph. D. "A Biography of Walter Ufer," in *A Place in the Sun The Southwest Paintings of Walter Ufer and E. Martin Hennings.* Norman: University of Oklahoma Press in Cooperation with the Denver Art Museum, 2016, 27-47.

—. "Victor Higgins" in *Pioneer Artists of Taos.* 2nd ed. Denver: Old West Publishing Company, 1985.

—. *Victor Higgins: An Indiana-Born Artist Working in Taos, New Mexico.* Art Gallery, University of Notre Dame and Indianapolis Museum of Art, 1975/76. [Exhibition with catalogue].

—. *Victor Higgins: An American Master.* Salt Lake City: Peregrin Smith, Publishers, 1990. [Circulating exhibition with monograph].

Porter, Dean A., Ph. D., Teresa Hayes Ebie, Suzanne Campbell [editor], with others. *Taos Artists and Their Patrons: 1898-1950.* University of Notre Dame and The Snite Museum of Art, 1999. [Circulating exhibition with monograph].

Porter, Dean A., Ph. D., with Mike Leslie. *Walter Ufer: Rise, Fall, Resurrection.* Oklahoma City: National Cowboy and Western Heritage Museum, 2014. [Exhibition with catalogue].

Simon, Hi. "The Art of Walter Ufer," *The Arts.* 15 April 1922, XII, no. 8, 108-109.

Smith, Thomas Gordon. *A Place in the Sun: The Southwest Paintings of Walter Ufer and E. Martin Hennings.* Norman: University of Oklahoma Price, 2016.

——. "Walter Ufer's Years of Critical Success," in *A Place in the Sun: The Southwest Paintings of Walter Ufer and E. Martin Hennings.* Norman: University of Oklahoma Press in Cooperation with the Denver Art Museum, 2016, 47-77.

Truettner, William H. "The Art of Pueblo Life," in *Art in New Mexico, 1900-1945 Paths to Taos and Santa Fe.* New York: Abbeville Press, 1986, 59-100.

Ufer, Walter Ufer. Letter to Miss V. R. Purinton, 16 May 1935, 35 pages. Ufer Papers, University of Notre Dame Archives, Stephen L. Good.

Whitney, Catherine. "Glimpsing Modernity," in *A Place in the Sun: The Southwest Paintings of Walter Ufer and E. Martin Hennings.* Norman: University of Oklahoma Press in Cooperation with the Denver Art Museum, 2016, 125-142.

White, Robert Rankin, Ph.D. "E. Martin Hennings" in *Pioneer Artists if Taos.* 2nd ed. Denver: Old West Publishing Company, 1985, 195-208.

INTERVIEWS

Dorothy Brandenburg and Dorothy Brenner [1995]; William J. Klauer and William Klauer, III [1993-2018]; Ted and Kit Egri [1974]; Benita Peralta [1995]; Dixie Gillespie [19974]; Rena Rosequist [1974-2016]; Forrest Fenn [1995]; Eya Fechin [1995]; Saki Karavas [1995]; John T. Higgins [1974-1980s]; Sara Parsons Mack [1974-1976]; Joan Higgins Reed [1974-1982]; Joseph Foster [1975-76]; Jane Hiatt [1975]; Mrs. Martin Hennings [1975]; Charlie Berninghaus [1975-1976]; Nelda Stark [1995]; Anthony Godfrey and William J. Klauer [1994].

PAPERS

Klauer Family Papers, University of Notre Dame; Walter Ufer Papers, University of Notre Dame; Papers from the Harwood Museum; Joan Higgins Reed Papers, Museum of Fine Arts, Santa Fe; Forrest Fenn copies of Kenneth Adams to and from Walter Ufer.

PERIODICALS

American Magazine of Art; Art Digest; El Palacio; Chicago Sunday Herald; Chicago Tribune; Chicago Examiner; New York Times.

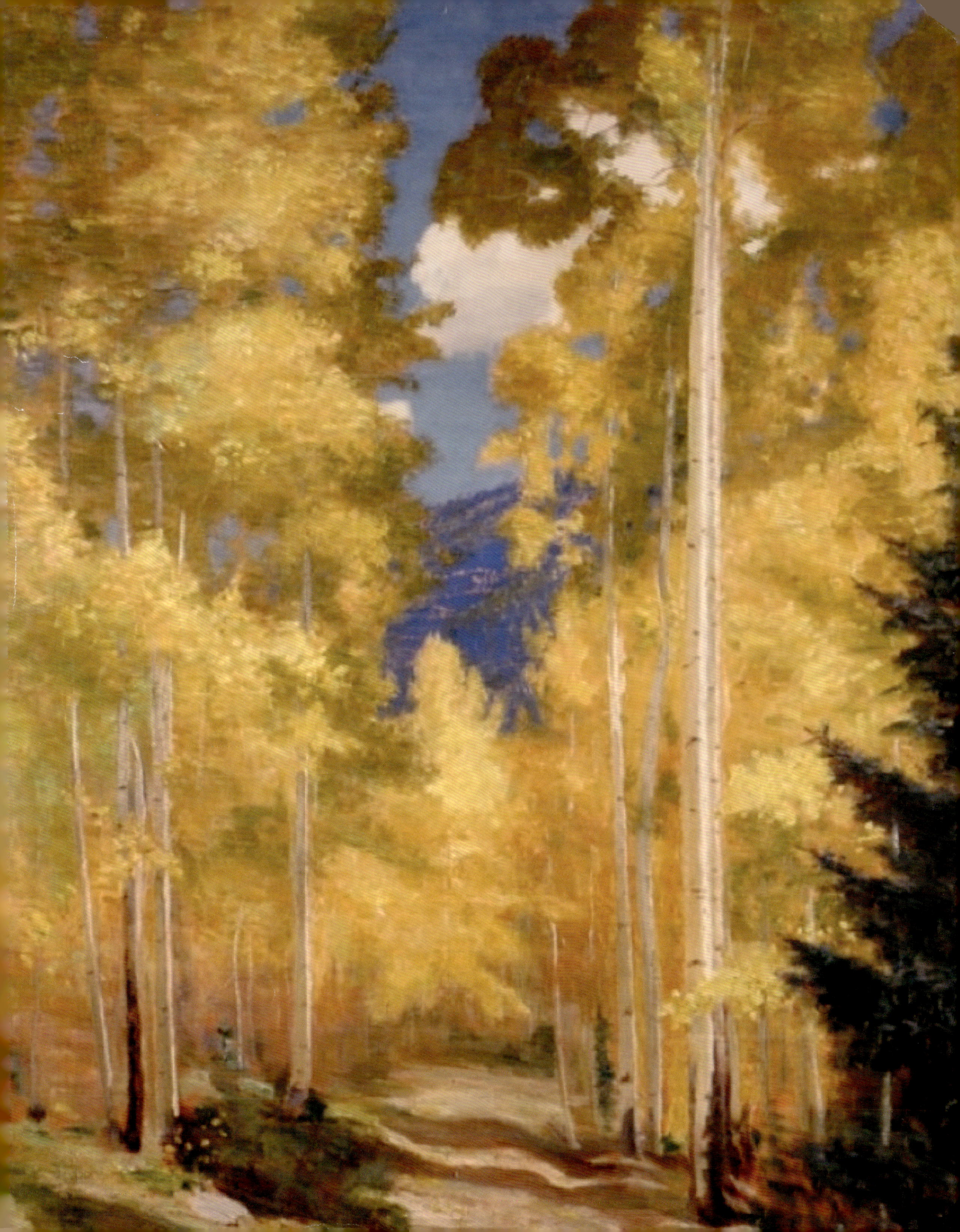